OWER

AND AMERICAN DEMOCRACY

PRIVATE POWER

& AMERICAN DEMOCRACY

GRANT McCONNELL

VINTAGE BOOKS
A DIVISION OF RANDOM HOUSE/NEW YORK

Library of Congress Catalog Card Number: 65-18761

Originally Published by Alfred A. Knopf, Inc., in 1966.

Manufactured in the United States of Ameri

VINTAGE BOOKS EDITION, AUGUST 1970

TO

Jane

ACKNOWLEDGMENTS

The process of preparing this book began many years ago. In one sense it started with discussions among colleagues in the federal civil service. In another sense it began over innumerable cups of coffee with the late Lloyd H. Fisher at the University of California. It continued in talk and argument with many colleagues and students at the Universities of Chicago and California. I am very indebted to all of these. There are particular debts to Wesley Calef, David Greenstone, Duncan MacRae, Michael Rogin, Peter Odegard and Gilbert White. Gerald Hewitt and Alan Seltzer have given help of a very concrete sort. Mrs. Eleanor Pettigrew has helped with unfailing efficiency and good spirit. The greatest debt, however, is to the individual to whom this book is dedicated.

I am grateful to the *American Political Science Review* for permission to use material which appeared in that journal and which now is incorporated in Chapter 5. I also wish to thank Alfred A. Knopf, Inc. for permission to quote from the works of V. O. Key in Chapter 6. The book would have been much more difficult to finish without my appointment to a Ford Foundation Research Professorship in Governmental Affairs.

G. McC.

CONTENTS

PRIVATE POWER

AND AMERICAN DEMOCRACY

INTRODUCTION

Since early in the history of the American republic organized interest groups have wielded a strong degree of political power. Such exercise of power by private groups has been perhaps the feature of political power most characteristic of American democracy. It was regarded by James Madison at the time of the ratification of the Constitution as the most serious problem of popular government. In the twentieth century it has received renewed attention and has aroused deep, although fluctuating, concern.

Two distinct currents of opinion have existed about the political power of private groups. One, which has found its most forthright expression in the Progressive tradition of American politics, has regarded their power as excessive and dangerous. At times, it has tended to seek the destruction, if not of the groups themselves, at least of all their power and even of power in any form. Much of the attention has been focused upon outright corruption. This preoccupation, frequently shared by wider segments of the public when wrongdoers in high places have been exposed, has placed the problem upon the seemingly simple plane of good against evil. The periodic exposures, however, have had little apparent effect and the cycle of public outrage, disgrace of some group of miscreants, and ultimate general boredom with the problem has been repeated again and again. For all its devotion to public virtue, the Progressive tradition has failed to develop either criteria by which that virtue could be known in other than the clearest cases or an analysis of power in a democratic society.

The other current of opinion regarding the power of private groups has been less sharply defined. Indeed, one of the curiosities of American political thought is that although private groups have been very strong and have had to meet loud denunciations, doctrines in their defense have been fragmentary and scattered; they have had no authoritative texts, unless recent apologias may be said to have acquired that status. Nevertheless, the defense of private-interest groups has its orthodoxy in the multitude of acts and statements of political figures who began to emerge during World War I. Industrial mobilization in that conflict greatly accelerated a number of already existing tendencies, the most significant of which was the widespread drive toward organization among economic rivals for mitigation of the rigors of competition. Moreover, governmental agencies assumed the task of organizing groups to formulate the consensus of agriculture, industry, or other apparently coherent segments of the population, thus relieving government of much of its burden and, through the very fact that these groups were voluntary, promoting freedom by indicating to government what their members wished. This kind of organization served efficiently for war and, with some lapses, was continued in peace. It became a cause in the crusade for which Herbert Hoover was the most articulate and influential spokesman.

The orthodoxy supporting the resulting political arrangements is an unstable amalgam of very different ideas. One is simply satisfaction with the performance of the economy and the general prosperity. Another is the vaguely expressed feeling that present arrangements are the result of much evolution and should not be rashly disturbed. Another is the belief that without the existing array of private organizations the nation might be subject to a host of evils culminating in anomie and totalitarian mass movements. Yet another is the conviction that these associations balance and counterbalance each other, with automatic benefit to society. The most important, however, has been a deep-seated faith in the virtue of small units of social and political organization. The roots of this faith lie in our agrarian past, but they have fed other parts of American life as well and have strongly influenced many aspects of political organization. The small geographical community, states' rights, and the centrifugal aspects of federalism have been conspicuous enthusiasms. However, small functional units—whether labor unions, farm organizations, or trade associations—have been celebrated on essentially the same grounds. By contrast, government, especially the national government, parties, and "politics" in general, have been deplored as threats to liberty.

Although both the defenders of the role of private interests and their antagonists in the Progressive tradition have valid arguments, neither has grappled with some of the most difficult and important problems. The first factor both ignored is that deference of government to private groups does not eliminate the phenomenon of power. Power exists in the hands of these groups. It is both inward and outward looking: it is power over the members of the groups and it is also power over matters affecting the larger community. The power over members is often substantial, sometimes affecting matters of great importance—the right to pursue a given means of livelihood, for example. Unfortunately, the governing systems of most private associations do not have the checks upon power or the protections for individuals that have developed out of long experience in the constitutional order of the United States. Indeed, these private governments exhibit the iron law of oligarchy and have regimes based upon a concept, albeit unacknowledged, of absolute democracy. As private and autonomous bodies having voluntary and homogeneous membership and limited purpose, these associations would appear to stand on different ground from public government. In point of fact, however, many of the most important private associations do not have these characteristics. Nothing in the countervailing power of other associations mitigates the consequences of this problem.

The exercise of power, outward and inward, by private groups and associations is profoundly affected by the narrow basis of their constituent organization. As Madison observed long ago, the smaller the society, the fewer probably are the parties and interests composing it; the fewer these parties and interests and the smaller the compass in which they act, the more easily do they concert and execute their plans of oppression. Far from providing guarantees of liberty, equality, and concern for the public interest, organization of political life by small constituencies tends to enforce conformity, to discriminate in favor of elites, and to eliminate public values from effective political consideration. The service of a multitude of narrowly constituted political associations is often genuine. However, this service lies in the guarantee of stability and the enforcement of order rather than in support for the central values of a liberal society.

In general, an organization with a given order of size and diversity is characterized by several other qualities. The ends of an association thus are directly related to its size. Similarly, the tactics preferred by an association are linked to its size and its ends. It is the same with the ideology by which the group defends itself and conducts its battles. A group having a narrow constituency will probably have relatively narrow and concrete ends, usually economic and material in character. These will be most readily served by direct and immediate action of the group itself, action that is more likely than not to be economic—for example, boycotts, strikes, or monopolistic agreements. It is noteworthy, however, that this predilection of interest groups for economic action does not necessarily exclude the use of public authority, where that authority can be successfully isolated from influences other than those of the group in question. Thus, governmental action by an administrative agency is preferred to legislation, group action is preferred to party action, and local and state governmental action is preferred to federal action. The ideology of an interest group may be *laissez faire* or "voluntarism," if this is feasible; alternatively, it may be "grass roots democracy" and the inherent virtue of small units. By contrast, a large constituency, such as that of a political party, will have large and rather general ends, which will be sought through political means—most characteristically, electoral campaigns.

Autonomy is essential to the preservation of power of groups with small constituencies. This is so of economic units with strong market power, as it is of all groups that have successfully brought about the insulation of particular agencies of government from the mechanisms by which government is otherwise held responsible to the large constituency of the nation. A large number of groups have achieved substantial autonomy for themselves and the isolation of important segments of government and public policy. The result has been the establishment of varying degrees of control and exercise of public authority by the private groups within the public areas with which they are concerned. This authority is available for reinforcement of the groups' own discipline and, at the same time, for exploitation of public policy in the groups' own interests.

In this process, government is kept informal, but by the same token it is often made arbitrary. Decisions made under such conditions are responsive to the power that can be wielded over the official agency. The process amounts in some situations to the capture of government. However, it is not "rule" as this is normally conceived; it is the fragmentation of rule and the conquest of pieces of governmental authority by different groups.

The fact that not all groups are organized and not all interests are represented has serious consequences. At the extreme they involve the virtual exclusion of some elements of the population from effective voice in affairs that deeply concern them. Other elements are placed at a relative disadvantage. With the absence of such segments from this important, although often obscure, arena of politics, the groups that have been successful are usually able to achieve accommodation among themselves by logrolling—a process to be sharply distinguished from compromise. Logrolling results in policies enforced by public authority, but these are more extreme than they might otherwise be.

The power exerted by private interests is uneven. It does not touch all areas of public policy and it does not everywhere exist to the same degree. The devices by which power is achieved vary greatly in detail. In state government and politics, there are many opportunities for private influence over or control of public policies. The small constituencies of states and the serious fragmentation of their political systems give functional groups—whether trade, farm, or professional—great advantages which they have nowhere been reluctant to seize. "States' rights" is the classic defense of the privileges enjoyed by local and other elites, although its effectiveness is wearing thin as the consequences for Negroes are perceived.

At the federal level the process has taken many forms and has been accelerated by several other influences. National crises of war and depression have brought about extensive devolution to private groups in business. The agrarian myth has given control of federal agricultural programs to rural elites. It has also influenced the development of informal systems of power affecting water and has given to commodity groups extensive powers over public policy affecting public resources of grass and timber. Progressive ideology, ironically, has established the conditions of isolation for important regulatory agencies, so that over time their policies have accommodated the desires of the regulated groups. It is impossible to state how pervasive the phenomena of the small constituency are in the great scope of national government, but they are very extensive indeed. Examples are to be found in a great variety of agencies and activities.

Fortunately, not all of American politics is based upon this array of small constituencies. The party system, the Presidency and the national government as a whole represent opposing tendencies. To a very great degree, policies serving the values of liberty and equality are the achievements of these institutions. Public values generally must depend upon the creation of a national constituency.

Part I

Chapter 1

The Open Secret

I

On Sunday, June 29, 1913, the *New York World* carried a story that loosed a nation-wide storm of indignation. "$200,000 spent by lobbyist in his work. Col. Mulhall outlines story of eight years of corruption he will prove by letters"—so ran the headline that set off the sensation. The story, which was scheduled for a long series of chapters in the *New York World*, was summarized in the first issue. The National Association of Manufacturers, an organization claiming to be a nonpolitical business and trade association, had always sought and often managed to secure control of the Committee on Labor and the Committees on the Judiciary of both the Senate and the House of Representatives. It was solely responsible for the creation of the Tariff Commission. It had given "financial reward for services rendered for political purposes" to some nine Congressmen and former Congressmen, as well as to the chief of pages in the House of Representatives, the "principal spy of the National Association of Manufacturers on the undertakings and movements of Members." The Association had waged relentless war against public officials and labor leaders who opposed its plans. Some Congressmen had been retired from office as a result of the Association's efforts.[1]

The story had been obtained by the *New York World* from one Colonel Martin M. Mulhall (his military title, it developed, was a fiction), who had long been employed by the Association as a lobbyist. On leaving the Association's service, Colonel Mulhall, in order, by the testimony in the *New York World*, "to render a service to the public by disclosing the identities and undertakings of the men at the head of the most powerful business organization in the United States and their allies among officials of the United States Government," and "to compel reform through legislation of the evils revealed by him," had brought to the office of the New York paper some 65 files each containing 400 to 600 letters, telegrams, and reports. The Colonel's public zeal was rewarded by a payment of $10,000 from the *World*.

Within days after the appearance of the summer Sunday's headlines, the House of Representatives passed a resolution creating a select committee to investigate the charges that had been outlined in the *New York World*. The files of material for which the paper had paid so handsomely were brought to Washington. On Saturday, July 12, the select committee began its investigation.

As the committee assembled for the first time, another investigation had been under way for rather more than a month on the other side of the Capitol. This investigation, by a subcommittee of the Senate Judiciary Committee[2] into a charge that a lobby existed and was maintained in Washington to influence proposed legislation, had been set in motion as the consequence of an earlier news story that had appeared in virtually all of the daily press. The author of *that* charge had been no less a personage and no less an expert on government than President Woodrow Wilson.

The President's statement read:

I think that the public ought to know the extraordinary exertions being made by the lobby in Washington to gain recognition for certain alterations of the tariff bill. Washington has seldom seen so numerous, so industrious, or so insidious a lobby. The newspapers are being filled with paid advertisements calculated to mislead the judgment of public men not only, but also the public opinion of the country itself. There is every evidence that money without limit is being spent to sustain this lobby and to create an appearance of a pressure of public opinion antagonistic to some of the chief items of the tariff bill. It is of serious interest to the country that the people at large should have no lobby and be voiceless in these matters, while great bodies of astute men seek to create an artificial opinion and to overcome the interests of the public for their private profit. It is thoroughly worth the while of the people of this country to take knowledge of this matter. Only public opinion can check and destroy it.

The Government in all its branches ought to be relieved from this intolerable burden and this constant interruption to the calm progress of debate. I know that in this I am speaking for the Members of the two Houses, who would rejoice as much as I would to be released from this unbearable situation.

On May 27, the day after the President's statement appeared, Senator Albert Cummins of Iowa, the Progressive leader, introduced a resolution calling for the Senate investigation. As amended and passed, the resolution sought an inquiry into the existence of the supposed lobby, the names of lobbyists and the methods they had used, the names of Senators on whom influence had been attempted, and the circumstances of the attempts. Moreover, the inquiry was to discover whether any Senator was financially or professionally interested in the items mentioned in the tariff bill before Congress and whether any Senator was connected, professionally or otherwise, directly or indirectly, with any person, firm, association, or organization engaged in manufacture or sale of such items.

On June 2, there began a solemn procession of United States Senators to the chamber in which the investigating subcommittee sat. Each senator, to a total of 91, appeared, was sworn by the subcommittee chairman, and addressed himself to eleven questions arising from the Cummins resolution. There were questions on the Senators' personal financial interests in legislation, their connection with firms or associations so interested, and the names of any lobbyists. But there were also questions asking whether anyone had attempted improper influence, whether money had been used to influence action on legislation, and whether the Senators knew of any lobby or lobbyist maintained in Washington to influence legislation.

The testimony each Senator gave followed the general outline given in the set of "interrogatories" established under the Committee's rules. Each began by indicating the nature and scope of his outside investments and interests. Some of these were in stocks and bonds, as might be expected with statesmen of substance; others had only the farms from which they had come to Washington. Then the Senators addressed themselves to the question whether they had ever been approached improperly. There was agreement here—and it was usually expressed with some firmness and feeling—no, absolutely not, in all the years each had been in the Senate. This had occurred no more to conservative Senator Penrose of Pennsylvania than it had to liberal Senator La Follette of Wisconsin.

As to the central question of the inquiry—the existence of a lobby in Washington supported by money to influence pending legislation—the answers, in view of the President's statement, were somewhat surprising. Senator after Senator stated that there was no such lobby. Senator Augustine O. Bacon, for example, when asked if he knew about a lobby, replied: "So far as that is concerned, I say, most emphatically, no; I have not known of any such thing—not the slightest. I have nothing even upon which any investigation could be based; no clue." Not all Senators were this categorical. Senator Borah was perhaps more typical:

I suppose in popular parlance we mean by "lobbyist" a man who is employed, paid professionally, to influence legislation concerning a matter not because he is interested in the matter, not necessarily because he thinks it is right, but because he desires to earn his salary, and is paid like a lawyer sometimes to argue a bad case, to do the best he can in the situation. That is my idea of a lobbyist, and I have not seen any around here this year, although they may be here.

However, a number of Senators, perhaps from an extreme of caution or concern for precise truth in an ambiguous area, gave names of people who had come to see them to argue for various features of legislation. Thus, Senator Reed Smoot had received calls from a rather large number of people who were concerned about various tariff matters. Their objects of concern included sweaters, face-finished cloths for coffins, carpets, machine tools, wire needles, iron and steel wood screws, clocks, chilled shot, grit and abrasive, zinc, lead, straw braid, cigars, sugar, and vegetable ivory. On reflection and after consultation with their records, other Senators were likewise able to compile extended lists of people who had particular worries on the tariff bill. The Goat Raisers of the United States had been in touch with Senator Warren; the National Farmers Union had communicated with Senator Kern; the American Wire Weavers' Protective Association had sent a representative to call on Senator Thomas; the American Sugar Bureau and the National Wool Growers Association had been represented in discussions with many Senators. Indeed, the lists of individuals who had paid their respects to the United States Senate in this manner included many names evocative of leadership in business, banking, labor, and agriculture.

But to name these familiar—even illustrious—names was not, in the eyes of the Senators listing them, to expose lobbying or lobbyists. The apparent inconsistency was probably explained away best by Senator Bacon, who had been most categorical in saying he knew of no lobby:

> I do not think that a man who comes here to represent an interest in which he himself is concerned which is to be affected by legislation, or who comes here for the purpose of presenting views why such and such measures should not be enacted into law, or why they should be enacted into law, is a lobbyist. . . . I think a man has an absolute right to be heard on any matter which is going to affect his interests. It is an unthinkable thing that he should be denied that right. . . .

This pageant of mildly indignant Senators was followed by the appearance of a number of men with interests affected by the tariff whose right to be heard it was unthinkable (to them as well as to Senator Bacon) to deny. It was abundantly clear from their testimony that the prospect of new tariff legislation had attracted to Washington a goodly company of gentlemen with definite opinions about the wisdom of parts of the proposed new law. There was, nevertheless, little in the testimony that could be taken as reflecting adversely on the personal integrity of the members of the United States Senate.

Then, abruptly, the figure of "Colonel" Mulhall intruded upon the scene. His revelations, as polished for appearance in the *New York World,* stood as "charges" against the personal integrity of members of the United States House of Representatives. There followed a polite contest between the investigative bodies of the two houses of Congress for Colonel Mulhall's appearance. The contest was settled amicably, both committees providing the Colonel with opportunity and limelight for the rendering of service to the public, the aim he had professed in the pages of the *World.*

The Colonel's revelations extended over many weeks of the stifling Potomac summer. He was asked the meaning of letter after letter in the large accumulation which had been brought to Washington. Various officials of the National Association of Manufacturers, all proffering their unstinted cooperation, testified to the goodness of their intentions and the purity of their methods. Expenditures of $20, $150, $12 were checked and explained. Comings and goings were recalled. Bit by bit and elliptically, events in Maine, Indiana, Wisconsin, and New York were retold. Senators and Congressmen questioned witnesses sharply as the good name of the United States Congress appeared to be involved.

Out of it all there emerged, at least for those patient but intense few who followed the hearings in their tedious detail, a number of things. The President had been quite right: at the first whisper of new tariff legislation, a small army of men had come to Washington to argue, cajole, and press for advantage. The battalions of the sugar and wool interests seemed the biggest, but perhaps they were only the most conspicuous; many others were present. And in a sense the *New York World* and Colonel Mulhall had been correct, too, although much too flamboyant and sensational for the facts that were finally established.

The National Association of Manufacturers had intervened actively in the politics of lawmaking and elections. A number of Congressmen had been elected and others had been defeated with the Association's help. The creation of the Tariff Commission had been at least partly its accomplishment. Several measures in which labor had been interested, such as an anti-injunction bill, had been lost in committee. The National Association of Manufacturers had rather more than concurred in these actions.

As to the charges of corruption and scandal, the facts established were not as far reaching as had been promised. There was the sordid little story of the chief of pages in the House of Representatives. Colonel Mulhall had given this House employee of two decades' service a regular "salary" of $50 a month and frequent meals and drinks at Fritz Reuter's hotel. In return for this largesse, the chief of pages had contributed information about the progress of bills in which the Colonel was interested and copies of the *Congressional Record* for the Colonel's employers. What else the salary bought was not entirely certain, except, perhaps, blank paper from the Congressional stocks for the Colonel's use and gladiolus bulbs from government nurseries for Mr. Emery, the secretary of the National Association of Manufacturers. There were also stories of the Colonel's success in placating labor leaders who threatened or were conducting strikes. But in these, again, the amounts of money spent were trifling, on occasion being little more than the cost of tickets to the circus, which several union officials had never seen before.

The allegation that a number of Congressmen had been "reached" by Colonel Mulhall on behalf of the National Association of Manufacturers was not proved. However, Congressman James T. McDermott of Illinois emerged with a tarnished reputation. He was reported on by the House investigating committee in measured but adverse terms, and resigned his office less than a year afterward.

For the rest, results were inconclusive. The public, tired perhaps from what had by now been more than a decade of sensation and exposure, was bored with the revelations. A measure was placed before Congress to require the registration of lobbyists (whose existence, at least, was thus officially certified). The bill died.

II

The tumult following the exposure of the activities of the National Association of Manufacturers was the first of a series of such incidents that has extended through the history of twentieth-century American politics. World War I put an abrupt end to concern over the National Association of Manufacturers, but the same sort of problem reappeared not long after the return to normalcy. In 1922, Congress found itself goaded to exasperation by a new organization, the American Farm Bureau Federation, and retaliated with an investigation. This Federation had had a meteoric rise to power among the more successful farmers of the nation and in just a few years had organized an apparently invincible bipartisan bloc in the Senate. When its lobbyists insisted that congressmen report their unrecorded votes directly to the Federation offices, however, Congress struck back. The story revealed in the investigation was in its way as startling as that which had emerged from the earlier inquiry into the National Association of Manufacturers.[3] Nevertheless, the investigation was as unproductive of concrete results as its predecessor.

In 1928 the Federal Trade Commission began a massive inquiry into the affairs of the private electric utilities. The investigation was precipitated by Senator Thomas J. Walsh of Montana, who argued from the Senate floor that the concentration of wealth implicit in the device of the holding company might carry with it political power as well. He wanted a Senate investigation, but his colleagues were fearful that the publicity attendant on such an approach might have detrimental effects on the stock market, and they succeeded in relegating the investigation to the more obscure forum of the Federal Trade Commission. The story that gradually emerged from the long succession of hearings conducted by the FTC went beyond purely financial matters, and for a time its revelations produced a deep sense of public outrage.

The electric companies, organized in the National Electric Light Association, had not only directly influenced Congressmen and Senators on a large scale, but had also conducted a massive campaign to control the substance of teaching in the nation's schools. Teachers in high schools and grammar schools were inundated with materials purporting to be aids to learning on such topics as the wonders of electricity and the romance of the kilowatt. Each pamphlet included carefully planted disparagement of public ownership of utilities. The Association took very active, if inconspicuous, measures to insure that textbooks that were doctrinally impure on this issue were withdrawn from use and that more favorable substitutes were produced and used. College professors, notoriously a needy lot, were given supplemental incomes by the Association and, in return, not infrequently taught about the utility industry with greater sympathy than before. Public libraries, ministers, and civic leaders of all kinds were subjected to the propagandistic efforts of the electric companies. Some of the Association's methods were above board, but others were subtle and disguised. The shock of discovery of this propaganda campaign, which had been in operation since shortly after the end of World War I, resulted in the widespread conviction that a process of corruption had been at work on the institutions that lay at the very foundations of the nation's being.[4]

Nevertheless, public attention turned to other things and the immediate results of the protracted investigation were meager. The National Electric Light Association disappeared from the list of associations in the United States, but a new name, the Edison Electric Institute, appeared to take its place. There was little at that time to suggest that a fundamental change had occurred. The campaign to dissolve utility holding companies persisted, however, and in 1935 the Wheeler-Rayburn bill to do just that came before Congress. A torrent of nearly 90,000 telegrams opposed to the bill poured in upon Congress and a new investigation into the lobbying campaign that had produced this flood was ordered. As many Congressmen had suspected, a large number of the telegrams were spurious, the product of large-scale expenditure by the electric utility industry. The Public Utility Holding Company Act of 1935 included a provision requiring representatives of utility companies or their subsidiaries dealing with the government to register with the newly created Securities and Exchange Commission. The provision was a partial realization of the suggestion for labelling lobbyists that had been made during the 1913 investigation into the National Association of Manufacturers.

In late January 1958, the Special Subcommittee on Legislative Oversight of the House of Representatives undertook an inquiry into the operations of the big independent regulatory commissions of the federal government.[5] The initial purpose was to see whether the Interstate Commerce Commission, the Federal Trade Commission, the Federal Communications Commission, the Securities and Exchange Commission, and the Civil Aeronautics Board had acted in accord with the laws under which they had been established. Considering the very broad powers granted to these agencies, the undertaking was important. Within a very short time, however, the investigators found themselves propelled into pursuit of corrupt influences within the agencies. Helped by a sensation-hungry press, the subcommittee's staff Director, Dr. Bernard Schwartz, prodded it into exposure of a rather sordid and petty set of relationships between members of the Federal Communications Commission and people in the broadcasting industry. On the one hand, an easygoing practice of accepting gifts and financial support from firms and individuals in the industry had developed in the Commission. On the other hand, there were distinct indications that some of the donors of this largesse had benefited from their generosity by favorable actions taken by the Commission. There was in particular a scandalous story of the assignment of a much-sought television channel in Miami, Florida. Several reputations were destroyed in the course of this investigation.

The subcommittee, having tasted blood, now turned to a much more tempting target, Sherman Adams, assistant to President Eisenhower. To the accompaniment of sensational headlines in the daily papers, the subcommittee established that Mr. Adams was a friend of Bernard Goldfine, a New England industrialist. Mr. Goldfine had paid hotel bills for Mr. and Mrs. Adams; he had given Mr. Adams a rug (or possibly several rugs) and a vicuna coat (the exotic origin of the latter item seemed particularly sinister as the story developed). It seemed also to be true that Mr. Adams had made a number of calls to several agencies with which Mr. Goldfine was having difficulty. The clamor that followed destroyed Mr. Adams' usefulness in government and produced his resignation.

The four investigations into political influence outlined above range over a half century of American history. Their details differ. The story uncovered by two is of improper, or seemingly improper, influence on Congress. Another revealed improper influence on education and public opinion, while the last exposed improper influence on administrative officers. Nevertheless, all of these investigations had the same preoccupation with corruption of public virtue by private power.

The record of exposure of this sort is one of almost tiresome repetition. The investigation of the National Association of Manufacturers went on in both houses of Congress and lasted more than two years. The investigation of the American Farm Bureau Federation and the National Electric Light Association both took place in the 1920s. In 1929 there was an investigation into the forces playing upon a tariff bill of that year. The 1935 investigation into lobbying on the utility holding company bill did produce a measure for the registration of lobbyists, which in turn became a model for a more general measure for the "control" of lobbying in the Congressional Reorganization Act of 1946. In 1949 and 1950 a select committee of the House of Representatives conducted a general investigation of lobbying, this time to examine the effectiveness of the 1946 provisions for control of lobbying. To nobody's surprise, effectiveness was found to be slight.[6]

In 1956 a special committee of the Senate undertook an investigation of political activities, lobbying, and campaign contributions.[7] This committee's major topic was campaign finance, but it also strayed into an investigation of lobbying by the oil and gas industry. The 1958 excursion of the Special Subcommittee on Legislative Oversight into exposure of "the influence racket," as Bernard Schwartz termed it, was in the same tradition.

This is by no means a complete catalogue. A comprehensive history would have to include the Pinchot-Ballinger dispute during Taft's administration, the story of Teapot Dome in Harding's, the uproar over mink coats in Truman's. The account would go on almost indefinitely if it were extended to state and local governments. There is probably no state in which it is not possible to find some political reporter or "Young Turk" legislator willing to explain, at length, "the system" as it operates in the legislature of his state.[8] These stories sometimes reach public print, but they have to compete for attention with their counterparts on the national scene.

III

There have been few more persistent themes in American political life than that of outraged virtue. Sporadically, but repeatedly and insistently, national indignation has erupted at revelations of corruption in public life. Sometimes these outbursts have been related to issues of major national importance. Sometimes, as in the discovery that television quiz programs had been staged and arranged for dramatic effect, they have been over issues so trivial as to be ludicrous. And sometimes, as in the McCarthy period, they have been genuinely sinister. But all have carried a common note of betrayal.[9]

Of the many objects of popular wrath in these recurrent moments of exposure the most frequent has been corruption of the political process itself. The incidents recalled in the preceding pages all had this issue as their foundation. The activities of Colonel Mulhall and the NAM, the efforts of the National Electric Light Association, the association of presidential assistant Sherman Adams and Bernard Goldfine, all stood as breaches of the democratic faith—a faith that seems at times to place almost impossible demands upon the integrity of the servants of a fickle and ungrateful public. All, moreover, posed a question about the realities of political power in a nation often seemingly given to the belief that private exercise—or even possession—of power is everywhere illegitimate.

The most characteristic form of the exercise of private power, to judge by the recurrence of public inquiries on the topic, has been lobbying. In the past this term referred exclusively to attempts to influence members of Congress and other legislatures; historically it has carried, moreover, the connotation of bribery and threats, a meaning it has not entirely lost today. Thus, the Constitution of California defines lobbying as improper influence through bribery and intimidation, a definition dating back to the nineteenth century, when the methods of lobbyists were particularly direct and uninhibited. Yet despite a political history that has often been lurid, California has found no occasion to use the provision for prosecutions in the courts. Definitions of this kind undoubtedly leave open the possibility that there may exist proper means of influence, but it is fairly clear that the view of lobbying as necessarily involving something improper is widespread indeed.

Perhaps the major change in the public's attitude toward lobbying is that implied in the broadening of the term to include foci of power other than legislatures. That the sort of influence investigated by the Subcommittee on Legislative Oversight was considered lobbying is fairly comprehensible. Federal regulatory commissions make regulations that have the effect of law, and it is understandable that they should become objects of lobbying attentions. With extensive ventures like that of the NELA, however, something rather different was brought into the concept. A House of Representatives investigation by the Buchanan Committee of 1949 and 1950 finally found the term "indirect lobbying," which assimilated into the idea of lobbying attempts to create a favorable but generalized public opinion for some particular cause. But, however great this extension of the concept of lobbying, the implication of impropriety, even of corruption and evil, remained.

There is something curious in this pattern of exposure which has been so nearly a constant of American political life: the sense of revulsion and surprise with which each incident is met. The revulsion is understandable; almost all of these incidents have involved something sordid. Moreover, all have provided ammunition for the ulterior purposes of one or more of the groups contending in politics. The element of surprise is somewhat more difficult to comprehend. What novelty each new revelation has had has been only of detail, and often even the detail has been known to many people before the ritual of purgation has begun. Still, the public sense of shock and surprise remains.

There are some simple explanations for this phenomenon, but they are partial only. Exposure of corruption is at once the obligation of journalism and the making of circulation. Wrongdoing and its flagellation are in the very definition of news. Certainly in the underworld of common motives there is a latent taste for sensation. And this, in turn, is related to the puritan moralism that is so strong a force in the American tradition.

Yet these factors, even taken together, do not adequately explain the persistent eruptions that have characterized American public life. Nor do they explain the resistance, the containing force, that has given these incidents their peculiarly explosive and sometimes dangerous quality. In retrospect it is difficult to escape the impression that there was in each case an unwillingness on the part of many people in official positions, whether in Congress or in administration, to proceed with the unmasking that was expected and demanded of them. It was often with a mixture of resentment and embarrassment that, when forced by zealots or by circumstances, they turned to the task they knew they could not escape. To one degree or another, members of the investigating bodies knew the facts they would uncover before their inquiries began. In some sense, the larger facts were common knowledge.

Thus, the existence of lobbying, of "pressure groups," of private power is a topic on which American thought has been deeply ambivalent. On perhaps no other subject in American political affairs has there been an equal uncertainty. Yet this is an area of politics in which American experience has been distinctive. Where European politics and European political thought have been cast in the mold of classes and class conflict, American politics has been largely free of class divisions and American political thought has had little to offer on this subject. This lack is the consequence, as Louis Hartz has said (echoing Tocqueville), of the fact that Americans were "born equal" without having had to become so.[10] There has indeed been a profound consensus on the large issues that in other countries have been subject to the overriding fact of class conflict. It is probably appropriate to see the uniqueness of American experience in its absence of a feudal past. Nevertheless, American freedom from feudal distinctions and class conflict has not preserved the United States from divisions of a different sort, which have provided much of the drama and, perhaps, most of the dynamism of American political life. But there has never been any real agreement or settled doctrine by which they are to be understood.

There have been many attempts to explain American politics in terms of class, but the Marxian formulas have fared ill over the long span. Socialism seemed for a period near the turn of the twentieth century to be a viable movement; there are even grounds for believing that the recording of its strength was seriously minimized by the mechanics of the American electoral system. Nevertheless, socialism as a movement was largely ended by 1912, though there was a brief renewal of class thinking during the worst years of the Great Depression, when it seemed possible that the economic order was in a process of collapse.

Furthermore, among the scholarly attempts to apply the categories of class to political phenomena in the United States, revisionism and redefinition have been so extensive that the meaning of "class" tends to be lost. The tests of class have often been subjective ("Do you consider yourself to be a member of the upper class, the middle class, or the lower class?"). The structures of class that have been set forth have become very elaborate ("upper-upper," "middle-upper," and so on). These characteristics of research in American class structure have helped to reinforce the everyday perceptions of many Americans that "class" in the European sense adds little to understanding political life in the United States. This is not to say that American history has been free of bitter conflict between various segments of society. Homestead, Haymarket, Pullman, Wheatland, Centralia—all are names that evoke memories of social conflict. It is relatively easy to assemble a list of events, including these and others, to support the argument that class conflict has been a major feature of American life; certainly the record of violence in America is as striking as that of many other countries. The facts of bitterness and conflict, however, do not establish that the lines of division are those of class.

In the large pattern of American politics the really persistent thread of conflict has been among units smaller than class. Even issues that have erupted in violence have been resolved within this context—that is, as particular issues—and have not had to await fundamental changes in government. This has been perhaps the greatest merit of the American political order. Virtually no definable group has been compelled for long to consider itself hopelessly outside that order. Where there has been exclusion of any substantial group, violence has frequently occurred, as is most dramatically illustrated by the violent strikes of the late nineteenth and early twentieth centuries. Where orderly access to power by small units and by organized groups has been possible, violence has been at a minimum.

By the same token, however, the accessibility to a share in power for almost any coherent and determined group has given American democracy some of its most serious and perplexing problems. The avoidance of a class basis of power has not put all individuals on an equal political footing. The phenomenon of power has not been banished. Some groups have used their opportunity with much greater effectiveness than others, for some, indeed, have been unable to seize the opportunity at all. Frequently, equality of political opportunity has become as much a mockery as equality of economic opportunity.

The particular consequences of this situation have stirred the American people again and again. The incidents sketched in the preceding pages illustrate the readiness of Americans to be shocked by what almost certainly are normal features of the political order that has evolved. Usually the outbursts of public indignation are triggered by discovery of a somehow underhanded trick or device. Corruption is the typical evil that is charged. The charge of corruption, however, is never as simple as it seems. Corruption of what? The question is seldom asked and difficult to answer. Certainly, bribery is an evil, and it has sometimes been categorically exposed. In some situations, however, it would be impossible to say definitely that bribery has occurred. In other situations it is clear that the intent and effect of bribery have occurred without the crime's having taken place at all; the clearest example of this is the giving of employment in an industry regulated by government to a government officer upon his retirement from the regulating agency. Usually, investigations into corruption emerge with far less lurid discoveries than initial allegations promise. This was true, for example, in the 1913 investigation of the National Association of Manufacturers and in the 1958 investigations by the Subcommittee on Legislative Oversight.

The tendency for public attention to focus upon the often trivial human failings of individuals in Congress or elsewhere in government service is the symptom of a deep uncertainty of expectations. Each time that attention is diverted to individual failings, as in a borderline case of petty bribery, the implication is that the problem is solely one of individual morality. And the conclusion is frequently drawn that the solution lies in the appointment of "better men."[11] The public is usually appeased when the individual culprits are punished by jailing or public disgrace. Nevertheless, the issue is much more general and political than the hue and cry in pursuit of some particular brand of miscreants suggests. Scandals over the exercise of "influence" are frequent, but are seemingly dependent more upon chance discovery and the popular mood than upon the actual occurrence of the phenomenon of influence itself. That phenomenon is probably one of the constants of political life in a democracy, as is suggested by the discovery of the exercise of power by interest groups in other lands[12]—which does not, however, diminish the degree to which this is a particularly American phenomenon.

The American response to the existence of private power has never been consistent. At different times one attitude or another has been dominant, but other attitudes have always been opposed. This national ambivalence explains in large part why the repeated outcries over corruption of the political process have never resulted in fundamental changes or reform. The immolation of a few exposed individuals has served to pacify the aroused public, but it has never struck at the heart of the problem.

There have been serious attempts to look at the phenomena of group power within the large context of the democratic system. These attempts, however, have tended to divide into the same two categories into which public attitudes have consistently fallen. To describe the two points of view is difficult because much of the vocabulary of politics is derived from the political life of Europe. Thus it is tempting to label one attitude "liberal" and the other "conservative," or to see one as "left" and the other as "right." Neither categorization is accurate, however. Both relate to systems of politics in which the class struggle colors virtually all issues. Where, as in America, that struggle was largely settled in the early years of nationality, the use of such a vocabulary can only be deceptive. The confusion to which it can lead is evident, for example, in the difficulty involved in discussing organized labor in the United States. If labor is regarded as a class, the terms "liberal" and "left" seem appropriate. But the program of labor in the United States, as well as much of its point of view, is more accurately described as conservative. Similar difficulties are encountered with other groups.

Nevertheless, the existence of extensive private power remains a problem in America. The instinct of mistrust for power wherever it exists is sound, however difficult the control of power may be. Since power is at the heart of all politics, it is inevitable that there should be sharp differences of opinion and even confusion about the part it plays in our common life. From time to time we have cherished the illusion that power need not exist, sometimes even that it is a myth. Parts of our political tradition seem to encourage these beliefs. They are dangerous, for they prevent understanding and contribute to the evils we would cure. Power is inescapably a reality; the forms it takes profoundly affect the ends it serves; the ends may well be other than those which are intended. In this lie some of the ironies of American politics.

Chapter 2

The Progressive Legacy

I

During the two decades divided by the year 1900 the problem of private power confronted the American people openly on a scale unmatched in the history of the republic. The corporation assumed its modern form and the institutions of transportation, exchange, and finance acquired an unprecedented influence over the affairs of ordinary men. Government appeared to do the bidding of those who directed the new behemoths of capitalism. A newly elected member of the United States Senate, on arriving in Washington, was told by one of his seniors, "Young man, tariffs are the whole of politics. Study them." This was not just cynicism; it was the practical wisdom of a political oligarchy whose power had endured for more than a generation. Yet there were other political topics of concern to members of this oligarchy. They included the control of legislatures and cities. They touched upon the distribution of the public lands and the content of the coinage. They bore upon the control of labor and its unions.

The response to the emergence of this power took different forms. By 1900 Populism, the greatest agrarian movement the nation had known or ever would know, had collapsed. There had been an incipient mass movement of workingmen in the Knights of Labor, but it too had disappeared. Marxian socialism had immigrated with the new tides of Europe's outcasts, and there was even a native movement of anarchosyndicalism in the new Industrial Workers of the World. These, however, were already locked in struggle with the forces that would before long reduce them to impotence.

All of these movements were symptoms of a deep and widespread sense of exploitation and disorder. They centered in those segments of the population with the most specific grievances. By the same token, however, these were groups apart from the main current of American life in the new century. Without doubt many people in that current, the broad middle class of increasingly urbanized Americans, saw nothing disturbing in the rise of the new aggregations of power. Nevertheless, the sense of an evil turn in national development was pervasive; the public's preoccupation with corruption was the most certain symptom. Although critiques by the Populists, organized labor, and even the Socialists influenced to some degree the more widespread uneasiness, it derived from an older vision, the vision of the public good. This vision, handed down by the founders of the republic, was one not often elaborated or easily defined. Yet it became the point of departure for a tradition of much importance to the development of American political life in the twentieth century.

The movement which assumed the role of defender of the public came after 1900. It had many aspects—so many, in fact, that it may be misleading to place them all within a single movement. Yet there were lines that connected them, and without minimizing their sometimes contradictory aspects, it is appropriate to use for them the term applied to the most conspicuous political movement of the time, Progressivism.

Progressivism was a movement of many paradoxes. Built on the foundations of Populism, it was yet more an urban than a rural phenomenon; speaking in the name of the mass of men, it was blind (when it was not hostile) to the organizations of labor; strong in language, it was weak in action. The most important paradox, however, was much more complicated and went to the very heart of what the movement meant. Essentially, Progressivism was an attack upon private power, reasserting the public's interest and decrying the "special" interests, sometimes in extreme terms. Yet the doctrines of Progressivism led to justification and acceptance of the evils it set out to destroy.

This paradox was slow to emerge; in one sense it took two decades, but it was present from the beginning. It accounts, perhaps, for the lack of accomplishment that has troubled some reformers; it certainly accounts for much of the apparent discontinuity in the history of American reform which Richard Hofstadter has seen in the beginning of the New Deal.[1] The story of reform—a word that is seriously inadequate for this strain of democratic thought, although we have no better—has been told many times. Yet it is necessary to look back to the varied parts of the Progressive movement and to seek what was common to them.

II

The political capital Progressivism began with consisted of a grievance and a theory. The grievance was a direct inheritance from Populism, which with all the certainty of rural fundamentalism held that a usurpation of political power had taken place at the direct expense of those who labor in the earth. In its earlier form the distress arose from foreclosed farms, low prices for farm products, and high railroad rates—and there was a common belief that behind these evils was the conquest of legislatures, railroad commissions, and the federal government by men of corporate wealth.

The theory inherited from Populism was the theory of "conspiracy," a notion that runs like a scarlet thread through the claims of American reform. In its most frequent form it amounted to an assertion that *any* power was usurpation[2]—a view, indeed, of considerably longer standing than Populism. As Henry Adams observed, it went back to the nation's beginning: "The great object of terror and suspicion to the people of the thirteen provinces was power; not merely power in the hands of a president or a prince, of one assembly or several, of many citizens or few, but power in the abstract, wherever it existed and under whatever form it was known."[3] The evil was *power in the abstract;* where power appeared in a democracy, it came only through conspiracy and corruption of honest forms of government.

Although some groups had hard, specific claims to make against the railroads or the trusts, the leaders of the Progressive movement were not on the whole representatives of those groups. Those with specific grievances were farmers and workers; the former, however, had largely withdrawn from politics and the latter were not included in the list of those for whom Progressivism primarily spoke. Pre-eminently the movement was middle class—and here was material for another paradox. Unlike the situation one hundred years before, power in 1900 was private power, and simple opposition to government would not serve to challenge it. To the lesson that a challenge of power can only be made by power the corollary had to be added that a challenge to private power sometimes could only be made by public power. But neither lesson accorded with the Progressives' ingrained distrust of power in the abstract.

The dark suspicion of things gone wrong through the concentration of power that goes with concentration of wealth came directly from the Populists, but it also had other sources. It would be difficult to say how much influence the criticisms of the Socialists had, but it is certain that some Socialist slogans struck responses that their parent theory could never evoke. The work of men like Gustavus Myers, moreover, brought to light facts that added to the picture being drawn by others. Perhaps as important was the legacy of Henry George. The peculiar unorthodoxy of George has consigned him to gathering oblivion, but his influence was considerable in formulating the questions that brought many to the verge of action in the Progressive years.[4]

Perhaps the effect of these influences might have been different if they had not converged as they did at the moment when technological change exploded in the printing industry. The Merganthaler Linotype was perfected in the last decade of the nineteenth century, and its consequence of cheap and abundant newspapers brought about a new technology of journalism and a new democracy of readers. Grievances against private groups provided material for the new journalism, but, inevitably, the issues presented were simplified for the vast new public to which the popular press addressed itself. "Muckraking" often was based on careful journalistic research, and much of it derived from conviction. Nevertheless, competition among the journals led to more and more sensational charges, until boredom and the law of diminishing returns finally brought muckraking to an end. Before David Graham Phillips made the ultimate charge, "The Treason of the Senate," in his series for *Cosmopolitan*, a long list of individuals and institutions had been treated to muckraking exposure: Carnegie, Schwab, Morgan, Vanderbilt, Rockefeller, Armour, Swift, Harriman, Astor, grain exchanges, oil, sugar, railroads, tobacco, packinghouses, banks, colleges, churches, the press, labor unions, cities, states, and the federal government.[5]

In the charges made against virtually all the institutions of American society there was one common theme—corruption. Various muckrakers had their own more elaborate theses to argue, but they agreed on one point: everywhere selfishness had corrupted original purposes of a higher nature. There has been a tendency in recent studies to explain the sharp intolerance which is an important undercurrent of American political life by reference to the rural Protestantism so evident in Populism and its kindred movements.[6] However, the need for simplification that derived from the new technology of journalism also tended to measure social phenomena solely on the scale of *virtue*—not the lowest common denominator, but the simplest. Quite as much as the bleak fundamentalism of the farmers, this accounted for the denunciations of the Progressive era. The political morality it developed was fully as harsh and intolerant, for all its secular basis.

The thesis of decay, however, was unsatisfactory. Corruption of such prevalence, disorder of such magnitude could only be explained by something more than the assumption of a slow-spreading decay. The theory of conspiracy was ready at hand and in one way or another it was invoked as an explanation. "The system," a term of sinister implications, was ultimately taken to be the evil, rather than the individual failings of policemen, legislators, editors, or clergymen. Thus Lincoln Steffens urged Theodore Roosevelt:

"The representatives and the senators," I said, "those that I know, those who come from States that I have investigated are picked men chosen for their tried service to the system in their states. They stand for all you are against; they are against all you are for. They have the departments filled with men they had sent here to be rewarded for antisocial services; and as vacancies occur, they will want you to support rascals of similar records." He nodded. He knew that. T. R. saw the machine; he did not see the system. He saw the party organizations of the politicians; he saw some "bad trusts" back of the bad politics, but he did not see the good trusts back of the bad trusts that were back of the bad machines. He did not see that the corrupting he resisted was a process to make the government represent business rather than politics and the people.[7]

Attack on "the system" has been a stock-in-trade of radical dissenters for much of our history. Although today we tend to associate it most commonly with Marxists, it has never been their peculiar property. "The system" was a perception of John Taylor of Caroline; many of the later Populists were also convinced of its existence. It passed readily over into the thinking of Progressivism.[8] This kind of explanation is partly the result of a common attempt to understand and find order in apparent chaos. It was also the result of a craving for simplicity, for reducing the diversity of things to clear-cut moral issues on which clear-cut judgments could be passed. In one way or another, however, "the system" was rarely considered that normal and to-be-expected web of institutions and relationships by which men are governed and their work is given meaning. The idea was, rather, that there existed a coherent, carefully thought out, and coordinated achievement of a singularly gifted, secret, and selfish band of plotters.

If this type of explanation often had its own beguiling simplicities, underlying it was a view of politics whose latent tendencies were not fully seen during the Progressive era, but which had important possibilities for later years. Of the many writings on political problems that appeared during this time, one published in 1907 best expressed the quality of the Progressive impulse. J. Allen Smith's *The Spirit of American Government* anticipated much of the argument in Charles Beard's *An Economic Interpretation of the Constitution*, but, lacking the latter's mass of factual detail, so appealing to American readers, it has been relegated to the role of its precursor. Smith explained his purpose: "to call attention to the spirit of the Constitution, its inherent opposition to democracy, the obstacles which it has placed in the way of majority rule. . . ."[9] Better than anyone else he provided the theoretical foundations the ardent pragmatists of the Progressive movement had refused to bother with.

The root of the evils with which American political life was troubled, Smith argued, was in the Constitution itself, and its origins went back to the nation's beginning. Some colonial institutions and most of the system of law were inherited from England, where they reflected the supremacy of the well-to-do minority. During the revolutionary period there was a drift toward democracy and a rejection of "the English theory of checks and balances." Some of this attitude was carried over to the government under the Articles of Confederation, but this was followed by the Constitution, "a reactionary document." The change was the work of wealthy conservatives; the democrats who had signed the Declaration of Independence were very slightly represented among the framers of the Constitution. As a result, "democracy was not the object which the framers had in view, but the very thing which they wished to avoid."

According to Smith, the system produced was undemocratic in both spirit and detail. Perhaps most important in his eyes was the difficulty of amending the Constitution. "All democratic constitutions are flexible and easy to amend. This follows from the fact that in a government which the people really control, a constitution is merely the means of securing the supremacy of public opinion and not an instrument for thwarting it." The independence of the judiciary and its power to review legislation were almost equally important, and these were inherently characteristics of aristocratic government. Checks and balances operated—and were intended to operate—against the majority will. Party, which had developed in spite of the framers' intention, was potentially a mechanism for insuring majority rule, but it had been so corrupted that the choice of candidates was made in the secret councils of the ruling minority. And in any event, party was doomed to frustration by the separation of powers provided by the Constitution. The general result was government by and for the wealthy interests.

This summary of the salient points of one of the most incisive books ever written about American politics does not do it justice. It is perhaps sufficient, however, to illustrate the coherent and forceful argument that Smith had to make. If there was a conspiracy it was, in his eyes, one that dated from 1787, had been in continuous existence, and was intermittently locked in struggle with the rising democracy of the masses (a word he used). Smith was one of those who had early been influenced by reading Henry George, but his work in places also had Marxian echoes (although his book was primarily political rather than economic).

Certainly, Smith cannot be taken as a characteristic figure of the Progressive Movement, although his book was one of the clearest statements to emerge from Progressivism. The significance of his work lies rather in the fact that he drew the full consequences from the majoritarian tendencies of Progressivism. More perhaps than any other American political writer of stature, he asserted majority rule qualified by few constitutional limitations as the principle of democracy. In one sense, therefore, his accomplishment was a muckraking of the Constitution and the whole of American political life.

Although *The Spirit of American Government* was widely read and had a strong influence,[10] majority rule was not the essential meaning of Progressivism. Dedication to majority rule perhaps went without saying among the Progressives, but emphasis upon it as principle did not accord with the dread of political power *in any form* that sometimes seemed to be the central motive of the movement. In Smith's quest of power for the majority, there was a sign of the pervasive and latent ambiguity of the movement. Power as it existed was antagonistic to democracy, but how was it to be curbed without the erection of a superior power?

This was the dilemma with which the other major Progressive intellectual figure, Herbert Croly, struggled. Like Smith a bit outside the mainstream of the movement, Croly was also willing to see the development of strong centralized power. His solution, the application of Hamiltonian methods to Jeffersonian ends, implied centralization of power not merely in government, but in *national* government, and this drive for strong national government was evident throughout the campaigns of Progressivism.[11] Like Smith, Croly saw the difficult amendment process as a barrier to the achievement of democracy in the United States. He even predicted that it would become the dominating issue of American politics.[12]

III

In the mainstream of Progressivism, however, the problem was simpler: to exorcise private power, rather than to oppose it with a greater. The program of Progressivism, wherever it was found, had this consistency: to restore honesty to government and society by returning government to the public.

Locally, this meant essentially the same list of reforms. Probably the first item everywhere was to exclude the corporate "interests" from politics—and nearly everywhere this meant primarily the ejection of railroad influence. The railroads, *bête noire* of the Populists, were perhaps no more than the first of the large corporations to attract public attention, but the fact remains that almost everywhere they were deeply involved in politics. The machine Robert La Follette set himself to unseat was primarily the railroads'; its director was a lumberman,

Philetus Sawyer, but the judicious distribution of railroad passes, the use of railroad money, the prominence of railroad men in party councils made it abundantly clear that the Republican Party of Wisconsin was neither more nor less than a railroad machine. In California railroad domination was even more complete. The Southern Pacific virtually owned both parties. Although his influence may well have been exaggerated, the Southern Pacific's political manager, William Herrin, rather than the legislature or the parties, was the proper object of lobbying. Hiram Johnson successfully ran for governor on the promise to "kick the S.P. out of politics." In state after state—in Iowa, where Cummins collided with the Burlington and the Great Northern, in Minnesota, the Dakotas, Nebraska, and Kansas—the central issue was the power exercised by the railroad political bosses.[13]

Why were the railroads so singularly active in political affairs? Probably because they were singularly vulnerable to the actions of government. Local communities, even whole states, had since the Granger period passed laws designed to harass the behemoths whose lines passed through them and on which they were so critically dependent. If Herrin of the Southern Pacific controlled the California legislature from San Francisco and if agents for other railroads similarly ran the Dakota legislatures from St. Paul, it was in no small part from conviction on the part of the railroad directors that this was their surest means of defense against an unreasonably hostile public. There was also the precedent that land grants from government, often given under the guidance of representatives of the railroad companies, had been essential to the railroads' development. Thus they had been involved in politics from their beginning.

The trusts, after the railroads, were the greatest targets of Progressive wrath, with the difference, however, that very little was done about the political involvement of the trusts. The Sherman Act was rarely invoked, and when it was, it was more often by the moderate Taft than by Roosevelt. The reason lay in the deep uncertainty of many Progressives about their objective. Ida Tarbell's *History of the Standard Oil Company* emphasized the ruthless competitive methods of John D. Rockefeller, but these were not the primary evils Progressivism sought to strike. Somewhat the same could be said of Upton Sinclair's *The Jungle;* clean meat was desirable, but again this issue was hardly central. Roosevelt voiced the Progressives' uncertainty when he made a distinction between the "good" and the "bad" trusts.[14] Once more the issue was posed in terms of morality, of that virtue for which Herbert Croly was so concerned. And yet the real issue was the power possessed by these new giants of industrial organization. Here the questions became more troubling. Should the economic logic of the Sherman Act be pursued? The economic logic of competition was not central, but it did seem to offer one solution to the problem of private power. Already in 1900, however, there were expressions of doubt that the solution would work.[15]

Another solution, reform of the political institutions themselves, was the alternative the Progressives preferred. Institutional reform was a standard program almost everywhere the Progressives came to office. The direct primary, the initiative and referendum, and a commission form of city government were the essentials of the plan. Together these reforms would return government to the people and drive the corporations from politics. The primary would upset the system by which a handful of men chose the candidates for important offices; the initiative and referendum would check the corruption of the legislatures; and the commission plan would smash the city machines. In larger outline, the program would spell the end of party corruption. But here intentions were not completely clear. Was *party itself* an evil to be destroyed?

The evidence seemed to indicate that the "special interests" had used the party organizations (usually the Republican) to fasten their control upon the people. Parties had provided the machinery by which the railroads, the trusts, and the other special interests had come to control the government. City machines had been corrupted by businesses (both good and bad); state organizations had fallen into the hands of men such as

Philetus Sawyer and William Herrin; the party organization of the United States Senate was Nelson Aldrich's personal machine, working for the high tariffs that benefited only the largest of the interests. To strike at the interests themselves, it was necessary to change the party system. The fault was not simply with one party; the evil was latent in both. Whichever party was elected, the interests were the real winners:

> The people vote for one party and find their hopes turned to ashes on their lips; and then to punish that party, they vote for the other party. So it is that partisan victories have come to be merely the people's vengeance and always the secret powers have played the game. . . . Under this boss system, no matter which party wins, the people seldom win; but the bosses almost always win. And they never work for the people. They do not even work for the party to which they belong. They work only for those anti-public interests whose employees they are. It is these interests that are the real victors in the end.[16]

Nowhere among the Progressives was there any great enthusiasm for party, but some were more willing than others to take the drastic step of changing the party system. La Follette, from early bitter experience in Wisconsin, was convinced that the political machine was itself a menace. He deplored "the unreasoning loyalty to party,"[17] and one of the first reforms he achieved in Wisconsin was the direct primary. Some Progressives took a more radical position. Herbert Croly, for example, was profoundly pessimistic about the prospects of party democracy.

> The two party system has serious, and, to my mind, fatal drawbacks. It can never get away from the initial vice of being no more than an attempt to democratize a group of undemocratic political institutions. Just in so far as a group of really democratic political institutions are created, the foundations of the two-party system are undermined.[18]

The remedy for an undemocratic government was not "to democratize the party which was organized to democratize the government, but to democratize the government itself."[19] The parties themselves could then be dispensed with. Croly was too sophisticated to accept a theory of conspiracy, but he was convinced that a deep derangement of the nation's political life had taken place. "The vast incoherent mass of the American people is falling into definite social groups, which restrict and define the mental outlook and social experience of their members. . . . The earlier homogeneity of American society has been impaired and no authoritative and edifying, but conscious social ideal has as yet taken its place."[20] The roots of the evil, then, were deep, and nothing less than a restoration of the principle of virtue, which implied unselfishness and, thus, a reduction of private power, would restore democracy.

The general Progressive conclusion, then, was that parties were a medium of special-interest power; to strike at the special interests themselves involved some kind of change in the party system. The logic of this approach was carried further in California than perhaps anywhere else the Progressives came to power. The first step was achievement of the initiative, referendum, and recall in Los Angeles in 1903. In 1909 the state legislature passed a direct primary law requiring a test of party affiliation for candidates seeking nomination. In the "reform" legislature of 1911 the initiative, referendum, and recall were adopted for the entire state. In that year also, the test of party affiliation for candidates seeking party nomination was weakened. In 1913 city and county offices were made subject to nonpartisan election. In the same year the requirement of an affidavit of party affiliation was removed from the Primary Act and the following statement was added: "Nothing in this Act contained shall be construed to limit the rights of any person to become the candidate for more than one political party for the same office upon complying with the requirements of this Act." This provision, the famous "cross-filing" device, was adopted with no controversy and its significance was hardly noted at the time, but it was not an accident; its terms appeared at several places in the state Elections Code. Moreover, parties were circumscribed by a set of provisions determining their governing bodies, times of meeting, and manner of operation so rigid and detailed that the private character of parties was virtually destroyed.[21] In 1915 a capstone to this anti-party legislation was offered in a measure to make all state elective offices, including that of governor, nonpartisan. The measure narrowly missed acceptance in a referendum vote.[22]

Different factors contributed to the steady development of the anti-party program. In California the most obvious was that the Progressives under Hiram Johnson developed their own political organization for which other parties would be rivals. Somewhat the same thing happened in Wisconsin under La Follette.[23] As the party of good government, of virtue, the Progressives almost necessarily were intolerant of opposition, but in both California and Wisconsin the regular party record had been a sorry one and, intolerance aside, empirical justification for the eradication of parties seemed strong.

With the passage of time, however—and it should be noted that antagonism toward parties evolved rather than stood as a matter of principle from the beginning—another line of reasoning developed. This lay in the prospect, or rather the hope, that science and management would solve the problems of government. In the high tide of Progressivism confidence in impersonal expertise took on an almost millennial tone. Thus Charles McCarthy, founder of that remarkable institution, the Wisconsin Legislative Reference Service, wrote in 1912: "If any praise is due the Wisconsin laws, it is probably because of the appointive commissions, the non-partisan spirit, the expert and the civil service law."[24] La Follette asked rhetorically, "How has it been possible that both the people of Wisconsin and the investors in public utilities have been so greatly benefited by this regulation? *Simply because the regulation is scientific.*"[25] Herbert Croly argued, "The administrative commissions are really free only to do right. Just as soon as they go astray the bonds tighten on them. They derive their authority from their knowledge, and from their peculiar relation to public opinion."[26]

IV

Enthusiasm for the administrative ideals of impersonality, independence, and expertise was not peculiar to the Progressives, nor were these ideals of recent invention. Civil service reform in the United States, for example, dated back to the Pendleton Act of 1883. Municipal reform as a movement was somewhat separate from the Progressive movement; nevertheless, it embodied the values of Progressivism. More, these administrative ideals were necessary consequences of the Progressive reforms. In the process of their evolution from Progressive logic, the inner tensions of the movement began to emerge.

Perhaps the most conspicuous sign of tension was that lack of achievement upon the national scene which has been the reason for criticism of the movement. Yet Progressivism had some accomplishments, and its ambiguities were more important there than in its failures. In national scope Progressivism's achievements in conservation were by all odds its greatest. To a remarkable degree this success was the work of Gifford Pinchot, one of Theodore Roosevelt's chief lieutenants. The son of a wealthy family, Pinchot took it upon himself to introduce the science of forestry to the United States, preparing himself by study abroad and practical experience in the United States for his chosen mission. With the transfer of the National Forests from the Department of the Interior to the Department of Agriculture and the establishment of the United States Forest Service as their guardian in 1905, Pinchot saw the first part of his objective attained. As chief of the new service, Pinchot laid down standards of professionalism and administrative integrity and efficiency that have made this service one of the most respected in the federal government. He went on to organize a series of conferences, commissions, and associations that made "conservation" the hallmark of the Progressive regime. Ultimately Pinchot became involved in a bitter controversy with Taft's Secretary of the Interior and, although forced to resign his post, did more than anyone else to secure Taft's defeat in his attempt for reelection. In the course of his stormy career, Pinchot stamped conservation upon the American consciousness and drastically decreased the pace at which the natural resources of the public lands were being dissipated.[27]

It was a remarkable accomplishment, one that would do

great credit to any administration. There has been a mistaken temptation to give the credit wholly to Pinchot and to treat the conservation movement as distinct from Progressivism. Nevertheless, the conservation movement was characteristically Progressive; its policy was no more than Progressive policy in the field of natural resources. Perhaps the most characteristic appeal of conservation was that of antimonopoly.[28] The essential principle, however, was contained in Pinchot's statement that "the natural resources must be developed and preserved for the benefit of the many, and not merely for the few"[29]—a statement he followed with the same denunciation of the special interests and the same emphasis upon virtue that ran through the entire Progressive movement.

When the Forest Service assumed custody of the transferred forests, Pinchot drafted a letter that went to Service personnel under the signature of the Secretary of Agriculture. Part of it read:

In the administration of the forest reserves it must be clearly borne in mind that all land is to be devoted to its most productive use for the permanent good of the whole people, and not for the temporary benefit of individuals and companies. All the resources of the reserves are for *use*. . . . In the management of each reserve local questions will be decided upon local grounds; the dominant industry will be considered first, but with as little restriction to minor industries as may be possible; sudden changes in industrial conditions will be avoided by gradual adjustment after due notice; and where conflicting interests must be reconciled the question will always be decided from the standpoint of the greatest good of the greatest number in the long run. . . .[30]

This language, more widely quoted within the Service than any other, became its high doctrine in subsequent years. "The permanent good of the whole people" and "the greatest good of the greatest number in the long run" are phrases it is tempting to regard as decorative clichés, but they are the terms on which a structure of administration has been built. Out of this language evolved justification for what has come to be known as "the multiple-use policy." The "greatest good" formula, in particular, is to be heard from even the most humble of the Service's officers.

The inherent problem lies in the *conflict* of uses, as was recognized in a revision of the first Service manual. The following language appeared in the edition of 1911:

> National Forest land should not be devoted to an inferior use so as to preclude a higher use. For instance, after the issuance of a pasture permit it may be found that the area covers the only available reservoir site for the water supply of the community. In such a case the District Forester should exercise his discretion and cancel the permit. The welfare of the community or the number of people benefited should be the factor determining a higher use, rather than the amount of money to be obtained for the use.[31]

This addition, however, was only more explicit recognition of the problem; the approach was unchanged. The first implication of this policy was its great reliance on discretion; the expert judgment of the Service should extend to matters of values. The second implication was that the test of numbers would be a sufficient guide to the exercise of that discretion and judgment.

Here, in the detail of regulations of one administrative agency —in microcosm, as it were—lie the basic ambiguities and perplexities of Progressivism itself. The Forest Service had emerged from its founders' determination that the special interests should be subordinated to some general public interest in the use of the forests. Its creation was part of a crusade against all too conspicuous evils: monopoly and waste of natural resources. But in the transformation of the movement from one against evil to one for good difficulties arose which the old righteous formulas of denunciation would not resolve. What was "the greatest good of the greatest number in the long run"? How should it be recognized? Who should determine "the highest use"? Antipathy to private power was no guide to the exercise of public power. Worst of all, a definition of positive goals did not automatically derive from the denial of private goals. The one was not the opposite of the other; virtue was not enough.[32]

So it was with the Progressive movement as a whole. Its primary accusation, that the special interests had amassed power, was undeniable. In their identification of power, the Progressives were correct more often than not. Yet in their extension into a theory of conspiracy of the discovery of business interests behind city machines, of railroads behind party organizations within the legislatures, of bankers behind the United States Senate, there was an illusion. These interests—selfish certainly and sometimes predatory—were in no massive combination, nor did they have a common purpose. Their agreement was based only upon the needs of logrolling, transitory in nature and pragmatic always. The vision of a public interest was wholly lacking; only the assertion of private interests was explicit. Had the conspiracy existed that the Progressives at times assumed, their attack would of necessity have been on government itself, something they never contemplated.

Progressivism did assert a public interest, but its vision of this interest was never clear. Destruction of private power was a clear enough goal, but what should take the place of such power? If public power, how should it be organized and exercised? If parties were to be emasculated, what would be left save government by the expert, government in the name of a public whose multitudes could never speak except through interest groups—the very instruments of that hidden government whose destruction constituted the Progressive mission? There were no answers for these questions.

In practice as well as in theory Progressivism faltered. The antimonopoly policy was applied in desultory fashion. The zeal for direct democracy via initiative and referendum brought reforms, but the results were trivial beside the promise. Government was returned to the people in some places, but where this took place nothing was left to politics; quietism, good government, businesslike management, administration were all that remained.

Perhaps among the Progressives, J. Allen Smith understood the movement best. He had drawn—ruthlessly—its fullest implications. Years later, looking back upon the movement, he said, "The real trouble with us reformers is that we made a crusade against standards. Well, we smashed them all and now neither we nor anybody else have anything left."[33]

V

What came of the Progressive movement? Was the result as bleak as Smith in his disillusionment believed?

With a movement as diffuse and as frequently contradictory as Progressivism, it is neither safe nor easy to judge. Moreover, since the tendency best illustrated by the Progressive movement reaches back into remoter stages of American history, it is not always clear what is properly to be called Progressive and what is not. Nonetheless it is certain that here was the zenith of reform, of the impulse, in secular form, for the achievement of virtue.

The simplest answer is to say that the goal was not reached. Certainly the narratives of the preceding pages would support such a conclusion. With some tolerance one might add, as does Hofstadter,[34] that catharsis was achieved, but this is faint praise for so much effort. Such a judgment, however, is too severe. If a fair estimate of the strictly moral aspects of the republic's health were to be made, it might very well show that in the years since the muckrakers were hardest at work corruption has greatly declined. Dismissal of Progressivism would also be mistaken on a different and probably more important score. The movement was too strong and of too long duration to be without effect. Moreover, as suggested earlier, it was not itself something discontinuous with the American past, but rather the intensification of an important trend in this country's politics. A generation of political dissidents was schooled in the Progressive era. Its leaders were in eclipse for almost two decades, but enough of them survived to join the next burst of reform when it came with the New Deal. In a multitude of ways the reforming ideas of the first decade of the twentieth century found their way into the actions of the fourth decade.

Actual consequences, however, are sometimes different from those intended. Some factors impinging upon a situation may not be taken into account; those that are may be misunderstood. So it would seem with the Progressive hostility toward parties. To a remarkable degree this hostility and the "reforms" it engendered were successful in impeding the development of party systems, most strikingly in California. The measures the Progressives wrote into the California elections code went far to make efforts to develop party organization sterile—as intended. Only in the 1950s when the most stringent of these measures were repealed and the Progressive program circumvented by extralegal organization parallel to the emasculated official party forms did that state begin to have a genuine party system.[35] In this sense Progressivism had succeeded, but it had based its program upon the theory that the political machine to be smashed was a party machine. In retrospect, however, it can be seen that the actual machine was purely a creature of the Southern Pacific and a few allied interests, not a party machine. Moreover, the conditions created by the antiparty "reforms" were at least as favorable to the growth of new pressure-group machines as any previously existing. Such a machine developed under the leadership of Arthur Samish, whose tenure of power was not broken until 1949, when a popular national magazine gave wide publicity to some very rash statements Samish made,[36] and the Internal Revenue Service secured his conviction on tax charges. The program designed to prevent political bossism and corruption only the more surely produced his machine.

But J. Allen Smith was correct in a more important sense. The administrative sphere of government has grown enormously in the years since the height of Progressivism. A long list of new administrative agencies has been added to those heralded early in the century as the scientific solution to the problem of ensuring the public interest. Some, like the Federal Communications Commission, the Civil Aeronautics Board, and the National Labor Relations Board, are modeled on the ICC and the Wisconsin commissions. These appointive, determinedly nonpartisan bodies were to be the solution to the dilemmas of Congress when it was faced with the problem of regulation in highly technical and complicated areas. But almost nowhere were these commissions equipped with guides to their conduct other than the very general Congressional admonition that their rules and decisions should be "in the public interest,"[37] and the "science" La Follette thought he saw at work in his own Wisconsin commissions has failed to develop to fill the void. The evils which the Legislative Oversight Committee found in the late 1950s were not intended, but it is not altogether unthinkable that they might have been foreseen long before they were exposed. The lack of principled guides to action led to a sense of the arbitrary character of the situation. In sheer self-defense, if nothing else, the commissioners were forced into a search for accommodation, and accommodation slipped imperceptibly into corruption.

Nor was the situation different in the ordinary agencies of government. The severity of the problem differed from bureau to bureau, but the effects of weaknesses in the Progressive attitude are to be seen in many places. They became clearest, perhaps, in that great administrative creation of Progressivism, the United States Forest Service, where virtual autonomy was achieved within a departmental structure and the demand for extreme administrative discretion was clothed in an appeal to science and a policy without standards—the so-called "multiple-use policy." Inevitably, with the formal channels of responsibility all but closed and with no effective or certain guides for action other than those personal to the administrators, the Forest Service developed its own informal lines of responsibility, its own political ties to a particular constituency. In short, simple insistence upon the virtue of administrators as wardens of the public interest led deviously but certainly to ties with the special interests, opposition to which had been the point of Progressive beginnings.

Chapter 3

The Search for an Orthodoxy

I

A curious feature of American politics in the twentieth century is the absence of any articulated body of doctrine that may be taken as an orthodoxy on the central problem of private power. This lack is all the more striking in light of the vigor with which the wielders of power have been attacked by critics and reformers from the time of the Progressives onward. In recent years a number of rather self-conscious attempts to state an American conservatism have, indeed, appeared.[1] The very ring of the word "conservatism," however, has remained somehow alien and uncongenial to American ears, and the various endeavors have been stillborn, whatever their abstract merits. Nevertheless, the persistence and growth of private power have posed an embarrassing problem for all who are involved in exercising it. The problem is authority. What justifies the existence of power; by what principle is it rightful? For, if it is not justifiable, power is properly open to attack and, if possible, destruction.

The pragmatic cast of American thought has done much to disguise the existence of this problem and to discourage confronting it. The term "authority" has an archaic sound and, when set amid the dialogues of current politics, seems laden with the dust of forgotten controversies. In some elemental sense, the mere fact that powerful private organizations have long existed creates a psychological barrier to questions that would touch the very roots of their being. The achievement of new levels of prosperity in the period since World War II has also contributed to a psychological disposition to escape the problem.[2] Historically, moreover, the context of discussion of private power has more frequently been economic rather than political. Nevertheless, there are indications that even economic discussions must be vexed by the apparent irrelevancies of politics.[3]

Confusion about this problem has probably been greatest in that area of American life in which private organized power has been clearest and greatest, that is, in business. By the beginning of the twentieth century the corporation had not only assumed many of its modern outlines, but it had at many points achieved decisive positions in political society. To a substantial degree it was still true that many corporations, even large ones, were dominated and personified by particular individuals, often very colorful men. The issue of responsibility for corporate action remained latent while men of the stamp of Andrew Carnegie and John D. Rockefeller were on the scene.

By 1900 most elements of the doctrine by virtue of which businessmen regarded themselves as moral, and by which public policy was being shaped, had become fixtures of popular thought. All were derivative. Underlying all was the value of work, as yet unexamined and uncriticized in the new world society. Much more on the surface, but perhaps almost as little examined in its new context, was the idea of freedom. Certainly it seemed as though liberty in that hour often meant nothing more complex than an absence of restraint by government, for all that Mill's famous essay had been widely printed and was still fresh. Of equal importance was the vision of an autonomous economy separate and distinct from other aspects of society; for fostering this vision the classical economists of the nineteenth century were neither wholly to blame nor entirely without responsibility.

Already some of the incongruities of the tenets by which business professed to live had emerged. The most conspicuous was exposed by the antitrust policy and the vicissitudes it encountered. The Sherman Act was passed in 1890 under the spur of intense hostility to the rapidly rising giant corporations, but the logic of the Act was thoroughly consistent with the dogmas of competition by which the problem of power was avoided. Nevertheless, the attempt to place the state in the position of arbiter of the economic game, which liberal theory seemed to assign to it, was widely rejected. In 1896, with the *E. C. Knight* decision, the Supreme Court validated a virtual monopoly in sugar and shook the hope that the antitrust policy could restore the dream of a society in which power would be a negligible factor in the conduct of economic affairs. Partial renewal of the hope came later, but while the antitrust policy thereafter continued in existence and to have discernible effect, it never assumed the position at the core of national policy which had been intended for it.

A less conspicuous but more curious incongruity was the tenet of individualism. Deeply rooted in the American ethos and in the conditions of life in a society from which the frontier had only just vanished, it had more immediately received support from the enthusiasm for social Darwinism. The craze for Herbert Spencer's ideas reached greater intensity in the United States than in England, but by the turn of the century it had passed.[4] The social application of Darwinism as it was popularly understood was perhaps too plainly in the interests of the new monsters of the corporate jungle—and too brutal. Nevertheless, emphasis on individualism survived far beyond the era in which it was possible to talk without irony or sarcasm about survival of the fittest in the business world. Even at the midpoint of the twentieth century a careful examination of business ideology confirmed that individualism remained a central strand in the business creed.[5] But the difficulty of reconciling this value with the highly social world of the large corporation was still to be faced.

One of the commonplaces of contemporary reflection on American politics is that the stock of political ideas by which the nation subsisted for the first half of the twentieth century came out of its first decade. One of the most gifted of political observers, perhaps reflecting this belief, has given his book the subtitle "On the exhaustion of political ideas in the fifties."[6] There is a measure of substance in the generalization if the focus is exclusively upon the array of ideas usually labelled "liberal," although even here the generalization is debatable. Much that emerged from the New Deal did find its origins in the Progressive era, and perhaps by the 1950s that particular storehouse had been emptied. In a broader sense, however, the period that followed the years of Progressivism produced a flow of ideas that may be quite as important for the quality of American democracy as those conspicuous in the first decade of the century. These later currents of thought were less apparent in that they found their way less readily into the ordered pages of books and were less the product of professional thinkers than the outcome of events.

A fact of first importance in the new century was the consolidation of the position of the large corporation. Despite the muckrakers' vociferous attacks on the new giants, prosecution of the antitrust policy was halting and uncertain. The Standard Oil Company was indeed successfully assaulted in the name of antitrust, and before the onset of World War I the incidence of antitrust suits was increasing. Nevertheless, a truer indication of the trend was the United States Steel Corporation's survival of a similar assault. Nine years separated the decisions on these two mighty firms, and therein, undoubtedly, lies some of the explanation for the difference of treatment. In retrospect, however, there was a measure of consistency in the two decisions, and that consistency illustrated the intellectual groping going on within the nation.

The picture of the creation of the Standard Oil Company laid before the public in the early century was Ida Tarbell's measured but utterly damning account,[7] an ugly story of ruthless competitive methods and conquest of virtually the entire oil industry. The process of acquisition was marked by the exercise of brute power in almost all its forms, and it left a trail of individual disasters among those defeated in contests with Rockefeller. The savagery of this process of creation was in one sense more important than the sheer fact of the subsequent existence of a huge monopolistic power. The existence of monopoly was the important fact for the Court when it came to rule against the company, but the methods by which that power was created and exercised were perhaps more at issue in the large political setting.

The United States Steel Corporation was created by a quite different method: negotiation within the offices of the greatest banker of the time, J. P. Morgan. The component units of "the world's greatest industrial corporation" were not wrested from those who had controlled them; indeed, much of the original argument against the Corporation was that it was built on grossly inflated values paid to Carnegie and the others, who unloaded outworn plants fit mainly for junking. Here was no story of ruthless competitive practices or the savage destruction of rivals. The difficulties from a public sense were, as the Commissioner of Corporations reported in 1911, liberally watered stock and the creation of monopoly. On the first score, the Corporation was capitalized and securities issued to a value of $1,402,000,000, while the underlying values discovered by the Commissioner's investigation totalled only $682,000,000.[8] The implication was certainly scandalous, but the issue of stockholder welfare was neither central nor, it seemed, of vital interest to the public.

The second issue, monopoly power, was more important. At the moment of its birth, the United States Steel Corporation controlled approximately 60 per cent of all crude and finished steel production in the nation.[9] This figure gradually declined during the years that followed, but the Corporation's power within the industry remained exceedingly strong. United States Steel was not in itself a monopoly, but a series of devices enabled the industry, under its leadership, to behave remarkably like a unit; and though some of these devices were in time dismantled by court order, the cohesiveness of the industry remained. But the Corporation never fell before an interdiction such as that which broke Standard Oil apart. The reason lay in the strategy of defense laid down by United States Steel's first Chairman, Elbert H. Gary. In essence this strategy consisted of recognition that the Corporation's power implied political involvement; he accordingly exercised his considerable political talents in convincing government that the power had not been abused.[10]

This was the crux of the matter. Gary successfully transformed the issue of the Corporation from the question of its power to the question of how that power had been exercised. At two critical points—once when President Theodore Roosevelt seemed to be wavering toward an attack upon the Corporation, and again when it was actually faced with an antitrust suit—Gary and his associates effectively maintained that the Corporation had behaved well. It was a remarkable performance, all things considered. Moreover, it established the pattern by which the Corporation's leaders have necessarily been politicians (or "industrial statesmen," to use a term preferred in business). But it also set the stage for a long contest with government. This contest had many episodes: the legal struggles to maintain a system of uniform prices with the "Pittsburgh plus" and the multiple-basing point arrangements, for example, and recurrent threats from the Anti-Trust Division of the Justice Department. As labor organization became inevitable in the industry, the Corporation acceded with a degree of grace that surprised everyone, but this, probably a reflection of the political sophistication of the organization's leadership, enmeshed the Corporation more deeply in politics. The explosions of 1952, when President Truman attempted to seize the industry's mills, and in 1962, when Chairman Roger Blough and President Kennedy met in face-to-face confrontation, were climactic incidents in the drama.[11] They were the direct consequences of the political nature of the organization.

An exceedingly difficult and important problem underlay all these events. So far as United States Steel was concerned, it might be put this way: If the Corporation could make decisions substantially free from the classic restraints of the market—that is, if it had power—what could justify its actions? Gary's implicit answer was that those actions were good. Later, in a different political climate, and with renewal of the antitrust threat and a diminished share of the industry, the Corporation tended toward the assertion that it had no power. This was no more satisfactory than the earlier one had been. The behavior of the industry seemed on numerous occasions to demonstrate the reality of power in the Corporation's hands, although appearances may have been deceiving about the degree of power that actually existed. The older alternative, that the power was exercised well, posed an even greater difficulty. By what criteria could such a claim be asserted? By what right could the officers of the Corporation determine the criteria? To these questions there was no visible answer save that the tenure of power gave the deciding to its holders, and to say this was to lay claim to a part of the power to rule.

The problem of the United States Steel Corporation's place in political society is only an illustration, if a particularly dramatic one, of an increasingly general and pervasive problem. Concentrations of market power in other industries than steel may have become even greater as the years went by. The important differences, however, were often matters of degree and of attention from the public.

During the early years of the new century there was another development that looked in the same direction. This was the rise of the trade association. A few trade associations had been formed just after the Civil War, but the movement acquired its first real strength in the same period that saw the rise of the

large corporation, beginning with the last decade of the nineteenth century. By the eve of American entry into World War I,
however, the formation of trade associations had become a social cause.[12] The spokesman of the movement was a lawyer,
Arthur Jerome Eddy, who saw in the multiplying trade associations "a radical change that is taking place in the commercial
and industrial world—the change from a *competitive to a cooperative basis.*"[13] To Eddy, the evil of the past was the old pattern of competition, secret prices, rebates and conspiracies—the
array of methods which had been used by John D. Rockefeller
in building the Standard Oil Company, but which were by no
means limited to such aggregations. A more civilized pattern
was emerging and a more righteous one: "the new is taking its
place, is winning its way in spite of ignorant clamor, regardless
of legislative enactments, in the face of hampering decisions; it
is winning its way because, fundamentally, *it is right—it is
progress.* . . . Only in the breeding of plants and animals do we
try to aid the law of natural selection, and even with animals
we are tender toward the sick and old—toward those nature is
trying to eliminate. . . . The human law should be not the survival of the strong, but *the survival of all*, of the best there is in
all, and, oftentimes, there is more of good, more of real value to
humanity in the weak than in the strong."[14] No radical of the
time ever made a more explicit repudiation of social Darwinism.

Eddy's solution for avoiding the warfare of competition
("and war is hell") was the open-price trade association, a device that came under cold scrutiny in an investigation for the
Senate by the Federal Trade Commission in 1929.[15] This investigation resulted in a recommendation that trade associations be licensed. However, the ideas Eddy expressed (in
franker and more extreme form than others then or since) were
more important than the particular institution he favored. He
was quite correct in seeing a widespread turning from the idea
of competition in business and the seeking of a series of organic
societies within the large society.

These ideas would have been less important if they had not

been in the air at a time when other influences were emerging. Among the most important of these was the development of the idea of scientific management. On its face, this conception was remote from politics. It was particularly associated with the work of an industrial engineer, Frederick W. Taylor, whose writings appeared between 1911 and the beginning of the war.[16] Taylor's methods were applied in many industrial plants, particularly in the steel industry. In a large sense, they came out of the same preoccupation with scientific management that pervaded Progressivism's view toward government.

In 1912 one of the more interesting undertakings of government got under way. At the suggestion of Charles Nagel, Secretary of Commerce and Labor under President Taft, a meeting of representatives of a number of local chambers of commerce and other business associations, along with several governmental officials, was held in the offices of the Department of Commerce and Labor. The group drew up a plan for a national organization of business groups. The Secretary of Commerce and Labor sent invitations to a conference in Washington to 2000 commercial organizations. The conference, actually attended by seven hundred delegates, was called to order by Nagel. President Taft spoke, Secretary Nagel gave an address, and the conference got down to work. Its achievement was no less than the formation of the Chamber of Commerce of the United States.

Nagel had had some hesitation about the enterprise, but he carefully checked it with the President, from whom he received support. The undertaking was at least partly motivated by the widespread feeling of businessmen that they were under attack. The Populists had been succeeded by the Progressives, and as yet Taft seemed to show as threatening a visage as Theodore Roosevelt. Nevertheless, Nagel's plan embodied an idea of a particular kind of relationship between government and business. Secretary Nagel stated in his address:

In our government we cannot discriminate. We cannot say we will communicate with this one and not that one unless there be some authority given which will enable us to do that, and for that reason it has been suggested not only that you organize so as to have a common commercial opinion to submit to the government, but that you get the sign of authority in the shape of a National Charter, which will enable every officer of the government to say, "This is the recognized representative of commerce and industry in the United States."[17]

The charter was not granted. The problem of authority which Nagel perceived (if a bit indistinctly) was not solved. Nevertheless, the boldness of his effort was little diminished by the lack of a charter. The voice of business would be authoritative if the new organization brought forth "a common commercial opinion"; and in any event, recognition had already been conferred by the initiative of Secretary Nagel and President Taft. Undoubtedly neither of these gentlemen conceived that he was experimenting in the institutions of government in any profound sense; yet that is what they were doing. The experiment was relatively inconspicuous only because it accorded so well with other developments of the time.

These trends might have had a different impact had it not been for World War I and the industrial mobilization the war effort required. There had never in history been such an experience. For a brief period mobilization reached into the uttermost parts of the economy and directly involved a large number of the nation's industrial leaders in the work of government. However, the particular outcome which is notable here is in the ideas of political and social organization which the experience nurtured.

The primary political problem of industrial mobilization on the necessary scale was to coordinate a multitude of independent producers of civilian goods into a cohesive and efficient machine for producing military goods. There were two principal difficulties: first, the somewhat technical organizational problem of communicating with the number of plants and managers involved; second, the problem of securing the acquiescence and cooperation of those many managers. These problems were solved brilliantly and in a manner that relied heavily upon the ideological developments that have just been mentioned. The initial (and crucial) step was recruitment of industrial leaders to participate in the direction of the machine. This not only provided a supply of skilled managers, but, more important, it coopted the power of many whose opposition might have been disastrous. But the solution was not as simple as this may suggest. Cooptation required an actual conferring of additional power on those industrial leaders who were already sufficiently powerful to be included in the wartime system.[18] It also implied intensification of organization among the multitude of producers themselves. The trade association movement was of great utility in this process. In fact, encouragement of such associations became official governmental policy, and the number of associations multiplied rapidly.[19]

The idea of first importance that emerged from this experience was voluntary cooperation by trade and industry—a theme stated and restated by every writer who has dealt with the history of this mobilization. For example, "It cannot be said too often . . . that the original feature of the War Industries Board was its successful, cooperative, democratic, self-control of industry for national purposes."[20] Members of a particular industry were brought together, through their established association if one existed, or, if there was none, through their established leaders to the extent such were quickly discoverable; their views about the needs of the situation were learned; government "requests," largely embodying the views of the industry, were issued; compliance with these requests was policed by the industry's own organization. This policing, it was generally understood, was by social pressure and by appeals to the patriotism and good fellowship of the individual units of the industry; officially there was little or no compulsion.

Thus voluntary organization and cooperation were the essential ideas of the time. By the official doctrine, they made for efficiency and flexibility; they preserved freedom; they contrasted with the methods of the enemy and his use of compulsion. The American method was at once more effective and more free. The War Industries Board and the Food Administration handed the task of mobilization over to the representatives authorized by the members of each industry. The representatives then gave their expert opinion on the sort of regulations that should be followed, and the government gave the regulations its blessing. (The Attorney General conveniently held that the antitrust laws were not involved where there was agreement between producers or traders and the government itself.)[21] The outcome was that industry cooperated and coercion was escaped. Here was the picture of a democracy solving its most critical problem without blemish to its ideal of freedom.

Another idea was also important, although somewhat less discussed, in the wartime period: the concept of efficiency. In a sense it came directly from the concepts of Frederick W. Taylor. Nevertheless, its application was different. This time it applied to the entire industrial machine of the nation viewed as a whole. This was perhaps most evident in the campaign for "conservation," an idea that had its root in—or at least took its slogan from—the Progressive era. As the official historian of the War Industries Board summarized the issue:

It was found that almost all industries were encumbered with an unbelievable amount of unexamined tradition, that resulted in duplication of effort, waste of material, and unnecessary expenditures of energy. Industry as it was, compared to industry as it should be for war purposes, was as a barracks to a modern hotel. Everywhere was found the superfluity of luxury and taste and the impedimenta of custom. . . .[22]

"Civilization is become anaemic with obesity."[23] This insight into the failings of normal peacetime ways struck deep into the minds of many of the industrial managers who for the first time found themselves governing an entire nation. The sheer technical possibilities were dazzling:

It is little wonder that the men who dealt with the industries of a nation, binned and labeled, replenished and drawn on at will for the purposes of war, and its train of consequences, meditated with a sort of intellectual contempt on the huge hit-and-miss confusion of peace-time industry, with its perpetual cycle of surfeit and dearth and its eternal attempt at adjustment after the event. From their meditations arose dreams of an ordered economic world.[24]

What might not be done in peacetime by application of war-time idealism, voluntary cooperation, and efficiency?

It became apparent, however, that voluntary self-regulation by the private associations of trade and industry was not quite sufficient. First, there was the difficulty that each industry had a few (officially, a *very* few) chiselers, individuals and firms that would not cooperate for the common good. They had to be disciplined. Moreover, there was a growing problem of co-ordination, however unpleasant it seemed. Consequently, commodity sections were organized in the War Industries Board, that is, actually within the government. Despite this seeming retreat from voluntary organizational methods, the essence of the idea was preserved and the evil of rigidity was avoided. Even overlapping was permitted:

> It was not the sort of overlapping that, for example, chokes Alaska by the formalism of thirty bureaus, but the overlapping, the inter-penetration of unjealous, cordial team-work, uncurbed by the hard-and-fast lines of statutes and regulations aimed at prevention of abuse of power instead of its efficient application. . . . The commodity sections were business operating Government business for the common good.[25]

The war did not continue long enough for all the implications of the industrial mobilization to become generally apparent. What seemed to emerge was simply the vision of freedom, co-operation, and efficiency as it has been outlined here. Nevertheless, other implications were there, and a few saw them. The clearest head was perhaps that of Bernard M. Baruch, who had led the whole mobilization effort. Speaking many years after the war and referring to some of the more effusive comments about the "spontaneous cooperation" of industry, he said: "What these witnesses are really referring to when they talk about spontaneity and cooperation in general public accept-ance of price fixing and all other war tasks is not that there was not compulsion behind the duty imposed on citizens. They are referring to the universal confidence that was placed by govern-ment in the people themselves to enforce the more or less arbitrary and distinctly sacrificial requirements of government."

The government, in other words, had sanctions and there was strong compulsion in the hands of the "cooperating" regulators within the industry.[26]

Although it was possible to ascribe the reality of compulsion in the mobilization to the harsh setting of a wartime situation and thus to see it as an aberration, it was more difficult to dismiss the equally important problem of legality. Actually, there was little legal authority for much that was done in the mobilization program. This was one of the fundamental, but usually unstated, reasons for seeking "voluntary cooperation." The freedom from formality and legal restraint thus achieved frequently became a source of efficiency and satisfaction to the administrators (as in the example of the contrast with the administration of Alaska). Nevertheless, the extralegal nature of the great enterprise was one of its essential characteristics. If it was given little attention, this was largely because the war created standards and aims of some degree of definiteness, objectivity, and popularity.

It is always tempting to repress the memory of times when behavior has not conformed to professed ideals. The experience of World War I has often been treated in this manner. Nevertheless, it was not a sealed-off part of history; the ideas that prevailed during the war did not disappear with the armistice or the demobilization. The wartime experience was of profound importance in the thinking of the principal participants, and some of them became crucial figures in the shaping of things afterward.

The most important of these men was Herbert Hoover. His misfortune to be president during a time of national disaster has obscured his real significance on the American scene. Although he can hardly be credited with originating the ideas for which he stood, he deserves to be recognized more than any other person as the spokesman for the view of politics under examination here. More, he may in time prove to have been one of the influential political thinkers in modern American history. In large part, this importance was the consequence of his education and early public service. His training was in engineering, a profession that has left its mark on various other thinkers on social issues. His first large-scale public task was organizing the relief of starvation in war-torn Belgium. More important, he was Food Administrator (he apparently originated the word "administrator") during the war. Under Hoover, precisely the same set of ideas was put into effect as prevailed in the War Industries Board. The Food Administration called for voluntary cooperation that extended even to the housewives of the land; industry committees were used to regulate themselves and to man the government; and the Administration's emphasis on efficiency went beyond anything seen in other parts of the mobilization.[27]

When Hoover became Secretary of Commerce, he had a well-formed vision of the society toward which he was working. He never described this vision in systematic form, but it is nevertheless possible to pick out its principal features. First, he believed firmly in what he termed individualism.[28] This idea was stated in terms that evoked nineteenth-century doctrines, but it was far from any real kinship to social Darwinism. Often it seemed to refer strictly to economic affairs, yet Hoover asserted insistently, "Our American individualism, indeed, is only in part an economic creed."[29] What was essential here was freedom, and this meant very simply absence of coercion—in war or peace this was the objective most to be sought. Throughout, Hoover's implication was that coercion comes only from government.

Perhaps the next logical step was that the opposite of coercion consisted of voluntary activity. The expression of this belief in its fullest implications lacked clarity, but Hoover had in mind matters that were definite enough. As a government officer, he wished to avoid compelling anyone; he wished to assist people to achieve what they wanted; this could be done only if the people organized themselves—in trade associations, trade institutes, chambers of commerce, labor unions, professional associations, farmers associations, and cooperatives—to inform government of their wants and needs.[30] He was quite aware of the possibility that such associations might form monopolies and use their powers to their own selfish advantage. Moreover, he did not repudiate the antitrust laws, although he had a deep disbelief in the power of mere laws to produce good ends. "National character cannot be built by law. It is the sum of all the moral fiber of all its individuals. . . . Legislative action is always clumsy—it is incapable of adjustment to shifting needs. . . . Three years of study and intimate contact with associations of economic groups convince me that there lies within them a great moving impulse toward betterment." Accordingly, the solution lay in encouraging trade associations to create codes of business practice and ethics. When each association had formulated its "code," the Department of Commerce submitted it to the Department of Justice and the Federal Trade Commission, and the latter promulgated it as a standard of fair practice. Such was "the strong beginning of a new force in the business world."[31]

Two other ideas were inextricably meshed for Hoover with this vision of cooperative and voluntary action. The ideal of efficiency, though not logically necessary to his primary conception, was very important to Hoover. As Food Administrator, he had campaigned unrelentingly against waste. Waste was categorically evil, and not just in a war setting. By the establishment of common standards in an industry—whether technical, as in the specifications for a particular product, or ethical, as in the agreed-upon limits to competition—efficiency was served and waste avoided.[32]

Another idea that ran through Hoover's thinking in the postwar period was that of decentralization. His views on this subject had appeared from time to time in the discussions of war administration, but they became much more conspicuous after he was made Secretary of Commerce. Voluntary agreement and self-regulation by trade associations (and presumably other groups, although Hoover was much less interested in the others) was by small groups; it avoided government and law. Whether decentralization was good because it avoided government in this manner, or whether avoidance of government was good because it promoted decentralization, was never quite clear in Hoover's writings. However, it seems probable that he regarded decentralization as something positive in itself and that it was closely linked in his mind to freedom. It also tended to merge with his view of efficiency.[33]

This summary characterization of the principal concepts of Hoover's thought does not do justice to the frequently intense moral tone with which they were stated, nor does it indicate the energy or the ingenuity with which he applied them during his most fruitful years. Most of all, it does not suggest the very great influence they had—influence not of the sort that comes from originality, but rather of the kind that results from expressing persuasively what is in the air and deeply congenial to the powerful and influential men of a given time.

Hoover's ideas had effects that outlasted the specific enthusiasms and devices he tirelessly promoted in the Department of Commerce. The most important related to the issue of organized power. Although Hoover did not face the issue squarely—at different times he joined both sides of the controversy—his fundamental position was that so long as common action was voluntary, the real test was whether power was used for good rather than for evil. The Sherman Act, for example, had been necessary to restrain attempts to crush competitors with unfair practices and destructive competition. However, "there is a wide difference between the whole social conception of capital combinations against public interest and cooperative action between individuals which may be profoundly in the public interest. The latter can improve business standards and eliminate waste in production and distribution."[34] This was the position Gary had evolved for United States Steel.

A second implication was one that Hoover would not have drawn himself; it was nevertheless present, however latent, in his thought. This was a spurning of mere law. Certainly Hoover had a distaste for the use of law. Law implied compulsion; moreover, it was formal and (in his word) inflexible. He had used law during his days in the Food Administration, just as other wartime administrators had when law was available. Yet this resort to law was obviously deeply repugnant to him, and he consistently emphasized cooperation and voluntary methods. Since there were too many people to address individually, they must get together in their own associations and agree—voluntarily. Then government could put its stamp upon their own informal, cooperative, and free decisions. Government would thus have achieved the purpose of a free people, and without coercion. Unfortunately, however, to turn government away from law is to turn it toward arbitrary action, and the removal of government from the direct making of decisions is not to relieve it of responsibility for actions taken under its encouragement.

A third implication, which Hoover apparently never saw, underlay his contempt for the use of law and legal methods. This was that a set of objective criteria existed and was universally perceivable. During the war, when the pattern of voluntary self-regulation developed, the problem was negligible. The objective of winning the war was clear and authentic, however arguments might develop about the most appropriate means of achieving it. With peace, however, this goal vanished; the inherent guides and limitations that had been available to the many advisory committees and functional associations working with government also disappeared. Yet the vision of what had been possible through voluntary methods in war persisted, and Hoover more than anyone else became the advocate of their use in peace. Toward what ends these methods should be used, and for whose benefit—these were not questions to be asked. Perhaps the answer was buried in Hoover's conception of efficiency. Waste was evil, coordination was good, and so were uniform standards. But Hoover never analyzed these notions in relation to the fundamental problem of criteria, and so the ambiguity in his thought was never evident. Had it been examined, an abyss would have been seen.

The Hoover era passed and a spirit apparently quite different came with the New Deal. Torrents of gall were poured upon the political grave of the Hoover administration. Nevertheless, some of the principal ideas of the New Deal were inherited from the Hoover era. The National Recovery Administration adopted methods but one step beyond those pioneered in the Department of Commerce under Secretary Hoover and by the Federal Trade Commission under President Hoover. Once again the trade association movement had a great new burst of energy, with government encouragement. The idea of voluntary cooperation was brought forth and stiffened with governmental authority for voluntarily agreed-upon "codes." Mr. Hoover retrospectively repudiated the affinity of the NRA codes to those of his own time, but the family likeness was unmistakable.[35] The New Deal era witnessed a burst of government-encouraged labor organization that gave pause to many who had been delighted with Hoover's voluntary approach to the politics of policy-making and administration. Yet this was but an extension of the Hoover logic—one, in fact, that Hoover himself had sometimes recognized. And there was a more concrete sign of continuity between the New Deal era and its predecessor. General Hugh S. Johnson, the first administrator of the National Recovery Administration, was a veteran of the industrial mobilization of World War I. He, like George N. Peek, his erstwhile employer in the Moline Plow Company during the postwar years and later the first administrator of the Agricultural Adjustment Administration, spanned the years between the war and the depression. The ideas that came out of the war, and not merely those of Herbert Hoover, colored the atmosphere throughout the years between the wars. Inevitably, they affected government and politics.

Other ideological currents, far more conspicuous, disguised many of the changes that took place during the New Deal. In particular, hostility between the abstractions of "business" and "government" became the axis around which much discussion and some decisions revolved. The result was a cloudy field upon which many struggles were conducted—often with battle cries of remarkable irrelevance—and of which we can only now see some of the realities. Despite seeming threats to its existence, the large corporation was not destroyed. But neither was its dilemma. Its power continued to exist—even perhaps to grow—yet there was no satisfactory answer to the conundrum of justification. Walter S. Gifford of American Telephone and Telegraph spoke nobly of his concept of "trusteeship."[36] The leadership of AT & T was responsible to the stockholders, the employees, and the customers, but how this responsibility was enforced was unclear. And the question by what standards the trusteeship was conducted or could be conducted was unanswered and, perhaps, unanswerable.

II

The change in the politics of business that occurred in the first part of the twentieth century was accompanied by a somewhat similar change in agricultural politics. As with business, the ideas about politics and agriculture which emerged during this time were deeply influenced by events. Inevitably, much in the detailed story was different from what occurred in business; nevertheless, there were enough parallels to suggest that events in both areas of politics may have been at least in part the product of some ideas of a general and widespread character.

Over the long span of American history many assumptions and beliefs about the nature of politics in the republic have been colored by its agrarian past. Although the period as a whole has been marked by a steady decline in the proportion of the population devoted to farming, only with the end of World War II did agriculture seriously begin to lose importance on the national political scene. The nation, which was 95 per cent rural at the time of the first census in 1790, had become only 30 per cent rural in 1960.[37] The change was not sudden; the point at which the part of the labor force engaged in farming was equal to that in other occupations was passed just a few years after the end of the Civil War. However, with the rapid westward expansion of the nation and the growth of the total population, the number of farmers actually increased until sometime in the decade between the census years of 1910 and 1920; thereafter the actual number of farmers diminished. Nevertheless, farm politics continued to bulk large in the nation. Indeed, it is arguable that the political importance of farmers actually increased for a time. This was in part the consequence of the peculiar advantages given the rural population by a federal system, but it was more particularly the result of the form of organization that developed among prosperous farmers during the twentieth century. This story has been told elsewhere, but some of its features may be recapitulated for the general light they cast on the making of modern American politics.[38]

Through the nineteenth century and for at least the first four decades of the twentieth it was widely believed in America that an especially intimate relationship existed between democracy and agriculture. This belief was seldom challenged because it was very largely unstated, and where most of the people of a democracy were farmers the assumption had the quality of a truism. Jefferson had been lyrical in his praise of farmers as the chosen people of God, to whom more than to others He had given virtue.[39] John Taylor ("of Caroline"), Jefferson's associate in Virginia politics, spelled out the benefits that might be reaped by a purely agrarian society in the new world.[40] With a seemingly limitless continent of land for the taking and the tilling, the republic might, by turning its back on the evils of cities and shops, achieve a pattern of free and equal small communities of upright farmers. To do this it would have to do away with the Old World laws of primogeniture and entail. It would have to guard vigilantly against the attempts of the city merchants and financiers to corrupt the essentially agrarian nature of the Constitution. But the benefits would be enormous. Men would have essentially the same interests, and the problem of social conflict would be solved before it appeared. In essence, this was just as economic an interpretation as that offered by Madison, but it was based upon a possibility that Madison explicitly rejected, striking at the *cause* of faction rather than its effects, by preventing the development of private power and interest groups rather than by balancing and counterbalancing them. Retrospectively, Taylor's vision is easily dismissed. In the context of his time, however, it was not absurd, and it is not wholly unthinkable that America might have resigned itself to a social pattern of subsistence farming. Given the great expanse of land stretching thousands of miles to the western sea, it was a vision that might have brought a society in which inequality and tyranny would have found no place.

Over the years of national development Taylor's and Jefferson's picture of the proper course had less and less relevance, yet elements in their thought have been echoed again and again in many places. The idea that farming was more fundamental than other ways of life often merged with the fundamentalism of rural Protestantism. What was simple was virtuous; and farm life was simple. Farming took place in the natural scene, under the very heavens; it was closer to God than other occupations. City life and city occupations, by contrast, were complex and corrupt; they were also removed from contact with the annual miracle of growing things.

Whether by logic or mere association of ideas, this vision of a righteous society carried with it great emphasis upon the small social unit. The value of the small community has been one of the most important political concepts in American history. For the most part it has been less a reasoned concept than a fundamental article of faith; but usually, it has been argued that a small social unit is more democratic than a large one and that a society formed of small self-governing units is more democratic than others. The meaning of this claim is often uncertain, since the word "democratic" is used to mean different things. In one sense this uncertainty is not important, for to many people local autonomy is by definition the essence of democracy and it would be useless to ask them for the meaning they intend; in this sense the only important questions are what are the limits of the locality and who is included within them.

In another sense, however, it is important to look at the reasons sometimes given in support of belief in local autonomy, since they relate to other values. Perhaps the most common argument is that since local people necessarily know more about local affairs they can govern themselves better than someone who is both physically distant and concerned with other localities as well. Thus the people of a small community will not only know their own problems and have a keen personal interest in their solution, but will also be personally acquainted with local officers and candidates for office. This knowledge will extend to details of terrain and to personalities and character. Moreover, since locally chosen officers will be responsible directly to the people of the locality and to no others, the government will be more responsive to the local people and hence more democratic.

Almost as important is the argument that local autonomy allows participation and discussion. In a large political unit, it is frequently contended, the individual is lost in a large mass and cannot make himself heard; the only participation open to him is an impersonal registration of his vote. In a small unit, by contrast, he can enter into rational discussion of issues and can make his voice heard; hence the political life of a small community is not only more responsible and more democratic because of greater participation, but is also more *rational*. This argument is as old as Plato.

Frequently these arguments are associated with a quite different type of argument, one not strictly concerned with the democratic nature of the small community. This argument holds that life in a small community is comprehensible and warm and human. Since relationships are not based on formal and impersonal rules but are informal and face to face, life is richer and more meaningful than in a large unit, and in this sense more *natural*. It is also implied that life is freer, since in a simpler and more comprehensible setting there is less need for law and compulsion. Difficulties and disputes can be adjusted on a personal basis and according to their true merits, without resort to the rigid categories of law.

Other contentions about the advantages of the small community stress its greater efficiency and stability, but on the whole the important arguments are those offered in support of the greater opportunity for democracy. They have been mingled with the long-existing American belief in the ideal of an agrarian society and have been brought forth in support of small political units of any kind. The nation's agrarian past has prepared a widespread receptivity for them.

As the twentieth century began, the conception of America as resting upon the foundation of a basically agricultural population was still vivid and little challenged. Nevertheless, a divide in history had been passed. Not only had agriculture become secondary in importance to industry and commerce, but the character of agricultural politics had been forever transformed. The Populist movement of the 1890s was the last agrarian mass movement the nation was to see. In retrospect, however, Populism did not offer a really radical threat. Its program was more political than economic, as was inevitable with a movement whose constituency included many different economic interests. But it was not for that reason either dangerous or irrational.

The reorganization of agricultural politics that took place in the twentieth century was not the product of any conscious or reasoned design. Indeed, realization of agriculture's diminished place in national life came slowly and long after the fact. Some leaders still hoped for a renewal of the old agrarianism of the 1890s and there was a tendency to look with alarm upon the flight of rural youth from the land.[41] If it was impossible to reformulate a general political party based on farming, however, it was by no means certain that the trend of events required the extreme narrowing of farm organization that followed. What occurred, in brief, was the rise of a completely new kind of political organization founded on only a segment of agriculture: the more prosperous part of the commercial farming population. This development was unforeseen and unintended, but it acquired all the seeming inexorability of a historical tide. Much of the impetus for it came from a set of ideas that were pervasive at the time, some of them indigenous to agriculture itself.

The important innovation of the twentieth century in agricultural politics was in education. By 1900 agricultural education had a long tradition going back at least to the founding of the land-grant colleges under the Morrill Act of 1862. This Act was one of the great landmarks of educational history in that more than any other action it established the trend toward democratization of education. The record of agricultural education to the end of the nineteenth century, however, was a rather sorry one of ineffectiveness and futility. In the first decade of the twentieth century a new device, a "social invention,"[42] appeared and spread across the farming areas of the nation: the county agent. The job of the county agent, or "county agricultural extension agent," to use his full title, was to bring to the farmers actually working the fields the best new lore of farming practice developed by scientific experimentation. Other methods of spreading this information had failed, but the agents' demonstrations on the farmers' own land began to show some promise of success. A widespread campaign for support of the county agents developed among business, philanthropic, and government circles. As a result, the county agent "movement" grew rapidly, first as a private undertaking and then in 1914, with passage of the Smith-Lever Act, as a part of the federal government's agricultural program. The manner of this transition was novel; the federal grant-in-aid appeared here for the first time, and the county agent acquired an ambiguous status through concurrent financial support from county, state, and federal governments, and from private sources.[43]

The county agent's work was avowedly, and in the beginning even determinedly, unpolitical. An important part of his educational method, however, was the formation of local supporting groups of farmers—a necessity, it was felt, since demonstration of good farming methods on each farmer's land was manifestly impossible. To gain widespread influence, as well as to mobilize local financial support, something more than individual demonstrations was necessary. Accordingly, the organization of local groups of farmers became a major part of the county agent's job. As the United States Department of Agriculture assumed a more active role in the county agent "movement," explicit instructions went out to the agents to work on the formation of these local organizations. In 1915 the Secretary of Agriculture stated: "These [local farm groups] are expected to take the initiative in securing local financial support for the agent, to join in his selection and appointment, and to stand behind him in his efforts to advance agricultural interests."[44] By 1921, the head of the office in the Department directly concerned with the work of extension openly took credit for the large-scale organization that had been created by the agents under his loose direction.[45] By this time, however, the fundamental fact of the situation was plain and should not have been missed by any reasonably alert political observer: what the county agents had organized with the aid of public resources and at the direction of the United States Department of Agriculture was not merely an array of local organizations of farmers devoted to education, but the most powerful private pressure group agriculture has ever produced, the American Farm Bureau Federation. The local groups, the county "farm bureaus," had federated into state Farm Bureaus, and these in turn had formed the national Federation.

A number of the ideas involved in this development are particularly interesting. First was the insistence upon voluntary action and organization. Farmers must be persuaded to do things for themselves and to improve their own lot. This was in the democratic tradition; it accorded, moreover, with the realities of the situation, for there was no power by which government could force the methods of enlightened agriculture upon reluctant farmers. However, the reality of voluntary action was sometimes complex. Even at the beginning of the county agent movement, before government was actively involved, an important part of the operation was the involvement of local banks and other creditors in persuading farmers to cooperate with the agents.[46] This sort of persuasion was less important, however, than reliance upon the most influential local farmers —who were, with few exceptions, the most prosperous and well-to-do farmers. The idea repeated most frequently in the formative days of the movement was that if the local leaders could be persuaded, other farmers would follow. Consistently, the instructions given county agents were to work with the local leaders.

Voluntary action above all meant organized action. The farmer has typically been a rather solitary figure. Physical isolation and the sheer numbers of farmers have made them difficult to reach and to mobilize under any but extreme conditions of adversity. Since there was no convenient organization through which they could be reached by the county agents, new ones had to be created. Existing organized farm groups, such as the Grange, the Farmers Union, and several lesser organizations, that might have been used, presented several difficulties. First, some of them, particularly the Grange, had elements of secrecy and ritual. What was necessary, in the eyes of the Department of Agriculture, was a "nonclass, nonsecret, noncommercial, and permanent institution open to all the farmers in the county."[47] Another requirement was that the supporting organizations be "nonpolitical." In some sense, perhaps an intuitive one, all these qualifications reflected an awareness of the fundamental problems posed by this method of governmental dealing with a segment of the population. How could government organize "voluntary" groups? How could such groups be limited to one part of the citizenry and yet be nonexclusive? How could they deal with government and yet be nonpolitical? Unfortunately, such questions had no answers.

The idea of voluntary action was very closely related to the long-standing agrarian tradition of small decentralized units and local self-determination. There was an implicit scale of freedom that went something like this: A small local voluntary group conferred the greatest degree of freedom; a small local governmental unit gave the next degree, a state governmental unit the next, and a centralized national government the least. Accordingly, the plan of administration which developed in extension work involved a maximum of decentralization.

Until the rise of the federal extension program the Department of Agriculture had relatively little direct contact with individual farmers. The Department's new relationship with them did not appear immediately, but its seeds were planted with passage of the Smith-Lever Act, as those concerned were perhaps vaguely aware, for an elaborate set of barriers was erected to prevent contact between individual farmers and the Department from becoming too close. The individual agents were made concurrently the employees of local counties and of the state colleges of agriculture. The federal contribution for their aid was channeled through the state governments to the colleges, which in turn usually had semi-autonomous departments of agricultural extension. Moreover, in the early days of the program the agents were also frequently employees of the local Farm bureaus. This plan effectively cut off any possibility of genuine direction of the agents by the federal government, yet maintained the flow of federal money for their support.

Such a situation involved a very particular view of the constitutional structure of the nation. It has seldom been made explicit, but quite clearly the makers of modern agricultural politics have felt that the federal system requires relegation of national government to a position of remoteness and weakness —an idea that has persisted to recent times. Perhaps its clearest expression was contained in a resolution passed by the land grant colleges' association in 1947: "It is a violation of the principle of our constitutional form of self-government for a Federal agency to by-pass a state agency having similar authority to work directly with local groups and individuals."[48]

The really important political idea, however, was decentralization. It was held up as an ideal because it was the method of democracy, but it was also maintained as a method of insuring conservatism among farmers. Bankers were helping in the cause, since farmers during the evil days of Populism had showed a lack of understanding of and even hostility for banks.[49] The Farm Bureaus were even held up as the device which had prevented American farmers from turning to bolshevism.[50] There may be some room for debate as to the actual effect of the extension system and the Farm Bureaus that grew up around it, but it is quite certain that there was a diversity of motives in the plan for decentralization.

In time the idea of "administrative decentralization" evolved. This came only after a massive structure of political relationships had formed and hardened and it was, perhaps, a rationalization. Nevertheless, it rested on a tradition of very long standing, that of the small social and political unit. This tradition pervaded agricultural politics in the years that followed; it also affected politics in other forms throughout America.

III

The most clearly articulated justification of private power in America came from organized labor. There are a number of ironies in this fact. First, it is doubtful that the welfare of American workingmen was as well served by the doctrine proclaimed in their name as their spokesmen believed. Second, this doctrine was more appropriate in some respects to business than to labor. Third, it was enunciated in the guise of explicit hostility to the idea of any doctrine.

The set of ideas that became the particular possession of the American labor movement during its critical formative period was given the name of "voluntarism." Although it was never offered as a formal or comprehensive system, it was not without coherence and was very rigidly adhered to. Samuel Gompers, who coined the term and who more than any other person formulated the ideas it embodied, insisted that his creation was solely the result of experience and historical necessity. In 1900 he asserted, "The American Federation of Labor has not indulged in any exhaustive or elaborate platform of abstract principle."[51] He reiterated this point tirelessly to the end of his long life in the labor movement. The organizations of labor were not the work of intellectuals or doctrinaires, but of honest workingmen striving to improve their own condition. They were not directed to some nebulous ultimate ends that could not be achieved, but to the alleviation of immediate and concrete evils. There was no worse delusion, as Gompers saw it, than doctrine itself: "Each ism has stood but as an evanescent and iridescent dream of poor humanity groping blindly in the dark for its ideal; and it has caused many a heart wrench to relegate some idealism to movements which do not move, to the dead ashes of blasted hopes and promises."[52]

The practical experience behind this attitude was actually quite definite. For almost a century, American labor had encountered resistance of the most stubborn sort from employers, courts, legislatures, and workers themselves. By the time of the formation of the American Federation of Labor in the 1880s it was reasonable to conclude with Gompers that the record of organization was one of repeated failure. The latest venture in broad working-class organization, the Knights of Labor, had become enmeshed in difficulties of objectives and coordination that could only have been solved by its transformation into a political party. That is to say, the only goals a diverse and large membership could have had in common were political and could only have been sought by political means. Nevertheless, the Knights' organizational difficulties were apparent, and Gompers pressed his own formula for labor organization and by so doing produced that death of the broader organization his theory had led him to expect.

Of the several principles with which the AFL began it would be difficult to say which was primary and which derivative. Certainly in retrospect it is fairly clear that one if rigidly adhered to would produce the others. Perhaps the first in point of institutional beginnings was organization based upon existing national craft unions. The second was insistence upon economic rather than political action. There was an insight of fundamental importance here; it has been outlined by the chief theorist of the AFL, Selig Perlman, in a much quoted passage: "It was indeed a new species of trade unionism that was thus evolved. It differed from the trade unionism that the native American labor movement had evolved earlier in that it grasped the idea, supremely correct for American conditions, that the economic front was the only front on which the labor army could stay united."[53] This has usually been taken to mean that workers in America would respond only to the most direct and concrete appeals. There may have been a measure of truth in this characterization of American labor; nevertheless, a more fundamental principle had been stumbled upon, as will be seen later.

In the eyes of Gompers and the other founders of the AFL every principle was eclipsed in importance by the principle of freedom. Gompers returned to this theme again and again with evident sincerity. "I want to urge devotion to the fundamentals of human liberty—the principles of voluntarism. No lasting gain has ever come from compulsion."[54] There were two elements in this conviction. First, devotion to liberty was righteous. Second, compulsion would not work. Many of the founders of the AFL had come from Europe and the vision of tyranny was vivid in their minds. In the New World compulsion could and must be avoided.

To Gompers and his associates, liberty seemed a simple thing, a first principle, self-evident, right, and true. It was the opposite of compulsion. But translating the principle into organizational reality involved very particular forms and ideas. The most important idea was scarcely ever examined, namely, that compulsion came primarily from the state. This conviction had a number of roots. Some were clearly matters of doctrine. Various AFL leaders had a Marxist background, and their picture of the state as characterized by force and compulsion persisted, although their later convictions were strongly anti-Marxist; the state still seemed to them to approximate the executive committee of the ruling class and the monopolist of force. Ironically, the very anti-Marxist development of the AFL leaders strengthened this perception, for the opposition to their own positions within the AFL—and from the outside, as well—came from the socialists. The socialists sought various degrees of state ownership of productive facilities. Thus the particular character of the opposition to the AFL leadership within the labor movement reinforced the leadership's anti-state assumptions. The socialist nature of the political opposition also hardened the acceptance of capitalism implicit in the AFL position.

In truth, however, there was much immediate experience to justify the view of the state that Gompers and his followers took. Labor's experience with the courts, in particular, seemed to confirm the severest cynicism as to their function, for the machinery of the law had repeatedly been twisted to labor's disadvantage. Whereas the Sherman Act appeared to be proving ineffective in dealing with the trusts, it was quickly and devastatingly turned against unions. The labor injunction was developed by corporation lawyers into a perversion of law and justice, and the courts were willing accomplices in the process.[55] In view of the courts' record in using the Sherman Act against labor, Gompers can perhaps be forgiven for terming the Act "that legislative monstrosity." Nevertheless, labor's attitude toward the courts and the law was much more hostile during Gompers' time than any likely to be taken today. The difficulty, as it was seen then, lay not merely in a particular law or a distortion of certain legal processes, but in a fundamental fraud in the entire body of law and the entire court system: "Place it in the power of the courts to take jurisdiction, to assume jurisdiction, or to have jurisdiction accredited to them, and they will leave no stone unturned to exercise it to the detriment of the men and women of labor, who, after all, in all times have been compelled to suffer the tyranny and the oppression of an oligarchy, under whatever name it might be known."[56]

Although the immediate reasons for the AFL leaders' mistrust of the legal system were strong, it is worth observing that it went beyond the idea that the courts had abused their trust or that the law had been perverted. In comments made by AFL leaders on the law and the courts was an implicit dislike for the very idea of law, and not merely for the law that touched labor. As one modern observer has said, the AFL made "a principled attack on law and on the state."[57] This attack was plainly related to doctrinaire acceptance of the nineteenth-century version of *laissez faire*, but it was also more obscurely related to the pragmatic strain of AFL thinking. And beyond this was a simple but firm conviction that the essence of law was compulsion.

The hostility to law in the judicial sense that was close to the heart of voluntarism extended to legislation with a rigidity that, in retrospect, is difficult to believe. Again, organized labor had some basis in experience for mistrust of Congress and its works. Not only had the Sherman Act turned out to be to labor's disadvantage, but those parts of the Clayton Act that were hailed as "Labor's Magna Carta" proved to be meaningless. Nor were these two acts labor's whole bill of specifications against legislation; the hostility had existed even before they were passed. Even as Sidney and Beatrice Webb were publishing their monumental work on trade unionism in England and discussing the method of legislation as one of labor's primary devices, the leaders of the American labor movement were opposing all forms of action involving law and politics.[58] Thus in 1895 one AFL leader even opposed sending a delegate to the International Conference of Social Work because this would embody political action. An AFL vice president asked in 1902 why there should be any wait for the slow process of the law, "when we can exert sure and certain economic power."[59]

Reliance on economic power—which largely meant collective bargaining (including ultimate recourse to strikes) and the boycott and a rather minimal reliance on friendly benefits—was the converse of hostility to the state and to political action. To see the "economism" of the AFL purely in these terms, however, is to miss much of its significance. Economic action was self-help, "the best help"; it represented the nearest approximation of individualism in the context of organization. Above all it was most congenial to solution of the very troubling problem of keeping the labor movement united in any organization whatsoever—a primary problem in the day-to-day thinking of the leaders of labor.

The AFL's record in the long struggle for social legislation in the United States was truly remarkable. Conceptions of social insurance were developed in Europe during the nineteenth century and were well established in a number of countries before the twentieth. Old age insurance, unemployment insurance, and even health insurance were recognized by this time in many places as quite free of radical taint; indeed, the great innovator in this field was Bismarck. The contest for social insurance in England came after the turn of the century, but was largely won before the beginning of World War I. In America, however, the story was very different. Although Americans watched the English controversy on social legislation closely, there was no comparable political movement for its enactment in the United States. In the labor movement, the response to suggestions for a system of social legislation was generally hostile.

One of the early controversies within the AFL on social legislation related to laws regulating hours of work. The limitation of hours had long been a major objective of trade unionism, and in the years just before World War II the eight-hour day was the goal of the most able and aggressive unions. In 1913, however, Gompers had denounced the idea of achieving this objective through legislation. A resolution favoring hours legislation brought before the 1914 convention was defeated. Presumably such legislation would have been compulsion. Nevertheless, the organization did not alter its existing approval for laws against child labor, and it continued to favor regulation of hours of work for women. This support was consistent with voluntarism in that it sought to protect the job market and did not threaten a weakening of any union member's loyalty to his organization. There were no children or women in the AFL.

On the greater issue of social insurance, the AFL was bleakly antagonistic. The array of arguments brought forward in opposition to state insurance, whether for old age, health, or unemployment, was at once long and abstract. All these forms of insurance were "paternal." They would increase taxation. They would create a special bureaucracy for their administration. They would require the registration of workingmen as a class. They would divide people into two groups: those eligible for benefits and those ineligible. They would be undemocratic; they would destroy freedom.

Old age pensions under a governmental system were discussed with some heat in AFL conventions beginning in 1902. Resolutions favoring such pensions were defeated in that year and each year thereafter until 1909, when a very mild and dilute form of approval was reluctantly given—approval which could count for nothing in any campaign before Congress.[60] Gompers returned to his practice of disapproving this form of insurance along with the rest on all the grounds outlined above. The debate on health insurance did not even produce transitory approval.

Unemployment insurance was the really big issue, and also the most revealing of AFL attitudes. When the British system was created in the years before World War I, much debate occurred in the United States, especially within the labor movement. Resolutions in favor of an American system of unemployment insurance proffered in AFL conventions were soundly defeated in the years before American entry into the war. Thereafter the issue lapsed, although there was some desultory discussion in the 1920s. With the onset of the Great Depression it once more came alive. After 1929 unemployment increased rapidly and the membership of the AFL dwindled. Nevertheless, a resolution favoring unemployment insurance was defeated in the convention of 1930, and a similar motion was defeated in 1931, a year which saw a 14 per cent unemployment rate. But the executive council of the Federation decided to study the problem further, and finally, in 1932, a resolution in favor of unemployment insurance was approved, although substantial opposition remained. In 1933 there was a unanimous favorable vote. History offers few comparable examples of doctrinaire rigidity in the face of adverse circumstances and in the name of pragmatism.

In one area of political action, the relationship between labor and local government, the dogmas of voluntarism were seemingly more flexible. The local organizations of the AFL unions established without hesitation alliances with the dominant political machines in most of the major cities of the country. In New York, Chicago, Philadelphia, Detroit, St. Louis, San Francisco, and lesser cities, organized labor cooperated with and even became part of the organizations that held political power.[61] Sometimes the machines were Democratic, sometimes Republican. This, however, did not demonstrate labor's impartiality toward the two parties so much as it did partiality for the holders of power, whoever they might be. Not infrequently these alliances between organized labor and city machines also involved collaboration with prominent local business interests.[62]

The sharp contrast between the attitudes of labor toward national and local government poses the question whether there was any genuine consistency in voluntarism. Was it in fact anything more than the pragmatism claimed for it? Was it anything more than a gloss for sheer opportunism? Certainly cooperation with city machines brought tangible benefits to many unions and their members. Using the power obtained by acting with these machines, unions were able to push through local laws on sanitation and safety, licensing of workers in skilled trades, and measures ending work on Sundays. They were also able to gain strategic appointments of their own people as inspectors and as examiners of license applicants. Nevertheless, the substantial advantages these measures brought labor are insufficient evidence of the thoroughgoing pragmatism (or opportunism) of the American labor movement. If such a trait existed throughout American labor, it would have resulted in a quite different attitude toward the actions and policies of the federal government. It is easily demonstrable that the lot of the American worker would have been far easier than in fact it was if a system of unemployment insurance had existed at the onset of the Great Depression.

It is much more probable that in terms of doctrine, however poorly thought out and unclear, voluntarism assumed very different attitudes toward local government and national government. It would be futile to seek clear and convincing statements of the rationale behind this at least superficially contradictory position. The leaders of labor have not been intellectuals; they have, indeed, often evinced mistrust of intellectual approaches to the labor movement. At this point, then, it can only be noted without explanation that voluntarism included a belief in action through local government while it rigidly opposed action through national government.

There was one other principle of cardinal importance to the American labor movement as it took shape under the leaders of the AFL: trade autonomy. This was, indeed, a restatement of one of those first principles on which, as we have seen, the AFL was founded: the necessity of building upon existing national craft unions. The political expediency of the original choice is quite evident. As time passed, moreover, it became clear that the national ("international") unions were the foci of power in the Federation. These unions have remained very jealous of the power they hold and have consistently fought attempts to change the structure of the American labor movement. It is accordingly tempting to see in the insistence upon trade autonomy nothing more than the rationalization of one of the accidental conditions of power.

As a principle, however, trade autonomy had deeper roots. In the eyes of Gompers and the other founders of the AFL, the national craft unions were given factors—hard, concrete entities; to interfere with them was to infringe liberty and the basis of voluntarism, an action hardly less evil than interference by the government. The American labor movement has therefore always strongly insisted upon obtaining unanimity in Federation voting. "There is no way whereby our labor movement may be assured sustained progress in determining its policies and its plans other than sincere deliberation until a UNANIMOUS decision is reached." This was Gompers's last message to the AFL.[63]

This insistence on an extreme degree of unity was related to another corollary of trade autonomy: rigid opposition to industrial unionism. Industrial unionism (save in a few industrial unions, such as the United Mine Workers, which happened already to be in the AFL) implied a heterogeneity of members, among whom unanimity would be difficult to obtain without compulsion. In all accuracy, however, it must be noted that the major proponents of industrial unionism in Gompers's time were his personal opponents, the socialists.

For all its seeming lapses and discontinuities, voluntarism was coherent. Although it has never had a systematic statement, a common thread ran through its different tenets. The deep hostility to political action involving the national government, whether through political parties or legislation, was linked to insistence on trade autonomy within the Federation. The belief in economic action was linked to use of municipal ordinances and public appointments for labor officials. Through all these positions ran a common theme: dislike of the formality of law, strong belief in small and coherent units of organization, and a particular vision of liberty.

Voluntarism has always carried the implication of a high degree of cooperation with business and industry, an implication which has at times been expressed in the same language and clichés as the doctrine of *laissez faire*. Certainly acceptance of such an economic vision was implied in voluntarism, but voluntarism was ultimately much more a political than an economic vision. At times it resulted in calls for very far-reaching change in the political order, more far-reaching, perhaps, than any of the AFL leaders appreciated. Thus in the "Portland Manifesto" of 1923 the AFL called for a trade unionism "whose purpose must be the extension of freedom, the enfranchisement of the producer as such, the rescue of industry from chaos, profiteering and purely individual whim, including individual capacity, and the rescue of industry also from the domination of incompetent political bodies. . . . Industry must organize to govern itself, to impose upon itself tasks and rules and to bring order into its own house." And in this reorganization, labor, of course, must be included.[64] In 1931, the President of the AFL, William Green, once more asked for functional representation of industry and "more economic government" to cure the ills of business.[65] These ideas were essentially the same as those of business, and it is not surprising that during the periods when they were most conspicuous and most explicitly formulated the degree of harmony between business and organized labor was greatest. Even in other times, however, the basic doctrine of American labor was congenial to the latent theory of American business.

IV

Is there any common political view in the doctrines and practices of these three large segments of American life—business, agriculture, labor? At times there have been conflicts among the three, occasionally bitter and sometimes violent. Moreover, many of the problems faced in one area have been particular to it. Nevertheless, the doctrines of all three reveal a number of common themes; together, these themes are sufficiently coherent to suggest that a very particular point of view has pervaded their development.

In one way or another, these three groups share an attitude toward government. Business and labor share quite extensive agreement in their hostility toward it. The ideology of *laissez faire* in business has been hardly more rigid than that of voluntarism in labor. Much in this common attitude can be traced to the doctrines of nineteenth-century economic liberalism, although to say this is to undervalue the distinctively political character of the attitude. Agriculture has been seemingly far less antagonistic to government; indeed, readiness to seek political alleviation of the economic problems of farmers has been a conspicuous characteristic of organized agriculture in the twentieth century. And even in the other two segments, there has been frequent recourse to the services of government. With labor such recourse has been principally through local government; with business it has involved a variety of forms, such as the tariff and various service and regulatory agencies. Thus, while there is some truth in the generalization that the principal organized groups in America have disliked government, it is also true that they have used it, willingly, under some conditions.

The most conspicuous item of agreement is a very loud and persistent appeal for liberty. It is very easy to discount this avowed devotion as propaganda and the use of an overworked cliché. To dismiss it thus, however, is to do injustice to the sincerity of those who voiced it and to ignore much of its significance. Several points should be noted here. First, liberty is seen by business, labor, and agriculture in very simple terms—as absence of compulsion. Second, compulsion is seen as coming almost exclusively from the state. Third, liberty is seen as an attribute not merely of the individual, but more especially of certain kinds of private association.

This emphasis upon the liberty of certain associations is very close to the second major item of agreement: belief in small units of association as the essence of democracy. This belief sometimes appears in the form of insistence upon the distinction between public and private organizations, with a strong preference for the latter on the ground that the former use compulsion whereas the latter do not. In the light of the experience surveyed here, however, it is evident that the distinction is frequently ignored. In practice it is treated as secondary to the question of size of units. Correlatively, federalism is preferred to centralism.

The third major tenet is less obvious, but may well be the most important. This is a dislike of law and formal authority, related in part to the view of liberty which is the almost axiomatic starting point of all these theories, for law represents compulsion. The dislike of law is also related to belief in the small unit of association, for law is rigid. Where it has been possible to harness the formulation and application of law to small units and private associations, however, hostility to law and authority tends to vanish.

Taken together these points of preference do not constitute a systematic political theory. Indeed, they have been extracted from the statements and actions of groups that have frequently asserted a commitment to pragmatism and a distrust for theory. Nevertheless, each point is related to the others; together they have formed a political logic that has had important consequences in the development of American democracy.

Chapter 4

The Constituency

I

Few of the tenets of American orthodoxy are more important or less examined than the belief in small units of social and political organization as the citadels of virtually all the values associated with democracy. Much that is central to the major issues of American politics turns upon the character of the constituency, particularly upon the size and shape of the political unit within which decisions must be made. Every moment of internal crisis, from the beginning of American nationality to the present, in one way or another has touched this problem. It was the crucial issue in the first days of the republic until the inspired compromise of federalism emerged. It was the vital question in the Civil War. It is involved today wherever the problem of civil rights is posed. Within what boundaries and to which unit shall an issue of substance be referred? To ask this in effect is to ask, Who shall rule? It is also to ask, What kind of policy shall be followed, and for whose benefit?

A fundamental problem of government is involved, and though it exists whatever the form government takes, it assumes particular importance when that form is democratic. Since political decisions in a democracy are referred in some manner to a test of numbers—an election, a legislative vote, a referendum, even an administrative decision—the definition of the constituency within which the count is taken is a matter of primary importance. Other problems of American politics are as important, such as the limits of government power over individuals. With most of these issues, however, the questions that arise are peripheral, and there is some basic sense in which the issues themselves can be regarded as settled. With the problem of the constituency, by contrast, there has never been any such settlement.

Most debates about the problem have centered on federalism. The texts of this discussion are endless. They trace historical origins and cite documents with arguments of much scholarship and subtlety; they have been economic, legal, or moral in emphasis. Yet in essence this is a political debate. Despite its long history, however, federalism remains what it was at the beginning: something of a mystery. The founders of the American federal system were themselves not entirely clear in their intentions. What they created was partly an inheritance from their recent past, partly a pragmatic compromise of contemporary issues, in which different men among them saw different virtues. In any event, their creation was not static; it changed as events and the shifting balance of political forces decreed. Moreover, federalism looked in two directions. In one sense it looked toward a greater degree of centralization, a larger unit; this was its meaning at the moment the Constitution was adopted. In another sense, it protected and preserved small units of political organization. Appeal to federalism as a principle consequently has served purposes almost diametrically opposed.

Federalism, however, is only one form of the problem of the constituency. The range of possible results from the appropriate design of electoral boundaries has been apparent to American legislatures for a long time; perhaps the most characteristic American contribution to the art of politics is the gerrymander.

Yet another well-known principle involving the problem of the constituency is that of "divide and rule."

There has been curiously little general analysis of the relationship between the constituency and political power. Since there are many conceivable possibilities for affecting the distribution of power by drawing constituency boundaries, it would be a very large undertaking to formulate, from the beginning as it were, the general principles involved. The most important dimension of the problem, however, is *size*. Because of the importance of the problem in American politics, one could reasonably expect to find a substantial body of discussion directed precisely to the question of how constituency size affects the distribution of political power. But this discussion is meager.[1] What does exist is a rather large body of doctrine, most of which bears only obliquely on the problem, but which taken as a whole amounts to an ideology of the small community. The roots of this ideology reach into the nation's agrarian past. They have produced the association so frequently made between individual virtue and the simplicity of rural life. This and other assumptions which have seemed to grow out of the particular conditions of American life have formed a conception of the small geographical community as the repository of social virtue.

The first of these assumptions is that the small community is natural. For most of human history most men have lived in such communities. In the scale of history large cities are deviations from the normal. By comparison with the life of cities, life in the small rural community is in accord with man's own nature. In the rural community man is close to the elemental aspects of existence—not two, three or more steps removed from the processes which produce the food by which he must live. Moreover, the rural community develops without human planning and is the result of an organic growth. In it needs for cooperation develop spontaneously among people living a common way of life. These needs are visible and comprehensible to all, so that there is no necessity for compulsion to meet them; thus if a member of the small community requires help, it must be given, not because some law or ruler commands, but because it is plain that at some later time similar need may strike those now being called to help.[2]

This seemingly simple picture of the small rural community as something natural carries several other important implications. Since the small farming community is natural there is no compulsion and in this sense its people are free. Here, probably, is the heart of the enthusiasm for small communities of any kind. They can exist without the array of formal institutions that are inescapable in cities or large communities.

The view of the small community as the natural home of freedom has been much more a direct perception than a general theory. If the community is autonomous, it is free; self-government itself is freedom—this has been the equation seen by small communities and new nations for most of history, and asserted today as vigorously as ever (and almost invariably without elaboration), as though a self-evident truth.

Such a view, however, contains several assumptions which bear closer examination. First, it assumes rationality among the people of a small community: they can and will perceive their own interests. Here again, direct perception has supported the assumption. The affairs of a small community are inevitably simpler and more comprehensible than those of a large community; rational behavior among the people of the former is, accordingly, much more probable than among those of the latter. And this contrast between simplicity and complexity has often been obvious from a local vantage point.

The second assumption is that the interests of the people of a small community will be identical. It is immediately obvious that in almost any small town there is less diversity of people than in a large city. There are fewer families, and these are frequently interrelated; there are fewer economic interests, and often lesser extremes of wealth and poverty; there are fewer religions and races. The same will generally be true of almost any dimension of social difference. This greater homogeneity is directly observable in most small communities and is repeatedly reflected in their cohesive behavior and their frequent mistrust of strangers.[3]

These two assumptions are bolstered by several arguments which tend to be made wherever the merits of small communities have been praised. One of the most common is that the members of a small community know much more about their own problems than outsiders do. The particular lay of the land, its history in detail, the intangibles of personal relationships— these are matters, often of essential importance, which in the nature of things can be known only to local people. In choosing public officials, the people of a small community thus have a great advantage when they are acting in a local election, where, in contrast with their situation in a national election, they can know the candidates by direct human contact. Quite possibly they not only know the candidates personally, but are familiar with their business records, credit, personal habits, and family histories as well. Similarly, the officials of a small community will know their community and their constituents—their histories, weaknesses, strengths, and needs. In such a setting discussion on the basis of accurate and detailed information is possible as it is not in a large community.

An even greater advantage is perceived in the deliberations of a small community. From Aristotle onward it has been argued that only in a rather small group is it possible to have any rational discussion,[4] the classic point being that unless the various speakers' arguments could be heard there could be no rational evaluation and that, accordingly, the range of a human voice limited the size of an effective deliberating body. Moreover, modern experience and study of crowd behavior have demonstrated the tendencies of any large group to irrationality, even when mechanical devices extend the reach of the human voice.

This emphasis upon rational discussion has been particularly strong in America, where the New England town meeting and the Quaker meeting have been cited endlessly as embodiments of democracy. The enthusiasm has been reflected in educational methods at all levels and has deeply affected even those seeming strongholds of authoritarian rule, the bureaucracies of modern corporations.[5] The pervasiveness of the town meeting ideal, even where its realization is only formal, is so great that the ideal plainly touches something very close to the heart of the dominant ideology.

Small communities other than geographical have also been celebrated as natural homes of liberty. The church, the trade union, associations of all kinds have been held in modern times to possess the same virtues as the small town or the farming locality.[6] The heart of the argument in each instance is the intrinsic value of smallness. A small community may be formed upon the basis of almost any dimension of social difference—function as well as geography, race as well as religion. A geographic community has some advantages through the daily propinquity of its members and their association with a particular bit of land, but even these advantages are not peculiar to such communities. Other forms of association are claimed to have in greater degree an equally important advantage: their voluntary character. A member of such an association is a member by his own choice. He has applied for admission and he remains by his own will. Even church membership is voluntary, and is symbolized by the sacrament of Confirmation. Moreover, it is arguable that by the act of individual choice a greater degree of homogeneity is achieved in these voluntary associations, and that consequently they offer an even greater degree of freedom from compulsion than does the geographic community.[7]

These are some of the essential arguments of contemporary "pluralism." Earlier pluralists also almost invariably assumed that freedom is to be found within the associations of the Western world, and were especially concerned with the threat posed to the integrity of the private association by the power of the state.[8] Nevertheless, there is a discontinuity between the older and the contemporary pluralist doctrines. The earlier was primarily a European phenomenon and enjoyed no substantial support in America, a land which would have seemed to be its most congenial setting. No major contribution to the large body of pluralist writings was made by an American thinker during the period when pluralism was strong in Europe,[9] partly because it was then most closely associated with the particular causes of the church and the trade union, while at that time in America the church was secure and trade unions were weak and inarticulate.[10] In any event European pluralism disappeared as a movement before the American phenomenon took shape.

This discontinuity in time between the older pluralism and that of today is paralleled by another discontinuity, one more of spirit than of argument. The outstanding fact is that what might be called classic pluralism was a liberal doctrine. It centered on opposition to the excessive power of the state as it was seen in the first quarter of the twentieth century. Perhaps the most fundamental point was that the state was to be regarded as only one of numerous forms of human association, standing on essentially the same ground as the church or trade unions. Each of these associations served some but not all human needs; the state, accordingly, could lay claim to no special authority over the others. In fact, on a number of scores, its claim was inferior to those of other associations. Thus it was not as old as the church. Even the trade unions, through a presumed continuity of history from the medieval guilds, could claim to be older. Geographically, the state was less extensive than the church, or the unions with their internationals. And the state had no superior moral purpose; the church had definite claim to a higher. Thus there could be no justification for state coercion of any of these various associations.[11]

The challenge to the state was always more important than its basis. Federalism was a desirable form of organization since it divided the power of the state and made it less capable of tyranny. Small geographical communities were good because, insofar as they were autonomous, they would check central power. Private associations were also desirable, since they too were opponents of the grasping central power. At its simplest, pluralist doctrine seemed to suggest that while the state relies on coercion, other forms of association do not. This has rarely been as explicit as stated here. However, other arguments were implicit and they supported the same position: Rational discussion precludes compulsion. Homogeneity avoids the conflict which may result in compulsion. Autonomy means self-government, which in turn *is* freedom. The small community, particularly in its rural form, is virtuous; and again, virtue implies freedom.

II

Enthusiasm for the small community of whatever kind has always rested on other grounds than liberty. They have probably been more important as motivation. Nevertheless, they have consistently been mingled with the argument of liberty and have been treated with a near-lyricism that has disguised their very different character.

Repeatedly, the small community has been portrayed as the guardian of "human" values. Here the individual has standing as a human being, not as a mere statistic. He can be seen as a creature of flesh and blood and he can see, touch, and feel his fellows. They meet face to face and they know each other not only by name and repute, but by detailed knowledge derived from long association. Most important, their relationships are natural.[12]

The small community (the argument continues) is a web of these personal, human, natural relationships. What must be dealt with in a large social unit by rigid rules, procedures, and precedents can in a small community be handled in humane fashion and settled on the basis of the merits of the individual situation, avoiding the procrustean bed of a system of law based upon analogies. In this sense the small community is at once more efficient and more just.[13]

But the really great virtue of the small community or private association is that it holds the prospect of fellowship. This is something more than an absence of restraint, formality, or impersonality; it is a positive relationship among the members of the community by which they are bound to each other in all the trials and joys of their common life. Real fellowship erases —or, at minimum, reduces to minor significance—the differences among them. It enriches their individual lives at the same time that it creates a common purpose. It builds on men's inborn impulses to cooperation and gives rein to the spontaneity of which they are capable. In a fellowship, no man is alone and apart. Each man's welfare is of concern to the entire community, and the welfare of the community is a concern of every man. The relationship between men is symbolized by special modes of address—"brother," "comrade," "neighbor," and so on.

This is one of the oldest dreams of man. It has been close to the heart of many religions and has inspired most utopias. It has been harnessed by most revolutionary movements, and has been implicit in the doctrines of conservatism. In one form or another it has been one of the most recurrent political ideas of history.[14]

Although the ideal of fellowship has an almost universal attraction, it has persistently met frustration in large political units. Fraternity has invariably been short lived in the hierarchy of revolutionary values; the human warmth and comradeship of new mass movements have withered in the sere winds of routine and bureaucracy that always follow the first stage of success. Relations among men in large bodies become impersonal and abstract, or else disordered to the point where every man's hand is set against every man. Only in small units can fellowship develop naturally and endure; only here can be found the congregation, the *Gemeinschaft*, the community.[15]

The vision of fellowship in the small community has been passionately defended and has often inspired an almost poetic eloquence. This very eloquence, however, tends to disguise the character of the values and prescriptions offered. And these are ambivalent.

In the entire fabric of argument extolling the small community there is, for example, an often inconspicuous but strong emphasis on order. This emphasis to a very considerable degree conflicts with insistence upon liberty as a characteristic of the small unit. Certainly there is no direct antithesis between order and liberty; even John Stuart Mill conceded that a broad measure of order and stability was a necessary precondition for liberty.[16] Nevertheless, liberty and order look in different directions, and an emphasis on one is always at some point in conflict with the other.

The emphasis on order appears in many different forms. Among the pluralists it is not always either clear or conscious, but rather implicit. Thus "human" values, warmth, face-to-face relationships, are all founded on the ties that bind man to man and to society, as is suggested by the very figurative nature of the concept of "belonging." The evidence of impersonality is of the same character. By the same token that decisions regarding individuals are made on an *ad hoc*, on-the-merits basis, they are open to the charge of being arbitrary. And this is scarcely compatible with the ideas of liberty and justice so eloquently stated in the best of pluralist writing.

This is not to say that all argument in favor of the small community is either disingenuous or founded on a preference for order over liberty. The devotion to liberty of the "classic" pluralists and of many American writers has been so evident as to be beyond question. But it is suggested that even the most liberal pluralists had a continuing concern for a sort of order to some degree inconsistent with liberty.

In other hands the argument takes on a different cast: order becomes the central problem, caused by the entrance of great new numbers of people into the life of politics in the modern era. This condition in turn derives from the great increase in population since the industrial revolution and the breakdown of social distinctions that has accompanied the cataclysmic changes of the modern age. With the breakdown of social distinctions there is a correlative dissolution of the routines and rules by which men live and which in other times have been the essence of order. One rule abandoned leads to a weakening of other rules; many rules challenged results in weakness of all rule. The consequence is disorder throughout society; authority is weakened not only at the highest levels of government, but in the ties that determine the personal relations between men. The family, the church, the shop, the community, all established institutions are undermined. The society that is left is subject to the tidal sweep of great mass movements. Irrationality takes over as the dominating force of politics. Individuals, left with the belief that all things are possible, strive for objectives they can neither see nor achieve. Here is the condition of *anomie;* beyond it lies the almost apocalyptic threat of totalitarianism and parabolic wars.[17]

This thesis appears, with numerous forms and variants, in many modern discussions of the mass society. In some there is a patent lament for the passing of aristocratic graces and privileges.[18] In others there is a very real concern for the preservation of the system of law, which has itself been important to the broader values of civilizations. These differences of concern are great, and it would be mistaken to assume that all discussions of mass society have a common purpose. But all share an underlying preoccupation with the disorders which seem to endanger a society characterized by large political and social units.

Although most literature on the mass society and its dangers is vague at many points, the fundamental value of preserving or creating small units within the large society is to maintain or impose discipline and rules upon the otherwise anomic masses of people.[19] If every individual had his place, with rights and duties deriving therefrom, a society would result approximating the status system of feudal times. But since this is impossible in an industrial era, some substitute in small communities of other kinds is sought. The suggestion that enthusiasts for small communities are seeking a return to a system of status would undoubtedly be denied, and with some justification. Yet it is not unfair to suggest that the advantages of order and stability that are the outstanding features of a system of status are just the virtues sought in other kinds of small communities in the modern era.

III

The situation, then, is that despite a very strong ideological attachment to decentralization and the small community in America, the justification for that attachment is founded on very divergent arguments. Although the ideology can be accounted for rather simply historically, it is important to examine the problem in its intrinsic terms. What are the political effects of decentralization? What are the inherent values of the small community? Curiously, these questions are rarely debated. Ideological support goes very largely to the small community ideal, even while many tendencies lead away from it in practice. The debate that does occur—and it is voluminous—relates to precedent, history, and constitutional exegesis.

Nevertheless, some of the most important and distinctively American contributions to political thought have dealt with just this problem—appropriately enough, for it has been a particularly American problem. The United States was the first of the modern democracies, for a long time the largest, and the first to launch the experiment of federalism. Almost from the beginning of American national history, the ablest political leaders realized that a commitment to liberty and equality implied a social structure free of the feudal orders of Europe and that this in turn posed a general problem of the political ordering of unprecedented numbers of people. For Jefferson, and even more for John Taylor, the solution lay in the agrarian democracy of small farming communities.[20]

The most penetrating of American discussions of the problem, however, was—and is—James Madison's. In a very broad sense Madison agreed with John Taylor's analysis, but disagreed with his prescription. The problem of modern government, in the eyes of both, was the tendency of men to fall into conflict among themselves. It is the problem that confronts virtually every new nation: how to make a unity out of a diversity of people of different backgrounds, interests, religions, and beliefs.[21] The conflict that arises from these sources—the "violence of faction," in Madison's language—is the cause of the instability, injustice, and confusion in public councils that have been the mortal diseases of which popular governments have perished everywhere. Madison noted that there were two methods of dealing with the disease: removal of its causes or control of its effects. Taylor's solution was the former. If the really important sources of conflict within a nation were economic (a point on which Madison and Taylor were agreed), the solution, said Taylor, was to give men the same economic interests, that is, to ensure that agriculture was their common activity. Here Madison differed. A removal of the causes of "faction" could only be achieved at the expense of liberty, he observed, since these causes were rooted in the nature of men. Differences in human opinions and abilities would always exist; unequal distribution of property, the most common and durable source of faction, must therefore follow. A solution was to be found only in controlling the effects of these conflicts.

The passage in which Madison makes this argument is one of the most celebrated in American political thought. It has had a widespread influence in justifying the array of interest groups that is so conspicuous a feature of the American political scene. Oddly enough, however, the solution Madison propounded in the same short essay has been given less attention. That solution was, very simply, large political units. It was, of course, offered in the immediate context of the New York debate on ratification of the Constitution, and perhaps the obvious special pleading in Madison's argument has robbed it of the influence it might have had in a different context. Nevertheless, Madison's explanation of his solution is the most illuminating treatment of the problem we have.

In the first place, Madison argued, since a large republic would involve representation rather than pure democracy, public views would be passed through the medium of a chosen body of citizens whose patriotism and love of justice would be least likely to sacrifice the true interest of their country. A far more important point, however, was contained in this passage:

The smaller the society, the fewer probably will be the distinct parties and interests composing it; the fewer the distinct parties and interests, the more frequently will a majority be found of the same party, and the smaller the compass within which they are placed, the more easily will they concert and execute their plans of oppression. Extend the sphere, and you take in a greater variety of parties and interests; you make it less probable that a majority of the whole will have a common motive to invade the rights of other citizens; or if such a common motive exists, it will be more difficult for all who feel it to discover their own strength, and to act in unison with each other.[22]

Although this is a very simple principle, it applies to situations of great complexity, and consequently is easily misunderstood. Perhaps the most common misunderstanding of its implications arises from a quite valid argument derived from it, namely, that in a large nation such as the United States many different interests develop and that in their mutual interplay they check each other and by their very multiplicity defeat any attempt by any one interest to dominate the whole. Moreover, by their number and individual strength, they stand as obstacles to assumption of total power, whether by a native pathological mass movement or a foreign organization. In different parts of his discussion, Madison emphasized this mutual checking of ambition set against ambition, and these passages lend support to the argument. Although, as will be seen later, some important qualifications must be made to this argument, the point is genuinely important and offers part of any explanation for the common failure of mass movements in America.

The operation of all organized interest groups in this manner has also been cited, however, as a general guarantee of liberty and a demonstration of political equality in operation. Although, as we have seen, the existence of different interest groups gives protection against the assumption of total power by a mass movement, it is much less than a guarantee of freedom or equality against other threats. To see why, it is useful to recall the specific problem to which Madison addressed himself. The issue was not simply whether there should be a large or a small nation, but how a nation should be politically organized. What are the appropriate constituent units within the nation?

The factor of first importance here is the diversity that accompanies size. In a small community there will probably be fewer different interests—economic, religious, ethnic, or other —than in a large community. Thus it may happen that a single economic interest, such as a particular farm product or a particular industry, is overwhelmingly the largest in the community. In the state, the relative importance of the particular crop or industry will be diluted by the existence of other interests; in the nation, the relative importance of the one interest will be even less. Thus, for example, the importance of dairy farmers will be greater in a rural county than in the state of New York at large, and the power of an oil company will be greater in Baton Rouge than in Washington, D.C. If decisions relating to dairy farming can be put in the hands of the counties and those relating to the oil industry in the hands of the states, the power of both interests will be much greater than if such decisions were put in the hands of the nation as a whole.

The effect of decentralization upon the distribution of power is not limited to the somewhat extreme (but certainly not rare) situation in which one interest is predominant in a community. Where several important interests exist in a small community they will have greater influence than if they were placed in a larger and more diverse community. The principle is the same. If those interests are in conflict, however, the power one of them may wield will be limited by that held by the others. Often, however, there is little such conflict among the important interests, and it is possible for them to cooperate.

What happens at the far end of the scale of power is just as important. As the most important and influential local interests gain power by being placed in a small sphere, the least influential interests lose power. In a purely democratic system many interests may be represented in a small community by numbers so small as to be less than the minimum necessary for defense of those interests in any setting. Thus Group A might command 10 per cent of all votes in the nation, yet because of an even diffusion of its voting strength have little influence as compared with Group B or Group C, each of which controlled only 1 or 2 per cent of the total votes. This could occur if the supporters of Groups B and C were each concentrated in a few communities. The latter two, for example, might be able to select several Congressmen, whereas Group A would have no material effect in the election of any. This situation would be most serious for Group A if the other two groups were opposed to its interests. But Group A is also adversely affected without such a coincidence of opposition to its interests, since it will have been effectively factored out of the political process and be left with none of the tokens of exchange in the bargaining that consti-

tutes so much of politics. To the extent that the units of government are small and autonomous, it can be expected that many
interests will be left without substantial political influence.

This principle applies with particular effectiveness in a situation where the means of power are democratic and a count of
votes is deciding. The chance of effective opposition to the
dominant interest developing is much less in a small than in a
large community, and the majority will be much more cohesive.
But the general principle will also tend to operate where the
means of power are not exclusively democratic and here it may,
indeed, be more effective. The efficiency of money or even
violence (if these are the established means of power) will be
greater where there are numerous small constituencies than
where there is a single large one, for, generally speaking, the
difficulties of using such methods are greater in a large than in
a small community.

Power in the small community (at least in most American
communities) is likely, moreover, to be informal. In a very small
community it is not only too costly to support a formal system
of government or to employ a policeman; it is also unnecessary.
The fact that a policeman is unnecessary does not, however,
establish the absence of power; the possibility of social compulsion remains and can be particularly strong. It is, indeed, a
form of constraint that has often been remarked upon in small
communities.[23] The emphasis laid by many enthusiasts for the
small community upon its orderliness is evidence in point.
Moreover, some sociological studies of small communities suggest rather strongly that a structuring of influence occurs frequently in such units.

The obverse of this is the very factor of impersonality, escape
from which is so commonly cited as the small community's chief
virtue. Yet impersonality is one of the principal factors which
in a large community provides access to sharing in political
power. In general, greater impersonality, formality, and impartiality are characteristics of large communities. Devolution
to local communities of the power to make decisions in a formal
sense is not necessary in order to maintain established power

relationships; simple denial to larger units of the power to treat such matters is sufficient. The informal structure of the small community will usually be able to suppress a challenge before it becomes overt. A highly discretionary system of voter registration in the South, for example, has been a principal means of Negro disfranchisement. Only a slight hint of economic reprisal for Negro attempts to register is necessary to repel them in a small community where relationships are face to face and "human." By contrast, in a large community, individuals will more frequently be unknown to each other personally, their relationships will be more formal, and intimidation will be much more difficult to effect and easier to prove if it does occur. There is a direct connection between size of the community, degree of formality of relationships, and ease or difficulty of enforcing patterns of subordination.

This is not simply an issue of power distribution; it is also an issue of freedom. Impersonality is the guarantee of individual freedom characteristic of the large unit. Impersonality means an avoidance of arbitrary official action, the following of prescribed procedure, conformance to established rules, and escape from bias whether for or against any individual. Impersonality, and the privacy and freedom it confers, may be despised, and the human warmth and community concern for the personal affairs of individuals characteristic of the small community preferred. Nevertheless, the values involved are different, and are to a considerable degree mutually antagonistic.

IV

To this point the force of the argument is that decentralization will generally tend to accentuate any inequality in the distribution of power that would otherwise exist *within* each decentralized unit. Quite obviously in the entire nation it should be expected that the groups so favored will be different from each other. Thus in a cattle-raising area, the stockmen would be favored; in a coal mining area, the coal industry would be politically strengthened, and so on. Accordingly, it might seem that the objective of diversity and the consequent mutual checking of interests that Madison saw as political virtues are best achieved by a large nation of small units. Thus (it might be argued) whereas in a given community one group might be strong at another's expense, that other group would in a different community be strong at the expense of the first, and so on. Hence it might appear that nationally the distribution of power among the various interests that compose the nation would be the same if there were only one large constituency in the nation. Such seems to be the assumption underlying the argument of many who are enthusiastic for small decentralized units of government.

What is the merit of this belief? Serious difficulties arise from the fact that it does not, even on its face, take account of the tendency to inequality of power within the unit. And if the unit has a large degree of autonomy this inequality may be a matter of importance. In a situation in which critical decisions on issues of policy are made locally the consequences can be very direct and apparent. If there is less autonomy and the issues of substance are not decided locally, the effect of small constituent units may nevertheless also be important—especially when one considers that this situation is very common.

The representatives chosen in small local units owe their choice to narrower and less diverse constituencies than if the units are large. They are accountable to these narrow constituencies and must, within limits, represent their demands. These will be narrower and more specific than those of larger constituencies. The effective constituency, that is, the part of the whole unit which is able to enforce its demands, is always less than the entire unit. To the extent that power is distributed unequally in the constituent unit, the effective constituency will be narrow. And it is in the small constituency that, other things being equal, power tends most to inequality of distribution. As a result representatives of small constituencies in a national forum will be more likely than representatives of large constituencies to take specific and extreme positions favoring the particular interests holding power in the constituent units. Where there is greater diversity within the units, the positions taken by representatives will in general be more diffuse, less extreme, and more open to compromise.

It is important also to recall that through the inequality of power distribution which is accentuated by a multiplicity of constituent units, some interests are seriously weakened and may be virtually factored out of the scheme of influence. In general, the interests discriminated against in this manner are of two kinds. The first is the interest of a weak minority which, if distributed evenly among many small constituencies, will lack the liminal numbers necessary to achieve any influence at all within these constituencies. Such a minority may be an ethnic group or any category of heterodox opinion. It should be recalled, however, that power is not always based purely upon numbers of people; other elements may enhance the strength of power-holding groups. The effect of a small constituency is to enhance the power of local elites, whatever their character or sources of power. Thus it should be evident that local minorities left without effective spokesmen in national councils may not necessarily be small or insignificant.

The other type of interest discriminated against in a system of many small constituencies is that for which support must inevitably be diffuse and which is not central or preoccupying for any group—the kind of interest most commonly called "the public interest." Active support for such interests must come from relatively small numbers of people with some sense of cause and dedication. These numbers, like those of the minority interests just discussed, may have no effect in small constituencies and, if they are to succeed, must have the larger numbers of a big constituency from which to draw enough people with the time, money, and drive to work for a cause the benefits of which will be shared by all. Moreover, only in a large constituency will there be a diversity of powerful interests and the mutual checking that follows from diversity. Such mutual checking may on occasion be the essential condition for the success of those who are defending a general or "public" interest. Thus, it is more probable that a general interest in conservation of natural resources will have effective support in a legislature composed of the representatives of large and diverse constituencies than in one whose members represent small and homogeneous constituencies. In the latter, the interests hoping to benefit from narrow, partisan, and quick exploitation of resources will more probably be successful. Thus the United States Senate can be expected more often than the House of Representatives to serve general interests.

Another difficulty derives from the fact that no individual has a single interest, opinion, or characteristic. He may have a very clear and dominant interest as a producer, but he will inevitably also be a consumer. He may also be a Catholic, a fisherman, and a stamp collector. Inescapably, people differ in many ways and there are many dimensions of social difference. To take explicit account of all these differences in a formal scheme of representation is impossible. Guild socialism was perhaps the clearest attempt to recognize such a diversity of interests, but even it was largely focused upon the interests of man as producer and consumer.[24] Whatever the historic reasons for the disappearance of guild socialism as a movement, it is fairly clear that the prospective chaos of its representative scheme would have spelled its defeat had there ever been an attempt to effect its plan of reorganization.

Nevertheless, the most common scheme of representation is based upon geography, and this tends to give special representation to particular interests in different localities where the power of those interests is concentrated. But the holding of power is itself one of the various dimensions of social difference. On this dimension the holders of power in the various constituencies will have in common that they are holders of power—a purely formal and largely empty consideration were it not for the tendency toward greater concentration of power in a small and homogeneous constituency than in a large and heterogeneous constituency. The holding of concentrated power in many respects assimilates the characteristics of *class*.[25] Although power and wealth are by no means inevitably associated, they are often found in the same hands, particularly in a society where values are heavily materialistic.

In consequence a decentralized system of small constituent units often tends to defeat the mutual checking of power by power that is a presumed purpose of decentralization. On many issues the various holders of power in the different constituencies of such a system can work together for their mutual advantage. It will be easier for them to collaborate since they will often have a common ideology. More important, however, much of the potential opposition to their policies, as we have noted, will have been deprived of effective voice. There will, indeed, be occasional conflicts among the various power-holding elites, but they will only be occasional and will tend to be limited in scale. Thus, to take a relatively simple illustration, textile manufacturers may favor protective tariffs for their own products, while industrial consumers of certain textiles (automobile makers, for example) may oppose them. Nevertheless, a *general* opposition to tariff increases from the standpoint of consumers is unlikely to emerge in a council whose members are selected on the basis of small constituent units.

It would be a mistake to suppose that the sort of collaboration among holders of power described here is solely or even primarily based upon ideological sympathy. Rather it is founded upon the nature of the demands which groups of narrow and homogeneous constituencies (and their leaders or representatives) have to make and upon the tactics that favor these demands. The demands will characteristically be narrow and limited in scope, although very possibly extreme in degree; given the narrow basis of the constituencies in a decentralized system, broad demands are impractical and doomed to defeat unless they are made in the context of a larger federation of such groups.

Logrolling is the tactic most appropriate to the ends of small and relatively homogeneous units within a larger system. It is both simple and effective for the leaders of such units to exchange support for each others' demands. While occasional conflicts of ends must be expected, it will much more frequently occur that the ends will not conflict at all. While the various goals will usually not be mutually shared, the opportunity for exchanging support is obvious and easily seized. This process, to be observed in almost any legislature, is not, it should be noted, a process of compromise; except in unusual circumstances it requires no moderation or tempering of demands. Given two interests whose objectives are intrinsically of mutual indifference, collaboration for support of the whole demands of each can be readily effected. Such cooperation will be all the easier where the work of negotiation has been given to professional leaders, who will have a common calling, however different their respective clienteles may be.[26]

The ease and success of this sort of collaboration are, however, far more dependent on the absence of effective opposition which would be present if the constituencies were large and diverse. As we have seen, such opposition is akin to class; it would have to speak in the interest of large numbers, of generalized interests, and of the interests of those in the lowest economic strata of the various constituent units. Yet these are the interests which are in effect excluded in the normal process of logrolling. Their absence from—or, at best, their ineffective presence upon—the political scene leaves a largely open field for the success of those more concrete and narrow interests whose mutual opposition is not great.

The assumption that the political structuring of a nation by large or small units is unimportant and that different groups existing in that nation will have the same influence no matter what the form of political organization is, then, mistaken. How the nation is politically organized is exceedingly important. Quite different results may be obtained with the same distribution of interests depending on whether the context they are placed in is centralized or decentralized.

V

The size of the constituency, then, is a central issue of politics. It is not simply a matter of whether a nation is large or small (although this is, indeed, involved); more important, it is a question of how a nation or a society is organized. The instinct that leads supporters of particular policies to favor units of a particular size is entirely sound; to a very great degree, their success or failure depends on the context in which decisions are made.

It should not be expected that a constituency of a given definition will always produce a particular policy or that any of the actions that emerge from it will be completely predictable on the basis of its influence alone. Representatives of the constituency will rarely be automaton spokesmen for their constituents' interests or desires; indeed, elected representatives frequently take pains to insist that they are not simple respondents to pressure from within their constituencies. Nevertheless, constituency influence will be persistent and strong. It need not take the form of overt pressure to be effective; any reasonably sensitive representative, whether of a congressional district, a labor union, or other social unit, will be aware of the needs and desires of his constituents and can be expected to respond to them. If he is markedly insensitive to them—at least to those of his constituents who hold power—he is likely in time to be replaced.

It would also be mistaken to suppose that the influence of the constituency is simple or wholly independent of other influences. Reciprocal relationships exist among a number of factors, among the most important being the size of the constituency, the tactical methods employed, ideology, and policy. Thus if a constituency is large and diverse, the tactics chosen will probably be political rather than economic, since the resources of the state will be necessary to satisfy the demands that all will make in common. Equally, a tactic of economic action such as collective bargaining, a boycott, or a cooperative will tend to create a narrow constituency, since only such a constituency can act with sufficient cohesion to assure the effectiveness of such tactics. An ideology of democratic participation, in which a high valuation is placed on a maximum degree of involvement of individuals in common affairs, comes most readily to and is most easily achieved in small units, which will tend to justify themselves by such an ideology. But the most important relationship is, as has been suggested earlier, that between con-

stituency and policy. Policies generally adhering to maintenance of the status quo and favoring the concrete interests of
existing elites will tend to be associated with organizations
based on small units; alternatively, large units will more probably produce policies favoring change directed to the general,
diffuse, and widely shared interests of a broad segment of the
population. The influence is not in a single direction in any of
these relationships. Accommodation of organization to particular tactical situations will occur, just as given organizations will
prefer certain tactics. A deep-seated particular ideology will
favor certain kinds of organization; an organization of a given
size will develop a congenial ideology.

Although such an ideology will generally serve the ends of
those who urge it, its claims cannot be taken completely at face
value. Thus the ideology of decentralization and small units
contains a mixture of incompatible claims. The claim that
decentralization and political organization by small units
(whether of a public governmental body or of a private association) will serve as guarantors of stability and protect against
mass movements is generally valid. The multiplicity of power
centers makes many obstacles for the development of such
movements; the tendency to stratification of power relations
and a pattern of informal authority within small units is a force
for stability. By the same token, however, the claims that small
units ensure democracy are erroneous. Except in the exceedingly simple sense that defines local autonomy (or the autonomy of any small units) as democracy, decentralization to local
or functional small units does not make for democracy; indeed,
in the sense that democratic values center about liberty and
equality, it creates conditions quite hostile to democracy. The
tendency inherent in small units to stratification of power relationships and to protection of established informal patterns of
domination and subordination is most alien to equality. The
insistence upon lack of formality and the constraint of law is
intended to demonstrate a protection of liberty. Actually, however, the absence of law and of the respect for the values of
impersonality and impartiality which law implies is a poor

guarantee of freedom; moreover, in the context of the power relationships that characterize a small community, it is an active threat to freedom.

The fundamental error of the ideology of small units lies in its ignoring of questions of power *within* the unit of organization. Although problems of power may in some respects be reduced in scale by decentralization, they are never banished. Stability and order may be preferred to liberty and equality, and under some circumstances, when a highly emotional and irrational mass movement threatens, stability can very justifiably be so preferred. But such circumstances are not common, and appear only in times of great extremity. Moreover, there ought to be some clarity as to just what the natural values of a small community really are.

Often there are good grounds in political life to coopt power where it is found. Existing elites may be recognized and some concession made to them on one score in order to gain their support on other scores. This kind of bargaining may take different forms. The most fundamental form in which it appears in the United States is federalism, by means of which substantial national resources are placed in the hands of such elites. The power of the elites is unchallenged, and is often enhanced by the new resources placed at their disposal. Very great gains have been made for national goals by paying such a price, but it should be clear that the process is one of bargaining and that a price has been paid.

Sometimes it is suggested that the problem is one of rationality versus irrationality. Thus the politics of a decentralized society is held to be rational. The demands that emerge from such an order are the concrete, definite, and limited demands of particular interest groups. They are usually for clear and hard economic advantage—an increase of wages, a lowered tariff, a subsidy. They are open to bargaining and do not individually represent a threat to the established political order. Many will cancel each other out, or at least appear to do so. On the other hand, according to this view, demands of a general character, less recognizably in the concrete interest of readily definable groups, are irrational. They are less likely to be promoted by well-knit organizations with disciplinary powers over their members. They are more likely to seek realization of these demands by political action, and they rely much more on generalized appeals and hence tend to be of an ideological character. Hence, the argument appears to run, general demands are characteristic of mass movements, which in turn are intrinsically dangerous and irrational; and apparently by transference the demands themselves are to be regarded as irrational. This view accords with the vision of a society in which a cosmic beneficence operates where only the hard, concrete (and usually economic) interests of clearly definable and well-organized groups have effect.

This vision would be closely similar to the eighteenth-century discovery of an invisible hand operating in the economy were it not that it perceives self-interest as pertaining to groups rather than to individuals. Undoubtedly, the large general demands condemned in this manner are less precise than those that are preferred. The aggregations of people who share in them are less easy to define than those in closely organized associations of a narrower character. Nevertheless, despite a difference of degree, the latter are abstract in the same sense as the former. To speak of the self-interest served by the demands of either broad or narrow aggregations is to speak in a collective sense and to pass over the often quite serious differences of individual interest that may exist inside either type of aggregation. Given the different character of the two types of demand, there would seem to be no significant difference in the degree to which either type of aggregation makes demands in the individual interests of all within it; the one demand, accordingly, may be quite as rational as the other. The real difference is that one type is broader than the other. It is consequently difficult to avoid seeing the argument that broad demands of large groups are irrational as itself a bit of ideology serving a spectrum of fairly narrow groups, usually of an economic character, whose policy objectives are directed to maintenance of the status quo.

The essential questions here relate to power. How is the distribution of power affected by different forms of organization? Who more probably gains by a centralized pattern? Who gains by a decentralized pattern? Certainly various factors influence the tenure of power, but the constituent context is one of the most important. Much more is involved, moreover, than the choice of intense power in a narrow context or diffuse power in a broad context (the big fish in a small pool or the little fish in a big pool), for certain interests are consistently favored in the one and slighted in the other. These interests, moreover, consistently represent particular types of values. Material values are much more characteristic of narrow than of broad constituencies; "altruistic," "sentimental," or "public" interests are more readily given expression and support in large constituencies.

It is important to note that the questions posed here relate not to the interests or values of different people (the population of one nation against the population of another) but to the values and interests of the same people (those of one nation, for example). Different interests and values of that people will be preferred accordingly as the nation is organized internally in units of different size. This is true whether the dimension on which they are organized is geographic, functional, or some other.

It is also essential at every point to remember that any people, any group, any aggregation of individuals, contains a diversity of interests and values. While a considerable degree of homogeneity of interest or value may be attained on one dimension, on other dimensions very substantial differences are inevitable. The achievement of relative homogeneity along one dimension may produce very discriminatory results on other, perhaps more important, dimensions. Thus the consequences of a choice for centralization or decentralization, for large or small constituencies, are to be found not merely between one defined group and another, but among the members of each group. If, for example, the basis of definition of the grouping is geographic, the different consequences of choosing large or small units will be found not merely between localities but, more important, inside all localities; the differences will appear on lines of class, race, belief, or whatever lines of division are important in the respective localities.

In a very important sense there is here a question of responsibility. It is *not* whether one pattern of organization is responsible and the other is not. The government or leadership of a large unit and that of a small unit can be equally responsible (or equally irresponsible). The important difference is that each is responsible to different bodies. Responsibility *to whom* is the significant question, not whether responsibility exists. The answer is, to a great extent, given by the definition of the constituency. If this is narrow, the responsibility will be to a narrow constituency; if it is large, responsibility will be to a large constituency. The narrow constituency will have less diversity than the large; as a consequence the policies followed in the two settings will often be different. In the aggregate, as in a nation, the two patterns will inevitably produce different results. And these will appear in the form of distribution of benefits to different groups and in the favoring of some values over others.

Chapter 5

---⭐---

Private Government

I

Massive endorsement of the private association as an essential of democracy is one of the most striking features of American political thought. Freedom of association has virtually become a fundamental guarantee of the Constitution.[1] The ideas of self-government and self-regulation have entered deeply into the doctrines of the political order, and they have been institutionalized to an unheralded degree. The private association, moreover, has been linked with the values of decentralization and federalism. It has also been pictured as the source of stability in politics and held up as the medium of the public interest. Most frequently, however, it has been seen as the guarantor of liberty. This is the most essential part of the general argument, and any examination of the doctrine must deal with this claim.

There is no doubt that pluralism belongs in the liberal tradition. The pluralist attack upon the state's assertion of unlimited power was one of the most incisive ever made. The defense of the private association against attempts to suppress it or to subordinate it to the state has almost always been a defense of liberty itself; the elaboration of this defense by pluralist writers has provided some of the noblest statements on constitutionalism and the limits of state action. Pluralist discussions of law carried important insights on the roots of law in sources other than compulsion. Moreover, the pluralists for the most part spoke out of a genuine dedication to individual liberty. Perhaps the most important aspect of pluralist doctrine in the present context is its adherence to the distinction between the state and society, a distinction closely related to that between the public and the private spheres of life.[2]

There can be equally little doubt that the preference of those American writers who are sometimes classed as pluralists is for liberty.[3] More conspicuously, however, the private associations of the United States have fought with great vigor to protect themselves from government encroachments. The organizations of business and labor have been the most vociferous in this regard, but perhaps the churches have made greater contributions; certainly separation of church and state is a more firmly established principle in America than in most countries.

When all this has been recognized, however, some very important questions remain. Since the private association has made its claim against the state in the name of liberty, how has the liberty of the individual fared vis-à-vis the private association? If the private association is to maintain the right of self-government and self-regulation, how is it governed itself? What is its conception of government within its own boundaries? These questions were not asked by the pluralists, and only comparatively recently have they been asked by more than a few others. Nevertheless, they are not easily avoidable today.

Since early in the present century enthusiasts for the private association have been confronted with Robert Michels' very troubling analysis of the sociology of membership organizations.[4] Ostensibly, his work dealt with political parties, and his concrete information related almost wholly to the social democratic parties of central Europe. The sweep of his work, however, was much broader, extending by implication to all organizations in which membership could be said to exist. Michels' thesis was one of the boldest and most provocative in all of social science: the "iron law of oligarchy"—who says organization says oligarchy. Nevertheless, for long periods of time, it has been ignored. Not that Michels was an obscure figure,[5] nor that his argument, despite its somewhat disorderly presentation, was easily disposed of. From time to time Michels' work has been rediscovered and the controversy begun anew.[6] Refutations have been offered, but the need for further refutation seems consistently to remain.

Michels' argument was phrased in perhaps too sensational terms. A generalization framed as an "iron law" invites the discovery of exceptions, particularly when it runs contrary to popular and cherished beliefs. Nevertheless, this "law" was supported with the citation of many factors of which increasing numbers of people have had personal experience. The argument rested, first, upon the characteristics of organization, and organization in the twentieth century was increasingly becoming the setting for the myriad activities in which Americans engaged. The situation was not new. Indeed, Alexis de Tocqueville, with his extraordinary prescience, had remarked during the previous century on the American propensity for forming associations. Where in Europe some large undertaking appeared, a prominent nobleman stood at its head; in America a similar undertaking would have an association of equals established for its furtherance.[7] This trait was incalculably more intensified in the twentieth century, when national associations were formed for everything from abrasives and absorbent paper to Zionism and zirconium; a thousand-page volume could do little more than list them and the addresses of their headquarters,[8] and it took no account of the multitude of local groups organized for seemingly every purpose the human mind could conceive. Thus many people had direct experience of the behavior of organizations, although few were willing to question the official doctrine about it. But such of those few who encountered Michels' argument found disturbing corroboration from their personal experience with many modern American associations.

Michels deliberately limited the scope of his work on private associations to the social democratic parties—those presumed to be most wholeheartedly devoted to a democratic ideal. If democracy existed in organizations, where more logical to look for it than among these parties? Or if it were not to be found there, what hope was there of finding it elsewhere?

Michels' entire work rested on a distinction between leaders and led that to a certain extent recalled the Marxist distinction between classes and was akin to ideas about the elite. The particular dimension he traced was formal organization. Organization requires leadership, since as a matter of technical necessity direct government by the membership is "mechanically" impossible. Moreover, because of their sheer incompetence without leaders, the masses or membership need, approve, and even crave leadership. The leaders control not merely by virtue of their superior abilities and the submissive tendencies of the masses, but also by an array of simple but crucial devices. The list of members, the files, the organization press—the apparatus of organization—all are in the leaders' hands.

To the extent that the "iron law of oligarchy" means that leadership is inevitable in organization it is a truism; but there is a much more disturbing implication in the argument. Leaders develop within a different milieu from members. They engage in different activities and come to enjoy a different status. Most important, they acquire different interests. Organization becomes conservative; leaders tend to identify their own interests with those of the organization and seek to preserve the foundations of their own position, thus laying the foundation for conflict of interests between leaders and led. The identity that is commonly assumed to exist among the interests of all within the organization is therefore false. And in contests between leaders and led, the former have virtually all the advantages.

Plainly, this argument is very sweeping. It is also very disturbing, particularly for those drawn to the pluralist belief that the freedom and self-determination of private associations are close to the essence of democracy. If private associations themselves should be undemocratic, as the Michelian thesis would seem to assert, how can they be essential to democracy?

Perhaps the simplest answer offered to this question is that the internal arrangements of the private associations are irrelevant to the question. In the first place, so the argument goes, the private associations as centers of power stand in opposition to the assumption of total power by any all-encompassing tyranny. With such associations in vigorous and separate existence, a sudden *Putsch* or mob action is insufficient to assume complete domination over the nation. Totalitarianism is defeated unless it can either absorb or destroy the private associations; hence, it is argued, private associations preserve democracy against the totalitarian threat.

The contention has much merit if the threat of totalitarianism is considered imminent. Certainly, twentieth-century experience indicates that totalitarianism is an evil greater than almost any other. By comparison with what went on in Hitler's Germany and Stalin's Russia occasional breaches of the democratic ideal inside private associations in America are insignificant. The force of this argument diminishes, however, if the threats of totalitarianism in America appear remote. On a lesser score, this ground for indifference to the internal arrangements of the private associations stands against the pluralist argument that the private associations are schools in democracy for the larger community. If such they are to be, they can hardly be other than models for behavior in the larger arena of national politics.

Another reason sometimes offered for dismissing Michels' charge is that the private associations are mutually countervailing—a modern gloss on the argument of Madison and his colleagues in the Federalist Papers. It tends to merge with the preceding contention that private associations are barriers to totalitarianism, but it goes somewhat further: by opposing each other, private associations supposedly check any overly greedy attempts by particular associations to extend their power. One association protects against another to the extent that in the large community democracy is insured.

This argument is relevant to the fear that one or more associations may exploit the general public. Except under special and unusual circumstances, however, it does not bear on the problem Michels posed. A trade union and a corporation may check each other in the making of decisions affecting the scale of wages and production costs; a high-tariff interest group may find itself confronted by a low-tariff interest group. Yet although each of these contests and the many others commonplace in modern political life may protect the economy and the polity from the extremist policies that might be followed if opposing or countervailing private groups were not active, they do not protect the members of any of these groups when they are threatened by their own organizations. To provide such protection, countervailing organizations would have to exist *inside* the associations, or, alternatively, there would have to be very nearly parallel or rival associations between which members might move without being deprived of the benefits that go with association membership.

In practice, however, private associations tend to be jealous of rivals. They seek to prevent the rise of competitors in the fields they have marked as their own. Often, when such rivals do exist, there is bitter conflict between them, conflict that has as its object the destruction of one or the other. Sometimes, when the conflict cannot be brought to this point, an accommodation takes place and jurisdictional boundaries are agreed upon, so that as a result the condition of monopoly is restored. An entire ethos within the American labor movement holds "dual unionism" to be the worst of sins, but this ethos is not unique to labor; it is found to some degree among farm organizations, veterans' organizations, and others. The appeal made to support this ethos is for unity. The fear is that with two or more organizations in a particular field, competition among them may lead one to appeal to a common foe, with consequent losses to the interests the organizations and their members share. In one degree or another many, if not most, private associations see themselves arrayed against some external enemy and are warring organizations.

If it is unrealistic to look for an escape from the problem through parallel or rival associations, there remains the first alternative: to look inside the associations. This, however, poses the question of how the associations govern themselves. Although the question is plainly relevant in view of the emphasis placed upon the private association as an essential of democracy, it is sometimes suggested that examination of the private association as a form of government is improper, probably because of the fear that such inquiry is a preliminary to suggestions for state regulation. But it can also be objected that the private association is not the same as the state and that the tests applied to public government are not applicable to the government of the private association.

Certainly state and private association are different, but the differences are hard to define. Both are to some extent based on territorial lines. The state, if it is a constitutional state, has, like the private association, limited ends. Both state and association exercise some form of authority. Each makes rules or laws (not infrequently the term "laws" is used by private associations for their own rules). These rules are enforced with penalties of varying degrees of severity, but some organizations' penalties are more severe than many punishments of the states. Fines, suspension, and expulsion, all exacted by private associations, are serious matters where the associations involved control the right to practice a particular trade or profession. This is especially true where, as with medicine, a large investment of money and years in education, training, and experience are also involved. Perhaps (at least for devout communicants) the most awesome penalty of all, excommunication, is enforced by the church, a private association. Of course not all private associations exist in spheres of interest with such degrees of importance. Yet some do, and where they do the problem of authority is substantially the same as it is in the state.

This problem is considerably more far-reaching than conflict between leaders and led, or the prospect of tyrannical leaders, for it is also a problem of conflict among members. Such conflict is very conspicuous in the state and constitutes a major part of the substance of politics. But it is far less apparent in the private association. Much of the ethos of these associations revolves about the belief that there are no differences among members, or at least no important differences. This is the tradition of the *Gemeinschaft,* expressed in the very language with which many associations cloak their proceedings: brotherhood, solidarity, fellowship, and so on. The members are likened to the members of a family, in which the ties of blood relationship reduce all transitory causes of dispute to insignificance. The roots of this tradition are ancient, and it is not to be despised. But not all associations have this communal quality. The distinction between the community and the more mundane society with narrow ends is familiar. In the latter, presumably, cohesion is markedly less than in the former, but since it exists for ends on which all members are agreed, there is no problem of government as found in the state. Different arguments thus apply to different kinds of association, but they arrive at the same conclusion: that the private association does not have the problem of government which the state exhibits.

Unfortunately for this conclusion, there are very genuine differences among the members of most associations, differences, for example, of age, opinion, taste, sex, religion. Some of these differences are trivial and do not represent conflicts, but others are important, some of them involving direct conflicts of both interest and belief. They occur even in the associations that lay claim to the quality of community, in some of which it would be difficult to claim that the tradition of community actually overrides the differences and the conflicts. In associations with narrow ends the absence of differences is also an illusion. In both types the problem of government does exist, and unless (as with hierarchical churches) there is a superior source of authority, there is also a problem of legitimacy.

Beyond all these factors, two considerations are stressed by the pluralists themselves. First, according to their argument, the state is but one of many forms of association. Accordingly, if it stands on the same ground as the other associations, and if its exercise of authority is open to question, so too is the exercise of authority in the other associations. Second, the pluralists correctly insist that the activities and ends of private associations are profoundly important. Some of them have moral purposes higher than the state's; the activities of some are in practice intrinsically more important than many state activities. Thus, while many associations have trivial aims, engage in activities of little general concern, and may be safely ignored, other associations are genuinely important to the large community. It is therefore unreasonable to assert that private associations are both important to the general polity and yet so unimportant that their political life may be ignored. Unless it can be established that problems of authority and government within private associations stand on different grounds from those of the state, examination of such problems in the private association is not only proper but necessary.

II

The initial difficulty confronting any attempt to examine the government of private associations is their great number. In the United States, as we have seen, they exist by the thousands. Many are national, but regional, state, and local associations are beyond counting, not merely because of their multiplicity but because they appear and disappear with the luxuriance of tropical vegetation. Indeed, even those that have attained national scope have different degrees of vitality, some being exceedingly vigorous while others are clearly moribund. Moreover, many organizations are associations in name only. Some bear titles which suggest large memberships, but in any realistic sense they have no members at all. This is particularly true of numerous "associations" and "institutes" with Washington offices which not infrequently consist of small rooms occupied by one or two individuals who may represent six or more organizations; the organizations may be little more than fictions used by individual lobbyist entrepreneurs. This is not to say that professional lobbyists do not necessarily represent genuine groups; some of the groups so represented are very real.

Still other organizations which maintain substantial office es-

tablishments and which claim many members are not membership organizations at all. In these, the so-called "members" are
no more than subscribers to a cause or to a service carried on
wholly by the office professionals. The "members" have no
voice whatever in the determination of organizational policy or
choice of officers, and there is no pretense that they do. The
supporter (a better term here than "member") may receive reports and information, and sometimes even a membership card.
Nevertheless, he is quite outside the organizational reality, and
his only recourse if he disagrees with policy is to end his support—a condition that is often quite openly stated. However,
the distinction between this and the situation in which safeguards are deliberately established to prevent a genuine membership from exercising influence on policy is in practice sometimes difficult to perceive. The motive for such safeguards is
usually to prevent enemies of the association from joining and
disrupting it or diverting it from its avowed objectives—as, in
somewhat analogous fashion, constitutional barriers are erected
against the subversion of a state. But there is a very great difference of degree in that the purposes and policies that the
private association seeks to defend are usually much more
narrow and concrete.

The governments of still other associations present problems
that fall outside the democratic tradition and can only be noted
here. The outstanding example is the organization of the Catholic Church. Although this is an organization of extraordinary
complexity with an involved political life of its own, it has no
presumption of democracy within itself. The principle of authority in the Church is, accordingly, much clearer than in
many other organizations: authority derives from God and extends downward on a hierarchical pattern. There is no problem
of deriving authority from the will of the members and, so long
as the faith of the communicants is maintained, the major problem of government is efficient administration. The same situation prevails in other hierarchical churches. The problem of
government is, of course, more prominent in sects which em-

phasize the role of individual conscience in the interpretation of divine authority.

Perhaps the most difficult problem is presented by the corporation, probably the most important form of private government in America today. The evidence of its role in modern life is pervasive and inescapable. In a formal sense, however, the corporation is a creation of the state, and presumably what the state may create it may destroy—or regulate. Nevertheless, many have claimed in recent years that here is in fact a genuine private government. The corporation makes rules, it is argued, and is thus within the category.[9] Moreover, in a realistic view, the part played by the state in the creation of corporations is minimal and unimportant. And, to understand the actual behavior of corporations, a political analysis must be added to the more traditional economic analysis.

These considerations have been very persuasively argued and they carry much force. Some of the major corporate units of American business exercise great power, and it is significant that business economists have been urging extended consideration of the corporation in explicitly political terms.[10] Concepts such as legitimacy, authority, power, and constitutionalism have now entered deeply into the discussion of the modern business corporation. Nevertheless, this approach exposes a serious dilemma. On the one hand, the corporation is today an intrinsic part of the economy and society. It is the dominant way of doing business and of producing and distributing most of the goods by which men live and earn their living. Its organizations reach deep into the patterns of daily life for millions. At different points it stands in opposition to the spirit of the nation's historic antitrust policy, but that policy has, to a significant extent, begun to give way. The brute fact that the corporation exists cannot be wished away. On the other hand, the existence of the modern corporation does not accord with long-standing conceptions of political organization, and no theory exists by which it can be reconciled with such conceptions.

The difficulty is apparent as soon as the corporation is regarded as a political body, that is, as having power. So long as one can maintain a fiction that the corporation is solely an economic unit exercising no power within the market, the problem is to some degree disguised. Even so, the fiction does not touch the difficulty of assessing political life inside the corporation, and it is this internal aspect that discussions of the corporation increasingly emphasize. Both critics and defenders of the corporation make the point that it is an association of people.[11] Whether it is a fellowship or a form of tyranny, however, it poses a problem of authority within itself. It possesses no claims, like the church's, to superior heavenly sanction. It can rely upon a theory of concession or delegation from the state, but to do so exposes it to the claims of external political control.

The traditional theory of corporate government—and it is of some interest that there is such a theory—is that stock ownership confers votes, which in turn control the choice of directors. In this sense, the government of the corporation has been derived from democratic theory. There was always a difficulty in that votes are attached to shares of stock rather than to individual human beings. This may have some precedent in the long-standing property-holding qualifications for the vote in the state, but the comparison is not really valid, since wealth is much more explicitly represented in the corporation than people. However, the theory at least was clear on one point: the constituency of the corporation's government consisted of the stockholders.

For some time (at least three decades) this theory has been untenable in the light of common knowledge about the realities of corporate life. The now-classic work of Berle and Means exploded the idea that ownership meant control in the large corporations of America.[12] Their demonstration of the actual separation of these factors created a sensation, but the demonstration withstood attack and in any event only confirmed what many observers had long sensed. The sheer size of the significant American corporations and the minute fractions of total stockholdings that any one owner might possess made obsolete the idea of simple control by ownership (except in a very few corporations, notably the Ford Motor Company). The development of numerous legal devices and the control of the proxy machinery by management made a mockery of any belief that management could be readily challenged by any faction of the corporate citizenry. Proxy fights occurred during the period following World War II in somewhat greater numbers than Berle and Means expected, but they remained exceptional.[13]

The question of control, once raised, proved a Pandora's box. As questioners sought to discover the reality of control, it became apparent that to a very large degree management was in control. By virtue of its possession of the proxy machinery, it was more likely to select the directors than the directors the management.[14] Uneasily, many observers felt that they had passed through the looking glass. In one sense they found themselves in a Michelian world: organization was indeed conservative in that the leaders of the corporation carefully and effectively preserved their positions, and were, in fact, virtually self-perpetuating. The files, the membership list, the control of meetings—most of the devices Michels noted as accruing to the advantage of leadership in a membership organization—were in management's hands. Moreover, the presumed "members" were either apathetic about the exercise of their rights of self-governance or quite frankly determined not to exercise them. Indeed, at this point the reality of stockholder "membership" was so blatantly contrary to the formal theory of corporation government that the Michelian analysis collapsed by virtue of its success as explanation: the question arose whether the stockholders were indeed entitled to the control the formal theory gave them. In the eyes of some critics, the stockholder was not only incompetent and helpless in his role of "member"; he was also irresponsible and deserved the powerless state to which corporate reality had consigned him.[15] In short, the stockholder could not be considered a member of the corporation at all.

This, however, was not the last of the questions unleashed by the initial query. Just who could be considered a "member"? What was the corporation's constituency? For a long time leaders of major corporations have toyed with these questions and have been tempted to proclaim that their responsibilities extend far beyond the welfare of mere stockholders. But then how far do they reach? To the customer? Certainly no corporate executive could be expected to exclude this group. To the employees? This is less simple, since the conflict of interest between stockholders and employees is rather obvious; moreover, too bold or aggressive an assertion of this responsibility might even arouse charges of unfair labor practices under the National Labor Relations Act, since it could be taken as an attack on unions. To the general public? But what is the general public? The trend of business thought has sometimes been to deny that this concept is meaningful when it is invoked by government.

A variety of motives were at work to release these questions. The muckrakers' attacks upon "the soulless corporation" invited the response that corporations had souls and were not merely machines for the enrichment of their owners. This was an especially tempting trap, and for a long time its dangers were not apparent; thus Judge Elbert Gary, first Chairman of United States Steel, insisted that his giant firm had not abused its power and had behaved responsibly, and the corporation's official historian even went so far as to assert that U.S. Steel *had* a soul.[16] With Gary's passing, however, whether because the danger in the position had become apparent or for other reasons, the firm's defense reverted to the blander assertion that it had no power. Perhaps there was also a motivation arising from a realistic sense of the behavior of corporations. Certainly it cannot have been very satisfactory to believe that the good that corporate leaders were convinced they were doing in the world was sheer inadvertence. At any rate, it is now almost fashionable for industrial chieftains to consider themselves statesmen and to enlarge in public upon the responsibilities they feel toward stockholders, consumers, employees, and the public. A few crusaders continue to struggle for "shareholder democracy," but their efforts are futile, and they are generally regarded with indulgent amusement.[17]

Although opinion may now be tending toward acceptance of

the view that corporation leaders have just such a broad constituency, the questions still do not end. The really difficult ones
remain: if, for example, there is a responsibility to a constituency that includes consumers, employees, and the public, how
is it enforced? What are the means of accountability? These
are very unpleasant questions indeed, and although the reply
is seldom made loudly, it seems to be that corporation leaders
are good men and make good decisions.

Obviously, this is a dangerous assertion. By what standards
are they good? By what criteria can it be said that they do
good? By what right do they claim to rule? What is this but an
arrogation of power? Here are all the questions that must con-
verge on power, and the questions have no answers. Richard
Eells, a former corporate executive, has stated very justly that
there is a constitutional crisis in the corporation.[18] The problem, in fact, is so acute that some sympathy may be given to the
critics who would rather turn their backs upon it and take
refuge in an extreme positivism which rejects the baleful notion
of power entirely.[19] Unfortunately, however, the problem of
legitimacy is not so easily induced to go away.

A number of points regarding the corporation are, then, quite
clear. Power is one of its principal characteristics, exercised not
merely over significant sectors of the economy, but over members of its own "family" as well. As might be expected, criticisms are not lacking that such power amounts to a form of
tyranny.[20] The Michelian theory of oligarchy in organization
seems all too well substantiated by the corporation, however
numerous the various pressure-group influences on it may be;
in fact, the reality is so plain that to dispute the thesis of oligarchy is scarcely worth undertaking. Second, there is no available theory by which this power can be regarded as legitimate,
and without some such conception there are no guidelines for
rendering it legitimate. Probably the only available ground for
exonerating the corporation's present form of rule is the fact
that stockholders generally find a ready market for their shares
when they are sufficiently dissatisfied to resign their membership. This view, however, rests upon the theory that sharehold-

ers are the only true constituency of the corporation, a theory that is today acceptable to few people. Until its constitutional crisis has been solved, then, the corporation cannot be used as a model of private government for analytical or any other purposes.

In many ways the corporation presents a peculiar problem, and is untypical of the many associations with which the United States is endowed. If corporations, churches, and the various organizations lacking membership in any realistic sense are excepted, the overwhelming number of the remainder are founded on a conception of authority which derives from the democratic ethos of the surrounding culture. In most, membership has a defined meaning, and the will of the membership provides the basis of authority.

Although genuine membership organizations of this sort are exceedingly numerous, they have similar characteristics and share the same problems, much of the similarity being the result of their mutual imitation of organizational form. Constitutions for new organizations are quite frequently simple copies of those of existing organizations, with only trivial changes of names and detail. This borrowing takes place even where the substantive interests of the organizations involved are very different; thus, for example, the constitution of the International Typographical Union was apparently based upon that of the Order of Odd Fellows.[21] Beyond this, it is to be expected that experience gained with organization in one sphere should be applied in others. The general conception of government in membership organizations, for whatever reasons, appears to be much the same. To understand the character of this conception, then, it is useful to follow the example of Michels and examine its operation in the practice of the organizations most devoted to the ideal of democratic association.

III

In the United States, as in a number of other countries, the associations which have most vociferously dedicated themselves to an ideal of democratic organization are the trade unions. Although their claim to superiority in this regard may be contested by various other groups, the unions are on the whole the most conspicuous claimants, and it would be mistaken to doubt their fundamental sincerity. They were born of a profound desire to establish democracy in the daily working conditions of industrial life. Whatever the American labor movement's aberrations in predatory unionism, the institution of industrial democracy has undeniably been one of its fundamental objectives. Here, if anywhere in the nation, the democratic vision should be clear and practice enlightened. What, then, are the conceptions at work, and how have they evolved?[22]

The source of authority in a trade union is the same as in a democratic state: the membership or the whole of the citizen body. In a small organization, such as a local, the membership (or a given portion of it defined as a quorum) meets and makes its own governing decisions. Ideally the presiding officer is no more than a moderator acting to preserve the conditions of orderly discussion and decision; the meeting itself is the sovereign body. Here is the ideal of the town meeting, of direct democracy. In a large organization, however, the meeting of the whole citizenry or membership cannot be approximated by these devices. The effective substitute is the convention, which has some similarities to a legislature, but also important differences. The delegates are not representatives in the same sense as are, say, members of Congress who meet continuously for extended periods. They are a much closer approximation to the town meeting of the citizenry.[23]

Accordingly, the convention frequently passes not only resolutions stating policies and "laws" or "statutes," but also constitutional amendments. This latter practice is not universal among trade unions, but it is nonetheless widespread. It underlies the fact that the convention in session is generally regarded as the embodiment of the sovereign power of the general membership and not merely as an ordinary legislature. An incident in the 1944 convention of the United Mine Workers will illustrate. At this convention the union's president, John L. Lewis, received a personal telegram from the Secretary of the Interior. Lewis referred the telegram to the convention and a reply was sent to the Secretary in the convention's name. A second telegram addressed personally to Lewis arrived, and he then proposed the following reply before the assembled delegates:

You do not seem to understand that our telegram to you was adopted by the unanimous vote of 2700 delegates elected by the mine workers of the nation in their home communities. This convention is the supreme authority of the Union. We are the employers of John Lewis and he is responsible to our orders. While this convention is in session we will answer his telegrams if we elect to do so. When we go home you can move in on him if you desire but watch your guard and protect your wind. We think he will go around you like a cooper around a barrel.[24]

With but one dissenting vote the telegram was adopted by the convention as its own.

The fiction that union leadership is no more than the servant of the assembled membership was perhaps transparent in this instance. Nevertheless, the underlying theory was consistent with the temper of the reply. Moreover, the existence of the theory sometimes has important consequences. Thus during the steel crisis of 1952, which resulted in President Truman's seizure of the steel mills, Philip Murray, president of the Steelworkers, persuaded the union to pass a measure forbidding the union leadership to accept a truce plan without approval of a special convention. As a tactical measure it almost precipitated extreme action by the federal government and Murray and the union leadership had to repudiate it hastily.[25]

While the convention is in session, then, the leadership in theory serves only as moderator. The leadership has no authority for independent action, and can only carry out the mandate of the collective decisions. To fulfill the many tasks facing it in a short span of time, the convention is compelled to rely on the work of temporary committees, but these too are merely the agents and servants of the larger body. This rationale also applies to the periods between convention sessions. In a great variety of provisions, from arrangements for election at conventions to requirements of ratification of officers' actions by the next convention, the pattern is made clear. From time to time, as in the examples given above, the fictional character of the pattern becomes apparent, but generally these instances are regarded as exceptional.

In theory, then, the union's executive body is a committee or group of officers of the whole membership as embodied in the convention. Although it may make a very real practical difference whether the officers are elected in convention or by referendum vote, the theoretical conception is not greatly different here. The officers are in theory definitely subordinate to the convention, a term which implies a body with constituent powers. The convention will usually dissolve at the end of its meeting. The president will often have power to summon a new convention, but its members then will be newly elected and possessed of a completely fresh mandate. Its authority, whatever the variations of practice, will be virtually unlimited, far greater than that of any legislature. And this authority in turn will serve to justify the leadership's exercise of power after the convention has been dissolved.

The officers, in fact, have very great power when the convention is not in session—real and authorized power, not normally considered as usurped. In some organizations the president's actions are specifically made subject to the approval of the executive board—of which he is of course the chairman. Some students have regarded this as a check on his power, but it is important to see that such a provision is intended less as a check on power than as a form of insurance that the will of the membership is carried out. Actually, however, such a provision is a very slight check in any sense upon presidential power.[26] Whatever the facts, it is quite clear that the purpose is not the division of power.

In a larger sense, the evaluation of private government in terms of its checks and balances is beside the point. For, as with the checks on executive power, there is little conception of checks and balances as a system. The convention is not a legis-

lature, and the executive is only an instrument of the general
membership as represented in convention; the executive board
is only an agent and the president is its continuing chairman.
These bodies do not check each other, nor are they intended to.
It is true that measures are taken in some unions for auditing
funds (in which experience has been most disillusioning) and
for the unseating of officers. But these devices are frequently
weak and have appeared as grafts on a scheme of government
to which they are intrinsically foreign. There is no *system* of
checks and balances here.

If we look within the government of unions—and most other
associations—for other important features of public government
in the United States, we find additional important differences.
The most striking is the absence of a bill of rights. In almost
any union constitution it is possible to cull a list of membership
duties which could stand as a "bill of obligations," but almost
never a list of members' rights comparable in importance to
those in the first amendments to the federal Constitution. Such
enumerations of rights as are found are apt to be those not
accorded to nonmembers; they are not the rights of members
against the association or its government. On the other hand,
the items of the "bill of obligations" are both numerous and inclusive. Thus, "conduct unbecoming a union man," "creating
dissension," "slandering an officer," and "undermining the
union" are frequently named as punishable offenses.[27]

There are rudimentary guarantees for trials and appeals.
They need to be viewed, however, against the common provision of penalties for members who seek redress of grievances
against the associations in public courts of law. The public
courts are generally unwilling to take jurisdiction over such
issues where there is a system of internal appeals and the entire
system has not yet run its course. Typically, the system calls for
an original trial by a trial committee of the local organization;
decision by the local; appeal to the president or executive council of the national organization; appeal to the convention, with
action by a trial committee; and final decision rendered by
majority vote of the convention. This system may in some stable

situations permit the development of a body of case law and a rule of *stare decisis*, but it is hardly conducive to either.

A discussion of United States government, or that of any Western democracy, would be very unrealistic if it did not treat the party system. In union government, however, parties have almost no place; the practice of most unions is, indeed, antagonistic to parties. In some organizations, parties are in effect forbidden by constitutional rules against circulating partisan electioneering materials or participating in "outside" meetings relating to union affairs. Thus, the Constitution of the International Brotherhood of Electrical Workers makes the following offenses punishable by fine, suspension, or expulsion:

Attending or participating in any gathering or meeting whatsoever, held outside meetings of a L.U. [local union], at which the affairs of the L.U. are discussed, or at which conclusions are arrived at regarding the business and the affairs of a L.U. or regarding L.U. officers or a candidate or candidates for L.U. office.

Mailing, handing out, or posting cards, handbills, letters, marked ballots or political literature of any kind, or displaying streamers, banners, signs or anything else of a political nature, or being a party in any way to such being done in an effort to induce members to vote for or against any candidate or candidates for L.U. office, or candidates to conventions.[28]

These provisions are somewhat more stringent than those in some other union constitutions, but the point of view is widely shared. Thus Philip Murray, one of the most justly revered of American labor leaders, warned the 1942 convention of the Steelworkers at its first meeting:

I do not want—as a matter of fact, I shall fight any attempt that is made to have little back room caucuses while this convention is going on. There is going to be one convention in the city of Cleveland and it is going to be held in this hall. We are not going to permit sharp practices and petty politics to be played in the Steelworkers. So if any of the boys are thinking right now of midnight sessions in strange places in the city of Cleveland, just begin to forget about it right now. There is only going to be one convention. . . . That is the democratic way to do business. . . .[29]

Statements in a similar spirit have been made by numerous other prominent labor leaders, and convey the orthodox doctrine. Some factionalism does occur in many unions, but it is generally deplored within them and tends to die out with the complete victory of some of the contenders. Only one private association of importance, the International Typographical Union, has an *institutionalized* system of parties. This organization, the subject of an intensive study,[30] is so atypical that it only sharpens the impression of an almost universal distaste for disunity and division within other unions.

The amendment process of many unions is also quite different from that provided in the United States Constitution, and ordinarily much easier to operate. Practice is somewhat varied. Although some union constitutions may be amended only by a two thirds vote, sometimes in convention and sometimes by general referendum, it is not at all uncommon for amendment to be by majority vote in convention. The distinction between constitutional amendment, ordinary legislation, and specific decree therefore tends to be blurred in such associations, and is not especially clear in some of the others. The common attitude toward constitutional amendment was expressed many years ago by John Mitchell, then president of the United Mine Workers:

The constitution of the trade union, moreover, has been evolved by and through the efforts of workingmen. The trade union is a government of workingmen, by workingmen, for workingmen and the framers of its constitution have been workingmen. Although the supreme law of the union was not formulated by highly paid constitutional lawyers, nevertheless, it represents in a clear and definite manner the ideals, purposes, and aims of the great majority of the members of the organization.

The faithfulness with which trade union constitutions represent trade union sentiment is due to the elasticity of these constitutions. The government of trade unions is loose and flexible and neither constitutions nor by-laws are rigidly fixed and immutable. The object of the leaders, as of the rank and file of trade unionists, has been to preserve the largest possible elasticity and freedom of movement to the ruling majority of the organization. In trade union management, there is no tyranny of the "dead hand." Even the most conservative unions are not bound by a blind, unthinking worship of an outgrown instrument, but adjust their form of government to the changing needs and exigencies of the times.

To a certain extent, therefore, the formal written constitution of a trade union is rather a statement of principles and a formulation of the present policy of the union than a hard and fast determination of its future laws. Trade union constitutions are easily changed.[31]

When all the foregoing features of trade union government are considered they fit into a remarkably consistent pattern. They are all derived from the same central conception of politics, sometimes termed "majoritarian democracy." The term, however, is a somewhat misleading description of the political realities of these associations, for it suggests that a very high place is given to majority rule. In actual practice, something more than mere majority assent is sought. The common stress upon "not washing dirty linen in public" and the frequent decrying of factionalism embody a goal far closer to unanimity than simple majority rule.

Unity is seen as the price of staying organized. The fear of organizational disintegration is recurrently the decisive factor in the framing of governing institutions, and although this fear may often be the immediate motivation, the arrangements that emerge are consistent with a particular conception of democratic rule. Even more important than fear of disintegration, however, is the belief that such devices as checks and balances and constitutional limitations are both unnecessary and improper. The argument may be summarized briefly: If power is good, why limit it? If power is evil, why have it? Since the organization is the total of its membership and since its goals are the common goals of its members, limitation of its power is not only undemocratic but also irrational.

IV

This conception of government seems to be pervasive throughout the array of American labor organizations, but it is not peculiar to unions. How widespread it is among other types of association is impossible to say in the absence of any thorough study of the multitude of American associations, but even the most casual inspection suggests that it is common to many farm organizations, veterans' organizations, and numerous others. What, then, is its validity?

If such a conception were offered for the government of the United States it is probably safe to say that it would be rejected by most people. It is incompatible with the actual practice of government in any large democratic society we know of. Moreover, many people would also reject the conception even if institutions compatible with it could be put into effect. The question accordingly arises whether there are peculiar characteristics of private associations that justify their accepting it.

There is no simple answer to this question. The unions and other associations are exceedingly varied, but they do have a number of common traits, and it is necessary to examine these traits one by one.

Perhaps first among the general traits of private associations is that emphasized in the word *private*. The implications of the concept of privacy have never been thoroughly and systematically explored, but it is safe to say that it is fundamental to Western traditions of government. It is closely tied to the idea of constitutionalism, which implies limitations upon the sphere of public government. Most typically, the distinction between *public* and *private* relates to the state and the individual. In the present discussion, however, the tradition of real corporate personality as developed by a long line of pluralist thinkers from Althusius to the early Laski is involved. Most of the pluralists of earlier times combined a deep concern for individual rights with enthusiasm and concern for the corporate personality of the association. If there is irony in their position, it has become apparent only in fairly recent years.

A second distinctive characteristic of these associations is autonomy. Almost all assert a right to be self-determining and self-governing. This may take the form of an appeal to the historical origin of the association in a spontaneous meeting of like-minded individuals. But it is often asserted where such an origin cannot be claimed. Thus the claim of autonomy is hardly less strong among those unions of the old CIO which were the direct creations of organizing campaigns under leadership provided by older unions. The claim and its presumption of rightfulness within the context of American labor ideology was one of the difficulties the CIO encountered when, some years ago, it "tried" several of its component unions for Communist domination and then attempted to destroy them by establishing new organizations to take possession of the convicted organizations' jurisdictions. Autonomy here seemed to reside in the international union rather than the federation, and it was asserted quite as much against the federation as it recently has been asserted by the Teamsters against both federation and public government.

Traditionally the claim to autonomy has involved a hesitancy to utilize public aid, even where this aid could be demonstrated to offer much to the associations' constituencies. Thus, during the long discussion of the merits of unemployment insurance the official (albeit challenged) position of organized labor was that less social security with autonomy for labor's organizations was better than greater social security provided through the medium of public government. The argument that what government might give government might also take away was in part founded on good grounds; it was also a rationalization of the desire for undivided member loyalties. If there was a nice counterpart here to the claims of *laissez faire* from the business organizations, it was also true that in practice the more conservative and consistent position was that of organized labor. Even organized agriculture, traditionally more willing than either organized business or organized labor to resort to public government, has attempted at various times to act autonomously. The Society of Equity sponsored a plan for farmers to withhold their produce from the market until the Equity-declared prices were met. The National Farm Organization has more recently attempted the same tactic. Here was good, if simple, imitation of business practice. It was also an attempt to maintain autonomy. The farm organizations have sought a similar goal with their cooperatives.

An important corollary of autonomy is the association's claim of the right to formulate its own constituency. Nearly every association lays down conditions for membership, affecting both entrance and continued membership. The conditions of eligibility are usually quite explicit, and oaths or pledges are frequently required of new members. Candidates for membership, even when they are solicited by the organizations, must come as suppliants or at least applicants, the formal decision on acceptance being made by the association.

A third important trait of these associations is limited purpose. They do not purport to concern themselves with all aspects of their members' lives. Sometimes their purpose is stated quite specifically, as for example: "To establish through collective bargaining adequate wage standards, shorter hours of work and improvements in the conditions of employment for the workers in the industry";[32] at other times the object may be quite vague. In either event, it is presumed that the association's objects do not encompass the entire range of the individual constituent's interests or preoccupations. He will have his own privacy, and he will, accordingly, have other loyalties. So a man may be a trade union member of a particular craft; but he may also be a church member, a Legionnaire, and a member of a team in the municipal bowling league, to say nothing of his place within his family or in a political party. The assumption is that no association will encroach on spheres of life other than its own.

A fourth trait, in considerable degree a corollary of some of the characteristics already listed, is homogeneity. Since the autonomous association selects its membership, and since its purposes are limited, within the scope of the association there will be only people of similar characteristics and like minds. Most important, there will be no conflicts of interest or grounds for legitimate conflict within the association; there is thus a presumptive absence of the basic political problem that other democratic societies of larger scope must resolve. If there is no conflict of interest or outlook, the only possible reasons for conflict will be error, personality, or something amounting to treason. The condition of homogeneity is precisely the solution Madison named in his famous argument in the Federalist Number 10, but felt compelled to reject as a solution to the problem of faction in the larger society.[33]

A fifth distinguishing characteristic is the voluntary character of the association. So, although the association may determine its own membership, the individual member also makes a decision to join or not. Typically he must actively request admittance. He is not a member automatically—as he is a citizen by birth in a state—but by virtue of positive choice. Initiation and probationary status serve to emphasize the element of individual choice in joining. Equally important is the individual member's right to resign. Resignation is the individual's ultimate recourse and the element that finally distinguishes the private association from the public body.

The voluntary aspect of private associations has repeatedly been held to place them in a very special relationship to democracy, one often so special that it is described as a necessary condition of democracy. Such a view was cogently argued by the pluralists of several decades ago; more recent writers have repeated the argument forcefully. Thus, V. L. Allen has argued that so long as individuals are free to join and to leave societies of their own choice, the essence of democracy is present even if there is no machinery permitting the members to control the societies.[34]

It should be apparent that these different characteristics of the private association to a very large degree overlap and rest upon each other. The meaning of privacy is impaired without autonomy. Homogeneity cannot be achieved without limitation of purposes, and voluntary choice underlies the entire arrangement. These, indeed, are all aspects of a single perception of the private association.

The conclusion at this point, then, must be that insofar as the conditions prescribed in this perception are met, the system of government that has been described earlier is proper and reconcilable with the goals and objectives to which we are committed in the governments of the United States and other liberal democracies.

V

However, a question remains: to what extent are the qualities so described actually found in existing unions and other private associations? How well, for example, have they maintained the distinction between "public" and "private"? Obviously, no precise answer in general terms is possible; it is apparent, nevertheless, that for many associations this particular distinction has been seriously blurred in recent years.

This is most apparent with labor unions. Until 1933, it could reasonably be argued that their private character was relatively unimpaired. The American labor movement had rejected political means of action, that is to say, the use of public government. Not only had socialism been decisively defeated within the labor movement, but positive legislation, however mild, was mistrusted. This was most striking with regard to social insurance: not until 1932 did the AFL so much as commend unemployment insurance. The only legislation commanding strong official enthusiasm was directed against labor injunctions, that is, it was legislation designed to curb state intervention in labor disputes. Organized labor sought its goals through the medium of its own economic bargaining power. It would be difficult to imagine a more thoroughgoing observance of the distinction between what is private and what is public.

With the passage of the National Industrial Recovery Act and its Section 7-A, however, and more particularly with passage of the Wagner Act and labor's acceptance and utilization of the provisions assisting labor organization, organized labor departed radically from its previous position. This was not just a matter of legal theory. Since the law conferred exclusive bargaining rights upon a union which succeeded in winning a government-supervised election, that union acquired a substantial measure of public power—power that extended to individuals and minorities which had not voted for the union in the election. The process of NLRB-supervised elections has been widely resorted to by American unions. The surrender of privacy so entailed was not fully apparent, however, until the Taft–Hartley Act was passed, and became even more apparent with passage of the Landrum–Griffin Act, which explicitly provided for public intervention in the internal affairs of unions. Although some unions have indicated a willingness to revert to the situation existing before the passage of the Wagner Act, the element of privacy is not likely to be regained.

Different situations prevail with other associations; it is nevertheless apparent that for many a question remains whether their private character has been preserved. Often, for example, the exercise of licensing powers is delegated to "private" associations, even though the coercive power involved is that of a state.[35] In the clearest case of this sort an association receives direct delegation; in other cases professional or trade associations are given the power to nominate personnel, virtually as a form of representation, to official licensing boards (bar associations, for example) and, on occasion, to policy-making boards. This is by no means unusual and is perhaps a growing trend.

A more perplexing question arises when a private association called into being by actions of government officials acquires the power to exert great influence over policy and administration, in the form either of membership on advisory boards of administrative agencies or of any exceedingly influential association's commanding the close attention of powerful congressional committees. Examples here are the American Farm Bureau Federation and the Chamber of Commerce of the United States, both of which had direct governmental encouragement in their formation. Obviously in such situations there is a shadowland between what is public and what is private. The years since the inception of the New Deal have seen much rationalization of this blurring, but clearly it is a concomitant of the growth of associational power during this period; clearly also, the blurring is incompatible with the previous conception of the private association.

These comments apply, too, to the private association's claim of autonomy. Labor unions, in taking an extreme position for *laissez faire* and freedom from social legislation, were defending their autonomy vis-à-vis government. In defending themselves from their own federations with which they have individually had occasional conflicts, however, the "international" unions are in a sense also defending their privacy. Not that this has been a matter of explicit discussion within the labor movement; but here, as with other matters of policy, labor's highly pragmatic leadership has behaved with a greater consistency than it has always been ready to acknowledge. The consequences of large units of organization do seem to have been visualized, however vaguely. If the locus of power within the labor movement is to be in the federations, the common form of action must be broad in character—almost necessarily a form of political action. Whether this takes the form of pressure for legislation, closely controlled administration, or political strikes, it weakens organized labor's claims to be uninhibited by governmental action. A similar set of considerations applies to the development of the American Farm Bureau Federation. Much of the early controversy about this association centered around the supposed differences between the county farm bureaus and the state and national federations.[36] It is significant that the particular compromise effected also involved a compromise over the distribution of power between the local and federal units of the association. Here, to an even greater degree than later developed in the labor movement, the drift of the gravitational center toward the larger unit inside the association meant a drift toward political action.

As for the third trait of the private association, limited purpose, the practice of some of our more important associations has evidently also departed rather far from the conception sketched above. Some trade unions have sponsored educational plans; others have developed housing and recreational resources for the benefit of their members. The activities of the United Automobile Workers and the International Ladies Garment Workers are leading cases in point. Almost all unions have long-established systems of friendly benefits—pensions, insurance, and so on—which, however advantageous they may be to their members, also serve the purpose of strengthening the members' ties to the organizations. Agricultural organizations have from their very beginnings sought to solve many of the problems of rural life through subsidiary cooperatives. Many associations seek to demonstrate their civic responsibility by resolutions on matters of citizenship, Americanism, and foreign policy, and by gifts to colleges, scholarships, and other means.

The fourth trait of private associations, homogeneity, is in some ways the most important. A membership united in interests, beliefs, and tastes is itself a solution to the most troubling problem of government, and the possibility of achieving such an identity is in some measure the peculiar governmental advantage possessed by private associations. Every such association must and does achieve it in some degree, yet none can achieve it completely. In the concept of homogeneity, in fact, lies a latent inconsistency with the characteristic of limited purpose. A single interest may be shared, but the complexities of human nature are too great for a homogeneity that extends much beyond this. Even where the boundaries of the association are fixed to coincide with the number of people sharing the one interest, divergencies of interest will arise and persist within the association. Examples are the differences between young and old in a trade union with a pension system, between employed and unemployed in any union during a depression, between producers of different commodities in a farm organization, between large and small producers in a trade association. There are serious grounds for doubting a claim of extensive homogeneity in any association that rests on the obvious differences in taste, ability, and understanding among men. Associations characteristically exaggerate the homogeneity they achieve.

The fifth trait of associations, their voluntary character, is probably the main justification of their forms of government. Here, it is evident that the penalties for not belonging to an association differ greatly in incidence and degree, and the severity of the penalty is an index of the association's power. The penalty for not belonging to a particular trade union in some communities may be forfeiture of the right to practice a trade; it may be the same with the right to practice medicine.[37] The penalty may be denial of the most effective means of access to publicly offered benefits, for example those administered by the Veterans Administration. When the right of resignation is accompanied by the availability of membership in competing organizations, the right is worth something. However, few trade unions are true rivals in any sense meaningful to their members; "dual unionism," as we have seen, is accounted a cardinal sin within the American labor movement. General farm organizations do compete in this manner, but their respective areas of strength are different. As for trade associations, it is clear that their fundamental rationalizing impulse is hostile to competition. Where their jurisdictions overlap and open warfare cannot quickly settle the boundary, consolidation or demarcation by agreement is soon accomplished. In fact, this pattern seems almost to be a law of behavior among our most significant private associations. The simple fact, then, is that often the private association is not voluntary.

The conclusions emerge that, first, the government of private associations is very commonly founded on a theory of absolute democracy; second, the validity of this theory rests on a series of assumptions about the peculiar characteristics of private associations; and third, these assumptions are seriously at odds with the facts about some of our most important "private" associations.

In assessing the significance of these conclusions it must be kept in mind that there are very great differences among the practices of different associations. These differences may be principally of degree, and yet be of great importance; thus although the governments of the United Mine Workers and, say, the League of Women Voters may have some similarities, to ignore the differences between them would be to produce a very false picture.

But if the existence of large differences of degree among

private associations is recognized, how widely shared is the theory of government that has been outlined in the preceding pages? No precise answer to this question is possible, but it does appear probable that the theory is very widely shared. The International Typographical Union is the only association of significance that has been offered as a great exception to the rule of the "iron law of oligarchy."[38] Virtually all others that have been made the subject of careful study have to some degree substantiated that "law." The examples of trade unions are particularly important, since these profess a special dedication to democratic methods, with institutions very generally framed on a strictly majoritarian pattern.

The reasons for the prevalence of this pattern of government in private associations are not easy to state. The reason most commonly offered is that most associations, certainly most trade unions, are in some degree warring institutions. According to this argument, such an organization needs to present a united front, and must not display internal disagreement, lest advantage be given to its opponents. The argument probably had some effect in persuading potential dissidents not to voice their dissent; it is not altogether obvious, however, that expression of internal opposition necessarily weakens the organization. Generally, trade unions have experienced most internal opposition at times when their most intense battles for organizational survival have been fought. In point of fact the times of peace are those in which tolerance of internal opposition declines.[39] The usual argument seems to rest on an assumption that any internal opposition can end only in complete victory for one of the contending factions, the defeated would-be leaders going over to the external enemy. Actual illustrations of such occurrences can be given, but they hardly support the contention that it is a necessary result.

Strong distaste for anything less than unanimity seems to be one of the principal characteristics of private associations. Perhaps the most common response to disagreement when it does appear is to attempt to suppress it, either by appeals for unity or by more drastic means. Some associations do attempt to confront the problem in a different manner. One of the more interesting devices was the elaborate system of referenda utilized until the late 1950s by the Chamber of Commerce of the United States in formulating its own positions on matters of national policy. On subjects the Board of Directors deemed to be "national in character, timely in importance, and general in application to business and industry," committee reports were sought and presented in pamphlets submitted to the membership. The committee recommendations were balanced by statements drawn up by the Chamber's research department, of reasons opposing the recommended position. The machinery for insuring the integrity of the balloting was elaborate. A two-thirds majority vote was required to commit the organization. The procedure had some large deficiencies as a democratic device, most notably the absence of genuine debate on the measures considered. Nevertheless, it was remarkable how frequently measures were adopted by majority votes of more than 90 per cent. This record is reminiscent of plebiscites elsewhere and suggests that the function served by the referenda was to proclaim policy rather than make it. The nature of the referenda themselves and their phrasing, however, indicated that the desire for unanimity had much to do with the results. The positions taken were, by comparison with the positions taken by other business groups on the same subjects, moderate, and the language in which they were stated was moderate.[40] This consequence of the drive for unanimity, however, is not common.

In general, the weight of available evidence on private associations is overwhelmingly on the side of Michels' "law" of oligarchy. Supporters of particular associations quite properly insist that there are significant differences among associations, differences which cannot always be seen merely by looking at constitutional provisions; the spirit and practice of some unions and other organizations are more democratic than their internal law requires. It could well be argued that the differences are more important than any general similarities that may be found among associations; some observers, in fact, seek to dismiss the question of democratic control of union governments as unimportant. It is claimed, for example, that the members of the Carpenters' Union may be quite aware of the undemocratic character of many of their union's practices, but are generally satisfied with the union nonetheless; the economic benefits it confers on its members outweigh any misgivings on other scores.[41] Nevertheless, when all these different arguments have been made, the really general fact is the prevalence of oligarchy in private associations.

In one sense oligarchic rule is what might have been anticipated once private associations were regarded as forms of government, for every government is to a degree an oligarchy. But the difference between public and private government does not lie here. Public governments have a long tradition of grappling with the problem of controlling and limiting power. Few topics have so occupied political philosophers over so many centuries. There have been many attempts to solve the problem by trial and error; consequently, a large variety of devices for checking and limiting power exists in public systems. The entire tradition of constitutionalism is discernible in the governing institutions of any Western nation.

With private associations, however, this tradition has not applied, and there have been few attempts to develop institutional restraints on governmental power or to seek in any way to limit it. There would appear to be no intrinsic reasons why such restraints should not be developed. A few American trade unions (the UAW, the Upholsterers, and the Packinghouse Workers) have instituted a device of independent boards to review cases involving individual members and their unions.[42] Some unions have managed to tolerate very lively factional disputes without major disaster; the Typographical Union, as we have noted, has even had a formal system of parties. Although these are relatively exceptional examples, they are sufficient to illustrate the possibility of constitutionalizing private governments. Experience, nevertheless, does appear to bear out the expectation deriving from the considerations set forth in the previous chapter that small political bodies limited in diversity of constituency are unlikely to develop constitutional patterns of internal politics.

The remarkable fact about private government, then, is not that it is oligarchic, but that it generally lacks the limitations that guard against tyranny and injustice to minorities and individuals. This lack, in turn, seems to be related to a deep and widespread illusion about the nature of politics in private associations. The illusion is that in any group homogeneity is ever complete or that unanimity is ever possible. Certainly a greater degree of homogeneity is possible in a private association than in a nation. Agreement within a private association can perhaps be more extensive and more concrete. Nevertheless, the difference is one of degree, and the problems of politics, of reconciling differences, and of limiting political power remain. The record of private associations in dealing with these problems gives little justification for the wishful view that the private association is the natural home of democracy.

Part II

———————⭐———————

INTRODUCTION

The object of most persistent concern for Americans as they have confronted the existence of strong interest groups in their midst has been the public interest. At times this concept has seemed vivid, as though it were etched against the horizon and clear for all to behold, standing in contrast to the sometimes insistent, sometimes devious demands of particular and special interests. Occasionally, it has seemed that the public interest was almost wholly defined by antithesis to these special interests, especially in earlier and simpler times, when the rapacity of railroads, bankers, land speculators, and all their kind was crudest and most glaring. It was self-evident in the Progressive era, when the promise of science in government and administration seemed brightest and "the greatest good for the greatest number in the long run" meant very simply that the people wanted what was good for them as revealed by the emerging administrative science. In even simpler terms, it was the vision against which the sordid practices of lobbyists from the National Association of Manufacturers early in the century down to the influence peddlers of the Truman and Eisenhower administrations were measured and condemned.

Gradually, however, the vision grew hazy and indistinct. Little action came out of the recurrent investigations of lobbying; the public indignation that each time seemed so strong soon cooled, and the scandals that developed every few years invariably were quickly forgotten. The reason for failure of congressional and public indignation to produce significant reform was in part the hard rock of the First Amendment and its guarantee of the right to petition the Congress for redress of grievances. In practice, the hallowed principle of liberty of expression seemed to give great favor to all the special interests but none to the public interest. But there were also growing doubts that the public really cared for what was presumably in its own interest. Thus, for example, a member of the House Ways and Means Committee, after watching the failure of efforts to generate public support for tax reform in 1963, remarked, "The average American doesn't mind other people having their own loopholes—he only cares about getting his."[1]

At another level there were currents of skepticism of a more searching kind. They had sources in the pragmatism and love of common sense that are supposedly such strong American characteristics. Perhaps there was no such thing as "the public interest," or if there was, perhaps it was unknowable—a condition in effect the same as nonexistence. These suspicions have always been latent in American thought, but their modern emergence dates, ironically, from that high point of the Progressive era, 1908, with the publication of Arthur Bentley's *The Process of Government*.[2] It was a knotty and often confusing volume, and there is little wonder that it had scant influence in its own time. Quite probably what Bentley himself wished to emphasize in his book was what he named in his title, *process*. Politics consisted to him of movement and motion; by implication, the supposed goals of politics were unimportant dross and confusion upon the underlying reality. Bentley's ideas were far from clear and they were lost in metaphysical discussion that gave a sense of profundity not least when it was most obscure.[3] But a later generation extracted something rather different from his book—namely that the significant units, the actors of politics, as it were, are groups. The political process is one of groups in action, sometimes competing, sometimes cooperating, but always pushing or pulling in some direction. Together they make the whole of politics a giant parallelogram of forces, with policy the resultant of their thrusts. Alternatively, they represent a continually changing but still stable equilibrium, with policy at any given time the price at which the equilibrium exists.

Such pictures of politics as mechanism had several strong appeals. First, they offered the satisfaction of a seemingly superior realism as compared with conceptions phrased in terms of a vague and inevitably controversial "public interest." They suggested that the analyst who thought in this way had greater toughness and freedom from sentimentality than his predecessors. Second, this new departure offered a method of thinking which avoided both the problem of weighing different values (a task apparently indistinguishable from the application of bias), and the problem of dealing in a purely static description of the lively world of politics. Whether for these reasons or not, however, it became very fashionable to reduce the account of political life to a mechanistic interplay of interest groups. Thus not so long ago one writer confidently said, "Assertion of an inclusive 'national' or 'public interest' is an effective device in many less critical situations as well. In themselves, these claims are part of the data of politics. However, they do not describe any actual or possible political situation within a complex modern nation."[4] It was a statement only slightly more assured than one of a few years earlier, that the public interest was a myth, albeit a necessary myth.[5]

The superior sophistication of the point of view which these statements typify would be more impressive if the skepticism that so readily dissolved the "public interest" had been applied to the groups whose behavior was being rehabilitated for the general estimation.[6] The existence of diversity and conflict of interest inside a nation was exceedingly simple to demonstrate and invoking it was an excellent device for mocking the pretensions of those who, like one corporation executive turned public servant, claimed that what was good for a particular corporation was good for the United States. Nevertheless, this sardonic attitude, which might have yielded additional insights if held consistently, disappeared when the analysis reached groups within the state. These were hard, they were reality itself, not "mind-stuff" or "spooks" like the other categories in terms of which politics had been analyzed before. The reification was the same that had characterized the thinking of the English and European pluralists, although the language garbing it was less elegant. The interests of superior reality held up in contrast to the abstract "public interest" were not mere self-interests, but *group* self-interests. As has been seen in the preceding pages, these group interests themselves embraced some diversity.

If this attempt to banish what seemed an unnecessary mystery failed, a greater mystery was perhaps created. This lay in the brute fact of nationhood itself. If groups were the only real social and political entities, how could there be a *nation?* Although the logical answer, that nations do not exist, seems to have trembled on the points of some pens, it has not been given. Rather the reply seems to have been almost Marxian: that larger entity, the state or nation, is nothing more nor less than the expression of whatever group interests have power. If one of these is sufficiently powerful, the nation is that group's own peculiar expression; if, as is more probable, there are numerous powerful interests, the nation is the combination of these, differences canceled and concurrences added.

Curiously, a notion of the public interest, or something much like it, tended to slip back into this scheme of things, in the guise of a belief that the result of the various group forces at work was beneficent. Sometimes this was no more than an operational definition. In such a form the implicit argument seemed neutral on the troublesome question of which values were good and which were bad. Inescapably, however, the neutrality did not extend to the question whether the result of existing forces was preferable to that of other conceivable forces; for practical purposes this was the best of possible worlds.

Perhaps the crucial step in the reasoning involved here was to take as given only those interests which found expression in organized groups having power. This assumption was not made altogether unconsciously, but neither was it given much examination. Thus, for example, the United States Department of Agriculture accepted the state Farm Bureaus as representatives of "agriculture" in their respective areas after they had been formed, with results that, while occasionally disturbing to some members of the bureaucracy, were taken as evidence of adequate consultation with farmers at large. When it became apparent in the 1930s that important parts of the farming population were not included in the consultation process, it was too late to challenge effectively the structure of power that had been created. Perhaps Herbert Hoover (to recall another example) had some sense that existing trade organizations did not include everyone having some interests in public economic policy; he did attempt to encourage the formation of additional organization where gaps were evident to him. The problem was not, however, especially vivid to him, if we are to judge from the policies he followed. The vague and latent conception of a corporate democracy of interest groups remained; the problems it posed were scarcely perceived.

In formal terms perhaps the most serious of these problems is the consequent blurring of the distinction between public and private. This distinction can be applied differently in different times and places to different categories. Certainly today property in some definitely liberal societies is not accorded the same sanctity of privacy as it is in others or as it has been in the past. The precise location of the distinction between what is private and what is public is much less important than its maintenance; nevertheless, it is necessary to look carefully at any change in the location to be certain that the basic conception itself is not destroyed. In the past no group of thinkers emphasized this more eloquently than the pluralists themselves. Their concern was with the encroachments of the state upon the private association. Today, the issue of maintaining privacy is quite as vivid, but the contemporary risks to privacy are different from those perceived by the pluralists of a generation ago.

More important and more characteristic of American government is the conquest of segments of formal state power by private groups and associations. Although it would be impossible to state with any precision what portion of the power of American government has been taken possession of in this way, it is certain that the portion is substantial and that the control involved is considerable. In the following chapters a number of illustrations will be given. In each instance, the reality is complex, but the essential fact in each case is the exercise of governmental power by what might otherwise be considered private groups.

The pattern by which this condition has developed varies, but several steps in the process are common. Local elites have become organized nationally, usually on a federal basis, and have then been able to assume the exercise of public authority within significant areas of policy. The public agency with a particular clientele is a familiar phenomenon. However, it is but one of various types of administrative body that serve the purposes of narrow groups. Typically, such an agency has been insulated from the influences of "politics," that is to say, of partisan politics. It has a considerable degree of autonomy within the general hierarchical pattern of the administrative structure. This autonomy implies some measure of isolation from the formal system of authority and from the means by which responsibility to the broad constituency of the executive is sought. Such isolation would mean extreme vulnerability to political attack in the legislature and elsewhere if an effective alternative scheme of representation were not provided by the private group. In return for special consideration of its interests, the private group supports and defends the agency from attack and from demands that general executive policy be followed.

Although power in the particular sphere of interest involved will tend to flow to those who actually are in direct contact with the members of the benefited group, usually the leadership of the private association, the relationship between public agency and private group is reciprocal, as is most clearly to be seen in origins of both agency and association. Sometimes the impulse for the establishment of a public agency of this kind comes from the private group. This is obvious and comprehensible. On the other hand, however, the impulse for the formation of the private group sometimes comes from public officials; some of the most important private groups have been formed in this manner. The reasons are mixed. The potential gain in support for the officials is a clear incentive. There is also a strong desire to avoid conflict and to gain a "voluntary" settlement of disputes in the making of policy.

The function of policy-making is often turned over to the private group in what amounts to delegation. That this procedure actually avoids compulsion is an illusion, since, given the oligarchic tendencies of organization, the private group will find itself exercising the compulsion the public official avoided. The private group, indeed, will have an easier task than would the public official, since the conflicts it will have to resolve will be both simpler and fewer. Nevertheless, the process exposes the members of the private groups to the vagaries of a power in which the compulsive force and authority of the state have been joined to the informal and social power of the private groups and from which no recourse may be possible. The public official, for his part, will by this process have successfully maintained his formal position and have cleared his desk of immediate work and trouble. Nevertheless, by his action he will have materially diminished his office and will over time discover that he has incurred a permanent debt to the group he has helped conjure into being and has endowed with authority.

There are many variations of this process in the United States. They differ in degree as well as in kind. There are great vertical structures of power by which large matters of public policy are in the hands of large associations working through committees of Congress and federal bureaus. There are local committees chosen as the most authoritative local leaders to make effectively final determinations on which of their neighbors shall benefit or be penalized by public action. There are advisory bodies working with official agencies to which they give advice that can be rejected only at considerable risk. There are private associations formally endowed by law with power to determine entrance into particular lines of work. The scale of their activity, its importance, and the degree of their power differ from group to group. Nevertheless, the pattern is very pervasive.

Not all the large consequences of this development are visible. In one sense, what prevails is a system of responsibility which rivals the system embodied in the formal structure of government. The problem posed here is not irresponsible government versus responsible government; responsibility exists in either system. The difference lies in the different constituencies to which responsibility is owed and paid. The largely autonomous public agency will have its own constituency whose demands and needs are made known by the concerned private associations and perhaps by carefully chosen citizens' committees or advisory boards. In another sense what is visible here is the rise of a scheme of representation alternative to the machinery of Congress, legislatures, President, and governors.[7] It is also a reformulation and redistribution of authority.

As a scheme of representation, this development is in many ways at odds with the formal plan embodied in the Constitution. To a very considerable degree it makes a mockery of the vision by which one interest opposes another and ambition checks ambition. The large extent of autonomy accorded to various fragments of government has gone far to isolate important matters of public policy from supposedly countervailing influences. Moreover, the picture of government as mediator among different interests is falsified to the extent that government itself is fragmented and the various fragments are beholden to particular interests. The pattern of federalism as a system of mutually limiting levels of government is also profoundly altered.[8]

None of these consequences have been intended. To a considerable degree, moreover, they are unacknowledged. Certainly they do not touch all aspects of government in America. They are nevertheless far-reaching. The chapters that follow will examine a variety of situations in which these effects have been particularly important.

✪

Chapter 6

The States

I

Few conditions of American political life have been more important in the distribution of power than federalism. Its effects have been different at different times, and invariably they have been complex. At the time of the adoption of the Constitution, federalism represented a great movement toward centralization. Moreover, the terms of federal relationships have been sufficiently fluid that considerable change has been possible within its context, much of the change centralizing in character. Over time, nevertheless, federalism has had a strongly decentralizing force. The perpetuation of the states as partially autonomous ("sovereign") units has clearly inhibited much change of a centralizing character that would otherwise have occurred. Considerably more important, however, federalism as an influence for decentralization has served to maintain and enhance a variety of systems of private power in the nation.

The strength of the states within the federal system is occasionally disputed and the supposedly much expanded power of the federal government deplored. This sort of evaluation, like its opposite, rests on a particular concept of the proper degree of centralization or decentralization. Even granting the relative character of such a valuation, however, it has been made abundantly clear in recent years that the states have not been weakened to the point of impotence.[1] Moreover, general belief in the merit of the states as autonomous units of government remains strong. The grounds for this belief are varied. Some (although probably not most) people feel direct loyalty to individual states as though to separate nations. The states, moreover, seem to embody the virtues of decentralization and smallness in an overly complex world. Occasionally, they appear virtuous just because, unlike the federal government, they do not deal with foreign policy or foreign aid and because they have almost nothing to do with national defense and cannot formulate or carry out a monetary policy. The most persistent and strongly held belief in the virtue of the states, however, is based upon a feeling that they are closer to the people and that power in their hands represents self-government more than does power in the hands of the federal government, a belief supported by virtually all the arguments advanced in favor of decentralization of any kind. Also, the states are perceived as presenting opportunities for experimentation and as sources of innovation in government. Certainly, a number of innovations have come from the states: the unicameral legislature of Nebraska, the initiative and referendum of Oregon, Wisconsin's regulatory commissions, the Georgia unit system, to name some outstanding examples. Yet the total list of such innovations is not long; the states' imitative tendencies are probably much more impressive. Sometimes partisans of decentralization to the states maintain that since state governments are closer to the people in point of geography, the people can know and understand them better. The fact, however, is that the state governments have a "low visibility" and are not well known even to their citizens.[2] Probably the strength of partisanship for the states vis-à-vis the nation is to be explained not so much by the reasons usually advanced as by a simple, unexamined belief that local autonomy *is* democracy—and by the intuitively understood advantages that accrue to local elites from autonomy.

Although there are very great differences in conditions in the fifty states, a common spirit pervades many of their political institutions. This spirit, different from that prevailing in the federal government, is largely the consequence of that decentralization the states represent. The institutions in which it is embodied give very great advantages to structures of private power and to private interests generally. These institutions are by no means unfamiliar; some of them have been under criticism by reformers for a long time. Their greatest significance, however, can be seen if they are regarded as features of a common pattern of power.

One of the first features of state government to emerge in any general survey concerns the quality of state constitutions. The most cursory glance at these documents reveals that almost all of them are entirely different in character from the Constitution of the United States. The difference is most apparent in the length of the state documents, the overwhelming majority of which are very long. The extreme example is Louisiana, with a constitution of 217,000 words. California follows with a book-length document of 70,000 words. The constitution of New York has 45,000 words and those of sixteen other states have constitutions of more than 20,000 words. Only eight state constitutions have less than 10,000 words, that is, approximately the length of the United States Constitution.[3] Almost as striking as their length is the frequency with which many state constitutions have been amended. As might be expected, Louisiana and California lead in this regard, with 407 and 335 amendments respectively.[4] There is no precise correlation between length and number of amendments, but there is a definite relationship. Even Vermont, with the shortest constitution (4840 words), has managed to make almost twice the number of amendments that have been made to the federal Constitution.

That most state constitutions are overly long is a commonplace among students of American government. And it is widely agreed that extreme length is a defect; constitutional revision is a favorite project of reformers in most states. The grounds for seeking revision, however, are usually of a pragmatic character: the terms of the documents are out-of-date, cumbersome, or otherwise inconvenient to those who must govern.[5] Despite the obvious justice of many of these criticisms, a more significant criticism might be that through their length, detail, and openness to change most state constitutions blur the distinction between what is constitutional and what is statutory.

There is irony in this consequence. In formal terms, the state constitutions stand as limitations on power rather than as grants of power such as are contained in the United States Constitution, a difference deriving from the character of the federal system itself. Ostensibly the state documents carry forward the tradition of limitation on governmental power. Yet the diverse motives that have led to the inclusion of a vast amount of detail and current policy within the protected categories of the constitutions have been self-defeating. Of necessity, they have given rise to a conception of the constitutions as mere outlines of governmental structure and policy, to be altered as the winds of political fashion shift and circumstances change. Unthinkingly also, perhaps, they have supported the cynical view that constitutional enshrinement of policy is no more than the tactic of particular interests that could not otherwise be defended. If this cynicism is justified, as it often is, constitutional provisions are properly open to attack and to ready change as the equilibria of power shift.

The explanation for the condition of the state constitutions is complex. One might expect that amending these documents is simpler than that of the United States Constitution, but special amending procedures are required by all states. In some it can perhaps be argued that no special majority is required, yet even in these (Arizona, Arkansas, Minnesota, North Dakota, Oklahoma, and South Dakota) special action by the electorate is necessary. In twenty-seven states a special legislative majority of two thirds or three fifths is necessary to validate proposals; other states have other provisions which place obstacles in the way of easy amendment.[6] The existing situation, then, cannot be explained by formal provisions that make amendment easy.

It appears that the constitutions are readily changeable *despite* provisions designed to make this difficult. In some degree, their length and openness to change are expressions of a general outlook which accords less sanctity to the state constitutions than to the United States Constitution. This suggests that in a very basic sense the spirit of state government may be considerably more majoritarian than its national counterpart. Certainly, many states have been deeply influenced by Progressivism and have incorporated measures such as the initiative, the referendum, the direct primary, and even the recall of judges, all of which bespeak an intention to democratize the processes of government in a highly majoritarian spirit. But the issue is very complex, and if the determination to give effect to the will of the majority is genuine, the reality is an ironic commentary upon it.

II

It is largely meaningless to lay claim to majority rule unless the constituency in which a majority prevails is defined. The most obvious illustrations of this proposition have for a long time been the state legislatures. For many years students of government have pointed to the highly unrepresentative character of these bodies when they are regarded as state-wide wholes. Most of the upper houses of state legislatures have been in some way based upon area as well as population. Often the constituent boundaries of their representative districts have been related to the counties, i.e., subdivisions created by the states themselves; perhaps the most notorious situation of this sort has been the California Senate, which has offered the contrast of one district in the Sierra with less than 15,000 voters electing one senator, and Los Angeles County with more than 6,000,000 voters also electing one senator. But the lower houses have also been seriously unrepresentative. As the U.S. Advisory Commission on Intergovernmental Relations summarized the condition existing in mid-1961, "In only 11 States did 35 percent or more of the population elect a majority of the members to both houses of the State Legislature; in only five of these States did the figure exceed 40 percent. On the other hand, there were at least seven states where less than 30 percent of the population elected a majority of the representatives to both houses of the legislature."[7]

This condition seemed impossible to challenge until 1962, when the United States Supreme Court handed down its decision in *Baker v. Carr*.[8] Before this decision, legislative districting appeared to be purely at the discretion of the legislatures themselves. The issue had been presented to the Court earlier as a consequence of its decision that it could not enter the "political thicket" surrounding the formulation of Congressional Districts, which it considered a matter for the state legislatures.[9] When the same plaintiff returned with a suit asking that his legislature be compelled to redistrict itself, the Court refused to hear the case.[10] Inasmuch as the legislatures controlled Congressional redistricting, the Court's refusal to deal with inequitable districting for state legislatures was tantamount to placing all districting beyond popular recourse. The state legislators were the very individuals who had succeeded under existing arrangements; their disinclination to disturb these conditions was too humanly understandable.[11]

Baker v. Carr changed the situation dramatically. In that decision the Court held that the courts do have a responsibility to see that the equal protection of the laws is extended to each citizen through equal participation in selecting his lawmaker. The Court did not say exactly what "equal protection of the laws" meant as it applied to the problem, and left immediate solutions to be passed on by the lower courts. But the issue was at least opened to change. In rapid succession, state after state undertook to adjust the boundaries of legislative districts to forestall court attacks. While it is too early to see what all the consequences will be, it is certain that ultimately a very substantial redistribution of political power will be effected.

Why have the state legislatures been so unrepresentative so long? The most important reason is the very strong American attachment to the value of localism—an attachment which in the legislatures takes several forms. In the lower houses it is common to give each county at least one seat. Where the state has many counties, however, the result is a serious distortion of representation; thus Iowa with 99 counties and 108 seats in the lower house gives its smallest county eighteen times the representation allowed its largest.[12] Limitation on the number of seats one district may have prevents sparsely populated areas from being overbalanced by densely populated areas; by the same token it prevents urban voters from having a voice commensurate with that of rural voters, an effect particularly evident in some of the upper houses. It explains, for example, the anomaly of the California Senate already cited, in which no county could have more than one seat and for which districts could not be composed of more than three counties. As in sixteen other states, this type of arrangement was justified on the ground that it is based on a "federal plan" similar to the federalism of the nation. The analogy would seem transparently specious, but it has been so persuasive that the plan was introduced as a great reform in California in 1926 with heavy popular support and has been repeatedly reaffirmed in popular referenda since that time.[13]

The other important factor explaining unrepresentative legislatures is that while the United States has become progressively urban, redistricting to take account of this shift occurs, at best, only at ten-year intervals after the taking of the national census. Some states have shown little enthusiasm for making the adjustments so plainly called for by changes in population distribution. Thus Tennessee, the state that occasioned the dispute of *Baker v. Carr*, had not adjusted the boundaries of its legislative districts from 1901 until the Court intervened, despite a provision of the state constitution that required reapportionment every ten years. But this situation was not unique. Delaware had undertaken no reapportionment since 1897; Alabama, not since 1880; Indiana, not since 1921; Connecticut, not since 1903, and then only for its Senate.[14] Illinois went from 1901 to 1955 without reapportionment and, when the 1960 census indicated further change was due, was unable to effect a reapportionment, so that in 1964 (to the horror of many people) an at-large election was necessary.

Unfortunately, court action in enforcing redistricting by the states can be only the first step in a long process that might lead to equitable apportionment. The efforts of the legislatures at reapportionment all too often fall short of the reformers' ideal of one man, one vote. And there remains the nicely developed American art of the gerrymander, which, while obviously more difficult to practice when the courts require constituencies to be roughly equal in size, is by no means banished.

The prospect for change created by the decision in *Baker v. Carr* should not be minimized. The tumult of activity it has precipitated among the states is itself impressive; the attention focused upon the problem may be more important still. Nevertheless, the most important part of the issue remains untouched. This is the problem of size of constituencies. These, for the most part, remain small, and a great many lack substantial diversity; indeed, they are often drawn to ensure homogeneity. Any justification for small constituencies on the grounds of difficulty of transportation has long passed. Another justification lies in the supposed values of local self-determination, which have been examined in earlier pages.[15] Until reform reaches this aspect of the problem, the results of reapportionment may be disappointing.

Although the long-frustrated desire for more equitable distribution of voting power in the legislatures is sound, there has been much confusion over the reasons for its importance. At times the reason appears to have been no more than an abstract and doctrinaire preference for symmetry in representation, so that the suspicion persists that in practical terms the issue may be rather unimportant. Certainly this suspicion has merit if it refers to any prospects for quick and major results from the changes in legislatures now taking place. The charges of meaninglessness and abstractness are mistaken, however. The genuine issue is important, for reasons which go close to the heart of state government as we have known it.

What is the significance of an inequitable distribution of voting power? Given the form in which the inequity exists, it might be (and frequently is) supposed that rural areas benefit at the expense of cities. Certainly it is evident that in many states representation of the countryside heavily overbalances that of the cities. The picture of a fundamental conflict of interest between town and country is thus easily conjured up. But this conflict may be less important than it seems. Issues that are solely rural or solely urban are not numerous, and there is some evidence that the conflict between city and country is less dramatic than it may have seemed; thus a study of voting in the legislature of Illinois, a state in which this division would seem particularly strong, indicates that urban and rural delegations do not vote solidly against each other.[16] The significance of inequitable representation lies elsewhere.

III

Another potentially important dimension of difference in the established distribution of voting power is that between the two major parties. This dimension very clearly is involved where the two parties exist as vital organizations. In a number of states the exaggerated representation given rural areas seems to have helped maintain the power of a particular party, usually the Republican. In Illinois and New York, for example, it is axiomatic that the Republican party is strongest in the areas outside the major metropolis, while the Democratic party must base itself on the big city.

Nevertheless, the consequences of particular partisan strength, even where they do exist, are not the really important aspects of the patterns of representation in the states. Despite the rather spotty coverage of the fifty states' political systems in scholarly analysis, there is sufficient evidence to indicate that parties are considerably less important than the frequency of reference to them in the press may suggest. Perhaps the basic general fact here is that vital two-party systems are not the rule among the states. The existence of one-party rule in the eleven Southern states has long been common knowledge. For the whole nation, different tabulations give different views of the incidence of the one-party phenomenon. A 1955 estimate was that 18 states had single-party systems.[17] A more recent list named 23 states as either one-party states or states with one dominant party. Of the remaining 23 (the officially nonpartisan states of Nebraska and Minnesota, as well as Alaska and Hawaii, were not counted), 14 additional states were considered to be two-party states only in a limited sense.[18] Even among the nine states characterized as having two-party systems, some systems have not been particularly impressive; California, for example, is included in this group although its two-party system is of very recent standing.

The meaning of these tabulations goes considerably beyond the evident conclusion that effective party competition is not the norm within the states. The figures only suggest the actual degree of weakness of many systems in the two-party category, and say nothing about the vitality of those many single-party organizations. And it is just here that their significance lies. In his landmark study, *Southern Politics*, V. O. Key demonstrated that one-party politics is no-party politics. At the end of his examination of the political systems of eleven Southern states, Key asserted that "the South really has no parties."[19] Instead, he found an array of varied factional systems. Factions differ from state to state. Some are based on networks of friends and neighbors, some on particular interest groups, but all are much less inclusive than genuine parties. They perform some of the functions normally thought of as belonging to parties, notably the selecting of leaders. But the general picture is of a disorganized and atomized politics.

The results achieved by this disorganization must be very troubling to anyone who takes at face value the orthodoxy of small local units as devices for democratic participation. In a memorable discussion Key indicated what these results have been in the Southern states:

Not only does a disorganized politics make impossible a competition between recognizable groups for power. It probably has a far-reaching influence on the kinds of individual leaders thrown into power and also on the manner in which they utilize their authority once they are in office. . . . Factional fluidity and discontinuity probably make a government especially disposed toward favoritism. Or to put the obverse of the proposition, the strength of organization reflecting something of a group or class solidarity creates conditions favorable to government according to rule or general principle, although it is readily conceded that such a result does not flow invariably. In a loose, catch-as-catch-can politics highly unstable coalitions must be held together by whatever means is available. This contract goes to that contractor, this distributor is dealt with by the state liquor board, that group of attorneys have an "in" at the state house, this bond house is favored. . . .

The significant question is, who benefits from political disorganization? Its significance is equalled only by the difficulty of arriving at an answer. There probably are several answers, depending on the peculiar circumstances in each case. Politics generally comes down, over the long run, to a conflict between those who have and those who have less. In state politics the crucial issues tend to turn around taxation and expenditure. . . . It follows that the grand objective of the haves is obstruction, at least of the haves who take only a short-term view. Organization is not always necessary to obstruct; it is essential, however, for the promotion of a sustained program in behalf of the have-nots, although not all party or factional organization is dedicated to that purpose. It follows, if these propositions are correct, that over the long-run the have-nots lose in a disorganized politics. They have no mechanism through which to act and their wishes find expression in fitful rebellions led by transient demagogues who gain their confidence but often have neither the technical competence nor the necessary stable base of political power to effectuate a program.[20]

What prevails in the South, then, is a pattern in which most political questions are relegated to the uncertain workings of a near-chaos of loosely organized local factions or are not treated within the political framework at all. So far as the political question of overwhelming importance in the South is concerned,

A loosely organized politics with no stable centers of power or leadership is in one sense admirably suited for dealing with the Negro question. A pulverized politics decentralizes power to county leaders and county officials and in some areas devolution is carried even further in that public officials do not cross the plantation boundary without invitation and government is left to the plantation operator in his domain. In a granulated political structure of this kind with thousands of points of authority there is no point at which accountability can be enforced. Private and semi-private acts of violence can be subjected to no real check. By the same token, a disorganized politics makes it impossible for a state really to meet the obligations that its leaders assert it undertakes with respect to a dependent people. Loud protestations that "we are doing something about the Negro"—which contains more truth than is commonly supposed—have no buttress of political program for dealing statewide with the race question.[21]

Obviously the South's political problems differ in many ways from those of other areas. Nevertheless, it is no longer so easy to say that what Key called "the Negro question" is peculiarly a Southern question, although states elsewhere have not been under the incubus of the "Negro question" in the same sense as the Southern states. The data on the incidence of one-party systems, moreover, suggest that some of the problems encountered in the South may have their counterparts elsewhere. In other regions, parties are not as weak—or, rather, as nonexistent—as they are in the South, but often they are very weak indeed.

The reasons for this condition, and its consequences, are somewhat different in non-Southern areas. Here, once again, we are confronted with the paradox of Progressivism. In state after state would-be reformers have erected legal barriers to the development of parties. Most of these barriers have come from the Progressive movement, which, as we have seen, was antiparty on principle.[22] They included the direct primary, the initiative, the referendum, and elaborate codes regulating the composition and government of parties. At every point these devices were intended to achieve the frustration of parties, a goal that has been to no small degree accomplished. As Key remarked in his general survey of American state politics, "Within a large proportion of the states only by the most generous characterization may it be said that political parties compete for power."[23]

Although weak-party systems outside the South have not had

the same effects of domination over Negroes, they nevertheless substantiate Key's general argument. If they vary from state to state and from locality to locality, it is because the underlying social patterns of power vary. The advantages of disorganized politics accrue quite impartially to whatever groups, interests, or individuals are powerful in any way. Where power is not organized in broadly based parties, lesser power organized in smaller and narrower groups suffices. If there is no formal political organization at all, the social and economic ties that exist everywhere are the most important political reality; in general, however, the individuals and groups that benefit from them are those who have some sort of stake in the maintenance of existing arrangements and, thus, are opposed to change. Such arrangements may, as in the South, be directed against change in the status of submerged groups, but such extremes will not always be found. Often, other influences such as the deeply believed-in egalitarian doctrines of the "American Creed," as Myrdal called it, have produced a social pattern much less bleak, and the political order is accordingly far milder in its discriminations. Nevertheless, the absence of significant party organization anywhere places strong restraints upon meaningful participation in politics by those whose economic or social bases of power are relatively weak.

Important differences among the states cannot be overlooked. There are genuine differences of degree in the cohesiveness and solidarity of parties from state to state; thus one study of a group of states has shown that conflict along party lines is more consistent in New Jersey than in Ohio, and more consistent in both of these than in California or Tennessee.[24] Without question a comprehensive study would permit a rank order among the two-party states on the score of party conflict. But there are also significant differences among the so-called one-party states, in which factionalism may be more or less well organized, however different the organization from genuine party systems. Thus Vermont has a bifactional system of some strength and durability. Interestingly, this bifactionalism seems to produce less demagoguery than appears where there are many factions.[25]

Perhaps the most interesting illustration of the effect of weak parties is the political pattern that prevailed in California between 1905 and the early 1950s. This was the period during which the Progressive "reforms" were undiluted and one-party rule by the Republicans seemed almost complete. During this time, there was only one Democratic governor, and he was not re-elected; the legislature was consistently dominated by Republicans. Yet registration figures indicated a heavy predominance of Democrats. The Democratic Party had almost no organization, a factor widely assumed to be responsible for Republican success. In reality, however, the weakness of Democratic organization was almost equalled by the weakness of Republican organization, for both parties, heavily inhibited by the restrictions in the state Elections Code, consisted of little more than labels. The processes of election campaigns, being largely free of party organization on either side, fell into the hands of smaller, less comprehensive organizations, for the most part well-financed groups. Money and publicity gained a heightened importance in elections to the degree that organization was lacking. The candidates who were elected thus were more likely to be Republicans than Democrats. Their success in the face of heavy Democratic registration depended heavily upon the absence of organization by *either* party. Had the Republican Party been strongly organized in this period, it almost certainly would have evoked organization by the Democrats, and it is reasonable to expect that in contests in which organization was the chief weapon, more elections would have been lost to the Democrats.[26] The more important consequence, however, was that interest groups were spared the compromises that might have been imposed on them by a stronger organization within the Republican Party. The largely non-party system that prevailed was ideally suited to the purposes of narrow interest groups with substantial financial resources. Had they chosen to act through either party in a well-developed system of organized politics, their favored candidates would have been defeated at least occasionally and their influence on policy would have been diluted by passage through the party medium. The strong influence of interest groups in the California legislature during this era is hardly to be wondered at. The powerful interest group machine organized by Arthur Samish in the 1940s was in no small part a result of party disorganization.[27]

Any comparison of the politics of the different American states is false if it subsumes all these diverse systems into a single pattern. It is of the essence of a federal or decentralized politics that various dominant purposes exist among the units making it up. These purposes and the interests to which they belong differ from state to state. Nevertheless, the disorganization of political parties in favor of other and lesser forms of organization does produce a fundamental similarity among the weak-party states. This consists of the heightened degree of power all confer on fairly narrow interest groups. Understandably, these groups vary in character. Some are more extreme than others in their demands, and some are perhaps wiser than others in their concern for public values. Thus a student of Montana politics has argued that the Anaconda Company, the strongest interest group in the state ("the company"), plays a stabilizing role in an economy and government that might otherwise be disorderly.[28] Whether this service and the close cooperation between Anaconda, the Montana Power Company, the state's three large railroads, and the sugar refinery companies are worth the costs so obviously implied may be another matter. Of Maine it has been claimed that "in few American States are the reins of government more openly or completely in the hands of a few leaders of economic interest groups" (a statement with parallels in studies of various other states). In Maine, however, the interests are timber companies, paper manufacturers, and developers of hydroelectric power.[29]

These examples suggest a number of different points. First, the interest groups which are important in the politics of a state are those which are otherwise important in the state; they are different in different states. Second, the interest group structure of politics is simple to the degree that the state is itself simple and undiversified. In California, where a diversity of significant interest groups exists, the political organization of interest groups is relatively complex; in Maine or Montana, where the important interest groups are relatively few, political organization is relatively uncomplicated. Third, the interest groups are generally strong when parties are weak and vice versa. This is perhaps most evident in the organization of legislatures, but it is noteworthy that interest groups may also take the place of parties in promoting political careers, particularly in the weaker, less competitive party systems.[30] Fourth, parties are likely to be weak where there is lack of diversity of interests in the state. This is not perfectly borne out by experience, since states like California have had weak parties while containing much diversity; here, however, the element of the antiparty Progressive "reforms" is obviously an added factor.[31] Weak parties and lack of diversity do, however, seem to be related.

It is apparent, then, that in a very large part of the United States, state politics does not provide the coherence of policy that might be expected from competitive party systems. There are strong grounds, moreover, for suspecting that to a serious degree state politics minimizes—or suppresses—the voices of significant elements of the state populations. Probably many issues are settled without controversy simply because the political context permits no ready challenge to the positions taken by entrenched groups. For example, a study of two sessions of the Illinois General Assembly showed that 73 per cent of all roll call votes were unanimous. Although many of the measures handled in this fashion were undoubtedly of limited interest, routine, or otherwise unimportant, it is difficult to believe that the treatment given all of them reflected underlying unanimity of interest among the people of Illinois. The result is certainly related to the party reality indicated by the fact that only 3.95 per cent of the votes in one session and 2.5 per cent in the second session were cast along party lines.[32] The appearance of consensus which the lack of division suggests is false and is in part the product of the political machinery itself. Inside the legislatures of states lacking strong party machinery logrolling, often managed by lobbyists themselves, readily avoids dispute and creates an illusion that there are no grounds for controversy.[33] The stability thus produced may be illusory in the long run.

IV

The character of state political systems is reflected in the pattern of governmental structure shared by most states; reciprocally, this structure has considerable influence in perpetuating the political system. The outlines of this pattern are common knowledge, and it has been the target of reformers for many years. Indeed, there is remarkably little disagreement among students of state government about the nature of the changes needed; for half a century demands have been repeated for fundamentally the same type of reforms, demands which have been collectively dignified as "the state reorganization movement." The subject, however, has been consistently treated as merely structural and technical in character, a very dry matter with little interest for the general public. Indeed, there are grounds for suspecting that tidiness has often been the reformers' highest objective; certainly the presentation of the argument for reform often suggests this value as the most important issue. Much more is at stake, however, as has been clear to the ablest analysts. V. O. Key, for example, has correctly noted the connection between political organization and the problem of state administrative organization.[34] Administration does involve politics, and in the states it is at least arguable that administration is the most important area of politics.

Perhaps the most conspicuous feature of state administration is the multiplicity of elective offices. Although there is considerable variety among the states on this score, most of their ballots have long lists of offices to be filled by direct choice of the electorate. Oklahoma leads with 15 agencies headed by elected officers; it is closely followed by Minnesota and South Carolina, each with 14. Eleven other states have ten or more. Only Alaska and New Jersey have the minimum of two. The offices commonly subject to election are those of Governor, Lieutenant Governor, Secretary of State, Attorney General, Treasurer, and Auditor. But other elected officers may be the Directors of Education, Agriculture, Labor, Insurance, Mines, and Land, members of Boards of Education, Public Utilities Commissions, Tax Commissions, Highway Commissions, Boards of Public Welfare, and others. South Carolina elects a State Librarian. The total number of individuals elected to administrative posts is accordingly large. North Carolina is pre-eminent here with 110 elected state officials. Nevada, a poor second in these sweepstakes, has 42; Ohio has 29 and South Carolina 28. Even New York, with a presumably well-integrated system, has 17.[35]

This feature of state administration is of long standing. In origin it recalls the long and gradual growth of governmental activities in the states. The tendency has been to treat each newly added function as something separate and unrelated to other functions. A majoritarian conception of democracy has, moreover, produced an insistence that the voters have the greatest possible degree of participation. The idea of providing additional checks on executive power by breaking up the administrative machinery has also been used to justify the practice of making administrative offices elective. The process and its justification are still to be seen and heard in many states. And the same process continues at a lively rate in local government, with the multiplication of special districts for single functions where population growth compels the establishment of fire and police protection and other services. In the states the reorganization movement has had some successes in reversing the tendency but, with a few exceptions, they have not been large. Despite the impetus given by the "little Hoover Commissions," which have studied the problem in some two thirds of the states since World War II, accomplishment has been meager.

The persistence of this pattern in the face of such widespread and determined crusading for reform is interesting, suggesting the presence of active resistance to change. This resistance can summon up a variety of justifications, but is actually based upon the advantages disorganized and ill-coordinated administration gives to narrow power-holding groups.[36] To groups that have established preferential positions for themselves in state government, the prospect of a centralization of authority in the governor's office through powers of appointment and removal is a serious threat. The multiplicity of elective offices, whether established by constitutional provision or statute, is a guarantee of the governor's impotence to require conformity with his own policy. Clearly it is also a check on power, and limits the capacity for evil in anything the governor might wish. But by the same token, it is an obstacle to coordination, and even more important, it is a limitation on the ability of the whole public to influence policy. Given the general absence of strong parties in the states, it is unlikely that all the different elected officers will be of the governor's party or faction. Although these officers are usually selected by the same general electorate which votes for the governor, the obscurity of many of their offices greatly diminishes the public's interest in them. Interested groups, however, pay great attention to some of these posts. Consequently the effective constituencies of some of them (such as directors of education, agriculture, commissioners of highways, and the like) are less than the general public and consist preponderantly of the groups most immediately concerned. The condition of a multiplicity of elective administrative offices thus tends to defeat democratic control of policy, and this, rather than coordination or orderliness of administration, is the main issue.

A second problem of administration that has troubled reformers is the sheer multiplicity of agencies in state government. An examination of the condition in 1950 by the Council of State Governments drew attention to the fact that Connecticut had 172 different agencies; Colorado, 140; Texas, 124; Ohio, 122, and so on. Oregon, moreover, had 78 major departments; Texas, 54; and New Hampshire, 47.[37] Some success in reducing these numbers has since been achieved, but the problem is perennial; new agencies develop soon after periods of reform, and the process tends to be repeated. Although this question has undoubtedly been given disproportionate concern because of a passion for neatness and economy, a genuine problem of accountability is involved. Beyond some point, completely separate identities in agencies which can only be coordinated and made responsible through the direct supervision of the governor's office result in irresponsibility, simply because the governor cannot give any of them sufficient attention.[38]

Despite the reformers' emphasis on the problems posed by many elective offices and separate agencies, change on both these scores would probably leave the fundamental problem largely unsolved: the widespread pattern of administrative agencies each of which is effectively accountable only to a narrow constituency consisting of the group or groups most directly and intimately affected by the agency's activities. Many different kinds of arrangements lead to this result, including the multiplicity of elective offices and agencies, but the extensive use of boards and other devices to make or advise on policy for administrative agencies is at least as important. Despite the diversity among these boards and commissions, they have one common quality: all to some degree limit the responsiveness of policy to the large constituency most clearly represented by the governor. In the clearest pattern of this situation a board is chosen, usually by statutory requirement, from members of a particular trade or industry—sometimes even *by* recognized units of the trade or industry—to advise or make policy for the state department or agency charged with public policy in the area involved. Often the official description of the board's powers does not correspond to the reality of the situation; thus a given board with policy-making duties may actually be no more than a rubber stamp for a strong professional administrator in the regular civil service. Often, however, a board legally invested with merely advisory powers is able to impose its policies on the line administrators. The latter condition is the more probable, since the board members are likely to have been chosen from the leadership, or on the nomination of the leadership, of well-organized interest groups with strong influence in the fragmented and substantially nonpartisan legislatures. In the long run only a strong governor can protect the strong-willed and independent line administrators, and strong governors are not common in the American system.

California has presented a particularly clear example of this problem. This is not a state unusually notorious for bad govern-

ment. It has great diversity and is even included among the
"two-party" states. Until very recently, however, its administration has been fragmented; in 1961 it had more than 350 agencies
presumably reporting to the governor. These agencies were
highly miscellaneous in structure and placement, but there
were in general two main groups: the departments with their
sub-units arranged in hierarchical pattern, and a great array of
boards and commissions. The position of the departments here
was particularly interesting, most of them being attached to one
or more boards with policy functions. Thus the Department of
Education was linked to the Board of Education, the Curricu-
lum Commission, and several others; the Department of Natural Resources was associated with the State Park Commission,
the State Board of Forestry, the Soil Conservation Commission,
the District Oil and Gas Commissions (six of them), and the
Small Craft Harbors Commission; the Department of Public
Works had the Highway Commission. The pattern was almost
universal, except for the many boards quite unattached to any
departmental structure.[39] There was some variety in the functions of these boards. Thus the State Board of Forestry, in the
official language, "prescribes general policies for the operation
of the Division of Forestry." Its members were chosen to represent the pine and redwood industries, forest land, livestock and
agricultural operators, and water users. The State Mining
Board "establishes policies for administration of the division
(of Mines). It consists of five members representing the mining
industry." In the Oil and Gas Division, "A board of commissioners is elected by oil and gas operators in each of five districts,"
its duties to include ruling on drilling and conservation. The
Department of Agriculture had a number of boards, including
the Agricultural Prorate Advisory Commission, a body with
considerably more than advisory powers in a field of great
economic importance to others than farmers.[40]

A number of things are conspicuous in this pattern. First, the
responsibility recognized and generally enforced was strictly to
the most interested groups. Second, the governor's powers of
supervision and control were minimal. Third, the boards' per-

sonnel was chosen by the regulated groups themselves. The extent to which this third point could go may be seen in the statutory language, as illustrated by the following example, perhaps extreme but not uncharacteristic. A local planning advisory committee was established in 1956. The committee was to

consist of seven members appointed by the Governor and serving at his pleasure, selected as follows:

(a) Three representing the counties, one of whom shall be a county supervisor, one a member of a county planning commission, and one a county planning director. The persons so appointed shall first be recommended for appointment by the President of the County Supervisors' Association of California.

(b) Three representing the cities, one of whom shall be a city councilman, one a city planning commission member, and one a city planning director. The persons so appointed shall first be recommended for appointment by the President of the League of California Cities.

(c) One a member representing the schools. He shall be a county superintendent of schools, and shall first be recommended for appointment by the President of the California School Trustees Association.[41]

California has been making heroic efforts to change the chaotic picture of its administration, but the dismantling of all the bastions of entrenched power that these illustrations suggest will be a large undertaking.[42]

Although not all other states have the consistent pattern of board influence and control by particular constituencies that has prevailed in California, many of them have comparable situations. New York, which is exemplary by contrast with other states on many scores, makes extensive use of advisory boards and councils in its various departments. Thus an advisory board consisting of representatives of the various branches of the insurance business exists in the Insurance Department. An advisory board of individuals associated with the supervision of cemeteries "assists" the Cemetery Board in the Department of State. The Advisory Council on Placement and Unemployment Insurance has an active part in administration.[43] But Alabama shows perhaps the extreme situation of this kind. Here, the State Health Officer is appointed by the State Board of Health, but this body is ex-officio the Medical Association of Alabama.[44]

In regulation of business particular representation of the groups regulated has been especially prominent. Some years ago a study of state regulatory agencies commented that banking and insurance-regulating agencies have been "to a significant degree creatures of the enterprises they regulate."[45] But the sphere that shows the most nearly universal control of regulation by the regulated through the medium of nearly autonomous boards is the licensing of trades and professions. The practice of giving public authority—sometimes formally but often in practice—to private associations of professionals is quite old. As early as 1859 the North Carolina legislature enacted that "the association of regularly graduated physicians . . . is hereby declared to be a body politic and corporate," with "power to appoint the body of medical examiners."[46] Other states followed suit, although by the 1920s some recession from this practice had occurred; a bit later, however, it was revived. North Carolina was again a leader with a self-governing bar act requiring all members of the legal profession to belong to the bar association.[47] The parade of other trades and professions in many states toward this ideal of "self-government" was sardonically summarized by one observer with the words, "the gild returns to America." By the 1950s, a study of state licensing legislation involving 927 licensing boards showed that statutory provisions required all members to be practitioners of the given occupation in 567 boards; in 140 of the others a majority of the members had to be practitioners. Appointment of some practitioners was required on most of the others. Moreover, direct selection by the association was required in 17 boards and appointment by the governor from an association list for 246 boards.[48]

The impulses leading to the creation of these agencies are largely the same. On the one hand all are justified by appeal to an ideal of professionalism and protection for the public. According to this argument, a given trade or profession is so technical that the public cannot be expected to discriminate between skilled and unskilled or between honest and dishonest practitioners. Moreover, the argument goes, the members of the trade or profession involved have a code of ethics arising from the corporate nature of the practitioners as a whole and including a specialized set of restraints on the practitioners for the public's benefit. Accordingly, it is argued, the public is best protected in technical areas through self-regulation by representatives of the trade or profession endowed with public authority. Undoubtedly many professional problems are difficult for non-specialists to understand; undoubtedly also, genuine concern for the public's welfare often exists within the professions. It is quite obvious, however, that the legal restraints exercised by licensing boards operate to the peculiar advantage of established practitioners of the skill involved. All of them administer regulations which limit entry to the vocation. Certainly in some professions, such as medicine and dentistry, such regulations are justified. But the list of activities frequently given state authority to regulate the qualifications of their members also includes barbers, hairdressers ("cosmetologists"), dry cleaners, funeral directors, cemetery salesmen, and many others. Even garage mechanics have attempted to gain such standing. Clearly, protection of the job market, which has been behind much trade unionism, forms a large part of the motivation to establish under state authority licensing systems effectively controlled by members of a given vocation.[49]

A number of conclusions emerge from this survey. First, the practice of securing special legal status to protect established members of a line of activity is widespread. What is sometimes slurringly referred to as "trade union mentality" is by no means limited to trade unions; its manifestations, indeed, are at least as far-reaching in some professions and businesses as in the trades. Second, the machinery of state administration has made an extensive accommodation to the demands of particular groups. Third, this accommodation has amounted to a parcelling out of public authority to private groups. This process is frequently indirect, as through the required appointment to

public bodies of representatives of particular groups; it is sometimes, however, quite direct and formal.

This system of protection for favored groups (and it should
be clear that only a minority of the people of any state enjoys
such status) has struck deep roots in state governmental structures. All the features of government and politics which render
the governors weak favor this system of protection. Wherever
possible, the various groups have sought to give their own
favored public bodies special constitutional status, although
such efforts may be self-defeating in that a multiplication of
constitutional provisions on such matters tends to erase the distinction between statutory and constitutional subjects. And
other features of established arrangements insure the perseverance of the pattern. "Earmarking" of public funds, for example,
goes far to render some boards and commissions impervious to
any requirement of coordination of public policy or effective
consideration of other than clientele needs. Sometimes the federal requirements contained in grants-in-aid help achieve this
result.[50] The most important factor, however, is the presence of
informal ties between the administrators and the interests concerned. Where virtual autonomy of boards or agencies is
achieved, the supposed antithesis between private and public
bodies tends to dissolve. Interest group and regulator develop
symbiotically and, under their joint influence, the legislature
becomes friendly. The process of government may become
quite informal.[51]

V

The spirit of state government and politics which emerges from
this discussion is remarkably consistent. At almost every point
it inspires a vision of democracy in which the people themselves
rule, in which there is no coercion, in which government is
servant rather than master. The vision pictures widespread participation in political life and a diffusion of power. It seems to
carry the torch of equality high among other values.

In general these ends are sought by the defeat of any tendency which might produce centralization of government or

political organization. Weakness of the governor, of central administration, of parties is at every point the goal. Yet paradoxically this does not mean weak government; the powers state governments exercise are often both strong and far-reaching. The actual target of all the devices surveyed here is not so much power itself as centralized power. The key to the paradox lies in the unstated assumption that power in the hands of particular citizen groups is not power at all. This, in turn, is related to an assumption that the matters on which regulations are enforced through the exercise of state authority affect others than members of the regulated groups to only a minor degree. It also implies that there are no differences of interest among the members of the groups most affected. If these assumptions were correct, it would be reasonable to suppose that no coercion is involved in the regulation of policy areas through public bodies dominated by particular groups. By this conception, the people would regulate themselves and thus be free, and power would not exist in any important degree.

This ideal of self-government can be seen in the various Progressive reforms that have sought the destruction of power—the initiative, the referendum, the direct primary, and all the legal restraints upon party organization. These, together with the deep mistrust for parties which is the hallmark of Progressivism in the states, have succeeded to a remarkable degree in keeping parties weak. The belief that parties serve a useful function only for national politics has prevailed far more extensively than is immediately apparent from press accounts of state politics. The altogether commendable impulse to discover meaning in politics tends to exaggerate the influence of parties, just as it does the differences between cities and country. The reality, however, is much more complex and more nearly bordering on chaos, for political organization in the states is more varied, more complex, and more fluid than any numerical summary of "two-party states" can suggest.

In what would otherwise be a political vacuum left by the weakness of parties, a great number of interest groups and narrowly-based factions of different kinds have flourished to provide such political organization as most states have. Some of these are tautly disciplined; others are quite loose. They by no means conjointly include the whole population or the sum of all the interests in any state, for very significant interests and very substantial categories of people are left outside the pattern. Important values are thus excluded from the political process that results. The illusion of unanimity disappears when closer examination reveals the existence of very real and sometimes fundamental conflict of interest. There is no more striking example of this than the long-term exclusion of Negroes from political participation in the South and the monumental façade of unity that has stood before this fact. The absence of controversy is too easily taken as proof of unanimity.

The weakness of parties is closely paralleled by the weakness of governors. Although it is perhaps no longer correct to consider the American governor a figurehead, much distance remains to be traversed before he can be regarded as a genuine leader or, more important, as the central medium for representation of all those interests which are widely shared but not reflected in the vaunted pluralism of interest groups and factions.[52] To an important degree the weakness of parties as the means of organizing the entire community is the basis for the weakness of governors. The governor is consequently reduced almost to the status of a factional leader. He can often wield the influence that derives from substantial patronage, but this power is often almost matched by that of similar patronage in the hands of other elected officials. Where parties are weak little more than mutual bargaining among the governor and these other officials is available for their coordination. The availability of patronage does give the governor a degree of power in legislation, but it is not commensurate with the need.

It is ironic in an era when state government has come to share fully in the complexities of modern life that, as one careful student has observed, "Curious as it may seem in many states, the governor is actually placed in the anomalous position of having far more influence with members of the legislature than with his own department heads."[53] The reasons, however, are clear.

Through the fragmentation of administration by autonomous agencies, each held effectively responsible only to narrow constituencies, and through a variety of devices precisely designed to block coordination and control by the governor, he is often reduced to impotence in the administration of which he is ostensibly the head.

The pattern of state government is quite different from that envisioned for the nation. It is not modeled on that drawn by the framers of the United States Constitution. The separation of powers has been bridged at many points through the influence of legislators over parts of the administration. Neither legislature nor executive is coherent or a unity. There may be checks in state government, but they are not the checks and balances of the United States Constitution. State constitutions have little of the sacredness of the federal document. Their length and numerous amendments give them the character of statements of present policy, like the constitutions of trade unions.[54] For the unities of party and administration, elements which have become essentials in the modern conception of American government, state governments have substituted the unities of interest groups leagued with legislative factions and administrative agencies. Government has indeed been fragmented and politics atomized. Yet power has not been abolished. The coordination of factions and autonomous bureaus generates important power from which appeal is very difficult. True, this power is not all of a piece, and it lies in different hands; but the separate structures of power tend to monopolize policy in significant areas for the benefit of only fractions of the people. Between these structures exist large gaps in which important interests and values are lost.

From time to time public attention is focused on scandalous situations in state government. The consequence of these moments of indignation—usually the work of journalistic enterprise—is a general conclusion that evil men have achieved high place and that corruption prevails.[55] These moments pass; state affairs recover their wonted obscurity and it is assumed that the wrongdoers have been exposed and punished. While corruption indeed exists, even by the most primitive definition, the real problem is less lurid and more serious.

In an abstract but very real sense, the problem is one of informality. Interpersonal ties, friendships, and relationships take the place of rules and formal procedures by reducing government and politics to small units. In legislatures, for example, logrolling is the product of the great complexities of established and anticipated personal obligations. The resulting web is woven from admirable human traits—friendship and gratitude—but rationality and concern for those not immediately involved are rare and slender threads in it. On another dimension, the problem is the dissolution of the distinction between what is public and what is private. One consequence is often to make the ways of government and politics humane and intimate, but another is to expose government to the play of favoritism and arbitrariness, and to make politics the preserve of those who are already economically or socially powerful. It is to surrender the peculiar functions of government to private hands over which many who must feel government power can have no influence. Self-government in this sense may enlarge the freedom of the powerful, but it may also diminish the freedom of the weak.

The political pattern of state government and politics shows the frequent convergence of the deep-seated belief in small units and the Progressive tradition. Progressivism has been dedicated to the eradication of special interest-group power, whereas often the stubborn insistence on small units has derived from an intuitive awareness that particular privileges are best protected in this manner. Ostensibly, therefore, it would seem that the two elements of belief should conflict. Nevertheless, the prescriptions of Progressivism, which in some states have been so fully institutionalized, have operated against the best available means for moderating factional power. Ultimately, perhaps, both Progressivism and the belief in small political units rest on an overly simple vision of majority rule. The difficulty is that there may be different majorities if the lines of constituent organization are differently drawn.

The particular form of political organization so prevalent among the states has probably contributed to stability. It has provided for the recognition of established power—for the most part, that of functional interest groups and factions formed about individuals. The organization of state politics and government has involved coopting these scattered centers of power, whose cooperation has been gained on a logrolling basis and has resulted in effective devolution to their hands. Where affairs of minor importance have been involved, such as the licensing of barbers, the cost has been minor, but with matters of greater importance, like the regulation of insurance, the costs have been considerable. By far the greatest problems, however, have been the product of the comprehensive pattern of many fragmentary constituencies controlling parts of government and in effect exercising public authority. The lack of coordination has entailed a waste of resources. The failure to encompass in the scheme of politics all the interests and values important to the people of the states may during the years to come diminish the stability the states have enjoyed in the past. Should this prove true, the federal system will come under increasingly serious challenge.

Chapter 7

Preemption: The Politics of Land and Water

From the earliest days of the American nation, something approximating a natural right to the untrammeled occupation and exploitation of land and its resources for private benefit has been asserted by people living near the areas where publicly owned resources are located. Simple proximity has been offered as sufficient ground for appropriation, the claims often being made good against counterclaims on behalf of government or the national community. In a large sense, the persistent success of demands for private exploitation has become a tradition, conferring a degree of legitimacy on a wide variety of actions that give control of land and land policy to limited groups within the general population.

Perhaps the turning point in this long and dark history came with the establishment of *preemption* as a valid principle. Although there may be room for debate about the singular importance of this step, preemption stands for much in the evolution of land and agricultural policies. Very briefly, preemption was historically the process by which unoccupied public land was taken and settled and later paid for at a minimum price without competitive bidding. It became a right with the passage of a Congressional Act in 1841, but before that it had become a well-established practice through defiance of law, acquiesced in by helpless or collusive officers of government. In one sense, it expressed the democratic drive toward equality because it benefited indigent but enterprising squatters. In this same sense, it was an important stage in the evolution of the homestead policy which culminated in the Act of 1862. In another sense, however, it was a continuing demonstration of frontier lawlessness, sanctioned by the capitulation of government and the non-Western parts of the nation in the 1841 law.[1]

Preemption as a means of acquiring public land on a preferred basis came to an end in 1891, when accumulation of evidence that fraudulent entries were common persuaded Congress to repeal the Preemption Act. In any event, as Frederick Jackson Turner was then noting, the frontier in the sense of a definable boundary of free land had disappeared; with it had gone most of the simple opportunities for appropriation of public resources. Nevertheless, the now century-old tradition of private expropriation of resources did not vanish with the disappearance of the frontier. Substantial holdings of public land remained, for all that they were discontinuous; perhaps more important, the gradual growth in government activities having to do with natural resources opened new and enlarged opportunities for private exploitation of those resources.

The transition from nineteenth-century profligacy with public lands was not abrupt. Scandal surrounded the work of the General Land Office through the early decades of the twentieth century, despite determined efforts by the Progressives to bring the old loose ways under control. Minerals and timber became the major sources of temptation for weak officials and over-eager entrepreneurs. The disposition of coal lands in Alaska precipitated a major political explosion in the Pinchot–Ballinger affair.[2] The revestment of the Oregon and California lands further tarnished the name of government handling of rich public resources.[3] There were lesser but still well-known scandals. The reputation of public officials and government generally fared badly in these incidents, but the guilt was widely shared by the citizens who had corrupted the men of government. More, a major fault lay with the tradition of free-and-easy disposition of land that had dominated nineteenth-century policy and was yet very much alive, still enshrined in mineral laws giving easy possession of public resources—laws that even today have seen only minor reform.

For all that the history of American resource policy has been repeatedly and deeply scarred by corruption, exploitation, and scandal, the central intent—the seeking of an ideal of free and largely equal men in an agrarian society—has been Jeffersonian (or, perhaps more strictly, Taylorian). Governmental restraints upon land entry were directed to equality of opportunity in the vast domain; by the same token, however, they were chafing because they hindered acquisition by the many who yet were land-hungry. The scandals were scandals less because they involved theft of the common property than because the land was acquired by unfair means. Monopolies were created in land and its resources, a condition that threatened the very roots of agrarian democracy and the promise of America as it had been seen from the national beginnings; here was the making of a landed aristocracy, an evil foresworn with the early abolition of Old World laws of primogeniture and entail. Hatred of monopoly in all its forms has been a particular passion in America, an attitude that pervaded the Homestead Act and its revisions. Very nearly as much as the alarm raised by the visible waste of timber resources, it brought about the conservation movement of the early twentieth century; conservation meant "antimonopoly" as much as it meant preservation or "wise use."[4] Hatred of monopoly, in turn, was based less upon a particular vision of the workings of the economic order than upon an elemental passion for equality.

The currents of continuity and change, each of which set in so strongly near the beginning of the twentieth century, are visible at least in retrospect in several pieces of legislation of that time. Acts of 1891 and 1897 authorized the creation of forest reserves, land in the national domain whose wealth should not be dissipated for the benefit of a few. These laws were followed by the creation of the United States Forest Service to administer the vast territory involved. In one sense, these developments formally set a seal on the passing of the frontier and heralded the end of uninhibited private exploitation of public wealth in resources. Yet for all their overtones of drastic reform and obvious break with the past, these actions showed a strong thread of continuity. The spirit of the Forest Service was Progressive; the agency in fact stands as the prime administrative achievement of Progressivism, imbued as it was with hostility to monopoly and dedicated to "the greatest good of the greatest number in the long run"—the slogan of Gifford Pinchot, who voiced it with all the fervor of an original discoverer.

Another law of similar significance was the Newlands Act of 1902, which made possible public support of irrigation of the West's arid lands. This law was more clearly in the nineteenth-century tradition of placing public land in the hands of individuals, but extended the tradition because the lands now available for settlement were those which could be successfully cultivated by investment in irrigation works. And yet the change involved in active governmental assistance to the new generation of settlers was plain.

Though these new policies faced in different directions, they had much in common—first the fundamental concern with equality, then the implicit development of a substantial administrative organization. What had been achieved before by the relatively simple distribution of land would now be sought through active governmental programs. Another common trait could emerge fully only after some development, for all that it had been implicit from the beginning: the high valuation set upon an ideal of self-determination. With the reclamation policy this was fairly evident in the emphasis upon small farming units, written into law in the "160 acre limitation" (the figure was clearly an inheritance from the old homestead law). With the Forest Service, however, there was at the outset a presumption of public rather than private purpose, of national rather than local action. Yet in time the very absence of criteria for discriminating among policies for forest administration that was implicit in the unelaborated "greatest good" formula left the agency politically exposed and vulnerable. The direct consequence was the agency's building of political support upon local holders of power. Its administrative doctrine and structure thus came to reflect and respond to a fundamental reality of American politics: power in the United States is primarily *local* power. The elites to which the agency responded were the local elites in the areas where the Service operated, and the values it came to serve were their values.[5]

Forests and reclamation, however, were only two among many policy areas relating to land and resources in which these convergent tendencies have been visible. The complexities of the twentieth century have enveloped the issues of land and agricultural politics, so that it is not often easy to state what is essential in them. In the nineteenth century the issue was most frequently the simple taking possession of public land; in the twentieth it has more often been the taking possession of public policy. This has not been peculiar, as will be suggested later, to the sphere of land and agriculture. But the process has perhaps been somewhat clearer in matters relating to land and agriculture than elsewhere; furthermore, agriculture is the natural home and point of origin of the central tradition, localism, and through it, of the self-determination of small units.

II

Of all the areas of policy relating to land and agriculture, management and regulation of the Western arid lands probably offers the simplest and clearest illustration of the principles and forces under review here. Certainly these lands present problems in an obviously continuous line of evolution from nineteenth-century practice. Although in modern times the development of active administration has replaced a policy of almost complete *laissez faire*, the fundamental issues remain the same. The results achieved by the introduction of a more positive governmental program are to a considerable degree extensions of tendencies dominant in the late nineteenth century. The new program was conceived as a reform and a protection for public values; yet the perseverance of the strong tradition of localism minimized the change involved. Indeed, it is quite possible that the introduction of active governmental administration accentuated the pre-existing tendencies of social and economic organization. It is true that certain peculiarities of the local situations have contributed to development in these lands, but they do not disguise a picture bleaker and starker than any to be found elsewhere.

During the decades after the Civil War, the paths of settlement gradually pushed westward to the hundredth meridian and then beyond. This line, which roughly coincides with the western boundary of the area in which unirrigated farming is possible, marked out, together with the line of the Sierra Nevada and the Cascades, a vast region of dry lands, in which the population must always be sparse and the agricultural product meager. Yet Congress did not appreciate this condition for a long time, and the policies of land distribution that had been appropriate in the Mississippi Valley and eastward continued to be applied here. Except in the widely scattered river valleys with good soil, cultivation was not practical, and great tracts of land were destined to remain of little use for farming. This land was not adapted to homesteading as it was understood elsewhere. The one economic use much of it offered was grazing. Although the land remained in the public domain and part of the national heritage, Western stockmen early established the practice of using it for their herds as though it were their own. At first this was simply a matter of running stock over the public land; by the 1880s, however, the manufacture of barbed wire had been perfected and vast areas of the public domain were enclosed with it. The authority for this appropriation by cattlemen or large companies was that of the frontier West in its most romanticized form, "Sharp's 45s"; as a historian of public land policies notes, the land was open to homesteading, but the settlers needed to be bulletproof.[6] Two companies in Colorado alone managed through application of these technological developments to enclose a million acres each. The sturdy pioneer spirit of self-help and independence which found expression in such methods brought conflict among the stockmen and, particularly, between cattlemen and sheepmen. The costs of the process included violence, loss of life, and serious destruction of the range through overgrazing—as well as the establishment of a Western conviction that the public lands were there for the use of those nearby who could take them and enforce possession.

The chaos of these conflicts and the rising sense of outrage in some Eastern circles over the appropriation of national resources combined to produce suggestions that these public lands should be leased, at least some return being made to the public owners and some care being given to the condition of the lands themselves. A Public Lands Commission appointed in 1904 reported that although the public lands are theoretically free to all citizens, "as a matter of fact a large proportion has been parceled out by more or less definite compacts or agreements among the various interests." The chaos resulting from lack of legal control had caused "the ruin of millions of acres of otherwise valuable grazing territory."[7] Bills for leasing and regulation, however, were successfully resisted by the stockmen on the grounds that they had fought out their controversies among themselves and that the government had no proper grounds for intervening. As these bills were reintroduced repeatedly during the second and third decades of the century, however, the principal opposition came from the sheepmen, who suspected that they were the principal targets of the proposals.[8] With the advent of the Hoover administration in 1928, a favorite alternative of the stockmen received official blessing, namely that the vacant public lands should be transferred to the states in which they were located.[9] From Hoover's standpoint, this was a thoroughly logical corollary of his particular theory of government; from the stockmen's point of view it was a device second in attractiveness only to outright ownership by themselves of the land in question.

The Depression and the arrival of a new administration combined with widening concern for the problem of erosion to produce a new legislative effort for reform and for regulation of the grazing lands. Even so, there was a determined effort to include in the reform bill a provision that it should not take effect in a state unless the state's legislature approved, and that administration of grazing on the public lands should be "co-operative," with state officials participating. This remarkable provision was deleted from the bill, but only after a struggle.[10] The measure, the Taylor Grazing Act of 1934, reflected the outlook implicit in this attempt; indeed, it reflected the history of these lands ever since the first stockman had turned his animals onto them. The lands were looked upon as private opportunity for those who lived nearby. If they could not simply be taken without payment of taxes or fees, they should be under state rather than national regulation; but, since this had proved impossible, the "national" regulation should be placed in the hands of the local people themselves—the justification being the familiar array of arguments that local people knew more about the problem and that local administration was more democratic.

The plan that took effect under the Taylor Act was in fundamental outline the same which the early New Deal was applying in business with the NRA and in agriculture with the AAA and other measures. A system of grazing districts was to be established within which permits for grazing were to be issued under the authority and regulations of the Secretary of the Interior. Fees were to be paid by the permit holders. Perhaps the most important feature of the Act was a requirement that the Secretary, in making his regulations for administration of the districts, should act "in cooperation with local associations of stockmen." An amendment of 1936 required that administrative officers of the government down to district graziers should be residents of a Western public land state, and that in their selection consideration should be given to "practical experience."[11]

The administrative system that emerged was much more the expression of these provisions than of the Act's avowed purposes—to prevent overgrazing, provide for orderly use and improvement, and stabilize the livestock industry. Whatever may have been in the minds of the bill's sponsors, the questions of control of the administrative structure, and through it of the lands themselves, were the central issues. The actual reform took place slowly. Before a district could be established, a hearing had to be held, the land withdrawn from all forms of entry, and an administrative body created. At first, conferences were held with ranchers (some government representatives encountered personal threats), and then state committees of stockmen were elected to advise on the district boundaries; thereafter organization of the districts could take place. It is noteworthy that in some areas the process of putting the Act into effect was still going on more than a quarter century after its passage.[12]

The first Director of Grazing under the Taylor Act, F. R. Carpenter, was a constituent of Congressman Taylor, an important Colorado cattleman, and a clearheaded student of political reality. He was at once concerned about the deterioration of the Western ranges—particularly as they suffered from overgrazing by sheep—and firmly convinced of the necessity of gaining the support of Western stockmen—particularly cattlemen. Acting on the Grazing Act's provision that there should be cooperation with local stockmen, he issued in his first instructions to the small Grazing Service staff orders for special elections of district advisors to assist in management of the grazing districts. The advisors were to be elected by local stockmen in order to provide a "practical local viewpoint." Their function, in the Director's eyes, was no less than to be the local governing agencies regulating the districts.[13] Ultimately, the electors of these boards were the permittees of the districts themselves. Carpenter likened the advisors to jurymen and emphasized their great wealth of local knowledge. Although the election rules were copied from the Colorado laws for school districts, it is worth noting that the grazing districts derived no authority from the states and were not parts of local government in any formal sense. Formally, they were simply advisory. Nevertheless, Carpenter took satisfaction in the fact that their advice was followed in decisions on 98.3 per cent of the more than

14,000 licenses issued during the first fourteen months of the Act's operation. The Boards' performance demonstrated, he felt, "the genius of the American people for organization if given an opportunity."[14]

The Grazing Service, the responsible agency in theory, was only a small body from the very beginning. Carpenter was fearful of entrenched bureaucracy and maintained a small staff. Moreover, like some other administrators of this period, he strongly believed in "decentralized administration." He had an office in Washington, but field headquarters were in Salt Lake City, and there were regional offices in the Western states. This degree of decentralization, however, was insufficient, and in 1941, when pressure for moving non-defense activities away from Washington was strong, headquarters was placed in Salt Lake City. At the end of the war a new Director sought to establish a range rehabilitation program which would have involved hiring a large number of new range specialists. The Director also attempted to raise the very low grazing fees to some realistic relationship to the value of the forage. The consequence was an explosion from Senator McCarran of Nevada, a strong advocate of livestock interests, and the administrative structure was reorganized, the Director replaced, and the Grazing Service dismantled. Its personnel was reduced by 79 per cent and the remainder consolidated with the old General Land Office to create the Bureau of Land Management. Once again, further "decentralization" had taken place. So limited in funds was the government grazing staff that the advisory boards themselves allocated range improvement funds for salaries just to keep administration alive. With the advent of the Eisenhower administration, the cry for decentralization was renewed, and another reorganization took place. It would be difficult to see any further gains to be made in efficiency or other public values from such reorganization. It is fairly evident, however, that the persistent demands were more political than administrative in character. The genuine objectives of the cry for "decentralization" were the weakening of any lingering ties of the bureaucracy to Washington and the larger public constituency.

This pattern of administrative reorganization would have been largely meaningless had it not been for the development of the "advisory" boards. These had been originally established purely on the basis of the Taylor Act's vague statutory requirement to seek the cooperation of local stockmen. F. N. Carpenter's objective, however, was plainly that something more than cooperation should be provided by the boards. By 1939, apparently, stockmen suspected that the administrative action which had created the boards would be undone by other administrative action, and the district advisory boards were given a statutory basis. But the development of a useful idea was not to be restricted to such a small theater of operations, and in 1940 a National Advisory Board Council was created at a meeting of representatives of various districts. Shortly thereafter, state boards were created. All of these bodies were outside of government and had no official relation to it. Nevertheless, they held substantial power and the Grazing Service could not well ignore them; indeed, the NABC and the state boards ultimately were given official standing in the Federal Range Code. This was a simple recognition of reality—that the various boards were the governing bodies. It was also the legitimation of a very ambiguous condition.[15] "Decentralized administration" had not only brought "home rule on the range," but had created a strong national interest-group organization which was a public body when it was convenient and a private lobby when that was expedient.

The ambiguity in the position of the District Boards pervades the governing system of the public grazing lands. In particular, it imparts a peculiar meaning to the "decentralization" which has been sought so assiduously. In effect, there are here two parallel orders of government. One is the public bureaucracy of civil servants responsible in theory to the federal government and the people of the United States. Obviously their sense of responsibility is colored by the insistence that they be Westerners and possessed of "practical" experience in grazing on western lands; this in no way diminishes, however, the direction of their formal responsibility. The second order of government is the system of boards elected by the permit holders, which formally have no power other than to give advice to the civil servants and their federal chiefs. Thus, the difficulty of the federal government's dealing directly with local government—a difficulty made much of by critics when the relationship is between large cities and the federal government—is minimized in public discussion. Although recognition of the Boards in the Federal Range Code compromises the private character of these bodies, the Boards, especially at the levels of their state and federal associations, are effectively private political bodies. The ambiguity of formal status extends all the way, however, since the state boards consist of district board members chosen by the boards, and the National Advisory Board Council members are similarly chosen from the membership of the state boards.

In this situation "decentralization" has meant that the formal public service of civil servants is weak, whereas the system of boards is strong. Whether it is correct to say that the boards are actually decentralized is open to doubt. Certainly the board system is decentralized in the sense that people in the various district localities govern in the districts. It is more doubtful, however, that this decentralization is of dimensions other than geographical. Plainly, interests other than stockmen have been factored out of participation in the governing of these lands. True, the Boards have always had wildlife "representatives" in addition to the members elected by the stockmen permittees; in 1961, moreover, Secretary of the Interior Udall called for representations of other interests—mining, timber, conservation, recreation, and wilderness.[16] But this has not brought an appreciable dilution of stockman influence.

Almost as important as this concentration of power—centralization—on the dimension of functional interest is a similar effect *within* the stockmen's ranks. Here it is important to note that, as with other groups of almost any category, homogeneity is not complete. In the first place, the stockmen using the Western arid lands are not the only stockmen in the nation; indeed, Midwestern, Eastern, and Southern areas are, area for area, vastly more productive in support of domestic animals than the western grazing districts. Wesley Calef has offered a dramatic comparison of the largest grazing district in Wyoming and areas of comparable size in other regions. An area in Indiana and Illinois of comparable size to this Wyoming district produces ten times more cattle than "this land of the cowboy."[17] Yet the producers in the Midwest do not have the peculiar Federal support enjoyed by the users of public lands in the West. The problem thus is not a simple matter of assisting an industry as a whole.

A second important dimension of difference among stockmen is between cattlemen and sheepmen—a historic source of conflict, some of it involving violence. There appears to be some ground for believing that the administrative scheme developed under the Taylor Act has favored the cattlemen, especially as regards the nomadic sheepmen. For many years before passage of the Taylor Act, bands of sheep based on no nearby landholding had wandered over large areas of the public domain. These bands were pointed to as the chief culprits in causing land erosion, quite probably a justified charge if prior rights to land use were assumed to belong to cattlemen owning nearby land. Moreover, it was evident that sheep can cause more damage to land than cattle. The competitive overuse by the nomads and the nearby residents was a major reason for passage of the Taylor Act. It nevertheless remains clear that a lessened intensity of use of the public lands was implicit here, and the impact of this decrease in use had to fall on some stockmen more than on others.

The difference of interest between cattlemen and sheepmen overlapped another important difference, that between old and new users of the land. The Grazing Act carried a statement clearly intended to give preference in the issuance of permits to old established stockmen who were landholders or holders of water rights nearby, effectively eliminating many of the nomad sheepmen and leaving most of the others in an inferior position.[18] The provision was placed in effect with a system of administrative priorities that gave governmental sanction to the informal pattern of "range rights" on which established cattle-men had been insisting for some time.[19] Essentially, this ar-rangement tied the use of public lands to ownership of neigh-boring land or to the control of nearby water. This was not a notable change from previous practice (save for the publicly sanctioned elimination of nomad bands of sheep), but it did mark a considerable degree of legitimation and formalization of what had been achieved through the use of various forms of nonlegal power. Moreover, it constituted a capture of formal power for the benefit of established stockmen to the exclusion of would-be newcomers. Certainly it was the best of two worlds for the established stockmen: it secured the benefits of the pub-lic lands as though they were privately owned, but largely avoided the costs of private ownership. Fees were paid for the arrangement, but they were largely spent for improvements on the lands for the users' benefit.[20]

A fourth, and perhaps more important, difference of interest overlapped that between old and new users of land: the differ-ence between large and small ranchers. From the beginning of the advisory council system, "the large-scale, aggressive, alert, politically conscious ranchers tended to seize the initiative and secure election to the advisory boards."[21] The large ranchers were not everywhere and always the only members of the boards, but in general the local boards reflected the existing patterns of social and economic power in their communities. When the state and national organizations of advisory boards were formed, a similar development occurred. At the national level, indeed, the process was particularly visible; a list of of-ficials of the National Advisory Boards Council showed a re-markable coincidence of positions in the board system and posi-tions held in stockmen's associations. The men who held posts in the American National Cattlemen's Association, the National Woolgrowers Association, and the state affiliates of those or-ganizations very commonly also appeared as officers of the NABC.[22]

The ranchers' associations completed the organization of power. These had, indeed, existed previously, but with their leadership on the now official boards and board associations, and with the boards possessed of semiofficial governing power, public authority was for practical purposes in the hands of the organized ranchers—more particularly of the larger and previously more influential ranchers. The important change that occurred with the appearance of the board system of "home rule" was not so much that the large ranchers acquired power they had not enjoyed previously as that they successfully transformed that power into a working approximation of publicly sanctioned authority. Concurrently, they made good on their demands for geographical decentralization of the new public bureaucracy while effecting a real centralization of their own power as a functional group. Although the Grazing Service and, later, the Bureau of Land Management attempted to assert its proper authority as owed to a constituency larger than the ranchers, the attempts were defeated. Perhaps there is a long-term possibility, given the still remaining formal responsibility of the public bureaucracy to the constituency of the nation as a whole, that the ranchers' power to maintain autonomous control of public land resources may be checked. But the long history of these lands hardly encourages optimism about such an outcome.

There are various results of this pattern of control. First, in a number of places the system of self-governing districts has hardened rather than diminished the control of influential— and generally large—ranchers. The local democracy of self-determining districts has been disappointing. A low rate of participation in the elections held in the districts has probably reflected the feeling of those eligible to vote that the paraphernalia of democracy could change the situation little.[23] Tenure in office has been long, and established leaders among the stockmen have tended to be the officers. While it is difficult to trace this concentration of political power in a few hands to a concentration in the flow of economic benefits, studies in a few specific grazing districts suggest that the two are at least sometimes related. In Wyoming District 2, for example, 43 per cent of the district's ranchers use less than 2 per cent of all the range forage; 13 of the ranchers at the other end of the scale use 44 per cent.[24] The Soldier Creek unit of Oregon District 3 has been the scene of a massive struggle between officers of the Bureau of Land Management and the organized ranchers. The issue has involved a proposed reduction in use and distribution of the reduction proportionately among the users. This conflict cost a number of public servants their posts and resulted in many years of defeat for reform efforts; more important, it resulted in maintenance of large-ranch domination of the use of these lands and perpetuated destructive overuse of the lands themselves.[25] Thus, the general interest in conservation of soil has, on occasion at least, suffered from the pattern of power deriving from the autonomous system of government of these lands. Finally, despite a number of fee increases and some change in their distribution, rancher-permittees have had not only the subsidy involved in low charges for forage, but also benefits derived from expenditures by their own directing of public funds for improvements such as fences, wells, and reservoirs.

III

The interest and significance of the Taylor Grazing Districts lie less in the inherent importance of the public grazing lands or the Western stock-raising industry than in the almost diagrammatic simplicity of their political system. The industry and the lands themselves are of only minor importance to the nation's economy. But in probably no other public program of substantial size are the elements of power and control so easily visible or so stark. These same elements are present in many other spheres of political life in America—indeed, the argument here is that taken together they constitute the characteristic form of power in the United States—but usually they exist in situations of great complexity and are far less obvious.

Where policy relates to land and agriculture, the principle of first importance is decentralization—specifically, geographic decentralization. As suggested earlier, geographic decentralization is only one of several possible forms of political organization by small constituent units. Geographic decentralization, however, has had and retains a peculiar importance in American political development. Decentralization in this sense has not only shaped the politics of rural areas, but has also done much to form the tradition of small units seen as democracy itself so frequently found elsewhere. It is therefore worthwhile to look at situations in which the patterns are more obscured and more confused by the accidents of political life.

One of the most persistently troubling parts of national domestic policy is the development and use of water resources. Because the technology of water management involves similar construction skills, whether the task is the building of an ocean jetty for protection of shipping or the construction of a river dam for flood control and irrigation, the issues of water policy have mingled problems of navigation and agriculture. A further inherent complexity of water policy is the frequent conflict between flood control and irrigation, between the requirements for abundance and those for scarcity of water. Both problems exist in America, often in the same river basins; the one is most typically the problem of the lower part of the basin and the other the problem of the upper part. Then there are the problems of cities located along the major American rivers, not infrequently directly on the very flood plains of highly erratic streams. In the arid parts of the land it has recently become clear that climate varies over time, with irregular periods of serious drought followed by wet periods marked by occasional floods. The problems of land and water, then, are inherently difficult. For this reason alone, shortcomings and failures have probably been inevitable. In the scale of the undertakings that have been attempted, moreover, involving on occasion no less than the reversal of stream flow and the altering of the natural features of whole river basins, it is inevitable that some of the shortcomings should also be large.

Nevertheless, the most startling fact about the history of water projects in the United States is the degree to which their shortcomings have been associated with administrative failures. Again and again these shortcomings have proved to be the consequences of inadequate study—of water flow, of soils, of factors other than construction technology (and sometimes even of this)—and of faulty organization. In 1959, when the Senate Select Committee on National Water Resources looked back upon this history, it found that in the fifty years preceding its own efforts no less than twenty different national commissions or committees had been charged with examining these problems and seeking solutions.[26] These studies were accompanied by an almost torrential outpouring of other studies and plans by federal bureaus, state agencies, and private groups. Despite many differences, most of these studies emphasized with remarkable consistency the need for coordination among the agencies dealing with water.

Perhaps the most common argument has been that a river basin is a natural unit and projects affecting it should treat it as such. Repeatedly, also, the study commissions have recommended reorganization and transfer of particular agencies from one jurisdiction to another. Thus in 1923 President Harding recommended placing the civilian functions of the Army Corps of Engineers in the Department of the Interior.[27] Congress rejected the proposal. In 1932, under a general congressional authorization for reorganization, President Hoover ordered the same transfer of functions. Congress nullified the order.[28] In 1937 two different official studies, one for the Senate and one for the President, advocated administrative reorganization; both sought relocation of the civilian work of the Corps of Engineers, the one in Interior and the other in a Department of Public Works.[29] Nothing came of either recommendation. In 1949 the massive report of the First Hoover Commission on Reorganization of the Executive Branch made the familiar recommendation about the Corps (though one of the task force reports recommended establishment of a Department of Public Works).[30] The Report of the President's Water Resources Policy Commission (the Cooke Commission) of 1950 carried a despairing note about the prospect for carrying the Hoover Commission's recommendation into effect, but underlined the need for coordinating different agencies in each major river basin.[31] A

House Committee in 1952 decided that the problems of water resources could not be solved by administrative reorganization, but then proceeded to emphasize state responsibility.[32] The Second Hoover Commission sought to strengthen measures to control the agencies short of general reorganization, but did recommend transferring the dam construction functions of the Soil Conservation Service to the Corps of Engineers.[33] In the same year a Presidential Advisory Committee on Water Resources Policy observed, "The greatest single weakness in the Federal Government's activities in the field of water resources development is the lack of cooperation and coordination of the Federal agencies with each other and with the States and local interests." It recommended interagency committees to plan and coordinate such activities.[34]

Several points appear from this cursory summary. The first is the long persistence of the issue of administrative organization, on which studies of water problems have repeatedly focused and about which they have made similar recommendations. Second, these recommendations have consistently failed of adoption. The necessary coordination has seemingly proved impossible to achieve. The technical difficulties of planning in a complex field have been matched if not overshadowed by those of bureaucratic organization. Stated in this way, however, there is a defect of disproportion that amounts almost to an absurdity. What accounts for such long-standing national incapacity to do what has been recommended so often?

In broadest terms the answer is that administrative organization in this area has involved political problems of great importance. Failure to achieve administrative reorganization has been the consequence of failure to solve political problems. Recommendations for administrative change have at every point been recommendations for *political* reorganization. If effective administrative reorganization had been achieved, political change would have been implied. But the relationship between administration and politics was more direct than this suggests. The conflicts over administrative reorganization have themselves been political conflicts involving the distribution of power and the allocation of costs and benefits. It is not that there were related administrative and political conflicts, but rather that the conflicts were the same.

As the summary of attempts to reorganize the federal agencies dealing with water problems suggests, the role of first importance in this history of conflict belongs to the Army Corps of Engineers. Nearly every proposal for organizational change has involved the Corps; most frequently these recommendations call for the removal of its civilian functions to some other agency. These functions—the design, construction, and operation of navigation and flood control improvements—are in military hands only by an accident of history which first gave the Army a civilian responsibility early in the nineteenth century. The military character of the agency is probably not of major importance; at most, it has afforded supporters of the Corps a specious argument that the large-scale civilian projects give Corps officers training useful for national defense (training that reaches only a few hundred officers at any time).

What is vastly more important is that the Corps of Engineers has enjoyed a remarkable degree of autonomy within the defense establishment and the entire structure of government. Over long periods of time, the Chief of the Engineers has been formally responsible not through the Chief of Staff, but directly to the Secretary. But this situation has entailed little supervision or review of the Corps' activities by the Secretary.[35] On the face of things, this is an enviable situation for any bureaucratic unit; it seems to imply that the agency is at liberty to do as it sees fit. More realistically, however, such liberty is very dangerous to the agency enjoying it and not to be envied in the slightest, for it would expose the bureau to charges of irresponsibility and arbitrariness whenever it could not adduce unassailable criteria for its choices and actions. Such charges, made before the formally responsible parts of government, would leave the agency politically helpless and unlikely to survive.

Plainly, however, the Corps of Engineers has had an excellent record of survival. Its history goes back to the nation's founding and it has steadily added to its functions. Though attacks upon it have been so forceful that three Presidents have supported movements to transfer its civilian functions, such efforts have been notable failures. Clearly, the Corps has been able to muster an impressive degree of political power in order to deflect these challenges. What are the sources of this power, and how has it been mobilized?

The first factor has already been underlined: the Corps' virtual autonomy within the bureaucratic structure. This is a negative factor, but it is important. Essentially it means that the Corps has not actually been responsible to the national constituency represented by the President. It has repeatedly been able not to respond to demands to coordinate its activities with other programs. The conflicts that have marked its history have, it is true, usually taken place in the context of particular regional conflicts, but the issues have been none the less national. It must be remembered that a direct connection exists between the national constituency and diversity, between the national constituency and the broad inclusive constituency in any given area.[36] If the Corps had been responsive to the wishes, even the orders, of the presidency, a quite different pattern of power would have existed and the consequences in distribution of benefits of the Corps' activities within various areas might also have been different. The record of presidential inability to make the Corps responsive to the presidential office has been reflected on occasion in the virtual defiance of a President's authority by the Corps. No more dramatic example could be found than the closely studied incident of the building of the Kings River dam in California. Although a memorandum from President Franklin Roosevelt to the Secretary of War said very curtly, "I want the Kings and Kern River projects to be built by the Bureau of Reclamation and not by the Army Engineers," the dam was built by the Engineers.[37]

A second element in the situation is the close relationship the Corps of Engineers has long had with Congress. This remarkably cordial association is the product of a long history in which the Corps has developed a series of procedures nicely designed to serve the constituent needs of a large number of

Congressmen and Senators. As the prospective builder of large and costly public works in the districts of these elective officers, the Corps has had much to offer to the job security of Congressmen and Senators. Since the Engineers' activities in navigation and flood control have costs that cannot readily be charged to their beneficiaries and accordingly are borne by the federal government, the Corps' cooperation in developing construction projects in particular congressional districts is especially valuable. The process of logrolling that goes on among Congressmen traditionally produces a rivers-and-harbors bill that is little more than a simple totalling of miscellaneous projects in a large number of congressional districts. This process has been so notorious that some cynics have taken rivers-and-harbors as a working definition of the "pork barrel."[38]

The peculiar structure of Congress and its corporate folkways have contributed greatly to the system of political power that has been built around the Corps of Engineers. There is no better recent documentation of Woodrow Wilson's nineteenth-century thesis that American government is congressional government, that is to say, government by congressional standing committees. Several committees of Congress have long regarded the Corps with "a proprietary interest" and have consistently acted as its especial guardians when moves for reform have been afoot.[39] The House Committees on Rivers and Harbors and on Flood Control and the Senate Committee on Commerce have been exceedingly reliable friends of the Corps, which has rewarded them with unsurpassed loyalty. These committees have regularly been composed of members from districts or states with opportunities for employment of the Engineers' talents. Although the reality of the situation is thus that only *some* Congressmen and Senators have a proprietary interest in the Corps, the latter has been able to assert with impunity that it is "an agency of the legislative branch."[40] This assertion, conjuring up as it does analogies with the General Accounting Office and the Library of Congress, would be merely absurd if it were not an approximate description of the actual situation at various times.

The third element in the Engineers' power is a number of interest-group organizations. It would be difficult to enumerate all the associations that properly belong on the roster arrayed behind the Corps of Engineers and its friends in congressional committees. Certainly, many local chambers of commerce would belong, as would various construction industry associations and a number of organizations specially formed for the promotion of particular projects: the Atlantic Deeper Waterways Association, the Ohio Valley Conservation and Flood Control Congress, and others. The crowning organizational achievement, however, is the National Rivers and Harbors Congress. This body, formed in 1901, continues as a thriving voluntary association with more than 7000 members, 50 state groups, and affiliations by state, city, and county agencies, water and land development associations, business firms, and various other groups. Among the individual members are government officials at all levels, members of Congress (honorary members, but some are active in the organization), officers of the Corps of Engineers engaged in rivers and harbors work, and contractors.[41] The good fellowship this organization promotes among these varied affiliates and individuals is reflected in a fine display of cooperation whenever projects of the Engineers are before Congress or when hostile reformers are seeking change.[42] Perhaps the barriers presented by the federal system, the separation of powers, and the distinction between what is public and what is private have seldom been so efficiently overcome as within the cordial and encompassing interpersonal relationships of the Rivers and Harbors Congress.

The fourth element in this system of power is the list of economic interests in particular localities that stand to gain from the Engineers' manner of allocating national resources. Some are navigation companies, some are construction firms, others are property owners in the flood plains of major rivers. By an odd quirk, some landowners seeking water for irrigation have been partisans of the Corps. The dams the Corps constructs can often serve for irrigation as well as flood control. And where authorization for construction of such dams has gone to the

Corps the taxpayers, rather than the landowners, have paid for the benefits to irrigation—a fact certainly of some importance in assembling the support which enabled the Corps to defeat President Roosevelt on the Kings River issue.[43]

The final element in the system is fundamental to all the others: the high degree of decentralization in the Engineers' planning and operations. This is only in part a matter of administrative organization; it is as much a matter of outlook and style. Structurally, the Corps is divided on a geographic basis into a large number of Districts, grouped in a number of Divisions. This decentralization insures that the head of each District Office is sufficiently close to the communities where work is being done that cordial relationships are maintained with community leaders. The officers in charge of these offices give speeches to local groups and otherwise see that friendly contact is maintained with locally important leaders and organizations.

The orientation to localities implied in this decentralized form of organization is directly related to the extreme degree of autonomy the Corps has asserted in the past, and has provided the basis of political support necessary to make good on it. Decentralization and local orientation have also been essential to the Corps' close relationship with key congressional committees. Congressmen are necessarily sensitive to the desires of powerful groups in their districts, and the close consultation and accommodation offered by the Corps' local offices ensures that Congressmen will be aware of the local services of the Engineers. By the same token, the Engineers' localism is particularly well adapted to the accommodation of locally powerful interest groups. This is not to say that *all* local interests are accommodated or served by the Corps. Not all of these are locally powerful—as for example the small farmers in the San Joaquin Valley who might have benefited from a plan of irrigation development other than that made by the Corps.[44] For the peak organization, the National Rivers and Harbors Congress, the localism of the Corps has undoubtedly been thoroughly satisfactory, since the basis of its own unity has been simple logrolling for the benefit of a great number of local-interest groups. Decentralization on a geographic basis and autonomy within the federal administrative system have essentially been different aspects of the same reality. A lessening of autonomy would have subjected the Corps to the demands of the President's constituency. A greater degree of centralization would also have tended to establish responsibility to a larger constituency. Actually, however, the established system has enforced responsibility to an array of localities and to the locally powerful interests.

The character of this system of power is also directly related to the policies the Engineers have followed and the values these have served. What emerges most clearly from all examinations of the Corps' operations is that the agency has been preoccupied with particular projects. It has also frequently been concerned with only one or a few of the various interests and values involved in its undertakings. It has only reluctantly and under the compulsion of competition from rival agencies acceded to the demands from groups outside its own constituency for benefits that could be achieved from its potentially multipurpose projects. It has persistently been charged with failure to conceive of its river projects in basin-wide contexts. These are serious but long-standing charges. It is difficult to escape the conclusion that the power system of which the Corps of Engineers is an important part is the significant reality and that the discriminations of its policy are inherent in that reality.

Although efficient political and administrative organization for water management would be very difficult even if only one agency was responsible for it, the problem is in fact much more complicated. Other agencies are on the scene and, like the Corps of Engineers, have their own political forces arrayed behind them. Each in some degree represents different values and each has different purposes and different technologies. None has so well-developed or so efficient a political machine as the Corps, but together they introduce much confusion and chaos into what might otherwise be a clear, if rather ugly, picture. On the face of things, the presence of these other agencies and power systems seems to indicate a real possibility of achieving that balance of interests modern pluralists hold ideal. Some recent experience suggests that the entry of a new agency with different goals may be a moderating influence and help to create a general policy more in the interest of a large constituency than previous policy. Other experience, however, indicates another possibility: logrolling instead of compromise and jurisdictional demarcation instead of cooperation in the general interest.

The second entry in the struggle to manage the nation's water resources was the federal Bureau of Reclamation (formerly the Reclamation Service). This agency, which came into being as a result of the Newlands Acts of 1902, has had a sectional character from its very beginning. Since its original and primary purpose was related to irrigation, its activities were limited by statute to the seventeen Western states. For a long time, the agency's effective headquarters was in Denver, but it shifted in the late 1940s to Washington.[45] Today it has seven regional offices, all in the West, and a district office in Alaska. Although the Bureau might therefore seem to be more decentralized than the Corps of Engineers, the contrast is more apparent than real. As has been suggested, the Corps managed to achieve a politically effective degree of decentralization, although it had to exist within the context of a national agency. The Bureau probably did not have the same degree of narrow localism built into either its structure or its ideology, and in contests with the Corps it has accordingly suffered a political disadvantage. This disadvantage is directly related to the Bureau's regionalism, an orientation that is, at any rate, broader than the local orientation of the Corps. At the same time it should be kept in mind that the Bureau's primary function in the development of irrigation, with its roots in the historically egalitarian land policy and its requirement for some degree of repayment by beneficiaries, has also handicapped it politically.

Nevertheless, the Bureau has enjoyed the great political advantage that the arid lands within its territorial assignment cover or include significant parts of seventeen states. This fact has given it the generally reliable support of a large number of Senators, support that has been most readily available when no rivalry with other water agencies has been present. Irrigation has often been regarded by the arid part of the Western region as the very basis of its economy; indeed, one assessment put it that "The development of the West since Daniel Webster's time is based largely on putting water to use for irrigation of land."[46] As it stands, the statement (made in a study requested by Wayne Aspinall, Congressman for one of these areas), is absurd, but it does reflect the importance attached to irrigation —and thus to the activities of the Bureau—in particular areas of the West.

Like the Corps of Engineers, the Bureau of Reclamation has had its own private-interest-group organization, the National Reclamation Association, formed in 1932 when the public agency seemed threatened in Congress. The Director of the Bureau, Elwood Mead, played a dominant role in its creation. The group meeting in 1932 feared that appropriations to the Bureau might be drastically cut, and—probably as disturbing —that the agency might be transferred to the Department of Agriculture. The Association today has some 4100 members in seventeen state associations. The members include officers of irrigation districts, canal companies, railroads, chambers of commerce, and businessmen.[47]

The National Reclamation Association, however, has not been an automatic supporter of the Bureau. When during the New Deal era electric power came to be an important element in the agency's program, Secretary Ickes sought to apply a policy of cheap publicly distributed power from the Bureau's dams. This policy and some appointments in the Bureau pre-cipitated a strong conflict between the agency and the Associa-tion.[48] The struggle is interesting for a number of reasons. First, an agency cannot rely on a supporting interest-group organiza-tion, even though the latter is substantially its creation, when the agency's purpose undergoes change. Second, the same un-reliability develops with the appearance of a potentially new clientele. In this instance, the old supporters, concerned primarily with irrigation, perceived the possibility of lowered charges on federally irrigated land if the proceeds from the sale of electricity were allocated for that purpose, whereas the Ickes policy would have allocated these benefits to the consumers of electricity. Third, the active role of the Secretary of the Interior represented a sharp prospective increase in the size of the Bureau's constituency and a strong measure of centralization of direction in Washington. Fourth, Ickes' proposed plan also created conflict between supporters of public and private distribution of electricity. It is noteworthy that in its struggle, the Reclamation Association acquired the support of the private utilities. All these features of the contest were closely related.

The most notorious aspect of water policy in the United States, however, has been the lack of coordination and the rivalry between the Corps of Engineers and the Bureau of Reclamation. Both have been builders of dams and on a number of occasions have come into head-on conflict, the best-known instance being the building of the Kings River dam. Here the Bureau had the support of a popular President, but the political resources of the Corps were too strong and the Engineers built the dam. This incident was a particularly disgraceful display of disunity in government and evoked widespread expressions of distaste. Accordingly, when the struggle between the two agencies reached a serious point over the much more important issue of a plan for the Missouri basin, both parties suddenly discovered that they had a common interest in survival.

The area drained by the Missouri and its tributaries has had a history of both drought and flood. At various times opinion has held that its climate has changed; only in fairly recent times has it been generally understood that it is subject to irregularly alternating moist and dry cycles. Public works for both irrigation and flood control have therefore existed in the area since rather early days. Different studies of the region, however, have repeatedly emphasized that its problems are exceedingly complex and interrelated, and most have emphasized that proper planning would require treatment of the basin as a unit, a point that has also been made about other river basins. Nevertheless, the Corps of Engineers continued to regard the area as a problem in flood control to be solved by flood control dams and levees—and as opportunity for construction projects. The Bureau of Reclamation, on the other hand, continued to regard it as a problem in irrigation to be solved by the building of dams and canals for irrigation—and as opportunity for construction projects. By the early 1940s, each agency had a collection of projects of its own design. Though the two "plans" were in part complementary, to a considerable degree they were in conflict. A major collision between two political aggregations of agencies, congressional supporters, and interest-group claques seemed imminent.

Instead, during the course of one short month, representatives of the Bureau and the Corps met and "reconciled" the two plans. The resulting plan was then hurriedly presented to Congress, which gave its approval and a mandate for speedy construction. For those observers who felt that the primary evil was conflict between the agencies and the highest good sheer harmony, the Pick-Sloan Plan (it was named for the respective chiefs of the Corps and the Bureau) should have been something of a revelation. Substantially, it was a simple consolidation of almost all the projects proposed by both agencies, with none of the inherent conflicts of purpose resolved and with specific glaring inconsistencies retained. The rationale of the reconciliation was very simply and transparently political. It was the sort of agreement that would not have been surprising had it been made by two sovereign powers confronted by a third at whose expense the two could collaborate for their mutual benefit. In the Missouri Basin, however, the third party consisted of the United States and those members of its broad constituency whose interests were not served by either agency within the territories that the jurisdictional settlement allotted to each.[49]

Peace, at any rate, might have been a result of the political settlement between the Corps and the Bureau had not a new champion been preparing to enter the lists: the United States Department of Agriculture, as represented by the Soil Conservation Service (SCS). In 1948 the Department issued a proposal for a vast new program.[50] Although the initial proposal related to the great prize, the Missouri Basin, the new conception had more extensive application. It was that flood control and poor agricultural conditions could best be served by "stopping the raindrops where they fall." Floods and erosion should be prevented by "project-type undertakings" in small watersheds, that is, at the headwaters of the streams.[51] As the idea grew, it seemed to become a panacea for all the problems of water in rural America (and even those of municipalities as well). Though water experts were extremely skeptical that action in the small watersheds could prevent major floods, as enthusiasts for the SCS scheme seemed to be suggesting, the general plan developed political strength and in 1954 the Watershed Protection and Flood Prevention Act passed Congress. Very quickly, the program mushroomed; for the fiscal year of 1955 its appropriation was a modest $7,250,000, but by 1959 this figure had more than tripled.[52] With the almost limitless opportunities in sight, the "take-off" point in program development had now been reached.

The passage of the 1954 Act came at an opportune time for the Soil Conservation Service, which was just then being sorely pressed by rivals within the Department of Agriculture which by now had the support of the Republican administration.[53] The SCS had unsuccessfully sought to build a political base in local soil conservation districts, bodies which were legally creatures of the states and which stood as units of local government. Despite the support of a private-interest-group organization, the National Association of Soil Conservation Districts, the agency was not faring well.[54] In the tradition of the Department of Agriculture, the SCS formulated its new program on the basis of a very strong localism. Not only should local initiative be relied on for starting projects, but planning and execution would be joint undertakings of local, state, and federal agencies, and private landowners and operators would have a

full voice. Here were foundations of great political strength in
any prospective contests. The other element, of course, was
that however much was said about the inculcation of technical
modes of treating land to prevent erosion, the really important
part of the program was the construction of dams—not large
ones, but a multitude of them. The construction industry could
not have been expected to ignore the new venture.

The emergence of the Department of Agriculture (especially
of the Soil Conservation Service) as a rival of the established
titans, the Corps of Engineers and the Bureau of Reclamation,
was not recognized immediately. That came later with establishment of an interagency committee to prepare a "comprehensive, integrated plan" for the Arkansas, White, and Red
River basins in 1950. This large area included all or parts of
eight Southwestern states, and was only somewhat less of a
prize than the Missouri Basin. Formally, a large number of
agencies were involved in the survey, but the major rivals were
the Corps of Engineers, which was already established with
authorized flood control projects in the area, and the Soil Conservation Service, which was seeking entry on a large scale. In
light of the Corps' openly expressed opposition to the whole
project and the jealousies exhibited by other agencies at an
early stage, the commission given to the study committee, composed of representatives of all the agencies, required unanimous
agreement for any action it should take[55]—the sort of condition
normally associated with negotiations between nations.

Behind the agencies engaged in these negotiations important
and different interest groups were aligned. The Corps had its
usual array of groups concerned with protection from major
floods. The Department of Agriculture had the support of upstream farmers, who were less concerned about major floods
than about the more frequent minor ones. The difference in
orientation proved critically important as the technologists
from the different agencies sought to take the first steps toward
fulfillment of the committee's mission, an integrated plan. No
agreement was possible on either standards of construction or
the allocation of prospective benefits and costs for particular

projects within the basins or at the Washington level of inter-departmental collaboration. An early attempt to write a "Memorandum of Understanding" between the Corps and the Department of Agriculture failed completely. This proposed treaty would have recognized particular zones of influence, but the remaining "zones of mutual interest" proved an insoluble problem. The Department of the Interior also sought to solve the problem by dividing the territory on a jurisdictional basis, the western part to go to the Bureau of Reclamation and the eastern part to the Corps of Engineers. This proposal also had to be dropped. In the end, after five years of effort, the committee produced a Report, which in light of its original commission could only be regarded as a confession of failure. The plans submitted were merely the collected and separate proposals of the various agencies.

As the Soil Conservation Service watershed program has grown, dam construction has become more and more the heart of the activity. Like the Corps of Engineers, the SCS has acquired a project orientation. The local watershed districts, formally organs of local government, have not been meshed with larger units of government and have preserved and probably intensified the narrowness of purpose implicit in small units and narrow constituencies. By the same token, however, the Service has achieved a strong political base after years of wandering in the political wilderness. One of the ironies of the situation is that some despairing observers have concluded that rational coordination of water plans would be better achieved by giving the problem over to the states. This is perhaps the measure of the degree to which the major federal agencies have themselves created their own political systems and relied upon utter fragmentation of the public.[56]

Ultimately, the most disturbing aspect of the record of water management efforts sketched here is the loss in public values involved. The process of policy making has been carefully attuned to the demands of localities and the separate interests of a relatively few groups of the general population, whether that population is conceived on a national, regional, or local basis.

Waste has been inescapable, whether of money or resources; duplication and mutual frustration of plans have been frequent. Perhaps more important, some important values have been almost wholly lost. Some of these, notably scenic protection and purity of water, have been of such general interest that they seemed to be no one's concern and hence unworthy of any consideration in planning. Thus during the 1950s a concerted campaign was mounted for a series of large projects of dubious economic value on the Colorado River, to be built by the Bureau of Reclamation. These projects would destroy the scenic grandeur of most of the as-yet little known canyons of the Colorado and its tributaries; one in particular would have inundated the principal features of Dinosaur National Monument with a fluctuating reservoir. Rather belatedly a number of national conservation organizations organized opposition to this one project. The opposition struck such widespread sympathy that one New England Congressman remarked he had received more mail opposing this dam than on any other subject—foreign aid, price supports, or anything else.[57] The conservationists were at a disadvantage in that they had to appeal to a national constituency of a diffuse character, whereas the Bureau had all the advantages of the locally oriented political machinery. A really massive national campaign was conducted by the conservationists, however, and the economic interest of a strong group of California water users joined in opposing the Colorado scheme. In the end, the particular dam was deleted from the plan, but the other dams were approved, and the great scenic resource of Glen Canyon has already been destroyed.

The outcries of the conservation groups have also done much to alert the general public to its interests in the quality of water. Pollution has long been a serious problem, and although its evils have been fairly obvious, until recently no agency dealing with water problems had undertaken to deal with it on a significant scale. The surge of conservation efforts in the 1950s, however, culminated in proposals for some new agency to deal with the problem. These proposals were sound in that it is usually necessary to create a new administrative structure to serve a purpose that is either new or in the interest of groups excluded from the established political structures of which older agencies are parts—even where the established structures might be considered to have clear jurisdictional authority to include such purposes in their work. The threat of a new agency was averted by the established powers in water matters, but Congress passed a new Act, the Federal Water Pollution Control Act of 1956, giving the new responsibility to the United States Public Health Service. This was a conservative choice, inasmuch as the Public Health Service has long had close ties to the health services of the various states and so could be relied upon not to disturb unduly the established power relationships. The subsequent Water Supply Act of 1958 authorized the Corps of Engineers and the Bureau of Reclamation to include storage in their reservoirs for municipal and industrial water. A 1961 amendment to the Water Pollution Control Act required these agencies to take water quality control into consideration. And in his natural resources message of 1961, President Kennedy supported the demand of the Senate Select Committee on National Water Resources for comprehensive river basin plans by 1970.[58]

By the early 1960s, then, there were some grounds for believing progress toward the development of a politically effective general constituency for the work of government in the affairs of water was in sight. With it there was hope for more rational planning for the variety of ends that are involved in this area of policy. Nevertheless, the record to this point has been unfortunate. The Senate Select Committee's recommendation for comprehensive plans was a repetition of what had been said many times before. Proposals for valley authorities, as in the Columbia and Missouri basins, had only brought tightening of the systems of power and temporary treaties of boundary jurisdiction among project-oriented agencies. Perhaps the growth of cities and the growing response to the national conservation organizations will accelerate the change. The difficulties, however, will continue to be great, and the task of adjusting policy to a broader, more inclusive constituency will be large. For a fundamental readjustment in the relationships of power is involved.

IV

In one sense agricultural politics is of a piece with the politics of land and water. All have their roots in a common past and all share a geographic foundation. The time when there was an identity among them, however, is now distant, and increasingly they seem separate worlds. Agricultural politics itself appears to disintegrate under examination into a welter of different contests and policies out of which chaos sometimes seems the only principle to emerge. Certainly the various discussions of this particular political universe often leave the impression that they are treating different subject matter. This very complexity, however, is a clue to the evolution which has occurred, for it is no longer true that agriculture is a single industry or even a distinctive way of life. Perhaps it was never true that all farmers were alike or had many common problems. Yet the differences among them are greater and more visible than in the past. In some degree, these differences are the consequence of technological advance and increase of specialization; they are also related to the form of political organization that has evolved.

During the period between 1896 and 1920 a major reconstruction of farm politics took place. The former year marked the final collapse of efforts to build a party of farmers. With the disappearance of the Populist Party, all chances for a broadly based agrarian party vanished. Abstractly and in retrospect, there were two alternatives for political organization among farmers at that point. One was incorporation within a general political party—to some extent the course followed for a time beginning in 1896, when the Democratic Party assumed some of the Populist demands and the latter became obliged to nominate the Democratic candidate for President. The other was to formulate a narrower and much less comprehensive organization. The long-term reconstruction took place upon this basis.

Save for its later and culminating phases, the development of the American Farm Bureau Federation occurred without plan or foresight.[59] By 1920, when the national federation was formed, however, all the elements of a new structure of power had been found and fitted together. As a whole, it was an anomaly: to state the situation as simply as possible, the constituent units were public bodies, but their state and national federations were private organizations. Attempts were made to escape the dilemma and its potential consequences by laying claim to the advantages of both statuses, public and private; but ostensibly the problem was formal, and Americans have seldom troubled themselves unduly over formality. Some critics did object and recurrent demands have been made that the relationship between the county farm bureaus and the county agents be officially ended. There have been orders to this effect and many struggles, yet pragmatism has prevailed and divorce (if it is that) has been both slow and gradual.[60] Like many other formal issues, however, this was neither meaningless nor unimportant. The distinction between what is public and what is private has always been a foundation of liberalism, and this was the issue here. If these statements and the issue as it was formulated are abstract, the underlying problem was real and often very concrete.

The Farm Bureau as a national organization was a spectacular success almost from its beginning. Virtually its entire original program became legislation. But suddenly there were no new worlds to conquer, or so it seemed, and the Bureau's bipartisan bloc in the Senate faltered from lack of direction and disintegrated.[61]

The performance of the Congressional "Farm Bloc" was the result of the Farm Bureau's sheer virtuosity in lobbying; it was also the first achievement of a new form of farm organization. It showed with unmistakable clarity what had occurred to the politics of agriculture. So far as the farmers were concerned, the parties were in eclipse. Just as it was evident that farmers were a declining minority of the population (the 1920 census was the first to betray a decline in their absolute numbers), agricultural organization had been reformulated on the basis of a narrowed constituency. Instead of representation by an agrarian party—or by the Republican or Democratic parties—representation of farmers was now by a general farm organization, as a class, and through a pressure group.

There were other farm organizations, of course. The Grange survived, and occasionally it seemed to give forth echoes from its own militant past. However, the disaster that had overtaken it many years before and the greater disaster that had overwhelmed the Farmers Alliance when it had transformed itself into the Populist Party were lessons in caution that the custodians of the Grange never forgot. The fraternalism of its peculiar tradition, with its ritual and vague religiosity, was the sanctuary into which it had retreated long before and within which organizational survival could be safely assured. It was an unadventurous policy, but the lessons of militancy had been bitter. The National Farmers Union was a little different. By origin, it was a direct heir of Populism, both in leadership and in tradition. Its two bases, among the wheat farmers of the prairies and the cotton growers of the Deep South, gave it an internal tension that was not relieved until the latter gradually crumbled, leaving the Union with a labile and frequently belligerent constituency of wheat growers. This gave the Farmers Union the advantages of relative homogeneity, but it also condemned the organization to a largely regional standing. There were also commodity organizations, but their time still lay in the future.[62]

For all that the Grange and the Farmers Union were regarded as general farm organizations, the Farm Bureau was something quite different, as its exploit of organizing the "Farm Bloc" clearly demonstrated. Such a frontal attack on the party system, however, was too much to make good on for any long period of time. The Farm Bureau ran into trouble in the House of Representatives, and before long the bloc organization of the Senate collapsed.[63] The Federation's power, however, had a foundation in the peculiar relationship between the county Farm Bureaus and the county agents. Most agents were publicly paid organizers and functionaries of the Farm Bureaus; at the same time they were the Department of Agriculture's only field service across the nation. In theory public and private servants concurrently, the county agents were effectively immune from Department orders and domination. The substantial national support given to the extension system was funneled through grants-in-aid to the states. Only trivial federal restrictions went with these gifts. The agencies for state supervision of the agents were the land-grant colleges of agriculture, which maintained their own independence from political direction. Even within the colleges, the extension system tended to be rather autonomous. In effect, then, the agents were most closely tied to the local counties in which they worked, where they were beholden to county government and even more to the Farm Bureaus they had organized and which they served as partial employees. Officially, their status was more than ambiguous: they were national, state, and local officials; they were also privately employed. Informally, however, there was little doubt where their effective political responsibility lay—to the locally influential farmers. And these were well knit into the Farm Bureaus.

The plan of organization which the Department of Agriculture recommended to the county agents was to take particular care to gain the support of the better farmers, that is to say the more successful and prosperous.[64] The "principle of leadership" has been one of the main tenets of Extension Service education, for seemingly excellent reasons. The more prosperous farmers would be the most likely to adopt new techniques; they would, moreover, be the most influential members of their communities and their examples would accordingly be the most likely to be followed. In addition, however, whether by chance or by intuitive design, this was a plan of proved effectiveness wherever some minimum change in the ways of traditional societies has been sought. As anthropologists have reputedly phrased it in advice to colonial administrators: Respect the native culture and work through the local headmen. The precept has worked as well with street corner gangs in city slums as with African tribes.[65]

Whatever success this method had in spurring the adoption of new farming methods, the technique had brilliant results as an organizing principle. County and local Farm Bureaus spread across most of the nation. There were several fundamental reasons for their success, entirely aside from the activity of the publicly paid organizers, the county agents. First, organization of the local Farm Bureaus followed the structure of the local informal organization and status systems, coopting the "natural leaders" of these systems. Second, however unintentionally, it passed over the lower ranks of rural society—the "poorer" farmers and those who were generally unsuccessful and without power; to this extent, it achieved an important measure of homogeneity. There were divisions among farmers on other dimensions, it is true, but in any given locality divisions along the lines of wealth and power were likely to be the important ones. The selective principle followed made it unnecessary to reconcile opposing claims between classes.

Here was the real value of decentralization and organization on a "grass roots" basis: it brought strength and stability. It avoided a "mass politics" with all of its presumed dangers of irrationality and radicalism. It made for informality and the avoidance of law, with its formalities and rigidities. With organization on a local basis the human warmth of neighborhood association was possible. By the same token, however, decentralization meant a narrowed constituency. It was, for the Farm Bureaus, a constituency narrowed beyond mere locality; it was narrowed also on a basis of "better farmers." It mobilized the social power of the informally structured local societies. And on this basis it made possible the national organization of the American Farm Bureau Federation as a federation of federations of local elites. Given the organization's relative class homogeneity, a strong national organization was possible through the system of logrolling that has been seen elsewhere. At the same time, decentralization of governmental administration meant that the national government was unable (as well as unwilling) to control its own employees, the county agents. In practice, this was the meaning of the best of both possible worlds, private and public, demanded by the Farm Bureau in its relationship with the Extension Service.

The practical significance of this structure of power did not emerge immediately when the national Farm Bureau was formed. There was the overly ambitious start of the "Farm Bloc" period; then agriculture entered a long depression and Bureau leadership faltered. There were, moreover, serious internal problems to be solved. In part these were sectional, the conflict of interest between the South and the Middle West; more fundamentally, however, they were conflicts between producers of different commodities. This was the issue aptly known within the Bureau as "commodityism," a disease even more serious today than in the 1920s and one which may ultimately bring down the organization.[66]

After a decade of groping, the Farm Bureau Federation came into its own with the inauguration of the New Deal. The Agricultural Adjustment Act was drafted in the Federation's Washington office. The measure required a system of local administration and its establishment was given over to the Extension Service. Administration here involved the allocation of benefits and restrictions, payments for restricting production, and restraints on production. This, the Department's first real "action program," was organized on the basis of local farmer committees and, not surprisingly, local Farm Bureaus were intimately involved. Here was a major payoff for the kind of organization that had gone into the Farm Bureau system. At this point, farm policy and its most important part, administration, had been taken into the possession of the private organization.[67]

The New Deal, however, had other impulses and encompassed other constituencies. A strong President was at the helm and, as President, he had a broad constituency that included poorer as well as better farmers, tenants as well as landlords, migrants as well as employers. A pragmatic movement, the New Deal was open to demands for dealing with the long-standing problem of soil erosion and the possibility of rural electrification. In attempting to cope with rural poverty, it was manifestly unrealistic to rely on the Agricultural Extension

Service, the agency on whose shoulders the responsibility would most reasonably seem to lie; even Extension Service spokesmen agreed that its agents' services had largely gone to the most successful farmers—as indeed had been planned from the beginning.[68] As often happens, to effect a change of policy or to serve a new clientele it was necessary to rely on a new administrative agency (as the introduction of new functions in water management illustrates).

To meet the problem of rural poverty, then, a new administrative structure had to be created. The major stream of agricultural policy in the New Deal and ever since has involved prices of farm products on the market and the problems of commercial farmers. Despite prevailing mythology, however, these farmers were only a part of the farm population. For many years approximately half of the farms produced 90 per cent of the products going to market, a division that remained remarkably stable throughout the period 1920–1940. (Since that time, the Department of Agriculture has changed the definition of "farmers" so that comparisons are difficult; certainly the redefinition suggests that the Department sees its constituency in fairly definite class terms and that noncommercial farmers are not among its "clientele.") Obviously, devices to rig the prices of agricultural commodities by government action had only minimal bearing on the problem of rural poverty, but this fact has not prevented justification of the price programs by appeals to statistics showing the low-income character of farming as a whole.

An administrative structure to accommodate the poorer farmers had therefore to be developed outside the Department of Agriculture. Efforts to deal with rural poverty had a number of such outside beginnings, in the independent Federal Emergency Relief Administration, the subsistence homesteads program of the Department of the Interior, and the Resettlement Administration. The last was headed by Rexford Tugwell, who was concurrently Under Secretary of Agriculture, although the Resettlement Administration was outside the Department of Agriculture. It was responsible for a number of experiments in cooperative farming and other projects which aroused ideologically based fears that traditional ideas of land ownership were being subverted. When the Resettlement Administration and the programs of the other agencies listed above were gathered together, the policy of experimentation lost force and support.[69] The Farm Security Administration was created to house these various parts and placed inside the Department of Agriculture —a step which was the beginning of the end of the program for relief of rural poverty, although this was but the year 1937.

Such bureaucratic reshuffling was of the essence of agricultural politics. Although administrative reorganization is an obscure topic of little general interest, it has often been the battleground on which the politics of policy has been fought.[70] Without attention to the seeming minutiae of administrative organization it is impossible to explain the destruction of the rural poverty program in the 1940s, when the entire Farm Security program was demolished in Congress under the lash of a campaign of unsurpassed bitterness waged by the American Farm Bureau Federation.[71] Although some quasi-Marxian explanations have been offered that this was a conflict between "big" and "little" farmers, the thesis will not bear scrutiny; the real issue was the Farm Bureau's power over the Department of Agriculture and agricultural policy through its control of the Extension Service.

Beginning in 1936, the liberal elements in the Department had sought to free it from the Bureau's stranglehold by establishing an independent field administration outside the Extension Service system and an increased measure of centralization. The system of farmer committees administering the AAA program in localities was officially freed from its bonds, but the ideology of decentralization prevailed and this remained a committee system. In the Farm Security Administration, however, a more centralized system was established. In 1938, moreover, after diplomatic negotiation at Mount Weather, Virginia, seeking a political settlement among the forces in agriculture, the Bureau of Agricultural Economics was made something of a central planning agency for the Department.[72] But the Soil

Conservation Service and the Rural Electrification Administration, both by then inside the Department of Agriculture, were also establishing their own locally based political organizations, the former through the systems of Soil Conservation Districts and the latter through local electric cooperatives. Although these were as yet weak systems, they loomed as serious rivals to the Farm Bureau structure of power. Both were opposed by the Farm Bureau, but the heavy attack fell on the Farm Security Administration and, to a lesser degree, on the Bureau of Agricultural Economics.[73]

When the Farm Security Administration succumbed in 1946, only vestiges of its programs continued and these had little to do with rural poverty—which did not, however, disappear. More than a decade later a study revealed that, despite general high-level prosperity, 40.5 per cent of all farm families had incomes of less than $2000 a year.[74] The long-term trend of migration from the country to the cities continued, and perhaps therein lay the prospect for relief of poverty on the farm (if not of poverty itself). A mild measure to deal with rural poverty was passed in 1955, but it had only modest results. General attention to the problem came in the early 1960s.[75] The emergence of a new program on poverty came with the interest and concern of President Johnson in 1964. The presidency, indeed, was the only source from which any concerted political effort to deal with poverty, particularly rural poverty, could emerge.

The story of Farm Security, however, was but one incident of an inconspicuous and confused drama. The Soil Conservation Service remained and, despite its leadership's crusading zeal, it was in continual danger until the mid-1950s. The SCS plan of local operation through Soil Conservation Districts was a clear attempt to parallel the Extension Service–Farm Bureau system of power. The Soil Conservation Service met opposition at both the Congressional and local levels,[76] though it had not achieved a seriously threatening position, since the local district organization, except in relatively few areas, had not taken root to the extent of coopting established farmer leadership. As one Service official remarked confidentially in the early 1950s, the system of

Soil Conservation Districts was "nothing but another government program," that is, a program controlled and directed by government officials. In other words the SCS had neither achieved its grass roots ideal nor created the basis of power necessary for survival in the wonderland of farm politics.

The Farm Bureau persisted in its drive to regain unchallenged control of agricultural policy and administration. Despite its great advantages, however, there were now serious disadvantages in its power position. Since its break with the New Deal beginning in the later 1930s, the rift had become wider and more serious. When President Truman won reelection in 1948, the organization was almost wholly at odds with the Democratic administration. The latter had drawn closer to the Farmers Union, which had long been doing its inadequate best to challenge the Farm Bureau. The alliance was in one sense a recognition of Democratic Party weakness in agriculture and of Farmers Union strength—which was good, however, only so long as the Democrats were in office; the option to move between parties was not open to the Union. By the same token that option, essential for an interest-group organization seeking to control policy, was also closed to the Farm Bureau, by now both ideologically and tactically committed to the Republicans.

Through the last years of the long Democratic tenure of office in Washington, the Farmers Union was influential at the highest level. Secretary of Agriculture Charles F. Brannan was a Farmers Union protégé, and the Union supported his plan for revising the general farm program. Yet the Brannan Plan was frustrated by the Farm Bureau and its allies in Congress. When the Republican administration assumed office, Secretary Ezra Taft Benson, though not a Farm Bureau official himself, was warmly regarded by the Bureau, which gave his general farm program its thoroughgoing support. But his reforms too were frustrated in Congress. Nevertheless, the Bureau of Agricultural Economics was at last broken up, and the Soil Conservation Service was now in serious danger. Its regional offices were closed, evidence, according to the National Association of Soil

Conservation Districts, of an intention to liquidate the soil conservation program. All the Association's ardor for soil conservation and "self-government" in rural life was poured into pleas to and denunciations of the new administration.[77] Ultimately, however, the Soil Conservation Service found its salvation (if not quite its original mission) in the great new program of construction projects on small watersheds, a rich lode that attracted new supporters in Congress and among private groups and gave the Service the role of Departmental leadership in the foreign wars against the Army Corps of Engineers and the Department of the Interior.

At this point, an important question emerges. Where has the locus of power in agricultural politics come to rest? One answer might be that it oscillates between two alliances, the Republican Party–Farm Bureau and the Democratic Party–Farmers Union. A superficial glance reveals a certain pattern here. The Democrats during the Truman, Kennedy, and Johnson administrations have had the support of the Farmers Union and have given the Union an effective voice in the choice of Secretary of Agriculture; they have also had the hostility of the Farm Bureau. The Eisenhower administration, on the other hand, enjoyed the friendship of the Farm Bureau and the hostility of the Farmers Union.[78]

This explanation, however, may be countered by a different theory, namely that the influence of political parties has grown to the point where party has become "the crucial decision group for farm policy."[79] This argument is based partly upon the apparent weakness of the two principal general farm organizations and partly upon a study showing a decline in bipartisanship in Congress and of voting among farmers.[80] The apparent decline in Congressional bipartisanship, however, is also explainable by the recent pattern of association between the general farm organizations and different parties. The evidence on farmer voting has little bearing on the behavior of party organizations.

A third explanation is at once more complex and more probably correct. This is that general farm organizations have diminished in importance while parties have remained weak in farm politics. What has been left out of the account so far is the extensive array of groups other than parties or general farm organizations that are involved in farm politics, groups so numerous and kaleidoscopic that an attempt merely to list them would be bewildering. They may, however, be roughly divided into two groups, business organizations and commodity organizations. Among the business groups are, for example, railroads, banks, processors and other companies of substantial size, some of which have been involved in lobbying and "influence" campaigns of doubtful repute. The most notorious such incident of recent years has centered about the remarkable entrepreneurial activities of Billie Sol Estes. His principal chronicler has argued persuasively that Mr. Estes's epic career was the direct outgrowth of the massive subsidies paid to firms and individuals loosely regarded as "farmers."[81] Other business groups active in farm politics include some familiar names: the National Association of Manufacturers, the Chamber of Commerce of the United States, local Chambers, the Association of American Railroads, the National Highway Users Conference, the National Tax Equality Association, and many others.[82] Some of these groups have had direct and concrete interests to be served in farm policy; others, such as the Farm Film Foundation and Harding College of Searcy, Arkansas, have been more purely ideological. To no small degree their activities overlap those to which the Farm Bureau has been increasingly devoted.

Although evaluation is difficult and uncertain, it is likely that the commodity organizations, within their own particular spheres, are becoming the most important groups for farm policy. Organizations such as the National Association of Wheat Growers, the National Milk Producers Federation, the National Cotton Council, and the American National Cattlemen's Association have been highly influential in formulating programs for their respective commodities. Thus, for example, four of the directors of the National Corn Growers Association were on the Feed Grains Advisory Committee to the Department of Agriculture when the feed grains program was being formulated.[83]

Insofar as policy on commercial agriculture is concerned, these associations have some of the same advantages over the Farm Bureau that the Farm Bureau had, and to some extent still has, over parties. They are more narrowly focused and have more homogeneous constituencies; they do not have the same need to reconcile divergent demands; they have the apparent appeal to their own constituencies of making support of the general farm organization unnecessary. Their approach is thus somewhat comparable to business unionism. The advantage of the commodity organizations, it should be noted, is particularly strong so long as they do not conceive that passage of new large-scale farm legislation is needed. The general price-support policy born of the Great Depression for the most part provides the framework of their demands, and they chiefly seek only amendments to this policy for the benefit of particular groups. In recent years, accordingly, they have often been at odds with the Farm Bureau's crusade for general policy change. The political decentralization of the nation plays into their hands. And, more specifically, their ties with the members of the congressional committees on agriculture (as a result of the character of existing congressional districting) have enabled them regularly to defeat Farm Bureau efforts to reorient agricultural policy.[84]

The general tendency of farm politics in recent years has been toward increasing fragmentation of policy and policy-making. Over a longer term, there has thus been a movement away, first, from the agrarian party of Populism to general farm organizations, and, second, from the general farm organizations to commodity associations to some degree leagued with specific business groups. To say this, however, is greatly to simplify the reality. The general farm organizations are neither dead nor dying. Each has great resources of strength in its affiliated co-operatives, marketing, and insurance businesses. These auxiliaries tie to the general farm organizations many farmers who would otherwise save their membership dues for the more narrowly focused commodity associations. Moreover, if it should appear that a number of the important commodity groups feel a need for new general farm legislation, the Farm Bureau's influence could increase considerably. Certainly, the general farm organizations would be more likely than the parties to be strengthened. In the meantime, the Farm Bureau and the Farmers Union will continue to play important roles in the formulation and propagation of ideology.[85]

V

The politics of land and water is not today the most important aspect of American political life. Save perhaps in some aspects of water policy, it directly affects only a portion of the general public. Many of the public lands have little interest for more than a relative handful of people. Farmers now have decreased in numbers to a dramatic degree. Nevertheless, this area of politics does have a peculiar intrinsic importance. What concerns the national supply of food and fiber is important to all the people. What affects the disposition of water and land enriches or impoverishes the nation. Beyond this, land policy is close to the heart of some deeply rooted beliefs about American democracy. It is thus one of the sources of prevalent political belief in other areas. Many transformations have taken place as these beliefs have been translated into policy elsewhere. Indeed, important changes have taken place in the politics of land and agriculture themselves as some of the consequences of these beliefs have gradually emerged.

One of the conspicuous qualities of this area of politics is its great complexity, which has increased with the passing years. The politics of the grazing lands has remained relatively simple, but those of water and farming have been marked by the entry of a bewildering number of participants. Although some of the incidents recounted in this chapter are important in themselves, they are essentially illustrations of some of the general qualities of political life in America. Little has been said here about the Forest Service and the cluster of political agents that form that particular system of power. Nothing has been included about the Tennessee Valley Authority, a regional agency that has taken brilliant advantage of American political reality.[86] Nor has the discussion touched minerals policy or mentioned the

politics of oil.[87] Many particular stories of farm politics have
been passed over. Among the most important is the shameful
history of policy on farm migrants; six decades of repeated examination of the conditions of this most exploited segment of
the population have not yet brought an end to a major failure
of the political process.[88] Yet each of these spheres of politics
is characterized by some of the same factors. There are differences of detail, complexity, and degree, but the political essentials are much the same.

What emerges as the most important political reality is an
array of relatively separated political systems, each with a number of elements. These typically include: (1) a federal administrative agency within the executive branch; (2) a heavily committed group of Congressmen and Senators, usually members of
a particular committee or subcommittee; (3) a private (or quasi-
private) association representing the agency clientele; (4) a
quite homogeneous constituency usually composed of local
elites. Where dramatic conflicts over policy have occurred, they
have appeared as rivalries among public administrative agencies, but the conflicts are more conspicuous and less important
than the agreements among these systems. The most frequent
solution to conflict is jurisdictional demarcation and establishment of spheres of influence. Logrolling, rather than compromise, is the normal pattern of relationship.

The success of logrolling and settlement by jurisdictional demarcation heavily depends on the exclusion of substantial parts
of the population and of important interests and values from *all*
these systems. Although it is not always true that a gain by one
group involves a loss to others, a logrolling agreement is most
readily achieved when interests and values of concern to others
than the two logrollers need not be considered. Some of the
consequences in land and water politics have been evil indeed.
The assumption that price policy is the central problem of agriculture is one; the lack of recent major efforts to deal with rural
poverty and migrancy is another; the discrimination of public
policy against the preservation of scenic areas is a third. The
list could be extended.

Decentralization of administration and policy-making has been a fundamental condition of each power structure; central direction has consequently been very weak. Since, as Madison observed, the small decentralized units are less diverse than the national unit, a narrower faction, usually based upon the established local social and economic leadership, dominates in each locality. The cult of decentralization is based upon a desire to abolish power. Nevertheless, the local elites are readily brought together on a federal basis and their differences are easily reconciled, since these differences are usually only that and not conflicts. Within each sphere of policy, power is not abolished but rather enhanced by decentralization. At the same time, decentralization means weakness of public officers in contests with private organizations and the elites these represent.

A large consequence is that important parts of government and the making and administering of policy within particular spheres have fallen into the hands of particular groups. Decentralizing of government land and agricultural affairs has meant not only emphasis on localism but autonomy as well. It has insulated the various systems in control of affairs in this area from the influence of the President and his constituency, the whole nation. By the same token, it has enforced the formulation of smaller and more partial constituencies. Usually, although not always, the private groups have gained the essentials of power.

Whether the public official or the private leader has control in this situation, however, is not a central question. One shrewd observer has recently noted, "Agriculture is the field where the distinction between public and private has been almost completely eliminated, not by public expropriation of private domain but by private expropriation of public domain."[89] This preemption of public policy and administration and their benefits in land, water, and agriculture explains much about American politics.

Chapter 8

Self-Regulation:
The Politics of Business

I

The commitment to decentralization in the politics of land and agriculture has a counterpart in the politics of business. It is not, as with agriculture, a belief in the virtue of small geographical units. The commitment of business is, rather, to the autonomy of functional units. Although the parallel is far from precise, it is yet close enough to suggest a significant degree of kinship in the common adherence to an ideal of small units. With some allowances, geographic decentralization and functional devolution raise the same issue, the appropriate size of the unit of organization—the issue of the constituency. As in farm politics, in business politics the ideal of the small unit has been seriously compromised by unplanned and unforeseen developments. These developments, however, have been in large part the consequences of application of the ideal to a complex society.

The claim to autonomy is the typical political demand in business. In its most traditional form—that government should not interfere in business affairs, that a policy of *laissez faire* should be followed—it is usually not seen as a political demand at all. Indeed, differing policies are often very simply condemned as "political," although it should be fairly obvious that a policy of nonintervention is as political as any other. Nevertheless, the demand is supported by the elaborate and long-standing rationale of classical economics. This imposing system of thought arose in intimate association with the cause of liberalism itself, and despite the abuse it has received from its detractors and defenders, remains one of the strongest defenses of liberalism. Even today, when much of business is conducted within a framework less friendly to liberal conceptions, the ideological defenses of business are framed in the terms of liberalism. It is very probable that without the apparent necessity of articulating business goals in liberal conceptions, the political practices of business would be much more bleakly power-oriented than they are. The contemporary appeal of corporate leaders to freedom and individualism, however inappropriate it may be from the spokesmen for the corporate giants, has been a moderating force of some importance to the general society.[1]

The specifically economic parts of historic liberal doctrine, however, are less important than the vision of an autonomous economy, and its corollary, an autonomous politics. Indeed, there has always been something unrealistic in this vision insofar as it was ever considered to be a description of existing conditions. The separation between politics and economics has always been primarily analytical. Nevertheless, there was a conception which, admittedly less than a prescription for the ideal society, formed a foundation for constitutional limitations. Moreover, the separation between politics and economics has carried a guarantee that the contests which are the daily life of politics should not become stark struggles that can only be settled by the total victory of one side or another. As one of the most acute observers of European politics has observed, "Once the political struggle degenerates into an economic struggle, its end, the achievement of power, instead of being the triumph of a policy for the State as a whole, valid for all members of the community, becomes the triumph of one group at the expense of another, subserving the interests of one faction as against those of another, and in the last resort against those of the whole."[2] The traditional apolitical posture of American business may not have been adopted with any clear understanding of this truth; it has nonetheless served to protect the community from these dangers.

The claim of business to autonomy, however, has had other meanings less reassuring for the future of a liberal society. Perhaps the most perplexing manifestation is the modern corporation. Although its roots are very old, the problem of the corporation is peculiarly modern. To a considerable degree the problem is associated with size, with the large corporation. Although it is tempting to say that the large corporation has been growing steadily in importance in America, the evidence is not clear and the case is disputed. The argument is only partly a matter of data. It relates to questions of power, and not only is power not ideally a topic of economic discussion, it is also a conception of much ambiguity and imprecision. Since the early 1930's there has been a feeling among some observers that a relatively small number of large corporations—numbered variously as 100, 130, 200, or 500—have control over a large fraction of the nation's wealth, and that some of these make decisions in some substantial degree free of the constraints of the market. Alongside these contentions, the charge that the power in question is growing is perhaps of secondary importance; if it is real on the scale suggested, the present power of large corporations may already be decisive.[3]

A number of distinct but certainly interrelated questions arise here. First, do any large corporations actually have freedom in the market to choose what prices they shall set, at what prices they shall buy, and so on? This is the question of "market power," and is much more narrow and specific than the vaguer "economic power." Second, do these large corporations (however many) have such a massive influence on the quality of American life that they form the social and political climate in a multitude of ways?[4] This might be termed "broad social power." Third, do the leaders of these large corporations constitute an elite, or part of an elite, which makes the important decisions on which the character of life (even the continuation of life) in America depends?[5] Fourth, do these large corporations exercise great power directly over the acts of government? This is the clearest form of political power. Fifth, are these corporations so completely self-governing and self-perpetuating that they must be regarded as a revolutionary species of social and political organization?

These different questions look in different directions and suggest different theories as to what has occurred in the "capitalist revolution" of the twentieth century. Some of the questions are so broad as almost to defy examination. The question of market power, moreover, is properly an economist's question, and on it only the judgment of economists can be acceptable. The other questions are to some degree also within the province of specialists, either economists or lawyers or both. Accordingly, it is worth quoting the measured summary of an economist who has dwelt on the problem at length:

Almost every one now agrees that in the large corporation, the owner is, in general, a passive recipient; that, typically, control is in the hands of management; and that management normally selects its own replacements. It is, furthermore, generally recognized that, in the United States, the large corporation undertakes a substantial part of total economic activity, however measured; that the power of corporations to act is by no means so thoroughly circumscribed by the market as was generally thought to be true of nineteenth century enterprise; and that, in addition to market power, the large corporation exercises a considerable degree of control over nonmarket activities of various sorts. What all this seems to add up to is the existence of important centers of private power in the hands of men whose authority is real but whose responsibilities are vague.[6]

Perhaps the clearest conclusion that emerges from such a summary is that the modern large corporation is a political body. It is obviously political at the point at which power is generally recognized as one of its primary characteristics. It is clearly political when it is seen to exercise appreciable influence over public policy. It is also visibly political when its partisans treat it as a self-governing society. A second conclusion is that the issue of corporate power in the large society is inextricably bound up with the issue of power within the corporate society. On the one hand, if it could be shown that the corporation had no power in the market or over matters of public policy, the problem of internal government in the corporation would have a relatively low order of urgency. On the other hand, if it could be demonstrated that the government of the corporation is linked to a discoverable constituency by some principle of legitimacy widely accepted as valid, the problem of corporate power in the large society would be only moderately serious.

However, neither of these demonstrations is possible today. For all that economists are reluctant to accept such terms as "administered prices" or even "monopoly" as descriptive of current reality, it is apparent that power in some degree short of the extremes suggested by these terms is a characteristic of some large corporations. Power that is less than total may yet be substantial. A. A. Berle, Jr., made this point some years ago: "In blunt fact, competition in an industry dominated by two or three large units is not the same as competition between thousands of small units. . . . herring do not compete with whales."[7] And this is a condition that prevails in a significant number of industries. At the same time, it is obvious that the corporation has no theory of legitimacy which can be applied to its existing practices of internal government. The official doctrine that the corporate directors are responsible to the stockholders is so irrelevant as to be ridiculous. The directors are, if reality is considered, effectively responsible to management, and management tends to be self-perpetuating.[8] The constituency of the corporation is defined in different ways by corporate leaders, but, given the lack of machinery for holding the corporation leadership responsible, the suspicion that the corporate claim to a constituency that includes groups other than the stockholders is a device for avoiding *any* accountability seems justified.

In this situation, then, the modern corporation is without any principle of legitimacy based on a constituency. It has no means by which consent can be said to be derived or reviewed. What other solutions are available? There are, in general, four possibilities. First, there is the assertion that the corporation does not have power. Although this seems to be the position adopted by some industrial statesmen it is not a position which is accepted by observers. Second, it is sometimes claimed that although the power of the large corporation is real, checks do exist and that these are generally adequate. The most notable of such suggested claims is the "countervailing power" of other large corporations and unions opposing the corporation from across the market.[9] Although this opposing power is real under some circumstances, in some of the most critical incidents involving the exercise of corporate power, this check has been unavailing.[10]

The most serious and most illuminating example of this is the history of events in the steel industry since the end of World War II. This is a record of repeated contests between the industry, led by the United States Steel Corporation, and the United Steel Workers. The outcome of these contests, with slight exceptions, has been a pattern of settlement in which the union has obtained higher wages and the industry has obtained prices sufficiently higher to cover not only the added costs of the wage increases but something additional. Perhaps the most startling feature of this history is that the effects of collaboration between labor and industry have been achieved in the face of genuinely sharp and even bitter hostility between the two sides. The incidents of this record include several of the most massive confrontations between industry and labor of modern times. One strike, that of 1959, was the largest single strike in United States history. Again and again, government was reluctantly enmeshed in the affairs of steel. Only in 1962 could it be said that government had any success, and here governmental effectiveness was far more apparent than real.[11] The fact of greatest importance in this history is that at nearly every point, settlement of the differences between the industry and labor was possible because other segments of the public were not parties to the settlement. There is probably no more dramatic evidence that the constituency of the industry and its corporations does not include all of "the lawful interests of each of the more than 185 million human beings who live in this Republic," as claimed by Roger Blough, Chairman of United States Steel.[12] It is also an indication that the beneficence of countervailing power is less than reliable.

The third possibility by which escape from the problem of legitimacy is sometimes sought by corporate leaders is the ultimately very simple assertion that the power of the corporation is exercised for good and not for evil. This assertion takes various forms. Perhaps the original form was offered by the reformed muckraker, Ida Tarbell, on behalf of U.S. Steel. With the implicit comparison of the Standard Oil Company in mind, she pointed out that the creation of U.S. Steel had left no trail of ruined competitors. Presumably nobody had been injured.[13] Even with U.S. Steel, however, this response has been too simple. The serious charges that have been levied against the Corporation have related to waste, inefficiency, technological backwardness, and uneconomic allocation of resources (none of these necessarily implying either viciousness or ruthlessness).[14] Another form this line of defense assumes is a very diffuse discussion of the corporate "conscience." Just as the conscience of a medieval Norman prince could be appealed to, so, it is argued, may the conscience of the corporation— later, perhaps, if not now.[15] If this analogy seems rather too frank, there is a more contemporary way of putting it, namely that business management will become "professionalized." The hope, in either case, is for some codification of good corporate practice arising out of usage. The difficulty, however, is altogether too obvious. By what standard—and whose—is that good practice to be known? No answer to this question is apparent.[16]

The fourth possibility for solution of the problem of legitimacy is some form of governmental action. Abstractly, this could take any one of a number of forms. Thus, outright government ownership is a theoretical solution, although inconceivable in any probable political context. The line of governmental action that has the greatest appeal to many Americans is the historic antitrust policy. Although the point is not often made explicitly, the strongest reason for its appeal is, in a broad sense, political. This is that such a policy, if rigidly pursued, would obviate the persistent problem of criteria. This problem, which hangs like a dark cloud over the large corporation today, also envelops governmental policy when it enters this area. By what standards and for whose benefit shall government act in dealing with business policy? This question becomes more serious and more perplexing with each additional increase of governmental responsibility. The one exception is the policy of enforcing limitation on the market power of private units in the economy. Such a policy if adequately pursued would restore the impersonal judgment of the market and make unnecessary the myriad conscious choices on the allocation of resources and the distribution of benefits of the economic machine. The assumption that the impersonal decisions of the market will produce efficiency is of secondary importance alongside this prospective escape from the problem of criteria.

Despite the strength of the argument for the antitrust policy, however, it is apparent that no thoroughgoing application of it is likely or even possible. The large corporation has been on the scene long enough to justify the view that it is one of the major established institutions of modern life. At this point it is understandable that some students should turn to the alternative of governmental regulation as a solution to the problem of the legitimacy of large corporations. Although the genuine advocates of such regulation are very few, it has an air of something approaching inevitability when the alternatives are considered in turn, as they have been here.

Yet the problem is far from simple. Perhaps the most important issue is whether the problem is broad "economic power" or the narrower and more specific evils susceptible of a relatively simple approach. Thus the invasion of individual liberties by business firms can conceivably be handled through the regular courts' extension of basic protection through well-established doctrines and procedures against arbitrary governmental action.[17] However, if economic power is seen as effective rule by a cohesive corporate elite, the problem appears to be without solution. Fortunately, evidence that this is the problem is insubstantial; it is far more probable that, given the character of American society, this elite is incapable of exercising political domination save in exceptional circumstances and for very limited objectives and very limited times. Perhaps there are occasions on which some member or members of this elite act on behalf of "the business community" in direct and large-scale political action (the behavior of steel industry leaders during the contest with President Kennedy in 1962 may be an example). Nevertheless, the judgment of Adolph Berle seems sound: "There is no high factor of unity when several hundred corporations in different lines of endeavor are involved. . . . Dominance by them over the political state in major matters is not a present possibility."[18]

Perhaps enough has been suggested in the preceding chapters about the pattern in other areas of politics to indicate that, although Berle is probably correct in dismissing this fear, the possibility of domination of government by business units in quite another manner may be genuine. Instead of a conquest of government as a whole, control of significant parts of it may be established by particular business interests. This, as has been seen, is the pattern appearing in other areas of government. In one sense this has happened wherever substantial market power has been established but autonomy has not been relinquished. Perhaps, however, this is not so readily recognized as the exercise of political power as where the stamp of governmental authorization has been achieved. In this capture of public authority in particular areas lies the most important problem. Since public authority is by definition not private, it is perhaps not correct to refer to this as an extension of private government. It is, rather, the formulation of separate narrow constituencies for particular parts of government. The problem is in essence the same as that appearing in today's large corporation, which is free of any control upon its management. Nevertheless, the problem of the corporation becomes much more visible when the character of governmental agencies is considered. This character, as will be seen, does little to diminish the problem of legitimacy posed by the modern corporation.

II

One of the unpleasant realities of government is its frequent and great preoccupation with war. In the modern era this preoccupation has extended over more years than we like to acknowledge. It is an almost ingrained conviction that the conditions of war or preparation for war are abnormal, whereas those of peace are normal. Nevertheless, war and the possibility of war have heavily influenced the character of government in the United States. They have also profoundly affected the pattern of relationships of business with government. The years of crisis and near-crisis, although aberrations in life as we would wish it, have been integral parts of our history and have left a stamp upon institutions that will not soon be erased. Among the many changes wrought by the influence of war is a much closer meshing of business and government, involving a major part of the directorate of the economy. And under modern conditions, the economy is intrinsic to war itself.

World War II was very different from World War I. It was greater in scale, American participation was longer, and the period of preparation (however inadequate) was longer. American industry and the American economy were vastly greater. Moreover, the experience of mobilization in the first war lay behind mobilization in the second. Despite all the differences, however, the fundamental political problems of mobilization were the same for both wars. In the organization of the economy it was essential to enlist the cooperation of industrial leaders, whoever they might be. Whoever had power that could obstruct had to be coopted. There was no time to discover and train new managers of industry, even had this been desired. All thought of social reform had to be postponed before the urgency of immediate production. Given the conditions and the necessities of the time, there can be little criticism of the determination to subordinate other considerations to the objective of maximum production of war material. Yet in the second war, as during World War I, this determination and the basic political decisions that followed from it had a strong influence in the set of political currents that continued after the ultimate victory.[19]

When the war began in Europe the United States was equipped with a blueprint, the Industrial Mobilization Plan, that had been evolved through successive revisions out of studies of the experience of mobilization during World War I. It contemplated a centralized administration under a War Resources Administration. The first step of this plan was the creation of a board to be transformed in time into the central directing agency. Its members were the Chairman of the Board of United States Steel, the President of the Massachusetts Institute of Technology, the President of American Telephone and Telegraph, the President of the Brookings Institution, a director of General Motors, and the Chairman of the Board of Sears, Roebuck and Company. Although this War Resources Board did not continue in being for long, and did not develop according to the Plan, its membership personified the political thinking that had gone into the Plan. War management required the cooptation of the highest business leadership and endowment of that leadership with great power. As things developed, however, with American opinion not yet committed to prosecution of the war and with uncertainty as to the immediate course of things in Europe, creation of such a centralized authority was premature and the prospective enthronement of the corporate elite was too abrupt. President Roosevelt and the board members themselves agreed that the original plan would not do. As the Battle of Dunkirk was being fought, the President created the Advisory Commission to the Council of National Defense. This Commission included William Knudsen, President of General Motors; Edward R. Stettinius, Jr., Chairman of U.S. Steel; Ralph Budd, President of the Burlington Railroad; but it also included Leon Henderson, a government economist; Sidney Hillman, President of the Amalgamated Clothing Workers; and Harriet Elliott, a political scientist from the University of North Carolina. Chester C. Davis, formerly Administrator of the Agricultural Adjustment Administration, was the final member. (His presence in the highest councils through the war helped materially to preserve wartime administration of farming matters for the Department of Agriculture.) Officially the Commission had only advisory powers, but in reality it exercised much actual direction.

Creation of the Commission was in a sense a step backward in that its powers of direction were insufficient for the need. Yet it was politically logical in that it was more broadly "representative" than its predecessor and more appropriate for an early stage in the evolution of administration for mobilization. The Commission gave way before the Office of Production Management in November 1940. A separate agency for price control (Office of Price Administration and Civilian Supply) was added the following April. These agencies had definite powers. The former was headed by Knudsen, with Hillman as his Associate Director. In January 1942 the Office of Production Management was supplanted by the War Production Board under Donald M. Nelson, who had been a vice president of Sears, Roebuck and then had been closely associated with the shifting agencies of war management; under this agency successful and large scale production finally began to appear. Although there was one more step in this evolution, the Office of War Mobilization in 1943, the appearance of the War Production Board represented roughly the stage at which the prewar Industrial Mobilization Plan had proposed to begin.[20]

This kaleidoscopic repatterning of administrative organization was at once narrowly administrative and broadly political. It was a purely administrative development in that a rapidly growing organization had to be pieced together and many technical problems of organization solved by trial and error.

It was political in the broadest sense in that consent for the application of increasingly stringent powers had to be secured gradually. But it was also political in that conflicts of interest and outlook were being fought out during this period. Many of these struggles were fought on the battleground of administrative form. At the highest level, there was the almost ideological contest over the role of "big business," of the influence and position given to men such as Knudsen, Stettinius, and Chester Davis, as against the recognition of labor as represented by Sidney Hillman. The crucial role of industrial direction in war probably made it inevitable that the influence of labor would diminish, as the declining part assigned to Hillman and other labor leaders indicated. Yet, the pattern of organization showed that even at this highest level, there was a fundamental theory which decreed administration should be "representative," that is, representative of economic interests as such.[21]

In an ultimately more important sense, the administrative growth that took place on lower and less conspicuous levels was the politically significant development. The mobilization establishment grew very rapidly and it swiftly came to bear on a multitude of specialized fields of economic activity. What was not actually or potentially war material seemingly proved (or was claimed to be) essential for the supporting civilian economy. At the manufacturing level was the heavy impact of priorities. At the distributing level was price control, and, with some commodities, rationing. Almost every industry and trade was involved and all suddenly displayed bewildering complexity. One example was rubber tires, a relatively small but exceedingly critical item. When the Office of Price Administration found itself compelled to establish price ceilings it discovered that the price structure on tires was extremely complex. It was in fact so complicated that merely to learn the going prices for tires was a herculean task.[22] Since problems of this sort were duplicated and reduplicated in the emergency agencies, it was essential that government acquire advice and expertise in very short order; it was also essential that it gain the active support of the industries whose facilities and activities had suddenly become essential to prosecution of the war. In general, two lines of solution were followed: the establishment of advisory committees and the employment of men from the industries involved.

Early in the development of the mobilization administration, Bernard Baruch met with members of the National Defense Advisory Commission and drew for them some of the lessons of his own experience in World War I. He laid special emphasis upon the Industry Committees he had organized then. Such committees, he felt, might solve some of the most troubling problems before the Commission. Donald Nelson, who was then serving the Commission, observed after the war, "I found out later that he was right, and it was, undoubtedly, too bad that we did not get around to the development of these committees until the War Production Board was rolling along."[23] The beginning of the committees actually came in June 1941, under the Office of Production Management (OPM). They were carried over into the succeeding agencies. There was some question (as well there might be in the light of experience in the NRA) about the legality of such committees. But John Lord O'Brian, General Counsel of OPM, secured a ruling from the Attorney General that the committees would not violate the antitrust acts. Each committee, however, had to be "generally representative of the entire industry"; it had to meet in Washington under the chairmanship of a government officer; and it was to be advisory only. By the beginning of 1942, Washington was beginning to be inundated with committee members. As Sidney Weinberg remarked, "Practically every industry in the country was ultimately represented, from brassieres to baby carriages." No order affecting industry could be issued by the War Production Board until it had been submitted to the committees. The process, according to Donald Nelson, resulted in "almost perfect meshing of the industrial and governmental gears in war production."[24]

The cooperation between government and industry that evolved out of the Industrial Advisory Committees aroused enthusiasm reminiscent of similar experience in World War I. The committees' record was "a story that is another heart-warming bit of evidence that our democratic way of life is worth fighting for."[25] Use of the committees avoided arbitrary and bureaucratic methods. The committees met before programs had crystallized and their help was obtained in basic planning. Meetings were informal, and in them industry was given "a place in the administrative process." The result was "government's receiving the advice and recommendations of industry on all matters including the review of orders, and in industry's receiving an opportunity to express itself continuously and thus assist in formulating administrative policy."[26]

It would be impossible to summarize the performance of all the industry committees (7000 were attached to WPB and 4000 to OPA). Certainly, many were of only slight importance, just as some trades had only slight importance to the war effort. Moreover, it is unquestionable that, as their enthusiasts proclaimed, there was much undiluted and unselfish patriotism in the service offered by members of these committees. Nevertheless, there was a persistent problem of bias, and often one of conflict of interest. The guarded approval of the Attorney General represented a relaxing of standards of antitrust enforcement. Occasionally, the committees were admonished by John Lord O'Brian. However, both business and government delighted in escape from the adversary stance, and the avoidance of compulsion. It seemed so "wonderful" to Donald Nelson that he fell to asking "if the same sort of willing cooperation between the government and business could extend beyond war into peace-time."[27] There was a surprising naiveté here, for the offices of the wartime administrative agencies were placarded with signs insistently reminding administrators that there were simple and direct tests for each of their decisions: "Will it build more planes?" ("more tanks?" "more ships?" "more guns?") The basic reality was just this, that the fact of war itself gave limits and, above all, the criteria of a visible purpose. Under these conditions the appeal to a common end had a definite meaning, but one that could not survive victory.

The other means for gaining the expertise and support of industry for mobilization was the temporary employment of leading businessmen in the directing agencies. This was the solution favored at an early stage in the National Defense Advisory Commission. The names of industrial leaders so coopted for membership on the Commission itself have already been mentioned. The appeal to come to Washington "and help run things" was one that no citizen, however critical of government he might have been in the past, could refuse. This joint appeal to patriotism and egotism was almost invariably successful. Nevertheless, for industrial leaders accustomed to very large salaries there was the difficulty that the rate of pay in government was low. The solution was service without pay, with (in most cases) continuation of private compensation by peacetime employers. The "dollar-a-year men," WOCs (without compensation), and WAEs (when actually employed, that is, paid only expenses on a per diem basis) became important figures in the management of the industrial mobilization. This device had been attempted during World War I, but it had brought scandal and had not been extensively employed. In World War II, however, it became common practice.

The numbers of dollar-a-year men and WOCs fluctuated markedly. In the early days of mobilization organization there were 34 in the National Defense Advisory Committee; however, this was 31 per cent of the total staff. In the succeeding agencies, the percentage declined to 8.8 per cent in March 1942 and to little more than 3.3 per cent in September 1945. Nevertheless, in the former month the absolute total was 1193.[28] Moreover, virtually all of the men serving without compensation were in high-ranking posts. The decline in numbers that came in late 1943 and continued steadily thereafter was a reflection of the facts that policy had been established and the line of development in administration largely determined. Without-compensation personnel were used in other agencies, although generally not on as lavish a scale as in the WPB and its predecessor agencies.

There was some sensitivity in various quarters about this sort of employment. The experience of the NRA was vivid, and both its opponents and proponents had the analogy in mind. An attempt was made to avoid placing WOC executives in posts where they would be dealing with the firms from which they were on temporary leave. This, however, created the difficulty that the expertise which was the ostensible reason for bringing such men to government was not being fully used, and exceptions were made to the rule. Another precaution was the exclusion of trade association officials from without-compensation employment. However, during the war such officials were seemingly omnipresent in the halls of the mobilization and control agencies, and their exclusion from this sort of job probably had little effect on their influence. These officials knew the businessmen-turned-bureaucrats personally and communications between them were often close.[29]

Criticism of these policies developed. The most notable came from the Committee headed by Senator Harry S. Truman.[30] The Committee believed that the inside information obtained by dollar-a-year men frequently gave their own companies definite advantages. Moreover, the Committee charged that the men taken from large companies discriminated against small business. The charges were not so much that there was deliberate favoritism on the part of the WOCs as that a "subconscious tendency"—a bias—was inherent in the use of such personnel in government. "In a very real sense the dollar-a-year men can be termed 'lobbyists,'" the Committee concluded. Nevertheless, the actual scandals that received publicity were not numerous and the practice continued. Donald Nelson was incensed at the criticism and insisted that he had never known a dollar-a-year man "who would have consciously put the interests of his own company ahead of those of the nation."[31] His response did not quite meet the criticism.

Most historians and other writers on this general experience have dwelt on the impressiveness of the achievement and on the dedication of the men who made it possible. With little question, such evaluation is just. Excellent work was done by many of the businessmen who came to Washington and served in discomfort and at real sacrifice. The advisory committees also undoubtedly often gave selflessly and in a manner which served the nation well. Some of the suspicions that were directed against men in these positions were very probably unjustified. More than this, however, the suspicions were too immediately concerned with outright corruption. The real issue was, as the Truman Committee indicated, bias. This was probably most often reflected in the consistent preference for large units of business over small, in the preference of some firms against others, and, in the later stages, in the determination of a multitude of issues in planning for reconversion. Serious undercover struggles for power went on increasingly inside the ranks of business as the end of the war approached. The public interest in these issues was seldom clear, and the presence of some representatives of business seriously handicapped the possibility of discovering it. Nevertheless, it is difficult to imagine other devices that would have served to meet the war emergency as well as those that were chosen.

In the largest sense, the particular devices of advisory committees and without-compensation employment were only part of the most important issue. Many essentially temporary personnel were employed in government during this period. Great numbers of businessmen were employed at regular government salaries on lower but yet important levels. A considerable number of these, for example, were salesmen without function in this greatest of sellers' markets. They were released by their companies and they gave of their special information to the government. Yet, it is likely that the issues debated by the Truman Committee and other critics applied quite as much to these "regular" governmental employees as to the highly placed dollar-a-year men. Like the latter, the ex-salesmen and their like planned to return to their own firms and, to these men, when issues arose on which the public interest was not overwhelmingly clear, they tended to follow long-ingrained ways of thinking. Over the long run, then, the impact of the general experience was a drawing together of business and government in significant areas. It perpetuated the dream that lay behind the now-defunct NRA and recreated visions in which the shibboleth of business–government hostility should be laid to rest and the authority of government placed behind the democratic self-determination of business. Donald Nelson was not alone with his dream of a cooperative, peaceful, noncoercive society in which business should regulate itself with the aid rather than the hostility of government.

The assumption that war was an aberration in the normal flow of life did not last long after the final victory in Europe. The machinery of World War II was indeed quickly dismantled and the wistful hopes for lasting cooperation among Americans dwindled in the familiar contests for advantage. In 1947, however, the Voluntary Agreements Act was passed, establishing a new network of industry advisory committees. The Department of Commerce created an Office of Industry Cooperation to facilitate the operation of these committees. The Act was in effect for a year and a half and then lapsed. Shortly afterwards, the Department of Commerce reviewed the industry committees that still functioned: 477 were still going. Most were narrowly technical (dealing largely with standards), but 77 were of "a broader type."[32]

With the outbreak of the Korean War, a new mobilization began. Although lesser than that of World War II, it was yet massive. The Defense Production Act of 1950 was rushed through Congress with little chance for hearings.[33] This Act authorized the use of advisory committees to gain the cooperation of private industry. Under the National Production Authority, an agency of the Department of Commerce, an elaborate system of committees soon developed. These committees numbered only 68 at the end of 1950, but by the end of 1952 they were 554.[34] In April 1951, the Munitions Board directory listed executives from some 22 different trade associations as members of the Board's own advisory committees.[35] Other agencies also enjoyed similar expert consultation.

The same issues that had vexed previous advisory committees arose during this period. However, they were rather more sharply delineated during the Korean conflict. Partly this was due to the fact that industrial mobilization this time was only partial and that an almost normal civilian economy operated alongside the war economy. It was also due, however, to the Celler Committee's forthright investigation of monopoly power. Most of the issues can be summarized either as questions of the representative character of the advisory committees, or as questions of the power exercised by the committees.

Some standards for establishing the committees on a "representative" basis did exist. Once it was granted, however, that the basis of selection should be something other than representation of the people of the United States (and if the broad principle had been followed, the Committees would make no sense), there was little solid ground to stand on. If the problem had been examined at all closely (as it was not), it would have been seen that a fundamental problem of government existed. This problem, how to organize representation, was unimportant only on the assumption that the committees wielded no power, that is to say, were not "representative" at all. The official history of the National Production Authority committees notes that there were pressures from "special interest groups" whose representatives were not permitted to participate in committee meetings, and that such pressures were communicated via Congressmen and Senators.[36] Apparently, the mark of a "special interest group" was just that it had been excluded from participation and did not wish to be excluded. One of the more difficult issues involving eligibility for participation in the industry committees was the question of participation by representatives of labor. A variety of arguments was put forward against this "pressure": it would inhibit discussion; if labor were to be permitted to take part, "there would be no way to bar other organized groups"; labor participation might result in something like the scheme of "codetermination" prevalent in Germany.[37] Labor was excluded. The arguments for exclusion of labor indeed had force. Most, however, also applied to the interests that were actually chosen for representation. There was some effort to preserve the idea that the committees consisted merely of individuals who happened to have needed expertise. The chief measure to this end was the exclusion of trade association executives. However, this rule was often broken. Moreover, the idea of representation was concurrently maintained. Ultimately, however, the real question was whether the committees exercised power or not. On this central issue, the Celler Committee discovered some striking discrepancies between official doctrine and actual practice. Thus, the minutes of the Pure Tungsten Swaged, Drawn, and Rolled Products Advisory Committee to the Office of Price Stabilization stated in 1951 that, "The purpose of the meeting is to arrive at a basis for pricing that is satisfactory to the industry and at the same time in conformance with the Stabilization Act." The minutes concluded, "Since the important parts of the regulation have been agreed upon, minor adjustments will be discussed by telephone, if necessary, after the forms have been received." A meeting of the Plain and Printed Converted Tissue Specialities Industry Advisory Committee to OPS closed "on a vote to omit the industry from any suggested alliance or affiliation with the graphic arts industry, and only if proper wording conveyed this sense would the industry willingly agree to be included in a printed and printing paper regulation." The Contract Motor Carriers Industry Advisory Committee to OPS felt no need to discuss the agenda for one meeting because it had been "quite fully discussed at a previous informal meeting of the group which was held in Chicago." Repeatedly, the evidence was strong that the "advice" given by committees took the form of granting consent to the proposed governmental regulations. In many instances, this consent was readily given—for the reason that the regulations had been formulated by the committees themselves.[38]

The Korean War mobilization also saw a renewal of the practice of employing businessmen without compensation. One of the principal devices for recruiting WOC administrators was the Chamber of Commerce, which provided assistance in soliciting a large number of major corporations for the loan of their personnel. In 1951, 876 WOCs were on the rolls of twelve defense agencies.[39]

At the end of the emergency, there was a spate of testimonials by the participants to the cooperative nature of the great undertaking. One businessman on a radio interview stated that "the lesson learned about the way in which this has been handled, particularly through NPA, would be a good thing to carry further." In 1952, a questionnaire was sent to 2000 committee members. The result was "a great testimonial"; 86 per cent of the members wished to continue the committees, for these had paid "worthwhile dividends." "They liked the relationship that had been established."[40]

The Korean War did not escalate into World War III; neither did it end. Rather, it dwindled into an uneasy truce that was neither victory nor defeat. And in the process the Cold War settled more pervasively into the ways of thinking and acting among Americans, both in and out of government. The inherent ambiguity of a large-scale war that needed but a partial mobilization, with two concurrent economic systems —one for war and one for peace—settled into still deeper confusion as the years of mobilization without war stretched on. The guideposts for policy had been clear and frequent in the prosecution of World War II; they were indistinct and infrequent in the Korean War; in the period that followed, they seemed almost not to exist. What had been a clear and then a hazy, but still visible, purpose vanished into a fog of uncertainty. Nevertheless, the machinery of consultation between government and industry that had been fashioned for the sharply defined ends of war was perpetuated.

It is impossible without an investigation more thoroughgoing than even those of the two Hoover Commissions to determine the scale and extent of *significant* collaboration between business leaders and government officials in the years since the Korean War. In 1955 and 1956, however, the House Committee on Government Operations conducted a questionnaire survey on the use of advisory committees in the executive de-

partment. The results of this survey indicated that there were
between 5000 and 6000 such committees.[41] By no means all
involved business leaders and many were relatively inactive;
some, moreover, were transitory (hence the difficulty of determining their precise number), and some, by almost any
test, were of slight importance or influence. The total, nevertheless, suggests the degree to which the practice had become
an ingrained way of government in the United States.

Perhaps the confusion of ends into which some of these
advisory committees fell during this era was greatest in the
elaborate structure of committees erected by the Department
of Commerce. In late 1953, the Business and Defense Services
Administration (BDSA) was established. This agency assumed
the residual functions of the National Production Authority.
Its creation was the outcome of plans laid by the leaders of the
new Republican administration before they took office. The
incoming Secretary of Commerce, Sinclair Weeks, had held
extensive consultations with prominent business leaders and
trade association officials to design the agency. According to
Mr. Weeks, the new agency was to "see to it that, while private business, of course, cannot dictate Government policy and
plans, it be placed in a position where it can effectively approve or disapprove of the implementation of such policy and
plans from the standpoint of their practical workability in
everyday industrial operation."[42] The plan of organization featured four devices: (1) giving to each segment of industry "its
own special division for receiving Government information
and service"; (2) the employment of WOCs "recommended by
various industries to represent them" as chiefs; (3) the appointment of three Assistant Administrators who would have direct
access to the Secretary and who would serve without compensation; (4) consultation with industry by means of an elaborate
system of advisory committees.[43]

Although this agency was the immediate creation of a new
Republican administration, and was in some respects almost
a reincarnation of the system devised by Herbert Hoover as
Secretary of Commerce, it would be a mistake to perceive

it in partisan terms. The ideas embodied here were in reality quite nonpartisan. The new organization was little more than an adaptation of the devices used in the just-ended Democratic administration and employed for many years in various parts of government, whatever the party in power. What was different in this case was the condition of the time, the continuing mobilization without war—and the old vision of adapting the business–government cooperation of wartime to peace, an ideal encountered several times already in these pages. Here, at last, was a substantial attempt to realize that dream.

The inherent ambiguity of the organization appeared in overt duality of purpose: the agency was to give service to business (in almost all dealing with Government); it was also to help achieve governmental ends in industrial mobilization and other economic activities. On the first score, one bureau official informed a business group that "In BDSA you have a powerful new megaphone for recommending measures which you believe the Government should undertake in solving your problems. You can make your views known while governmental policies are being discussed and formulated."[44] Here was a direct "pipeline" to government for businessmen. On the second score, the agency had the function of allocating materials and products required in the military and atomic energy programs; it had the duty of making recommendations on applications for accelerated tax amortization, applications for Federal loan assistance, stockpiling, and other matters. Thus it was at once regulator of business and representative of business to government.

This duality might have been merely a curious anomaly had it not been for the devices of organization and operation listed earlier. The calculated use of WOCs led to serious confusion of functions and responsibilities. There was not here, as there had been in previous situations, a clear understanding that the justification for the employment of WOCs was that their expertise was otherwise unavailable to the government. The explicitly given justification this time was that the WOCs were *representatives*, as was nowhere clearer than in the process of choosing a Director for the Aluminum and Magnesium Division of the agency. At an aluminum task group meeting held in 1954 at the Waldorf-Astoria Hotel in New York, it was decided that, according to the minutes of the meeting, "The Director's position [is] to be staffed by the three integrated producers—Alcoa, Kaiser, and Reynolds in that order. The succession dates for this position to be approximately February 1 and August 1 of each year. . . . The Deputy Directors' position to be staffed by representatives of nonintegrated companies from the aluminum industry."[45] As the Celler Committee observed in its report, "In BDSA for all practical purposes the selection, if not the actual appointment of WOCs has been delegated to industry."[46]

Since the WOCs were temporary and rotating personnel, there was a persistent problem of allegiance and responsibility. With the best will in the world, the WOC who had been selected by his industry and firm as their representative had divergent calls upon him. Thus Mr. Leonard Pasek, for a time Assistant Director of the Pulp, Paper, and Paperboard Division, first of the National Productive Authority and then of BDSA, had for a long time been the Washington representative of the Kimberly–Clark Corporation, a large maker of paper. Since he continued both public and private functions concurrently and on salary from Kimberly–Clark, he was faced with the necessity of carrying on his duties for the corporation by working at the firm's Washington office evenings, Saturdays and on occasional days taken away from his government office.[47] Difficult as Mr. Pasek's problem of allocating time must have been, officials in his position had yet more serious problems. Thus Mr. Bernard L. Orell, Vice-President of Weyerhaueser Sales Company, affiliate of the large lumber producer, became Director of the Forest Products Division. Under his direction, the Division was able to report to a conference that it had successfully intervened with the Tariff Commission, the State Department, the Treasury, the Export-Import Bank and various other agencies in such matters as plywood imports, financing of foreign manufacturers, government purchases of lumber products, and general Forest Service policies. The Division under Mr. Orell's direction claimed a "batting average" of 0.875 on these undertakings. If Mr. Orell sensed any ambiguity in his responsibilities, his superior, the Administrator, was greatly pleased with the success obtained by this division.[48] The Administrator, Mr. Charles F. Honeywell, was, in fact, quite generally inclined to enthusiasm over the sort of industry–government collaboration BDSA fostered. On one occasion, he addressed a meeting of representatives of the chemical industry called to consult on the disposal of spent sulphuric acid in the Chicago area by the Department of Defense, a matter on which the industry felt a strong interest. He characterized this as a "town meeting approach."[49] However intuitively, Mr. Honeywell came very close to the heart of the matter, the small constituency.

The Department of Commerce network of committees and task groups, the employment of WOCs, and the holding of conferences of industry groups (sometimes with WOCs from those industries as presiding officers for the government) constituted perhaps the most remarkable venture of government–industry collaboration to occur in peacetime. The total effects are difficult to assess, for they have occurred in a multitude of specialized fields on matters sometimes quite esoteric, as some of the examples given above will suggest. Nevertheless, the Celler Committee was definite in its conclusion about what, in general, had happened: "In operation, the organizational arrangements of BDSA have effected a virtual abdication of administrative responsibility on the part of the Government officials in charge of the Department of Commerce in that their actions in many instances are but the automatic approval of decisions already made outside the Government in business and industry."[50] The Celler Committee disapproved. But what else was this but self-regulation and self-government of industry?

Perhaps the perseveration in the Department of Commerce of the ideal of industry collaboration with government will seem understandable in view of the long-standing tradition on which the Department itself was founded and the direction given it at a formative period by so strong an individual as Herbert Hoover. As the Department of Agriculture cherished its own peculiar grass-roots "philosophy," so the Department of Commerce embodied its own particular ideal of the responsibilities of government. Experience in the government elsewhere, however, casts doubt on the peculiarity of Commerce doctrine. The Department of the Interior, in particular, offers evidence that the ideas and institutional developments under examination here were not the patented possessions of the Commerce Department. The remarkable system by which administration of the Western public lands was effectively released to local ranchers has already been discussed. The Department of the Interior, however, has been much more than an agency for transmitting governmental authority to local ranching interests.

In the National Petroleum Council the Department of the Interior has possessed a supporter and guide on oil policy and administration that could only be envied in the Commerce Department. This Council was established in 1946 in connection with the creation of an Oil and Gas Division in the Interior Department. It was essentially a continuation of the Petroleum Industry War Council, which had served like similar councils attached to the War Production Board in World War II. In the face of persistent controversy and opposition to the new Council, it is probable that the indignant response of a later Chairman of the Council is correct: "Contrary to the thought that some want to propagate, the idea for the National Petroleum Council did not come from within the industry. It was not something that the industry conceived and sold to the Government. It was just the other way around."[51] Although the idea may not quite have originated with President Truman as the Chairman suggested, the initiative in at least a formal sense did come from government. In view of government sponsorship of the Chamber of Commerce of the United States and the Farm Bureau, it is not surprising that governmental officers should have originated the Petroleum Council. Nevertheless, these analogies and the extensive use during the war of WOCs from the industry do suggest that the question may not be an important one. Industry and government were fundamentally agreed and often very nearly indistinguishable during that period.

The Petroleum Council in some respects surpassed its prototypes in the Department of Commerce. Most notably, its membership consistently included a high percentage of the genuine elite of this important industry. Among its members were chairmen of the boards or presidents of Standard Oil of New Jersey, Standard of California, Standard of Ohio, Texaco, Superior Oil, Gulf Oil, Sinclair Oil, Hunt Oil, and so on through most of the roster of important firms.[52] The list of members, is, in fact, so impressive that it is difficult to imagine Interior Department officials, even if they wanted to, ever taking positions contrary to those adopted by the industry in its own organizations, such as the American Petroleum Institute.[53] Nevertheless, this impressive representation in the Department of the Interior of the oil industry, an industry notable for its political skill and influence, brought out problems that only infrequently reached the surface in the Commerce Department network of industry–government relationships.

Perhaps the most important of these problems was the fundamental issue of self-government. How should conflicts *within* the industry be resolved? At the time of the founding of the Petroleum Council and subsequently there were protests from "independent" marketers of oil products that this type of organization fostered monopoly and discriminated against the smaller units of the industry.[54] The oil industry, like others, is not a simple monolithic unit. A problem of government, of resolving conflicts of interest, plainly existed here, and it was not avoided by devolution of public authority to a private consultative body. The difficulty was aggravated by the size of the Council, sometimes more than 80 members. Much of the Council's work had to be done by committees, and these inevitably narrower groups posed the question of self-government even more acutely.

Nevertheless, there was genuine sensitivity to the problem

in the government and in the Council. A major reason for the large size of the Council was the desire[55] that it be representative of the industry as a whole. The problem of self-government also raised the problem of the Council's status as a public or a private organization. The operating expenses of the Council, for example, were met from the beginning by voluntary contributions from companies and individuals in the industry. Once more the analogy with the Farm Bureau seems vivid. The same issues of participation of trade association officials (probably more open and extensive in oil matters) and the use of WOCs that plagued the Department of Commerce network also appeared in the relationships between Interior and the Council. The substantive functions of the Council included the making of recommendations on—in effect, supervision of— voluntary agreements on the allocation of transportation facilities and equipment. In this, the purpose was "to make Government control unnecessary."[56] Perhaps in the exercise of this and other powers, the Council decided wisely. Once again, however, the problem of criteria arose: by what standards could *any* decision the Council made be justified?

The Department of the Interior has also had the assistance of a variety of other advisory committees. These run through the metals from the Aluminum Industry Advisory Committee to the Zinc Industry Advisory Committee.[57] Elsewhere in the government, the use of advisory committees has also been extensive. As might be expected, the Department of Defense has had the largest list. For the most part these relate to items of procurement interest. The roster includes such charming titles as the Industry Advisory Committee on Bacon, the Industry Advisory Committee on Peanut Butter, the Industry Advisory Committee on Steel Shanks, the Power Cranes and Shovels Industry Advisory Committee, the Steatite Subcommittee, and so on almost without end.[58] The Treasury Department has been generally more modest, but during the 1950s some of its committees were drawn directly from private associations. Thus there were the American Bankers Association Government Borrowing Committee, the Investment Bankers

Association Government Securities Committee, the National Association of Mutual Savings Banks Committee on Government Securities and the Public Debt, the American Life Convention and the Life Insurance Association of America Joint Committee on Economic Policy.[59] This was perhaps a more direct, and certainly a franker, method of committee selection than any found elsewhere in the government.

Undoubtedly, most of these committees are above reproach. It is altogether probable that for the most part they are simply what they were originally intended to be, sources of expert knowledge, whether it be on the supply of zinc or the technology of peanut butter. Many of them have met infrequently and have had little or no influence on public policy in even the small areas of the economy with which many of them deal. Yet a number of points about this array of advisory groups does appear important. First, there is the sheer fact of their great number. It is not true that they pervade the whole government; they are used by some agencies to a much greater degree than by others. Nevertheless, their use has increased vastly and has spread through the government in the years since Herbert Hoover first entered public service. Second, some of these groups have achieved a strong degree of influence over—even control of—public policy in particular areas. It is often difficult to determine where the distinction between advice and the making of policy lies. The orthodoxy discussed in Chapter 3 has deep roots in some agencies and in these the distinction tends to be lost sight of. Third, where advisory groups are actively relied upon by government officers, or where the industry groups aggressively press their views (conditions that by no means always exist), there is a persistent possibility of capture of the governmental unit and governmental policy by the organized industry acting through the medium of the advisory group. The more frequent the use of such validating groups, the more likely such capture becomes. Fourth, the lengthening years of crisis and a deepening involvement of government in economic affairs have brought more detailed and more fragmented organization of economic affairs. This

situation has been directly reflected in policy formation. Like
the politics of land and water, the politics of business has been
characterized by a multiplication of interests and an ever-
increasing complexity.

One advisory group, however, would seem to pose a question whether the last point is altogether valid. This is the
Business Advisory Council (BAC), one of the more remarkable
groups ever associated with the government. The Council was
formed in 1933. Officially, it was advisory to the Department
of Commerce, but its functions have ranged far beyond the
concerns of that Department and have touched many parts of
government. Perhaps it has advised the Department of State
most frequently after the Department of Commerce. According
to the by-laws of the Council, its membership was restricted
to 60 active members, each of whom might serve as many as
five successive years; thereafter members were eligible for
"graduate" status. The roster has always been distinguished.
Although the Council has always included some representatives of small and middle-sized business, the predominant
membership has been drawn from the world of large corporations. The Celler Committee observed in 1955 that among the
active and graduate members of the Council at that time "were
representatives from 2 of the 4 largest rubber manufacturers,
3 of the 5 largest automobile manufacturers, 3 of the 10 largest
steel producers, 4 of the 10 largest companies in the chemical
field, 2 of the 3 largest manufacturers of electrical equipment,
2 of the 3 largest manufacturers of textiles, 4 of the 16 largest
oil companies and 3 of the largest glass manufacturers."[60] Moreover, the men chosen to represent these firms were usually their
board chairmen or their presidents. Understandably, the names
have been very well known. The last chairman of the BAC
(while it still held that title), for example, was Roger M.
Blough, chairman of the board of United States Steel. His immediate predecessor was Ralph J. Cordiner of General Electric.

The Council met six times a year. Some of the meetings were
in Washington, but others were held in the more attractive
settings of Sea Island, Georgia, Pebble Beach, California, Hot

Springs, Virginia, and similar spots conducive to calm and reflection. The expenses of these meetings, like other costs of the Council, were met by private contributions. At these meetings it was customary for high government officials to appear and to discuss important problems of public policy before the Council members and their wives. Confidential advance economic information was presented by the officials at such meetings. For this reason, presumably, the press was excluded, as were other uninvited members of the public. One of the interesting features of the Council, in fact, was the discreet obscurity in which it operated (or, in the words of the Celler Committee, "the aura of secrecy" that enveloped it).[61] In addition to the meetings, the BAC prepared reports on a variety of matters of public policy. Some of the topics were: labor policy, foreign trade, manpower mobilization, monetary policy, fiscal policy, and antitrust policy. Most of the reports were not made public. The other function served by the Council was recommendation of men to serve the government. According to the executive director of the Council "a great number" of government officials were so selected; these included "two or three Assistant Secretaries of Defense."[62]

On the few occasions on which public attention has been drawn to the existence of the Business Advisory Council and its operations, sharp criticisms of it have been made. The majority of the Celler Committee, for example, saw it as a means of avoiding the constraints of the antitrust laws. Somewhat the same issue arose in a different form in 1961, when Mr. Cordiner was Chairman. His firm was indicted for price-fixing in the electrical industry, although through his ignorance of what was going on in his company, he avoided the prison terms given other electrical industry officials. In the eyes of critics Caesar's wife at this point was not above suspicion. Partly as a result of this incident, but more as a result of the criticisms current after the Celler Committee's report, Secretary of Commerce Luther H. Hodges suggested changes in the Council's manner of operation. Hodges particularly sought membership for additional representatives of small business and an end to the exclusion of reporters from the Council's meetings. This intervention by a member of the Democratic administration was partially successful, but it was apparently quite disturbing ideologically to the businessmen on the Council. Under the leadership of Roger Blough the Council declared its independence from government. As an independent body, it assumed the name of the Business Council and took office space outside the Department of Commerce.

In a formal sense, this action settled a question that had existed since the Council's beginning: was the Business Advisory Council a public or a private body? In 1951, Secretary of Commerce Charles Sawyer had declared that the Council was "not in any sense an official body." In 1955, however, when the Celler Committee sought to obtain records and information from the Council, the Department of Commerce changed its mind. After some reflection on the implications of the demand from the congressional committee, the Department decided that the BAC was a governmental body and that its files in the Department could not as a matter of executive privilege be released to an arm of Congress.[63] In reality the Business Advisory Council was both public and private. The distinction had been hopelessly lost.

On the face of things, the issue was unimportant. As the Business Council, the same group of top business leaders continued to have the services of the same staff, which they continued to pay, and to have much the same access to the same governmental officials. Nevertheless, a matter of fundamental importance was at stake. This was the very conception of liberal government itself. It was the same issue that prevailed wherever private groups of advisors assumed actual policy-making functions. The issue of formality has throughout been intimately associated with questions of power and responsibility. Where these groups actually assumed power and exercised authority, responsibility of government became responsibility to the constituencies of the groups the advisory groups represented. The many references to "representation" as a quality of the groups encountered in these pages indicate the degree to which it was, perhaps unconsciously, assumed that the BAC and the various Industry Advisory Committees *would* exercise power.

The Business Advisory Council, however, presents another perplexing problem. Given the wide range of its mandate and the elite quality of its membership, was the BAC (and its successor, the BC), a "peak association," a directorate of big business effectually controlling the economic policy of the nation? Certainly, if a search were to be made for a top executive committee of corporate business, no more likely body could be found than the Business Advisory Council. Nevertheless, such an interpretation would probably be mistaken. The Council included a number of disparate elements. Not only were some representatives of small business actually members, but some of the representatives of big business had interests in conflict with each other. Moreover, the recommendations of the Council have not always been put into effect. Thus, its views on antitrust policy (a matter of particular concern to the BAC) have not resulted in the changes recommended in its report.[64] In view of the secrecy of the Council's operations, it is difficult to say how often such failures have occurred. Yet, the Celler Committee probably made as strong a statement as could legitimately be made about the Council, when it observed that "its advices and recommendations do reach into the farthest confines of Washington's bureaucratic structure."[65] As a lobby, it has undoubtedly been unusually efficient. As a social body it has conferred much prestige upon those selected for membership. Nevertheless, membership on the National Petroleum Council has probably been more important than membership on the Business Advisory Council to Mr. Eugene Holman, Chairman of the Board of Standard Oil of New Jersey; much the same thing could probably be said of other figures of high stature in business. The influence of business upon public policy is great. Some of the means by which it is achieved have been traced here. However, the reality seems to be that multiplicity of intimate contacts with government is the essence of the process. By the same token, it is probable that this influence, like the business interests it serves, is rarely united and is most often fragmented. Public policy would seem to reflect this.

From time to time, various government officials have sought to enforce rules and procedures that would guarantee the integrity and the public quality of agencies utilizing the services of WOCs and advisory committees. The Department of Justice has written opinions and established rules of operation. The different Congressional investigating committees have also had this concern. Nevertheless, the rules have consistently been broken and it is not too much to say that they have had little effect. In the Department of Commerce, the prevailing orthodoxy has inculcated a belief that the erasure of the distinction between private and public status is desirable. The belief is rarely explicit, but it is strong and pervasive. Although some of the other Departments have a less clearly articulated doctrine of voluntary self-regulation, their practice is often as far-reaching as that of Commerce. A secondary source of confusion is the preoccupation of many critics of the practices of business representatives in government with the antitrust problem. Antitrust is indeed involved, and it is important. It is, however, only an aspect of a much larger problem, a problem of politics rather than of economics. Failure to perceive the problem of how the nation is to be politically organized, to what constituency or constituencies government is to be responsible, is serious; yet it is better to have raised the issue as a question of antitrust policy than not to have raised it at all. President Kennedy issued an executive order in early 1962 somewhat limiting the use of advisory committees and making a few requirements of procedure.[66] As before, however, large escape clauses exist and there is little ground for believing that the practices that have taken such deep root and spread so widely will disappear.

III

The examples of collaboration between government and business that have been given so far might be summarized as expressions of the orthodoxy described in Chapter 3. But it is one of the curious ironies of American politics that the other clear, and to some degree opposed, tradition—reform and Progressivism—has by its own peculiar route brought about results remarkably similar to those of the orthodoxy. These results have appeared most clearly in the independent regulatory commissions.

The commissions date from 1887, when the Interstate Commerce Commission was created. This was well before the advent of the Progressive Movement, but in some respects it was an almost typical Progressive reform. It was designed to bring monopoly power under popular control; it was intended to be expert; and it was built to be free of "politics." The ICC was followed by the Federal Reserve Board in 1913, the Federal Trade Commission in 1914, the U.S. Shipping Board (later variously renamed) in 1916, the Federal Power Commission in 1920, the Federal Radio Commission (later the Federal Communications Commission) in 1927, and, in New Deal days, the Securities and Exchange Commission, the National Labor Relations Board, and the Civil Aeronautics Board.[67] The forces that brought about the creation of these agencies were varied. One force behind establishment of the Shipping Board, for example, was the incipient American entry into World War I; once again war conditions had an important influence on the development of governmental institutions. Chaos on the radio waves led industry itself to demand regulation by a Federal Radio Commission. For the most part, however, popular desire for regulation in the public interest (as seen in Progressive terms) was the more important and the more consistent motivation. A number of reasons have been given for adoption of the independent commission form, but perhaps historical accident was as strong as any. The ICC was given this form, and under the first chairmanship of the very able Thomas M. Cooley achieved a prestige that made it the model for the commissions that followed. Certainly, it seems probable that Cooley's strong direction did much to create the aura of legalism that has surrounded these bodies, sometimes to their bene-

fit, but often to their vexation. To the reasons commonly offered
for the peculiar independent commission form might be added
the advantage it offers of swift relegation to decent obscurity
of issues that have become overheated in the glare of public
controversy—an advantage most politicians esteem highly.[68]

The independent commission long ago became established
with that degree of solidity and seeming immortality known
only to old-line government bureaus. The commissions have
successfully passed the test of survival; nevertheless, they have
drawn recurrent criticism—some trivial, some serious, some
damning. The literature of investigation on these agencies has
grown to great volume, perhaps out of proportion to their importance in relation to other parts of government. However,
a few of these examinations stand out to the extent that they
deserve comment. In 1937, the President's Committee on Administrative Management opened the issue of their structure as
it had not been opened before. The Committee termed the
independent commissions "a headless fourth branch of the
Government, responsible to no one, and impossible of coordination with the general policies and work of the Government
as determined by the people through their duly elected representatives."[69] This criticism appeared in the context of a discussion devoted to the difficulties faced by the President in
controlling more than 100 different agencies. Retrospectively,
the Committee at times seems to have been preoccupied with
the problem of administrative tidiness. Nevertheless, it did
have a fairly clear perception of the largest issue posed by the
commissions, responsibility.

In the same era there was also a quite different approach to
the independent commissions, again a critical one. This was
made by the Attorney General's Committee on Administrative
Procedure. This distinguished group focused, as the Committee's title suggests, upon the process by which administrative
agencies operated, rather than upon their organization. Unlike
some other studies of "administrative agencies," the Committee
study covered a number of other governmental bodies as well
as the independent commissions. The test of an administrative

agency, in Committee eyes, was that it held the power to determine private rights and obligations.[70] With the particular concern indicated by this definition, it was understandable that the report of the group was attacked as being too legalistic and too little concerned for the achievement of the ends of public policy. Perhaps there was a lawyer's bias in the Committee's work and a tendency to measure the administrative process by the standards of the judicial process, particularly in dealing with the independent commissions, which bore some analogy to the courts. Nevertheless, the hostility aroused by the Committee was too intense. The hopes aroused by the culmination of its work, the Administrative Procedure Act of 1946, were also too high.

The differences of orientation toward the problem of the independent commissions in these two reports is interesting. The first sought solutions by reorganization. The second rejected "mere change in the administrative structure, and sought reforms of procedure."[71] These approaches to reform reflect two fundamentally different—although properly complementary—assessments of the underlying problem. As the problem has become clearer in the years since the New Deal, it has become evident that the first approach is political, the second legal. When Congress created the independent regulatory commissions it was reasonable to hope (whatever may have been in the minds of Congress) that in time the commissions would build a body of largely consistent precedents out of which general principles would gradually emerge. By such a process, criteria would develop and the problem of bias would be solved. This process would meet a major part of the problem of fairness to individuals and also provide the order which is essential to effective administration. To the extent that this process did not develop, however, it was also reasonable to look for means for referring the basic value choices to the people. Typically, this means would consist of legislation by Congress. With the commissions, however, it has been assumed that the subject matter is so involved and abstruse that Congress is largely unable to deal with policy choices in the forms in which they appear in these fields. Thus, the question, how responsible to the public are the Commissions? has become very relevant.

Except among scholars, there has been great reluctance to confront this fundamental question. Reorganization of the commissions and placement of their functions within the departmental structure, recommended by the Committee on Administrative Management, was rejected by Congress. In 1949 the Hoover Commission decided that "the independent regulatory commissions have a proper place in the machinery of our Government, a place very like that originally conceived," although a small number of relatively small reforms were desirable.[72] The Second Hoover Commission in 1955 did suggest establishment of an administrative court, but this proposal had no success.[73] Nevertheless, the problem remained and it briefly exploded in a seriocomedy of exposures by the Legislative Oversight Committee in 1958.[74] A number of students re-examined the problem and, as a result, the issue of the commissions is very much alive today.

Criticisms of the independent commissions contain some quite different implicit theories as to what is wrong. Perhaps the most obvious criticism is the seemingly simple protest against *any* governmental regulation. This, however, is very deceptive. In general, this criticism is not seriously made by the regulated industries themselves. Some industries, including the radio industry, the airlines, the railroad and trucking industries, and the oil companies, have actively sought regulation.[75] When, a few years after establishment of the Interstate Commerce Commission its abolition was proposed, a very prescient U.S. Attorney General wrote to a railroad president in a letter much quoted since then, "The Commission . . . is, or can be made, of great use to the railroads. It satisfies the popular clamor for a government supervision of railroads, at the same time that the supervision is almost entirely nominal. Further, the older such a commission gets to be, the more inclined it will be found to take the business and railroad view of things. . . ."[76] Industry organizations have indeed often proved staunch defenders of their respective regulatory agencies. Thus, in 1948 *Railway Age* asserted flatly that transportation "has a natural tendency to become monopolistic," and that the "only sensible policy for government is to recognize this [and] regulate accordingly." The vocal denunciations of regulation still heard from some industry spokesmen are, as Huntington has remarked, a part of maintaining the myth of regulation as something imposed on industry.[77] This, of course, is not to say that all members of any industry are agreed upon the substance of regulation, however monolithic the industry is made to appear by its appointed spokesmen.

A second group of criticisms relate to various details of organization and inefficiencies of operation; criticism of the large backlogs of work in the commissions is typical. These matters are seemingly most easy to deal with, for they appear superficial. Nevertheless, it is likely that delay, inefficiency, and indecision are all related to the more fundamental difficulties of the commissions.

A much more important charge is that the independent commissions have failed to "make law." A federal judge has recently stated the difficulty: the commissions have failed "to develop standards sufficiently definite to permit decisions to be fairly predictable and the reasons for them to be understood."[78] The case for this legal diagnosis of the problem is very strong. Thus, the Federal Communications Commission has been deeply involved in scandal in the award of licenses for broadcasting. Given only the "public convenience, interest, or necessity," as a guideline by Congress, the Commission has been confronted with the necessity of formulating its own criteria for choosing among applicants. This it has been unable to do, with the result that its decisions have appeared to be based on whim or, even worse, bribery.[79] Similarly, the Civil Aeronautics Board has been confronted with exercise of large-scale discretion with little guidance from Congress. One of the most important of its duties is the assignment of routes among various airlines. Judge Henry J. Friendly has asserted that in seventeen years of existence, the Board arrived at no understandable criteria on this activity.[80] Here he was saying in specific terms what an outraged ex-member of the Board itself had asserted, that the Board had "almost no general policies whatever," and that such policies as did appear changed "suddenly, without notice, and often with no explanation or any indication that the Board knows it has changed policy."[81] Even this severe criticism was not substantially different from a statement by a chairman of the CAB: ". . . the philosophy of the Civil Aeronautics Board changes from day to day. It depends who is on the Board as to what the philosophy is."[82] This was painfully close to a confession that the Board's decisions were wholly arbitrary. At this point, the whole issue had been reduced to a question of power, in this case the power to determine appointments to the Board.

When serious scholars and active participants in the decisions of the commissions have been able to make and support such statements, it is almost irrelevant to ask what the substance of the decisions and policies of the Commissions have been; the presumption of bias and, as has been seen, even the suspicion of outright corruption are ultimately unanswerable. Yet, it is worth noting that specific charges of favoritism have not been lacking. Thus, the Civil Aeronautics Board has been faced with charges of discrimination in that it has generally denied certificates to new airlines. It has favored scheduled passenger lines over all-cargo lines in rate structure. It has discriminated against surface lines seeking to enter air transportation.[83] Similarly, the Interstate Commerce Commission has generally favored the railroads over the trucking firms. In particular, it has interpreted identical regulations on rate structure differently for the railroads and for the motor carriers.[84] Examples could be added at some length.

So long as the problem of the commissions is viewed in these terms, the solution indicated by Judge Friendly is incontrovertible: a better definition of standards. If the operations of the commissions are to be anything other than the playthings of sheer political power, this is the only answer. Unfortunately, however, this may be tantamount to saying that if the problem is to be solved it must be solved. Two questions of great importance remain unanswered. The first is whether it is technically possible for the commissions to develop standards giving reasonably precise meaning to such Congressional guides as "public convenience and necessity," "just and reasonable rates," "undue preference or prejudice," or "unfair methods of competition." Judge Friendly has persuasively argued, particularly with the example of the long-and-short-haul clause of the Interstate Commerce Act, that solution is thus possible.[85] His judgment deserves respect.

If the question of technical feasibility of better standards can be solved, the already long record of the independent commissions nevertheless indicates that in many areas it has *not* been solved. The second question thus becomes highly important: is it *politically* possible to develop the needed standards? At this point, where the issues of procedure encounter the issue of structure, the problem of criteria and the problem of power meet.

The outstanding political fact about the independent regulatory commissions is that they have in general become promoters and protectors of the industries they have been established to regulate. Attorney General Olney's prophecy to the railroad president in 1892 has not only been fulfilled by the ICC; it has gained the stature of a general rule of independent regulatory commission development in most fields. This is easy to understand where regulation has been sought by the industries themselves. Here the analogy with the NRA is obvious; it is less obvious with industries in which regulation has been instituted as the result of external forces and by the Progressive impulse. Marver Bernstein explains the process thus: independent commissions have a characteristic life cycle. In the period of a commission's gestation, agitation develops for reform of a condition that is causing widespread distress. The agitation is denounced as "socialistic" and a heavily ideological struggle occurs. Ultimately, however, the fervor for reform reaches a peak and the regulatory agency is established with a very vague and general Congressional mandate. Such were the origins of the ICC and the SEC, for example.

In its youth the commission has a crusading spirit. It encounters, however, the by now well-organized resistance of the industry it has set forth to control. The industry has superior knowledge of matters relating to itself and is determined to defend itself day in and day out against the apparent threat. Moreover, the legal standing of the commission may be uncertain and serious action may have to await Court determination of its validity. Even more serious, public concern over the problem quickly wanes and the commission is left without the strong political support that had brought it into being. Congress is happy about the disappearance of agitation and conflict, and the President is presumably freed of responsibility. In its maturity devitalization characterizes the commission. It achieves acceptance and loses its reforming zeal. It settles down to routine operation of established policies and more and more assumes the role of manager of the industry, of course serving the interests of the industry. Changes in commission personnel will now have taken place and the new appointees will probably be wholly acceptable to, if not indeed the nominees of, the industry. Those permanent staff members who remain will have become wearied by struggle and more and more responsive to the suggestions of industry members that they should get along together and forget past strife. These appeals, combined with the attrition of the former struggles, become strong indeed. In old age debility sets in and the primary task of the commission degenerates into maintenance of the status quo in the regulated industry and the commission's own position as the industry's recognized protector.[86]

This process has been remarked upon in one way or another by many students of administration.[87] It is by no means confined to the independent commissions; it is also familiar to veterans of active administration in many long-established governmental bureaus. Why, then, has the process been so particularly associated with the commissions? First, it is probably somewhat more severe in the commissions than in most other agencies. This is somewhat uncertain, however, since the commissions have generally attracted more attention than have bureaus better hidden from public observation. Second, the independent commissions have very large discretionary power, which has not been tempered and restrained by the development of rules and standards of a firm character. Third, the commissions are formally and in reality more independent than many other agencies.

Their independence is probably the crucial political issue regarding the commissions. Originally, independence was conceived quite simply as a matter of independence from partisan politics. To different degrees it was enforced not merely by overlapping terms of commissioners and appointment of members of both major parties, but by independence from the presidency as well. The judicial model was influential, but freedom from "politics" was also an important motivation. Unfortunately, what was achieved was not freedom from all politics, but freedom only from party and popular politics. The politics of industry and administration remained. In terms of the present analysis, independence substituted a small constituency, that of the industry itself, for a large constituency, that of the whole nation. Thus, it is incorrect to charge that the commissions have been irresponsible. They quite obviously have been responsible—indeed, particularly responsive—to the industries with which they have been associated. The question of responsibility is always meaningless unless it is asked *to whom* the responsibility is paid.

The fallacy of the organization of the independent regulatory commissions thus has two faces. On the one side is the assumption that standards could and would be developed by the commissions. On the other side is the assumption that the commissions could and would be independent of all political influence. Neither assumption has been justified. Under the disguise of antiregulatory rhetoric, the fiction has been maintained that the commissions' formal responsibility to the general public is the responsibility actually paid. Perhaps the legalists' contention that better definition of standards is really possible is correct, insofar as the diverse claims *within* the regulated industries are concerned. But analysis of the character of private government indicates that standards for regulated industries that meet elementary tests of fairness to weak and strong alike are most unlikely to emerge from the existing organization of the commissions. At best, it would seem reasonable to hope only for more *certain* standards—which, however, may be expected to serve the interests dominant with the industries. Even this less sweeping improvement would be dependent on accentuation of existing tendencies toward domination of the regulated industries by a few elements within them. No standards adequately reflecting the array of interests other than the industries themselves that are affected by the regulations are likely to emerge from the political context of independent commissions. The actual constituencies of these commissions are no more than the industries regulated.

Much of the context of recent discussions on the independent commissions is directed to reform.[88] Accordingly, it is fair to pose a question similar to that raised earlier about the legalist solution of better definition of standards: Isn't suggesting the political solution of reorganizing the commissions to make them responsible to a larger constituency tantamount to saying that solving the problem would solve the problem? Unfortunately, the answer to this question is also probably affirmative. The web of relationships between the regulators and the regulated and the influential committees of Congress is so complex and strong that it is unrealistic to expect reform except after great effort and much determination. Solutions actually offered are likely to take the form of minor internal reorganization and the selection of better personnel for commission membership, as James Landis recommended to President Kennedy before the latter took office.[89] Nothing in such recommendations, however, will meet either of the basic problems of the commissions.

The most curious feature of the independent commissions' history is the degree to which these expressions of the Progressive drive have produced the same phenomena as the agencies that emerged out of the orthodoxy of group self-determination. The commissions have exhibited the same accommodation of governmental bureaus to the industries with which they deal, sometimes even to the point of virtual fusion of public and private bodies. They are characterized by the same uncertainty of standards, sometimes to the point where they appear hopelessly adrift. The independent committees practice the same informality of operation and relationships —in extreme cases to the degree that corruption is difficult to disprove. There is the same drive toward autonomy of the conjoint regulator-regulated political systems. Finally, these systems have followed the same development of narrow constituencies.

The Progressive impulse has waned and the slogans of self-regulation are perhaps heard less than they once were. Nevertheless, the ideas of self-regulation are probably more pervasive than ever. Certainly, the phenomena of self-determination and self-regulation in business are more widespread than when Herbert Hoover was Secretary of Commerce. The most striking recent evidence of the strong vitality of the ideas of self-regulation came out of a re-examination of the workings of the Securities and Exchange Commission. This agency is somewhat unlike its fellows in that self-regulation has been an explicit part of its doctrine from its very beginning. The essential part of this doctrine is that the securities business should police itself, with the SEC largely standing by and keeping its shotgun behind the door, as SEC Chairman William O. Douglas once put it.[90] Thus, although the Commission has issued some regulations of its own, most of the controls exercised over the trade in securities have been those of the exchanges, which are intrinsically private clubs.

By 1963 the securities market had grown substantially and the number of stockholders had increased vastly. Moreover, a number of scandals had enveloped the stock market and public feeling was rising. A sweeping investigation of the market followed. To no one's surprise, the SEC itself concluded, "Our firm conviction is that self-regulation, an essential ingredient in investor protection, must continue in a strong, forward movement."[91] Perhaps the most interesting novelty of the study was its examination of the internal governmental systems of the various private self-regulating bodies. Although this examination was less than penetrating, it was at least an acknowledgment that problems of government persist even where public authority has been abdicated. A more important element of the entire investigation, however, was the call for extension of self-regulation. Regarding the over-the-counter market, for example, a variety of small reforms were proposed, but the major thrust of the recommendations was that the National Association of Securities Dealers should undertake a more aggressive policy of regulation of this market.[92] Accordingly, when legislation was drafted to deal with the problem, one of its quite logical provisions was a requirement that all broker firms should be members of a registered securities association. This and the requirement that the associations should establish rules and regulations over their members had, as the Senate Banking and Currency Committee noted with satisfaction, the support of all the national and regional exchanges as well as the National Association of Securities Dealers and the Investment Bankers Association.[93]

Perhaps at this point the assimilation of Progressive reform into the orthodoxy was complete.

IV

Only a portion of the large and complex world of business politics has been touched on here. The web of relationships between business and government is exceedingly intricate. Some of the political organs of business are concerned with seemingly trivial matters; some are largely ideological. Yet those which seem most clearly ideological, such as the National Association of Manufacturers and the Chamber of Commerce, occasionally concern themselves with concrete matters of policy. Like the Business Advisory Council, they occasionally become active in matters of large-scale policy such as taxation, foreign trade, labor, and fiscal policy. For the most part, however, the really effective participants in business politics are those which direct their energies almost wholly to hard, specific matters of immediate economic concern to business firms. Where the units of business are numerous and small, this provides the advantage long ago discovered by the American labor movement: that concrete and immediate economic demands are the strongest basis for maintaining organization. Thus, for example, the ideologically oriented Conference of American Small Business Organizations dissolved without substantial achievement, whereas the National Association of Retail Druggists has thrived and succeeded in establishing its remarkable scheme of retail price maintenance by legal enforcement ("fair trade").[94]

The greater advantage possessed by largely homogeneous business groups with concrete demands is the close tie with government units which can be relied upon to lend public authority to policies determined by the private groups. Establishment of such a tie, relatively simple under American conditions, has been frequent. Moreover, this is an efficient use of power. Thus while a certain fiscal policy or the election of a particular presidential candidate might appear advantageous to a given industry group, much more reliable and direct benefits may be gained by using available resources of influence to create a governmental administrative agency to care for the industry's interests vis-à-vis the public. This, of course, is not to say that business groups avoid taking part in contests over large matters of public policy or in electoral politics. Many do, but the extent and intensity of their participation are probably less than is frequently assumed, in accord with the widespread business distrust of "politics."

A conclusion that must be drawn from this examination of business politics is that the noisy denunciations of government heard from business spokesmen are not to be taken at face value. It has been seen repeatedly that in day-to-day affairs, business and government are not only not hostile but so closely meshed as frequently to be indistinguishable. Yet the fulminations are persistent and fervent. What can explain them? The

first element of the explanation is that business is not a monolithic entity. The measures enforced by government on behalf
of some business groups are adverse to the interests of others.
Second, whether the issue is understood explicitly, intuitively,
or not at all, the denunciations serve to establish and maintain
the subservience of governmental units to the business constituencies to which they are actually held responsible. Attacks
upon government in general place continuing pressure on
governmental officers to accommodate their activities to the
groups from which support is most reliable.

Third, and probably most important, is that business attacks
upon government are directed at any tendency toward the
development of larger constituencies for the governmental
units. This is the really essential key to the politics of business,
as it is to almost any area of interest-group politics. The autonomy of established units of association is the basis of most
power relationships. To change the constituency, particularly
by increasing its size and diversity, is to destroy that autonomy
(at least until the new constituency is stabilized and delimited)
and to weaken existing power relationships. Thus a changed
constituency will undermine the position of the officers of any
association and at least pose the threat of challenge by dissi-
dent leaders. But much more important is the inevitable dilution of the established leaders' informal power that will occur
through the addition of other elements. At a minimum, some
compromise with the new elements will be necessary to the
extent of directing a portion of group resources to the achievement of new goals, the ends of the enlarged group very probably becoming less specific and more difficult to attain. At a
maximum, some of the goals of the added elements may conflict with the ends of the established group, with a resultant
serious weakening of the power the group previously enjoyed
on the large political scene. That wider power had been dependent on walling off the particular area of concern to the
group and maintaining its isolation from the claims of other
groups. Autonomy is the means of preserving established
power.

Thus, an industry that can effect its own disciplinary system and establish its own rule over its area of concern will have strong reason to fight off governmental intervention. This supposes, however, that the private governmental system *is* established and efficient. Such a system should be recognized as a form of rule. It involves the power and the claim of a right to make decisions within the area walled off and declared autonomous. Two difficulties usually stand in the way of achieving this degree of autonomy. First, discipline upon the units of the industry may be difficult to impose. Second, external threats to the autonomy of the industry may develop, and its claim to the exclusive right of making decisions within its area may be disputed. Here public authority may be very useful if it can be seized; but the need for autonomy remains, and the governmental agency which bears the public authority must be isolated from constituent elements other than the industry itself. Given the autonomy ("independence") of the agency, its decisions in time become those of the industry; they are thus validated and are enforceable on dissidents within the industry. Moreover, the external demand for public intervention on the exercise of private power is seemingly met and the public agency becomes a means of combating attacks from other parts of government and other segments of the public.

Thus the avowed hostility of business toward government may or may not be genuine. It is genuine where governmental action seems to threaten the autonomy and the system of rule established by a unit of business; it is false where a governmental agency is responsible purely to that unit. Hence the railroad industry is largely content with regulation by the Interstate Commerce Commission, the securities trade is pleased to see extension of Securities and Exchange Commission policing, and the oil industry is happy to cooperate in the operation of the National Petroleum Council. Few industries or businesses, however, approve of any aggressive operation by the Anti-Trust Division, although this agency is the true protector of the avowed ideology. Only dissidents to the rules and discipline of the various systems of private government approve of Anti-Trust.

The modern large corporation is in some respects no more

than a special case in the pattern of business politics. It seeks
autonomy and defends its political boundaries with determination. Its leaders are genuinely concerned to protect the corporation's power against the threats occasionally posed by the
Anti-Trust Division. Yet they are glad to serve the government
as WOCs and to collaborate with agencies or units of agencies
exclusively concerned with matters in which their particular
corporation is interested. Both positions are consistent in that
they serve to protect or extend the corporation's power. Where,
as with numerous firms, substantial power is held by a corporation, a system of rule exists. In the words of Eugene V.
Rostow, the large corporation is "an autonomous body politic
in a legal order of decentralized power."[95]

The large corporation on the face of things relies to a greater
degree than some trade associations upon maintaining the
character of a private body. The associations more readily participate in the work of public agencies, though obviously large
corporations share in this participation by their membership
in the associations. In a larger sense, however, the private
character of the great corporations is seriously compromised
by their power. When it develops power to make choices without the limitations once imposed by the market, the corporation is exercising governmental power, and this is, to some
degree, public in nature. That it exercises power over only a
fragment of public concerns does not distinguish the corporation from other governing bodies, a number of which are also
thus limited. An outstanding characteristic of American government and politics is great fragmentation. The problem of
the large corporation as government would not arise if there
were definite and unchallengeable criteria for corporate managers to observe. There are none, however, and the managers
are left only with the claim that their actions are good—a
claim without clear meaning and amounting to little more
than an assertion of the power to rule.

The breaking of the boundary between public and private
merely becomes more obvious where trade associations and
industry organizations actively participate in government. The

trade association that is linked with a government agency through or as an advisory council visibly destroys the boundary. The process, however, is not intrinsically different from that of the large corporation. Indeed, it may not be necessary for the trade association to capture a public agency. Walton Hamilton has observed that the functions of a regulatory agency "may be very much the same whether it is set up and operated within an industry itself, or is maintained as an arm of the Government."[96]

A decline of formality accompanies the destruction of the distinction between public and private. Although this has the genuine merit of making government friendlier and more "human," it magnifies the danger of arbitrary and discriminatory action. It is not mere coincidence that largely autonomous agencies of government have developed close informal ties with particular constituencies and have failed to develop clearly defined standards to guide their actions. The problems of criteria and power are intimately connected.

In an era when the claims of any elite have no sanctions of birth or title and criteria have no external and objective basis, the problem of responsibility in government is paramount. Responsibility involves both standards and the control of power. The standards may be developed by experience over time or they may be given by decisions of the formally representative organs of government. The devolution of such decisions to informal and less than comprehensive units of government will always leave a cloud of doubt over the legitimacy of any standards chosen. Where power is unchannelled by any standards, responsibility can only take the form of institutional reference to some constituency. But constituencies may be large or small. The constituencies in the politics of business are small.

Chapter 9

Autonomy:
The Politics of Labor

I

Until 1932 the politics of labor exhibited a consistency, almost a purity, of pattern unmatched in other major segments of American politics.[1] Preservation of the autonomy of the established national (officially, "international") unions was central. Union autonomy was to be defended against employers, government, and even labor's own federation. It implied emphasis upon job control, concentration upon hard economic issues of immediate concern to the unions' constituencies, reliance upon the unions' own economic strength, and rejection of "politics," whether this was taken to mean partisanship or the seeking of legislation. All these were pursued in the name of liberty and were continually and rigidly defended as pragmatism. There were lapses, of course. Support of La Follette's presidential candidacy in 1924 was probably the largest, but even it was half-hearted. The issue of socialism was present, but after the first decade of the twentieth century it was muted and of little importance.

On the eve of the New Deal, at the very darkest point of

the Depression, the thread of consistency snapped. The most obvious sign of the break was perhaps more apparent than real: the passage of the Norris–LaGuardia Act with organized labor's support. This Act, which at last brought the evils of the yellow-dog contract and the labor injunction under control, was paradoxically still consistent with voluntarism, for it freed the organizations of labor from some of the most damaging forms of interference by arms of the state. In the sense that unions had been seeking only freedom from governmental intervention, the Act represented no breach with the policy labor sought; unions now were able to exercise their economic strength unhindered by the hostility of judges. Nevertheless, the Act was legislation. Although it merely undid the previous power of courts to behave as good Marxists insisted they must —that is, as agents of the ruling class—the idea that political institutions might not only be neutralized but might even be seized began to be thinkable.

A more authentic sign of a break in the tradition of voluntarism was the 1932 AFL convention's support of demands for unemployment insurance administered by government. This issue, already two decades old, more than any since the defeat of socialism in the AFL, had been the battleground on which voluntarism had been defended. The issue was again contested in the 1932 convention, but the times were too desperate for the ideologists of voluntarism to hold the line. Actually, the astonishing feature of the struggle was that they had been able to win so many times; the issue had been fought in 1929, 1930, and 1931, while unemployment grew and despair spread.

The arrival of the New Deal provided a vast impetus for what has generally been interpreted as a redirection of American unionism. The first sign was the inclusion of Section 7 (a) in the National Industrial Recovery Act. This guaranteed the right of employees "to organize and bargain collectively through representatives of their own choosing." The Act had the support of the AFL, and President Green of the Federation followed it up with a letter to affiliates calling on them to take advantage of this "revolutionary" measure by organizing.[2] The opening effort was to be a great organizing campaign in Detroit, but the campaign turned out to be less than energetic.

At this moment no greater issue faced the labor movement than its own size. Depression-born unemployment had reduced its ranks dramatically since the beginning of crisis in 1929; by the time the low point had been reached, the membership rolls totaled less than three million members. Few of the mass-production industries had any organization at all, despite the growth of the automobile, rubber, oil, and similar industries in the period of prosperity just preceding. The problem was actually of long standing and was in one sense merely aggravated, though on a large scale, by the Depression. At the end of World War I, organized labor had had a membership approximately twice its size in 1930; the decline had been steady throughout the 1920s. Reasons for the decline were complex. Certainly one was that the membership at the close of World War I was swollen by the nearly automatic organization accorded under wartime contracts; some portion of this at least could reasonably be expected to fall away. Another was the "American Plan" campaign of employers (the open shop with public relations touches).

Whatever the strength and importance of these influences on union organization, a substantial part of the explanation for the decline in membership lay in the outlook of the AFL unions themselves. On the face of things, this outlook was characterized chiefly by lack of aggressiveness, if not outright defeatism, illustrated by the Federation's half-hearted efforts to establish unions in the automobile industry. A union, the old Carriage and Wagon Workers, had achieved a substantial toehold in the industry by 1920, but it was charged with jurisdictional encroachments by several metal trades unions and was expelled from the Federation. In 1926, a year after a convention of the Metal Trades Department of the AFL had called for new organization of the industry, an organizing campaign was launched; the Federation itself was to be in charge. Resistance from employers developed, but the jealousy of the established crafts was probably a more serious obstacle. Although many in the labor movement recognized the principle of mass organization in the industry—industrial unionism—as the key to the situation, the respect that had to be accorded established unions robbed the new campaign of vitality before it was well begun, and the onset of the Depression killed it.

In a large sense what had happened to the AFL during the years between World War I and the Depression was that its constituency had narrowed. The constituency when the AFL was formed had been very broad, at least in the sense that virtually all workers for wages were regarded as organizable ultimately into separate national unions. This goal, however, was vague; the cold reality of the labor movement was that it consisted of established unions for the most part based on the skilled crafts. What Michels has called the conservative basis of organization soon dominated these organizations, and no body in the official labor movement was capable of making the vision of the large constituency of wage workers a reality. The responsibility of labor leaders was to a variety of much narrower constituencies. These constituencies did extend beyond the actual membership of the various unions, but even so a great mass of workers were left without organizations to which they might have had recourse. The Industrial Workers of the World had been an exception, but this frightening organization had been effectively smashed in the antiradical repression after World War I. The AFL, as the example of the automobile workers suggests, was the remaining possible matrix of organization, but its loose federal form prevented it from taking vigorous action. In effect, the automobile workers and others in mass-production industries were outside its constituency. Moreover, many of the workers over whom the established unions had once asserted jurisdiction and the right of ultimate organization were by 1932, in any realistic view, also outside the actual union constituencies.

There was a close, though not always easily visible, connection between the shrinkage of organized labor's constituency and its reliance upon economic methods. Except in municipalities, labor had not followed the examples of business and agriculture in establishing its own parts of public government. Representation of a kind, it is true, had long existed in the federal government. Pressure from the Knights of Labor in the late 1870s had resulted in formation of a Bureau of Labor. From its beginning, this agency was devoted to the gathering of statistics and other information, first from a vantage point in the Department of the Interior and then in the Department of Commerce and Labor. The AFL succeeded in gaining separate departmental status for Labor in 1913, but the new Department's powers did not develop in the same manner as those of its counterparts elsewhere in government. One reason was that the first Secretary, William Wilson, was a former United Mine Workers official and was deeply committed to the doctrines of voluntarism. Thus, for example, he felt it would be wrong for Congress to give his own office greater power in industrial disputes, arguing that legislation to this end would give "to the Secretary of Labor the power he should not have—power to organize, direct, and concentrate public opinion so as to compel the employer to give conditions he does not want to give or the employee to accept conditions he does not want to accept. Both of them are wrong and should never be incorporated in the laws of the U.S."[3] Moreover, to Secretary Wilson labor meant organized labor, even when this amounted to only 6 per cent of the working class. His position was essentially that taken later in a different field by Herbert Hoover: "The Department is usually under a necessity of turning to the labor organizations that exist and such as may come into existence for definite and trustworthy advice on the sentiments of the wage earning classes regarding their common welfare."[4] Apparently the AFL leadership liked the former view as well as the latter and did little to gain more effective power for the Department. The one important Bureau with which the Department was endowed was that of Immigration and Naturalization. Understandably, immigrants hardly ranked as its clientele.

The Department of Labor had a brief taste of significant activity during World War I, especially through its Employment Service. With peace and a Republican administration, however, the principles of voluntarism were reasserted by a new Secretary, James Davis (also a former unionist), and the Department was redirected to the accumulation of statistics. Cautious ventures in conciliation of industrial disputes placed a premium upon not alienating the partisans of any side. Probably Department officials could not have followed any other policy. Labor unions were not only weak politically; they had no desire to become strong. By the 1930s the Department of Labor was subject to Washington jibes as "the Department of Labor Statistics"—a cutting characterization in a power-oriented city which assumed that the significance of any group could be measured by the weight of the part of government it owned.

Despite the doctrinaire "pragmatism" of organized labor, passage of the Norris–LaGuardia Act and the National Industrial Recovery Act released (or at least was followed by) a burst of new organizing activity. This was most notable in the United Mine Workers, a union which long before had fought and won the issue of industrial unionism within the AFL. It had a membership long accustomed to risk and hardship and so, perhaps, was more open than others to rough and drastic measures. It was also endowed with leadership of an unusual caliber. Even before President Roosevelt signed the NRA, John L. Lewis was conferring with his lieutenants over plans for a great new organizing campaign. Lewis and his aides took vigorous part in formulating the NRA code for the coal industry, from which the first of a succession of agreements emerged. The union achieved the check-off, as well as other benefits. A new spirit of aggressiveness animated the organization and its rolls grew dramatically.[5] The Amalgamated Clothing Workers under Sidney Hillman and the International Ladies' Garment Workers under David Dubinsky also caught the note of opportunity and mounted organizational campaigns.

For all the clarity with which these signs pointed to a new era in labor history, the really great breach in voluntarism came with passage of the Wagner Act in 1935. This Act had direct continuity with the now-defunct NRA. Nevertheless, it went far beyond that little-lamented experiment, at least insofar as labor was concerned. In providing a solid administrative structure for carrying out the public policies that employees had the right to organize and that collective bargaining was the proper method of regulating industrial relations, the Wagner Act created the basis for an entirely new unionism, one which could assume that government was not only not hostile but was actively assisting labor organization. The Act's requirement that employers engage in bargaining and the enumeration of unfair labor practices by employers spelled out its meaning in considerable detail. For the first time at the national level labor unions had a genuine handle on government.

The change of direction involved in organized labor's support for and achievement of the Wagner Act was great. The new policy was at odds with most of what labor leaders had been asserting as right for decades. It seemed to repudiate the mistrust and hostility for government as the inevitable tool of employers that had been reiterated endlessly at AFL conventions since the Federation was founded. And yet it is possible to exaggerate the change. The change the Wagner Act promoted and validated was the establishment of trade unions as fully legitimate institutions on the American scene. Although the achievement of this standing took more time, effort, and even violence, the outcome was virtually inevitable once the Wagner Act was on the books and finally in operation. This cannot be minimized. Nevertheless, the change must be seen for what it was: the alignment of government on the side of trade unions in their search for institutional security. Security for unions as organizations within the constitutional framework had been the object of organized labor's greatest struggles from the 1880s onward, and it is scarcely too much to say that this was the meaning of most of what labor had done to the date of the Wagner Act. This is not to deny labor's further goal of material improvement in the lot of union members and potential members or the genuine improvements in conditions it actually achieved. The major struggles to this point had simply revolved about the prior matters of union recognition and union security. The Wagner Act was the climax to these struggles. The issue was the same; only the means of resolution was novel to the labor movement.

By the same token, however, the Act did not deal with matters of substantive interest to individual workers. It did not directly touch wages, hours, or working conditions; it did nothing to establish pensions or unemployment insurance. Organized labor had, it is true, supported the Fair Labor Standards Act. This support, however, was belated and derived largely from the consideration that by limiting the ability of employers in areas such as the South to pay grossly substandard wages and to impose grossly excessive hours of work, the Act would assist in the unionization of workers in other regions. The aims of the Social Security Act, as has been seen, gained the blessing of the AFL only after decades of controversy and during serious crisis; in the actual drive for the Act the contribution of labor was far less than proportionate to the interest of organized labor's membership in its purposes.

The break in voluntarism, then, was real and substantial. It did not, however, signify destruction of the tradition. The building and maintenance of organizational strength remained at the center of labor's objectives. The achievement of benefits for members and for workers in general, the ostensible justification for everything else, continued to be reserved for economic battlefields. This whole pattern, of course, is much more visible in retrospect than it was at the time. In the middle 1930s the most conspicuous feature of the political scene was the personality of the first Democratic President since Woodrow Wilson, a figure whose charismatic brilliance blinded observers to the finer details of what was taking place. Franklin Roosevelt acquired the reputation of a labor sympathizer; by association his was a pro-labor administration. Sponsorship of the Wagner Act by allies of the administration seemed ample demonstration that labor shared in the exercise of power. The ideological fog that enveloped the time, moreover, obscured many of the genuine issues, and the outcries of employers did nothing to clarify matters.

The agency of government to which organized labor now could have recourse, the National Labor Relations Board, was thoroughly unlike the Department of Labor. It was modeled at least in part on the ICC, the FTC, and the other independent regulatory commissions. Thus it might have been expected that in time the agency would serve labor as some of the other independent agencies served their own clienteles, and indeed, for a number of years the NLRB appeared to be doing just this. Given the long-standing hostility of many employers to collective bargaining and to any avoidable dealing with unions, and given the Wagner Act's injunctions against expressions of this hostility, the Board made many decisions against employers and in favor of labor.[6] This apparent partisanship, however, was simply what was required under the policy of the Wagner Act; it was not favoritism of the order that developed from the discretion given some of the other independent agencies. Moreover, it was implicit in the Board's structure from the beginning that once employers generally came to accept the policies of the Wagner Act the Board would prove to be less a partisan of labor than it appeared in its early days. In actuality, the Board had a double constituency—management as well as labor. This reality, however, was some time in appearing.

The other great change that affected labor during the New Deal era was the vast increase in organized labor's constituency. Industrial unionism was obviously the key to organization of the big mass-production industries as yet largely untouched by unionism. But the craft unions of the AFL were bitterly antagonistic to this sort of mass organization. Their hostility was doctrinaire and rigid, but it was not wholly irrational. Its rationality had two bases. First, change in the constituent foundation of any organization is profoundly disruptive to that organization, not least to the security of its leadership—a truth as clear today to state legislators faced with reapportionment as in the 1930s it was to unions threatened with a flood of newcomers. Second, a very real tactical advantage accrued to organizations with small constituencies and limited objectives. Thus, a union with a relatively small number of skilled craftsmen could demand—and get—substantial economic benefits from an employer who also used the services of a large number of unskilled workers. The cost to him of granting a rather large increase of wages, say, to the small skilled group would be minor in proportion to the cost of enduring a strike that would close down his entire plant. The situation might be quite different if he were confronted with a possible strike for relatively small benefits for a large number of workers. Obviously, however, enjoyment of this tactical advantage depended on the existence of a small constituency in the union and its holding to very narrowly construed objectives, however extreme these might be in degree.

The rise of the Committee for Industrial Organization (later renamed the Congress of Industrial Organizations) was the major feature of a near-revolution within the labor movement. For all the prominence of personalities in the formation of the CIO it is difficult to imagine how except by revolutionary means (revolutionary, that is, in the context of existing labor organization) the constituency of organized labor could have been enlarged on the scale it was. Nevertheless, it is notable that increase of membership occurred not only in the CIO, but in the AFL and the independent unions as well. Total union membership, which in 1930 was 2,900,000, rose to 4,300,-000 in 1935 and to 8,500,000 in 1940; of this last figure, 4,900,000 members were in AFL unions and 2,800,000 were in CIO unions.[7] The explanation for this dramatic growth obviously cannot be simple. The energy that went into organizing campaigns was an essential fact. Behind this, however, was the fact that the CIO leaders had burst asunder the chains that existing AFL organization and ideology had bound about the labor movement.[8] Related to this was the great change in the attitude and action of government, specific in the influence of the Wagner Act and the NLRB, but also general in the widespread impression that the national administration was favorable to labor organization. And at nearly every point in labor history at which union membership has changed markedly, the help or hindrance of government has been intimately connected.[9]

This relationship was at no time more dramatically evident than during World War II. Total union membership in 1945 reached 13,400,000. It was apparent once again during the Korean War. Membership had indeed increased between these wars, but the increase was gradual; in 1950, however, the total touched 14,500,000, and by 1953 it reached 16,500,000.[10] As had happened in earlier times of national crisis, the role of government in economic affairs grew enormously during both of these wars. Although it was already settled national policy that union security in war production should be protected, one of the large and difficult issues of administration during World War II was the degree to which it should be guaranteed. The compromise evolved by the War Labor Board was the maintenance-of-membership formula,[11] which, though it was not the enforcement of the closed shop that organized labor would have liked, was still substantial assistance to union organization. Government contracts and war-induced prosperity added to the ease with which unions acquired new members.

During the war it would have been correct to say that labor had achieved a new status in society and that unions had won their fundamental objective of legitimacy. Moreover, an important number of labor leaders had begun to turn to politics, avoidance of which had been so conspicuous a feature of voluntarism. Although officially the AFL took its traditional nonpartisan stance in 1936 and 1940, organized labor became largely a captive of the Democratic Party. Labor's Non-Partisan League (whose name evoked the old voluntarism even while the organization gave support to Democrats) was formed in 1936, and for a number of years noisy ideological battles were fought over purely political issues. Individual union leaders made no secret of their commitment to the New Deal, although John L. Lewis, the most prominent among them, gyrated wildly in his affiliation. In 1944, the CIO Political Action Committee was formed for the specific purpose of supporting Roosevelt and other liberal candidates for political office.

Nevertheless, the war marked a turning point in the politics of labor. Perhaps the first sign was the decline of labor's influence in government. In a formal sense, that influence was short lived. Although the National Labor Relations Board had apparently favored organized labor, it could hardly be regarded as labor's part of government in the same sense as, say, the Agricultural Extension Service was organized agriculture's. Participation (or, perhaps, representation) in administration really came to organized labor when Sidney Hillman was appointed to the National Defense Advisory Council in 1940. Although the NDAC existed only briefly, Hillman was appointed to the successor agency, the Office of Production Management, as Associate Director General. His status there was at once coordinate with but also below that of the Director General, William S. Knudsen—an arrangement that pleased few partisans or administrators. In the reorganization that followed the Pearl Harbor disaster, the transition from OPM to the War Production Board, Hillman was omitted from the top directorate. Although he remained in the new organization as director of its labor division, representation of labor in the higher levels of government had ended.

Progressively, as time went on, the sense grew among labor leaders that they were being left out of the direction of the war. It is difficult to say to what degree this belief represented reality and to what degree it was deflation of a previously unrealistic assessment of their importance. Some of their demands were far-reaching, although these were for little more than had been achieved by businessmen. In 1942, for example, Philip Murray demanded "full and equal representation of labor in all government agencies dealing with war problems."[12] Even business was seldom this explicit in pressing for such a theory of governmental organization. A large number of "labor–

management committees" in war production plants were created, but many of these were ineffective on any level other than the trivial.

Labor was represented, however, on the War Labor Board, certainly an important agency. This, like its predecessor, the Defense Mediation Board, was tripartite; that is, it had four members representing employers, four representing labor, and four representing the public. Although the War Labor Board was generally regarded as successful, much of its success must be set down to popular support for prosecution of the war, the no-strike pledge from labor, and the skill of some Board members. Moreover, in the need to preserve industrial peace and to prevent inflation the Board had very genuine policy guides. Nevertheless the Board was an embodiment of ambiguity. What was that public which the "public members" were presumed to represent? Of what did its interest consist? How were these members to act if the other two groups disagreed? How if they agreed? These were questions to which the answers were unclear in the extreme. During World War II, however, they were avoided; the slogan of victory seemed to give sufficient guidelines. The dilemmas could not so easily be avoided in a later war, but during the war with Hitler the Labor Board was assured in its behavior, and its assurance underlined the fact that organized labor had achieved status but had not won power on the scale to which business was accustomed.

At the end of World War II, then, a very persuasive argument could be made that voluntarism was dead as the guiding outlook of the labor movement. The movement's constituency was vastly increased and membership was still growing. Labor had dropped its reluctance to participate in electoral politics and had plunged actively into repeated drives for legislation. It had had notable successes in the legislative arena, successes which in turn had built organizational strength and could be held to have benefited labor's membership. Moreover, labor leaders had gladly participated in the crucial work of administration and had vigorously sought greater participation. Labor had seemingly dropped its old rigidities and had, at the minimum, adopted the pragmatism of business which welcomed the services of government. Unlike business, however, organized labor at this moment had the qualities of a social movement—mass membership, dedicated leaders, and a great fund of enthusiasm. Difficulties had arisen; the necessities of war and the antagonism of employers had given labor setbacks. It seemed reasonable, however, to assume that these would be temporary and that labor would move onward in its evolution as a broadly based movement.

Nevertheless, for all that a genuine change had occurred, these trends could not safely be projected indefinitely to support either an assertion that voluntarism was now a thing of the past or a prediction of organized labor's future direction. In point of fact, the change that had occurred was not nearly so great as it seemed.

II

The atmosphere into which organized labor emerged at the end of World War II was very different from that of 1939. It was vastly more conservative in spirit and far less congenial to labor's aspirations. A massive retreat to purely private goals preoccupied most of the population after so long and intense a period of concern with the abnormalities of war. Labor inevitably shared in this mood and sought to seize the gains it had been denied by the wartime restraints of government. A wave of strikes occurred in 1945 and 1946. They resulted in substantial short-run gains, but these were largely lost in the general galloping inflation. A greater cost of the strikes to organized labor was the hardening of hostility directed against it. Moreover, difficult as it was to appreciate at that time, both Franklin D. Roosevelt and the New Deal were dead. And further, a substantial number of the new millions who had entered unions during the war years had little zeal for or commitment to the labor movement. Few of the new members had shared in the bitter struggles for union recognition; most had joined simply to meet the conditions of holding well-paying jobs on projects operated under government contracts. This new membership accordingly did not bring the same degree of loyalty or strength to the labor movement as the previous wave of members. These were intangible factors, but they were important.

The first shock of realization of the new conditions confronting the labor movement came with passage of the Taft–Hartley Act in 1947 by the first postwar Congress, the Eightieth. This measure—which but for the fact that the United States Senate changes its composition less abruptly than the House of Representatives might have been much closer to the "slave labor" act shocked labor leaders proclaimed it to be—was more than anything else a limitation on the organizational strength of unions. The Act somewhat diminished union security (although not as much as seemed probable at the time of passage), and this touched the most sensitive nerve in labor's leadership. But the rank and file was much less troubled by the measure, a factor that accounted in no small part for the second shock when, despite President Truman's reelection in 1948, efforts to repeal the Act failed conclusively.

Ironically, the Taft–Hartley Act was to no small degree the product of a mode of thinking to which the labor movement had contributed heavily. A frequent comment during this era was that labor had become too powerful. Sometimes the feeling was expressed through the metaphor of a pendulum, which had swung too far toward the labor side and now must return toward the business side; sometimes the metaphor was of a set of scales. Implicit in both figures of speech was a theory of balance between two definable extremes and two reified entities which constituted the whole of the reality involved. Although this theory was seldom elaborated, it was often implied, and it served as the framework of thinking about and justification for the action that was taken. Indeed, it was probably the more influential for not being explicit. Its invocation was a measure of the degree to which the orthodoxy of neopluralism had seized the mind of America.

The Korean War added to labor leaders' sense of frustration. Administration for mobilization in this war was modeled on that of World War II. Representatives of the labor movement were accordingly placed on a large number of administrative and advisory boards, the most important from labor's standpoint being the Wage Stabilization Board. Unfortunately, despite the tacit assumption that the experience of World War II could be used as a guide, conditions now were very different. In particular, there was the entirely new problem of partial mobilization: only part of the nation's productive resources was needed for war purposes, and a large-scale civilian economy existed alongside the war economy. Thus the impact of wartime regulation and restraint fell very unevenly, and the single test of contribution to the war effort could not be made at every point. Under these conditions, labor representatives on the Wage Stabilization Board felt justified in seeking wage increases. Denial of the increases sought, labor's sense of not being included in direction of the war effort at a sufficiently high level, and a generalized sense of diminished status in national politics led to disruption of the Board by the labor representatives, who walked out of it in 1951. Concurrently, labor representatives on other agencies also walked out.[13] Thus was disrupted what now amounted to the traditional plan of organization for wartime industrial mobilization. The walkout and labor's manifest bitterness produced the desired results: the Wage Board was reconstituted and the Truman administration made a very large, although tacit, concession to organized labor. It was a substantial but, again, short-lived victory, for in 1952 the struggle over wages and prices in the steel industry resulted in a massive political defeat for both labor and the Truman administration. Although the outcome could be regarded as a large economic victory for labor, politically this was a great turning point. Henceforth, union leaders could not be sanguine about their prospects as collaborators in the work of government at any very high level.

This gloomy outlook was confirmed by the subsequent election of a Republican administration and the events of the Eisenhower years. Perhaps the most important political development affecting labor during this period was the direction of public attention to the unions' internal problems. These problems were by no means new, as we have seen.[14] By all odds the greatest was the character of union government. To a very large degree, however, that issue was lost sight of in the general hue and cry for exposure of corruption and gangsters in the labor movement. This was essentially the same process that had occurred many times previously in other fields of American political life: the pathological fascination of corruption for Senators, Congressmen, and the press largely obscured the fundamental issues that were ultimately responsible for the various titillating delinquencies.

Much too late leaders of the labor movement undertook to clean their own house. Pious resolutions had been passed by the AFL deploring wrongdoing in unions, but the hard rock of union autonomy had always stopped effective action. In 1940, for example, President William Green of the AFL expressed the degree of forcefulness the Federation was prepared to bring to the problem:

> Our national and international unions are autonomous bodies, chartered by the American Federation of Labor, governed by their own laws and administered by the officers of said organizations. . . . We have never assumed and never will assume dictatorial policies toward national and international unions affiliated with the American Federation of Labor, but with all the power we possess we appeal to the membership of every International Union affiliated with the American Federation of Labor to keep the American labor movement clean. . . .[15]

By the early 1950s, however, the scandals were a bit too generally known. The affairs of the International Longshoremen's Association in particular were well aired by a New York State Crime Commission, and the consequent newspaper publicity forced action by the AFL. In 1953, after issuance of an ultimatum, the Federation expelled the ILA and chartered a new organization to take its place. With financial help from John L. Lewis, the ILA won the contest with the new union by a substantial margin in two different representation elections supervised by the NLRB. Here was corroboration of a sort that the old voluntarism had been right.

Nevertheless, continuing public disapproval of the labor movement's scandals led to the adoption of a series of codes of ethical practice by the AFL–CIO a year after their merger. Unfortunately, this gesture largely served to lend support to the public belief that corruption and gangsterism were much more prevalent than in fact they were. Early in 1957 the United States Senate appointed an investigative committee with the mouth-filling title of Select Committee on Improper Activities in the Labor or Management Field. The McClellan Committee, as it understandably came to be called, looked into some of the darker recesses of the labor movement, uncovering some stories new to the public and others more familiar. The Teamsters, the Bakery Workers, the Textile Workers, the Operating Engineers, the Carpenters, and a number of other unions were held up to public gaze as tainted with corruption or, at best, given to practices of an unsavory sort.[16] Only a fragment of the labor movement was investigated, but it was large enough that, whether by intention of the Committee or not, the public obtained an impression that the movement was thoroughly rotten. Yet the revelations were more extensive than the apologists of labor were willing to concede.

Passage of the Landrum–Griffin Act (the Labor–Management Reporting Act, 1959) was the direct outcome of these exposures. This measure, which required the filing of financial statements, regulated trusteeships over locals by national unions, and specified the intervals between elections and the rights of members, was governmental intervention in the internal affairs of unions on a wholly new scale. Although there is little evidence that unions have been weakened by the Act, many union leaders look upon it as a serious threat to the labor movement.

These major landmarks in the relationship between organized labor and government diminished any sense that henceforth labor could safely rely upon government in matters affecting union security. In the period after World War II it could be reasonably argued that government was more likely to hamper than to assist the exercise of union power. The efforts of labor's leadership to share in the exercise of public authority at a high level had failed. The significant labor legislation of the era was antagonistic to the power of unions—to a degree generally exaggerated by union leaders, though the trend was unmistakable. Moreover, public bodies, notably the McClellan Committee, had seriously damaged the labor movement's reputation.

Two quite different conclusions can be drawn from this reasoning. On the one hand, it could be concluded that the labor movement made a fundamental error when it accepted positive governmental assistance during the New Deal era. Thus, while adoption of the Wagner Act and use of the NLRB's certification process had been useful in gathering in a large new membership, unions had laid themselves open to government regulation when the fortunes of politics changed. According to such reasoning, the restraints of the Taft–Hartley and Landrum–Griffin Acts were the price paid for the benefits of the Wagner Act. On the other hand, the conclusion might be reached that the labor movement had not engaged sufficiently in political activity. Thus, if unions had devoted more of their energies to political indoctrination of their membership, the voice of labor might have been louder in Congress and the two restraining measures might never have been passed. Moreover, with more vigorous political activity, labor might have enjoyed greater influence with the executive branch of government.

It cannot be said that the labor movement adopted either of these rather clear alternatives. Various leaders adopted each position. Thus, after failure to repeal the Taft–Hartley Act following President Truman's reelection, there were rumbles from some union leaders (such as John L. Lewis) that the Wagner Act as well as the Taft–Hartley Act should be removed from the statutes. At the same time, other leaders (like Walter Reuther) were seeking greater labor efforts in the political arena. Thus the position of the movement as a whole has been ambiguous. It is probably correct to say that labor would welcome favorable legislation and that it is not ready to turn its back on the use of government. However, favorable legislation is probably definable as legislation that protects or enhances union strength. The degree to which the labor movement is prepared to commit resources for the passage of other legislation is probably very limited.[17]

The situation is rather similar in partisan and electoral politics. Since 1932 it has been axiomatic that "labor" is Democratic. The commitment, although clear, was informal during the 1930s, but in 1944 the CIO formed the Political Action Committee for the explicit purpose of reelecting Franklin Roosevelt. In 1948 the PAC had the assistance of Labor's League for Political Education (AFL) in campaigning for Truman's reelection. Official commitment of both AFL and CIO came when both endorsed Adlai Stevenson in 1952. The merger of the two federations brought the creation of the Committee for Political Education, which was active in the 1960 presidential campaign on behalf of John Kennedy. Organized labor spent substantial sums raised by special contributions on these elections. Thus, through the 1950s the national political committees of the AFL, the CIO, and of ten individual unions spent a total of between $1,500,000 and $1,750,000 in each election.[18] By 1962, President George Meany of the AFL–CIO was asserting, "Political action is labor's most important activity at this time."[19] On the face of things, the abandonment of the strictures of voluntarism against partisan politics would seem to be complete.

Nevertheless, some important qualifications to any such conclusion must be made. First, some labor leaders retain Republican affiliations. (Whether the Goldwater candidacy in 1964 has seriously changed this situation remains to be seen.) Neither the federation nor individual unions levy political tests, and it is unthinkable that they would try. Second, it remains official doctrine that labor should be nonpartisan—even in political education. The first constitutional convention of the AFL–CIO in 1955 affirmed "labor's traditional policy of avoiding entangling alliances with any other group and of supporting worthy candidates regardless of their party affiliation."[20] Third, it is at least arguable that organized labor's commitment to the Democratic Party is the product of labor's political weakness rather than of any fundamental decision to support the Democrats. Thus it can be said that ever since the New Deal era labor has had no alternative to support of the Democratic Party, and that so long as existing labor legislation is on the books it must seek friends in public office. Given the powers of the National Labor Relations Board, for example, the stake of union organizations in the character of appointments to the Board is great, and only one party can be regarded as friendly to the labor movement. Given labor's inability to isolate the NLRB from influences other than its own, the choice of remaining aloof from partisan politics is not open.

Ultimately, the political weakness of organized labor lies in the unions' inability to control the votes of their members. This was dramatized by labor's effort to defeat Senator Taft in 1950, a venture which met overwhelming failure. Additional evidence has made it plain that members' loyalty to unions does not extend to automatic acceptance of union-approved candidates.[21] Campaigns by labor have indeed had some local successes. The United Auto Workers, for example, have acted very aggressively in Michigan politics, and have probably played a larger political role than other unions. Their success, however, was in no small degree the consequence of the fact that the UAW was able to act in the absence of a developed party structure and to serve the functions of a party in a city where the union bulks unusually large. Even in this situation, however, the union has had to compromise and has had some failures. A recent comparison of the political pattern in Detroit with those in other cities suggests that unions are less able to act effectively in political campaigns where strong party machinery already exists.[22]

The avoidance of politics which was so prominent a feature of the old voluntarism certainly no longer characterizes the labor movement in the United States. Unions and union leaders are involved in both legislative and partisan politics, and labor involvement in local politics is probably at least as great as it has been in the past. If political action is taken as the test, it may appear that voluntarism is dead. But appearances may be deceptive. Although resolutions on particular matters of public policy are passed by federation and union conventions, few of these have been able to muster the subsequent energetic support of labor organizations that is essential to their translation into legislation and that indicates serious commitment. On the whole, the measures that do receive this sort of attention are those which affect union security and autonomy. The entrance of organized labor into electoral politics is real, but it is sporadic and uneven. And it is rather plainly the consequence of necessity. Ever since the Pandora's box of political action was opened in the 1930s, there has been no way to close it upon the ills that were released.

III

If the labor movement has departed from voluntarism by resort to political action, it has also deviated from its old principles in matters of organization and economic action. The creation of the CIO unions by organization from the top was a very large break with tradition. The trial and expulsion of Communist-dominated unions and the CIO's attempt to destroy them was an even greater break with the tradition of national union autonomy. Although this venture was hardly a thoroughgoing success, it was followed by the expulsion of other unions from the AFL–CIO for corruption. Here too, however, invocation of the only direct penalty in the power of the AFL–CIO proved inadequate to achieve the result intended.

On the face of things, labor also made radical departures in economic action. In the new setting of the period following World War II, a number of the CIO unions bargained with employers for establishment of pension and welfare plans. The practice rapidly spread, and by 1960 there were more than 24,000 pension plans and more than 94,000 welfare plans providing various benefits including life insurance, accident and sickness insurance, hospitalization, dental benefits, and sick leave.[23] The "escalator clause," a means by which wages would be kept even with inflation, was introduced in 1948 and spread to the contracts of numerous unions. In 1955 the campaign for a "guaranteed annual wage" began; it ultimately produced supplemental unemployment benefits achieved through bargaining with employers. There were also demands for profit-sharing plans, a number of which were successful, and for long vacations and provision for early retirement. Going even beyond these were demands that unions be permitted to examine the books of companies and that wage increases be made with no increase in the prices of the products involved. It is notable that most of these innovations were pioneered by the United Auto Workers, the most politically aggressive and successful union.

All these were marked changes from the one-time limitation of union objectives to better wages, hours, and working conditions. Some were more radical than others. Certainly the demands to look at company books and to prevent price increases were very far reaching. These demands, however, did not have the same degree of seriousness as the others and they were not won; they are probably best regarded as bargaining devices and as means of influencing public opinion. The demands for pensions, welfare plans, and profit-sharing, on the other hand, were very serious, and at different times during the postwar period became the central objectives of union strategy.

Various reasons impelled unions toward such demands. Before the end of the war, "fringe benefits" of various kinds had been the gains easiest to make in the face of the government's program to restrain inflation. The unions had become accustomed to this extension of the horizons of collective bargaining. Moreover the membership of some important unions was aging and was expressing concern for personal security. When the coal miners won the Miners Welfare and Pension Fund in 1946 the attendant publicity placed pressure on other unions to seek something comparable. At least equally important for the unions themselves, however, was an institutional consideration curiously akin to one that had been discovered by some business firms long before—namely, that the existence of pensions made workers reluctant to leave jobs to which the pensions were tied. For unions, particularly those with aging membership, pension systems offered stability. By giving members an increasing stake concurrently in the existing union and the existing jobs, a pension plan tied them to both union and employer. From the union standpoint, making union membership a qualification for benefits was probably more important than a maintenance-of-membership or union-shop clause in guaranteeing the union's continued existence,[24] a consideration all the more important with the preclusion of the closed shop by the Taft–Hartley Act. In one degree or another all of the various welfare plans have this function. Thus it is hardly true that these new objectives of union bargaining lead away from voluntarism. Although the conscious motivations of labor leaders in seeking pension and welfare benefits have been varied, it remains true that such devices have served the end of union security.

Voluntarism has always been heavily colored by the unions' need for institutional preservation. "Job consciousness" has indeed always been one of voluntarism's conspicuous traits. This has always been one of several characteristics, however, and unions have never been comprehensible simply as economic institutions. They have concurrently been political bodies, even when they have been most narrowly preoccupied with wages, hours, and working conditions. Politically, their most important characteristic has been narrow constituencies. This has been the political meaning of the much-noted job consciousness of the old AFL. In the postwar drive for pensions and welfare plans essentially the same factor is visible. In a broad social sense, enlargement of the benefits of the Social Security Act would have been preferable to the private welfare plans in a number of ways. First, it would have made benefits available to a larger constituency. It would also have improved labor mobility and made it less costly to individual union members. And it would have relieved the unions of a persistent problem

of managing increasingly large funds, which has at once made
unions more cautiously conservative and created temptations
for weak or venal officers. Nevertheless, the new devices have
enhanced the institutional security of unions, and in this sense
they may be indications that voluntarism is not wholly a thing
of the past.

Much of the argument that a fundamental change in the
character of the American labor movement has occurred since
1933 must rest on the characteristics exhibited by the unions
that have developed and grown large in this period, particularly the unions of the former CIO. Understandably, the smaller
craft unions can be expected to behave along the old lines of
voluntarism. A craft union with a small membership cannot
hope to act effectively in politics or be expected to forego the
tactical advantages of concentrating its energies on the narrow economic interests of the craft. On the whole, unions of
this sort have continued to exhibit the traits of what Robert
Hoxie termed "business unionism"—that is, voluntarism.[25]

The union with the best claim to vitality based upon ability
to increase its membership is the Brotherhood of Teamsters.
Whereas most major unions have lost members since 1955,
the Teamsters have made marked gains, despite opprobrium
heaped on them by Congressional committees, the press, and
the general leadership of the labor movement. The union's
growth in membership is the product of the special position of
power deriving from the fact that very few articles of commerce or industry do not at some time move by truck, and
also from the remarkable view of its jurisdiction contained in
the Teamsters' constitution. That document specifies a long
list of worker groups and then adds, "and other workers where
the security of the bargaining positions of the above classifi-
cations requires the organization of such other workers."[26]
It might be expected that this nearly all-encompassing jurisdictional claim would lead to the making of broad social demands and to political action, but the Teamsters have been
intensely particularistic and have largely avoided political
action.

The explanation is that this is a "business union" *par excellence*. Its leadership has always emphasized wages, hours, and working conditions. No other union has demonstrated so decisively that such a narrow range of interests is compatible with an intensive accumulation and exercise of power. Its broad constitutional claim of jurisdiction is a reflection of the union's almost obsessive concern to protect its outposts and then its outposts' outposts. A consequence is that to guard its own security the Brotherhood of Teamsters often appears more willing to collaborate with employers than with other unions. Certainly it seems true that the union is moved far less by any idea of solidarity than by the logic of its own power as an autonomous organization.

The notoriety of the Brotherhood of Teamsters rests primarily on a long series of investigations which have revealed an intricate set of relationships between the union's leaders and underworld figures and business ventures of dubious morality and legality. These ventures and relationships have been traced in hearings and reports of ponderous length; the McClellan Committee hearings alone ran to 58 volumes.[27] The stories brought forth in these investigations of sweetheart contracts, paper locals, dubious loans and partnerships made national headlines for many months, and inevitably the outcome was legal pursuit of the presumed evildoers.[28] The whole thing made splendid newspaper copy, but it obscured the issues of genuine public importance.

These issues revolved around the problem of business unionism itself. Certainly not all business unions are corrupt or engage in the practices the Teamsters have been charged with. Nevertheless, the particular forms of enterprise of which this union has been accused are rather clearly the particular pathology of business. Other aspects of the Teamsters' business unionism are more important, if less sensational. Certainly the union's propensity to collaborate with business in restrictive practices is more important than any collaboration in corrupt arrangements for the enrichment of leaders, however serious these may be. Perhaps the classic example of restrictive practice dates from the days when Dave Beck was head of the Western Conference of Teamsters. By refusing to make deliveries to Seattle filling stations which Beck regarded as "excessive," the Teamsters eliminated "cutthroat competition" in the business and earned the good will of established units in the industry.[29] The union presumably made gains of some substance for its members in return. It is less clear that this type of arrangement ("Dave Beck's little NRA") has served the public well.

Although the Teamsters have been avowedly nonpolitical in accordance with the best precepts of voluntarism, the union has not been especially hostile to the use of government when it has seemed that particular governmental powers might serve its interests and the interests of its industry. Thus, while former President Daniel Tobin of the Teamsters disapproved of the labor provisions of the NRA, he liked those of its features designed to fix rates and trade practices. The union, moreover, has sought governmental regulation of small owner-operators of trucks who have not been under union contracts. The Teamsters have been in considerable agreement with the American Trucking Association, and it is clear that their common goal is a reduction in the scale of operations of independents.[30] Indeed, at one point Beck expressed a complaint reminiscent of complaints sometimes made by business leaders:

We feel as if we are orphans in this industry. We are the only transportation industry in America without its own regulatory body. The railroads have the Interstate Commerce Commission. The airlines have the Civil Aeronautics Board, and ships have the Maritime Board. Yet our industry must be regulated by the railroad-dominated Interstate Commerce Commission.[31]

James Hoffa, Beck's successor as Teamster president, has continued the policy of collaboration with trucking firms and promotion of organization among truckers themselves. He has not achieved the sort of governmental regulation longed for by Beck, but this may be in large part because he has even more reason than Beck to be personally distrustful of government. However, the Teamsters' power under his regime has grown by rigid adherence to the voluntaristic principles of economic action, autonomy, support of the industry, and strict limitation of interest to the narrow constituency.[32]

The Brotherhood of Teamsters, however, can be regarded as unique in various ways. It has singular advantages deriving from the strategic position of its industry. Its membership may be more given to cynicism than many others. Its tradition is deeply rooted in voluntarism, and it has a web of relationships with industry of unusual complexity and long standing. Accordingly, it may not be the most significant union in which to seek evidence of the trend of things in the labor movement.

The United Mineworkers of America has contributed to the development of the labor movement to a degree perhaps greater than any other union. It fought out and won the issue of industrial unionism more than two decades before that issue was confronted by labor as a whole. When that time did come, the Mineworkers provided in John L. Lewis and Philip Murray the two greatest leaders in the reconstitution of the movement. This union also provided a large part of the money that made the CIO a reality. Under Lewis's leadership the UMW became an important political force, although its influence was diminished by the later estrangement of Lewis from Franklin Roosevelt. It is an organization that might well be expected from its record to be in the vanguard of any movement away from labor's traditional voluntarism.

Developments of the postwar era do not fulfill such expectations. Since the late 1940s the coal mining industry has been mechanized to a degree that amounts to a technological revolution, a revolution the union has not only permitted, but has actively fostered. One of the consequences is a sharp decline in the number of coal miners. These, the backbone of the union, numbered approximately 400,000 in 1948. Within ten years their number had been reduced by half, and the decline continues.[33] The UMW has won a remarkable financial return in its Welfare and Retirement Fund for its cooperation in mechanizing the industry. This fund, supported by a rising levy on each ton of coal mined, quickly rose to magnificent proportions and supported an impressive system of welfare benefits. Although it later encountered difficulties, it created benefits on a scale seldom rivaled and won repeated skirmishes with the American Medical Association.

Even more impressive, the UMW provided the leadership that has brought prosperity to the industry itself. The great increase in mechanization of the mines has been the major factor in this prosperity, but in union and management eyes alike the union-fostered organization of the industry has been equally important. The UMW has held that the industry's central problem has been excess capacity—the counterpart to the problem of too many miners. With organization in both industry and union, excess of both capacity and miners has been eliminated in recent years, with a resultant increase in both profits and wages.

The union has saved itself from what otherwise might have become a disastrous situation. It has earned the praise of coal operators as the industry's savior. But it has also earned the curses of the more than 300,000 miners of the Appalachian coal areas who have been forced out of work in a fifteen-year period.[34] Large numbers of these miners remain in the valleys once dominated by the now abandoned mines. It is thoroughly believable that the UMW acted in a manner best calculated to insure its survival. The miners who remain in its constituency enjoy prosperity that their fathers might have found difficult to believe. But the choices made by the union to narrow its constituency and to collaborate with (even to force organization among) the coal operators are clearly in the mainstream of voluntarist tradition. For the union it is an old tradition; the conspicuous political ventures of the 1930s suggested more of a break than actually occurred in the union's economic policy.[35]

Somewhat the same impulsions have been apparent in another union which would seem at least superficially to have a thoroughly different character: the International Longshoremen and Warehousemen's Union. This union developed in the 1930s from a split-off from the International Longshoremen's Association, and under the highly aggressive leadership of Harry Bridges soon transformed the situation of West Coast longshoremen. Where before they had been subject to the degrading insecurity of the shape-up (as longshoremen continued to be on the East Coast), hiring was placed on an impartial basis through union-operated hiring halls. Wages and working conditions improved markedly, but only after bitter struggles with employers. Bridges was attacked as a Communist in a series of legal campaigns that today seem difficult to believe. Everything about the union seemed tinged with ideology, and it earned a reputation as a radical organization. Employers seemed bent on its utter destruction.

Nevertheless, after the Soviet Union entered World War II, the union undertook to support prosecution of the war and established a record of cooperation as marked as its previous seemingly implacable hostility to capitalism. From the cooperation with employers that developed in this period there gradually emerged a pattern of collaboration with employers. This collaboration did not occur immediately, but after an ideological crusade against Bridges and the ILWU in the late 1940s by employers and the United States Government collapsed, the plan for an accommodation between union and employers developed. This plan, like that of the United Mineworkers, involved acceptance by the union of mechanization on the docks and gradual reduction of the union's rolls. A substantial price was exacted by the ILWU from the employers, but the essential facts were that the union and the employers reached a long-term settlement and that one of its conditions was the union's agreement to the deliberate contraction of its constituency. The results were highly favorable to those who remained within the constituency, but were admittedly different for those who were now outside. Bridges, the notorious radical, explained in a statement of remarkable candor: "You can't go getting mad at the employer because under our system he's in business to make profits. So you have to try to work out a solution within the system, and ours is admittedly a pretty selfish solution."[36]

A prominent feature of each of these narratives is the attainment of fundamental agreement between union and industry for the common enjoyment of benefits gained in some degree at the expense of those outside their joint constituency. Collaboration on this basis has been no less possible for a combative organization like the Mineworkers and an ideologically colored union like the West Coast longshoremen than for a business-minded union like the Teamsters. All have arrived at positions of remarkable similarity in this respect—suggesting that differences of ideology and style may be superficial. The record of another union, the United Steelworkers, however, indicates that this explanation is inadequate.

The steel industry has been widely regarded, rightly or wrongly, as peculiarly and fundamentally important to the general economy. For this reason and also because steel is unquestionably of central importance in wartime, government has been repeatedly and heavily involved in the industrial relations of steel—an involvement deriving as well from fear of inflation and of the consequences of protracted strikes. Nevertheless, industrial relations in steel since the end of World War II have followed a pattern in which industry and union have engaged in one bitter dispute after another and settlements have featured higher wages, higher prices, and defeat for the government. This pattern began in 1946, when a post-strike settlement resulted in dissolution of the public machinery for controlling inflation. There were no strikes in 1947 or 1948, but increased wages were followed by increased prices; results in 1949 after a 45-day strike were similar. There was no strike in 1950, but in 1951 and 1952, during the Korean War, a particularly sharp contest between union and industry resulted first in disruption of economic stabilization machinery, and then in its destruction. Feeling ran high between the two contending parties. The union was convinced the industry should have no price increase, but was determined to have higher wages for itself. In the outcome the wage increase was accompanied by a price increase generally regarded as larger than necessary to meet the cost of the wage increase. A strike by the union enforced both demands in the situation.[37] So the pattern continued for the rest of the decade; its culmination was the largest single strike in American history, that of 1959.[38]

The degree to which results of the frequently hostile relationships in steel were similar to those of the often friendly arrangements in the industries mentioned earlier is remarkable. Certainly, neither corrupt leadership nor sheer ideology can explain the general pattern. Recently, some unions have indeed sought longer vacations, paid holidays, and more relief time, and have opposed overtime, in order to spread work in the face of the effects of automation. To this extent there is resistance against the shrinking of union constituencies. In a very broad sense, however, it is clear that some of the most important traits of voluntarism remain. Although the rhetoric of some unions has undoubtedly changed, the economic behavior of even those unions least likely to proclaim the virtues of voluntarism is directed toward organizational survival and the benefit of narrow constituencies. If there is an important change, it is that constituencies are becoming narrower.

IV

By the 1960s a condition approaching crisis had overtaken the American labor movement. That "crisis" is the appropriate term is sometimes disputed, but certainly many observers and participants in the movement are deeply troubled.[39] With its apparent change of direction in the 1930s great fervor developed and widespread hopes arose that the labor movement was on its way to a transformation of American society. But as the greatly enlarged movement gradually settled down to a bureaucratized existence, the fervor abated and disillusionment took its place. It was a new illustration, perhaps, of the insight of Gompers when he spoke of the relegation of "some idealism to movements which do not move to the dead ashes of blasted hopes and promises."[40]

Nevertheless, there were other signs of a more objective

character that all was not well with the American labor movement. The first was that the growth of union membership had stopped. Following World War II union membership had increased slightly more rapidly than the increase in the civilian labor force, a growth that continued until 1953. In the following year, however, union membership as a percentage of the labor force began dropping. The decline has continued on a slow downward curve from 28 per cent in 1953 to a bare quarter.[41] There has also been a decline in absolute numbers since 1957. Although these figures indicate no catastrophe, they are not signs of good health in a movement that has always presumed that ultimately it would include most of the working class.

This failure to grow is a reflection of a series of particular failures. Thus it reflects the failure of a much-heralded campaign to organize in the South. It reflects the similar collapse (or perhaps simple abandonment) of a campaign to organize agricultural workers. More important than either of these is the continuing lag in organization of white-collar workers during an era in which the ratio of white- to blue-collar workers is steadily increasing.

There are other signs of the membership decline. Most apparent but also most difficult to measure is the decline of dynamism in the labor movement. As the low attendance of members at local meetings reflects, it is no longer possible to generate the enthusiasm of members. And union leaders have only limited ability to gain the voting support of members in public elections except where they can demonstrate that issues are of the most immediate concern to labor. Various reasons have been offered in explanation. Unions are much more efficient organizations than they were in the 1930s, but they are also much more bureaucratic and impersonal. And the leaders who formed the new industrial unions of the CIO have, like their counterparts in the older AFL unions, grown older. With this bureaucratization and aging has come increasing attention to the problems of internal government in the unions. Intellectuals and liberals have been more and more articulate on this subject, and union members have themselves proved restive under their established regimes.[42]

Some observers have also emphasized factors external to the unions. The most dramatic of these is automation (a term frequently used loosely to cover mechanization and improved technology). There is a sharp difference of opinion as to whether automation results in a net destruction of jobs, but it is clear that it does eliminate some jobs on which particular unions have relied for maintenance of their membership rolls in the past. The examples of the Mineworkers and the West Coast longshoremen support the argument that unions cannot handle the problem and at the same time maintain their membership. Automation has also been a factor tending to make strikes difficult or even, as in the telephone industry, nearly impossible. The availability of strikes as tools in collective bargaining has also been diminished by a strong and apparently growing public intolerance for strikes on any substantial scale. The continuation of a large pool of unemployed, the conviction of young workers "that union seniority systems and attrition programs for dealing with automation are conspiratorial devices foisted on industry by labor organizations, whose sole concern is to guard the vested rights of their own dues payers," and the hostility of Negroes to unions are among the factors that are claimed to have made both unions and collective bargaining obsolescent.[43]

The implicit prediction is a gloomy one for the labor movement; nevertheless, if it is that unions are going to wither and die in America, it may be too far reaching. As Philip Taft has observed, crises for the labor movement have been heralded before and have in time proved exaggerated insofar as sheer organizational survival is concerned. Moreover, there are good reasons to believe that many unions of craft workers and many in the service trades may continue to go along much as they have in the past, bargaining to improve wages, hours, and working conditions for their limited constituencies. While some of these constituencies may shrink, others may grow to a limited extent. Even industrial unions such as those in mining, steel, oil and textiles, in which automation is a vivid prospect, will still have the same basis for existence, despite continually smaller memberships.

But to say all this, is not to deny the reality of a crisis. Whether or not this is the proper term, it is clear that a sharp reevaluation of the labor movement is under way in many circles. To no small degree this reevaluation is itself the crisis. Until comparatively recently the labor movement had the apparent stance of a challenger to the established order of things, speaking on behalf of men at the lower end of the social spectrum. The voluntarism of Gompers and his successors belied this, but until World War II unions still had to fight for recognition and acceptance, although they accepted the economic and political order within which they existed. This struggle did much to disguise the nature of voluntarism. But recognition and acceptance have recently become general. One of the most striking facts about the labor movement today is that, as one close student puts it, employers do most of the work of maintaining union membership through enforcement of the union shop and deduction of union dues from wages.[44] By 1960 almost three quarters of union members were covered by agreements providing for union shops; 78 per cent were under agreements with checkoff provisions. Some of the unions without such provisions are in the construction industry and control access to jobs through control of hiring.[45] In short, unions need no longer engage in the struggle that has been their principal preoccupation in the past and which has given them the air of crusading organizations.

While unions were afflicted with deep insecurity and doubt whether they could survive in the face of the bitter hostility of employers and the erratic unreliability of members, it was understandable that maintenance of organization should be an ultimate consideration in union policy. This was a large part of the practical meaning of the old voluntarism, and it often gave a stern and bitter quality to industrial relations. With that issue now largely settled, the other qualities of voluntarism are returning to the surface, notably the tendency of unions to collaborate with employers in arrangements that are mutually gratifying but of doubtful advantage to those outside their respective constituencies. Although this tendency can occur under peaceful and friendly conditions, it can also appear, as in steel, where there is genuine hostility.

The willingness of certain unions to accept solutions that require a virtual casting out of some of their members (to say nothing of potential members) is equally striking. These solutions may well be justified in terms of abstract economic efficiency, and may even be forced upon the unions. Nevertheless, they are at odds with the aspirations for self-government and self-determination within unions. The democratic presumptions of the unions may have substance, but they are repudiated when the unions themselves participate in the liquidation of a part of their membership.

The issue of political action is obviously deeply troubling to union leaders today. Many labor publications are heavily given over to political news and political appeals. Much of the energy of prominent leaders goes to political matters, at local, national, or international levels. Some of the most vigorous leaders quite plainly wish for a greater role in politics for the labor movement. Thus, Joseph Beirne, President of the Communications Workers, has placed strong emphasis upon greater political participation by the labor movement.[46] External observers, particularly those who are most troubled by the present situation of the labor movement, share the view that union goals are too narrowly economic.[47]

Despite the frequently intense desire of some union leaders to enlarge the political and social horizons of their organizations, however, the labor movement is ill constituted to realize their hopes. The national unions remain the foci of power in the movement, and they are all founded on an exclusive basis. The constituency of each is narrow and more likely to be further narrowed than broadened. For such organizations the logic of voluntarism remains compelling. The evidence of attempts to achieve important results by political action is disappointing to those who would transform the labor movement by sheer political campaigning. The United Auto Workers have been in the best situation to achieve political results; nevertheless, even that union has had only limited success and has had to return to aggressive economic action as its principal tool. The difficulty has been stated by the then President of the United Steelworkers, David J. McDonald: "I firmly believe the type of unions which exist today will not suffice for the future." He asked for "entirely new ideas of organizing and different types of organization."[48] Such new ideas of organization, if intended to achieve results upon the political scene, could only involve a broader constituency for the labor movement.

The break with voluntarism which came in the 1930s was real. It involved the labor movement in the creation of a greatly enlarged constituency and in political modes of action. If the voluntarism of Gompers and his associates and their immediate successors is regarded as at heart an antipolitical creed, then perhaps it is correct to say that the break with voluntarism was almost complete. Despite the doctrinaire quality of the rejection of political action in the old AFL, however, this rejection was probably never the heart of the matter. The autonomy of narrowly constituted organizations has always been more important, as could be seen in the apparent inconsistency of the craft unions' deep involvement in local politics at the same time they supported the Gompers antipolitical position nationally. More recently, labor has been willing to act in national politics, but most of its political involvement has been directed to the goal of organizational security. When legislation affected organizational matters, as with Taft–Hartley, or where appointed governmental officers had important powers over organizational issues, as with the National Labor Relations Board, organized labor willingly entered the political arena.

Just as large corporations secure in the exercise of their own market power have asserted the doctrine of *laissez faire*, whereas other business organizations have resorted to the use of governmental authority, organized labor has at different times and places either insisted on the wrongfulness of political involvement or engaged in legislative and political campaigns. To the extent that private economic power proves reliable, it may be expected that both business and labor will renounce politics and insist upon the antigovernmental strictures of *laissez faire* and voluntarism. To the extent that private economic power is unreliable, whether for purposes of internal discipline or defense against external influences on their spheres of interest, it may be expected that business and labor will seek the use of government.

Labor's deviation from voluntarism, then, has been less dramatic than it has seemed. Many labor leaders do indeed show a deep ambivalence on the issue of political participation. It is notable, however, that the historic goal of organizational security has to a very large degree been achieved for many unions. With this achievement, it is increasingly open to labor to conclude treaties of collaboration with industry in which the classically narrow goals of voluntarism are those of the labor movement. If there is a further step it is that units of government be used to enforce these ends along with those sought by industry in their collaboration. There are already signs of such a step.

Chapter 10

The Quest
of the Public Interest

I

Power is an exceedingly diverse and complex phenomenon in America. Almost everywhere elusive to analysis, it is especially so in the greatest of the democracies. The theories about its nature, its sources, and its holders are varied, and some are deeply at odds with others. At one extreme is a view that power is highly concentrated in the hands of an elite the unity of which has steadily been growing and which acts largely without regard to the supposed values of a liberal society. In its most recent form, this has been termed a "power elite," woven of the highest leadership of the large corporations, the government, and the military.[1] The great decisions are made in these higher circles and what lies beyond their reach—or, perhaps, concern—is unimportant. At the other extreme is the view that power is so scattered, balanced, and counterbalanced as to be almost nonexistent; what it amounts to is no more than a bewildering array of "veto groups," each having the capacity to block the ventures of the others.[2]

Some evidence can be cited for each of these differing views. The exchange of posts between industrial and military leaders has been noted by many observers since the end of World War II. President Eisenhower gave this often close relationship special emphasis when, on leaving office, he warned of a "military-industrial complex" which might take complete control of government. Some of the evidence presented in earlier chapters could be cited to suggest the growth of such an insidious power: the close affinity between industrial leaders and civilian and military managers of mobilization, the meshing of industry advisory committees with public authorities, and the extensive penetration of government by without-compensation personnel from industry. On the other hand, the sheer multiplicity of organized groups in private life, many with heavy influence sometimes amounting to control of public agencies and many with marked power through ties to particular congressional committees, suggests that American institutions are studded with so many barriers to action that stalemate is the essential reality of politics in the United States.

Neither of these perceptions is adequate. The "power elite" today rather obviously suffers from internal disarray. It lacks the organization and unity necessary to give it the capacities which are feared from it. Perhaps such organization would be impossible under any circumstances save a total mobilization unprecedented in either world war of the past. The military-industrial complex has been unsettled to some degree by Secretary of Defense McNamara. The façade of unity within the military establishment has repeatedly been broken in contests such as that over the TFX experimental plane.[3] The reality seems to be that the military-industrial complex is not one but many complexes. Moreover, although on occasion massive industrial challenges to public leaders are made—the outstanding example being United States Steel's attempt in 1962 to nullify President Kennedy's economic policy—"big decisions" are few.[4] Indeed, the great decisions themselves seem to be the largely unanticipated consequences of previous and lesser decisions made under pressure from a great variety of circumstances and participants.

On the face of things, then, the actual fragmentation of the elite lends plausibility to the view that power is really illusory. But this conclusion does not accord with the evidence presented in these pages. Repeatedly during the past half century, relatively homogeneous groups have been effectively organized and have assumed a strong degree of power over particular areas of public policy through close collaboration with segments of government; and one cannot dismiss as unimportant or insignificant the areas where such power has become a reality. Perhaps the decisions made in these areas pale beside such hypothetical choices as "war or peace" or "capitalism or socialism." Such choices, however, are beyond the power of even that elite imagined by the most apprehensive critic. In their absence as genuine issues, the matters dealt with in the areas of government and policy discussed here are the very substance of politics. Some are more important than others; some seem almost trivial. But each in itself has a degree of importance; and collectively they encompass a substantial part of our common concerns.

The pattern of power discussed in previous chapters is probably the most characteristic form of power in contemporary America. And more examples might have been considered. The relationship between veterans' organizations and the Veterans Administration is a conspicuous omission.[5] The history of the Food and Drug Administration, both when it was part of the Department of Agriculture and more recently when it has been in the Department of Health, Education and Welfare, would have been illuminating.[6] The entire area of housing policy and organized real estate interests has not been mentioned. Only a cursory look at state government and policy has been possible, and here, as might be expected, is a sphere in which private organizations, some of them national in scope, are more effective than in the federal sphere. Thus, for example, the National Council for the Accreditation of Teacher Education exercises legal powers delegated by boards of education in 29 different states.[7] And nothing has been said of local government, where a similar system may be even more deeply rooted.

The existence of an array of narrow-interest-centered power structures within the open framework of American political life is no secret. It is not a hidden government, it is highly visible to anyone who spends time in Washington or who reads news beyond the headlines. It is obscure, certainly, but its obscurity is the result of dullness, routine, and the general acceptance of a largely unarticulated orthodoxy. It is apparent in the press only when, from time to time, weak public servants adrift on the beaconless sea of their own discretion are discovered to be corrupt. Even in these recurrent scandals, the venality of the weaklings usually proves petty, and the scandals quickly lose their interest and are soon forgotten. The underestimation of the significance of this pattern of power, however, is also partly a product of the cautious language used to describe it by scholars who are familiar with it. "Clientele relationships" (or, even less happily, "clientalism"), the term usually applied to the phenomenon, not only confers an aura of professional respectability on the participants in these relationships; it also obscures the fact that they are power relationships and misses the most important facts about them.

The first conclusion that emerges from the present analysis and survey is that a substantial part of government in the United States has come under the influence or control of narrowly based and largely autonomous elites. These elites do not act cohesively with each other on many issues. They do not "rule" in the sense of commanding the entire nation. Quite the contrary, they tend to pursue a policy of noninvolvement in the large issues of statesmanship, save where such issues touch their own particular concerns. Indeed, it could be argued that some genuine benefits to the nation might be conferred if these elites could fuse into one. Their assumption of control of parts of government is not the result of conspiracy; numerous examples have shown that private groups that exercise control are as likely to be created by public officials as the posts of public officials are to be established by private groups. Almost invariably, moreover, these structures of power are built with good intentions to serve the ends and means of democracy.

This would constitute capture of government if it were comprehensive and if the consequences of the process were more clearly foreseen by those taking part in it. Some of the results of such capture do appear in some areas of government. Some of the elites that have assumed power in this manner are among those Marx might have named as the ruling class. Nevertheless, the multiplicity of these elites and their separation from each other in organization sharply distinguish the reality from Marx's perception. A secondary distinction is that whereas most of the power structures moved by these elites are focused upon particular economic interests, some are noneconomic in character. The latter—the conservation groups are an example—are usually at a disadvantage in maintaining their own cohesion and are compelled to imitate their opponents' form of organization in order to be effective within the American context.

However, the control of particular agencies in government by narrow private groups, although genuine and perhaps the logical culmination of the development traced here, is not the whole or even the essential part of it. Where sufficient power over the constituency of a particular elite can be established without using the compulsion of public authority, it is sufficient to wall off the area of concern to the elite and to insulate it against forces from without; and if government is, or appears to be, such an outside force, the wall will exclude government. This is in accord with the tradition of *laissez faire*, and the arguments derived from that doctrine are of great assistance in mantaining autonomy; but they may sometimes produce a policy less effective in maintaining autonomy than a forthright utilization of public authority would be. A large corporation is frequently so strong within the market that it can rely upon its own private power and need only ensure that public authority is weak. Some corporations, however, are quite willing to make use of public authority when the need appears, particularly when wartime conditions magnify its force. There is thus an important continuity in the assertion of corporate freedom from government intervention and the capture of a segment of government. This continuity consists of autonomy and the preservation of the power to govern within the particular area of concern.

A similar continuity is evident in the insistence of labor unions on reliance solely upon their own economic strength in some situations and their willingness to use state and local governmental powers in licensing. The same thing may be seen in the rejection of government-supported health insurance by the American Medical Association and the exercise of examining powers by state medical associations. The principal difference between business on the one hand and labor and professional groups on the other is that business is generally more pragmatic and perhaps less rigidly attached to the ideology of *laissez faire*.

Autonomy is fundamentally a conservative principle. It appears as the thread of consistency in the behavior of organizations and groups simply because it is the condition of their being; its preservation is necessary to maintain their power. But this is not to say that autonomy is necessary—or even always useful—to protect the power of individuals within the scope of the group's power. Autonomy protects the power of a group, particularly an organized group, and this power is at once power over matters of common concern and power over the group's members. However homogeneous on one dimension a group may be, it cannot escape differences on other dimensions, whether these be of age, race, religion, or some other. The existence of these differences, usually overlooked in the general acceptance of the group's own assertion of unity, creates a political problem which may not be important in some organizations, but which when the groups are taken collectively is important. The recognition of a right of autonomy, self-determination, or self-regulation may be expedient, given the group's power. But it does not eliminate the power over its members which the leadership of the group may have; indeed, it is more likely than not to enhance that power. When, under the guise of serving an ideal of democracy as the self-government of small units, the coercive power of public authority is given to these groups, their internal government becomes a matter of serious concern.

This is, first, a problem of the constituency in that the conditions and qualifications of membership may exclude significant numbers of people who are affected by the group's actions and the public regulations it influences or actually formulates; thus the exclusion of Negroes by some unions has been a serious issue. But comparable, if less dramatic, issues have appeared in other organizations; farm groups, for example, have informally but effectively drawn their constituencies so as not to include the rural poor, among whom the major problems of the farm population are concentrated. Second, there is a problem of actual government within most of these associations, a problem at once of how well the various interests within the membership are accommodated, how well individual members' rights are protected, and how well the responsibility of leaders is maintained. Unfortunately, the governments of most associations illustrate well Michels' "iron law of oligarchy," and the institutions of their political systems provide few checks or limitations upon the power of leaders. Nor do they provide any but the most rudimentary means for taking account of differences among members. On both these scores, the principal restraint seems to rest in the leaders' intuitive capacity to perceive potential hostility that might result in rebellion. A major reason for the widespread pattern of unchecked leadership power and irresponsible government among these associations is the myth of unity most of them profess to believe. This, in turn, is related to the small constituencies on which they are founded; relative homogeneity on one dimension is usually regarded as extending to other dimensions as well.

Why has political organization in the United States so often been based on small constituencies? The answer lies partly in historical origin. In general, although the actual membership of a group or association may grow, its category of eligibles—that is, its potential membership—will narrow. This is a consequence of the imperatives of organization, which has an easier task of internal government to the degree that dissidents are excluded and homogeneity is achieved. It is almost a truism that this is an era of organization and bureaucratization. The constituency at the time of beginning is thus probably larger than it will be later. For whatever reasons, the original constituencies of many groups today have been relatively narrow; the development of the Farm Bureau is a clear example. The labor movement also illustrates the point; to encompass a larger constituency than was actually being served by the unions of 1933, entirely new unions had to be established at the cost of a revolution within the movement.

A second explanation for the prevalence of narrow constituencies is that they enjoy tactical advantages in contests with external opponents. Thus the United Mine Workers Union has enjoyed general peace and prosperity since it accepted accelerated mechanization of the mines and a smaller membership. A third explanation may be found in the orthodoxy that organization by small units is the essence of democracy.

Despite these strong tendencies toward smaller constituencies, opposing tendencies place some limits on the narrowing process. Some of these are economic and social. The creation of an increasingly national market, for example, sets bounds on the degree to which unions may decentralize their operations. This development long ago forced local unions to join with each other to prevent workers outside their respective geographic boundaries from disrupting local union organization. It should be noted, however, that the nationalization of union organization was not complete and, moreover, took place upon another narrow dimension, that of craft. Even today, the craft basis of organization has not been superseded in many fields. Similarly, the vast improvement in roads and other means of communication inevitably erodes the certainty attributed to the parochial values of particular areas. Southern faith in the validity of states' rights is undoubtedly under such pressure at the present time. Beyond this, there are more purely organizational pressures. Thus a difficult choice is presented to union leaders today: should they seek to operate upon a wider field (i.e. politics) and dilute the intensity of their power, or should they narrow their efforts and intensify their power within the lesser field? Organizational dangers have helped produce smaller constituencies in the International Longshoremen and Warehousemen's Union and the United Mine Workers, but they have tended to lead the Communications Workers in the direction of political action and, implicitly, a larger constituency. The circumstances of these unions are obviously quite different.

The constituency occupies a central position in the present analysis. The defense of autonomy is thus to be seen as the defense of particular constituent boundaries. Autonomy has no clear meaning in a given situation unless those boundaries are known. The meaning of responsibility, in turn, is empty unless the constituency to which responsibility is owed and actually paid is known. It is necessary to specify the *actual* constituency, since many organizations pretend to speak for constituencies larger than those in whose interest they customarily act. Thus the American Farm Bureau Federation publishes *Nation's Agriculture* and the Chamber of Commerce of the United States publishes *Nation's Business;* the Farm Bureau asserts it is the voice of American agriculture, and presumably the Chamber regards itself as a similar spokesman for business. Such claims are patently excessive. Behavior is a better guide to the actual constituency. "Business," "agriculture," and "labor" are all abstractions, and they can only be misleading when regarded as reified political entities.

Although the constituency is the central conception of the present study, one or another of several different factors could be so considered. In general these factors imply each other and tend to appear together. They may be listed as (1) size of constituency, (2) character of ends, (3) character of tactics, and (4) character of ideology. They might be conceived as arranged in a circular relationship, one leading to another, that to the next, and so on.

The constituency (if this is taken as a point of beginning on the circle) may be large or small. If it is large, it will probably be heterogeneous; if it is small, it will probably be homogeneous. To the degree that it is homogeneous it will be cohesive, but it will also have efficient power over matters of common concern to the constituency. Accordingly, the ends it most probably seeks will be narrow, specific, concrete, and usually material in character. If the constituency is large and heterogeneous, its ends will be large, general, and sometimes vague. Correlatively, narrow and concrete ends dictate limited tactics, most typically economic. If the ends are large and general, the tactics will probably be overtly political. Finally, narrow and specific ends will produce an ideology of small units, whereas general ends will produce an ideology of large units. Thus we are led back to the character of the constituency.

In general, the political units examined here have shared the characteristic of resting upon small constituencies. They have on the whole had limited ends; their tactics have been limited and often more economic than political. Where they have been openly political, they have relied upon group self-help through the exercise of well-isolated segments of public authority rather than upon action through political parties and elections. Finally, they have all shared an ideology of small units. Sometimes this has taken the form of "grass roots" local democracy, but it has also assumed the form of *laissez faire* and insistence upon the autonomy of economic units. Vis-à-vis the nation as a whole it has glorified the separatist aspect of federalism and disparaged the public as a reality.

The politics of both land and water has shown a persistent tendency toward the maintenance of small constituencies. The loose and general constituency of the Farmers Alliance gave way before the narrower Farm Bureau; the Farm Bureau has had difficulty in standing off the challenge of even more limited commodity groups. The private associations and groups supporting the various agencies in water politics have been very narrowly based. Business has been conspicuously devoted to the autonomy of the corporation or, where business firms have individually been without substantial market power, to

well-knit and homogeneous trade associations. Labor organization has proceeded beyond national unions only so far as a
loose federation.

Similarly, the groups surveyed here, with some differences
of degree, have generally had narrow ends. The Farm Bureau
in much of its history, for example, has been concerned with
the prices of major commodities. Its present distaste for
measures akin to those it once sponsored is not merely an
appreciation that the Depression conditions which seemed to
justify them have disappeared; it is also the result of a sense
that price supports can be maintained only through government action and that, since other organizations are in the field,
this may not serve to maintain Farm Bureau organization.
Exclusive control of public agencies in agriculture has not
been possible to the extent once hoped for when the Extension
Service was the only field service of the Department of Agriculture. Prices and moderation of the rigors of competition
have been the outstanding preoccupations of business organizations. The trinity of wages, hours, and working conditions
is nearly sacred among American labor unions.

The tactics of the various groups have on the whole been
tailored to their ends. Labor has shown the simplest pattern.
For much of its history it resolutely refused to follow any but
economic methods on the national scene, considering the benefits of social insurance as too costly in terms of organizational
weakness for the component unions, although local unions
have readily supported city machines for control of licensing
and other benefits. Various farm movements such as the Society of Equity and, more recently, the National Farm Organization, have attempted to use the purely economic tactic of
holding goods off the market to raise prices; this tactic has
not been successful and other farm associations have willingly
had recourse to public authority by capture of segments of
government. Business groups have, where possible, relied on
their own economic power, but have frequently used governmental agencies where this was more expedient. In general the
use of government has depended on a particular group's capac-

ity to isolate the relevant governmental agency from influences other than its own and to establish itself as the agency's constituency—at once giving an air of validity to its own ends and endowing it with the added disciplinary power of public authority over its own members.

All these groups have a strong commitment to the orthodoxy of small units. This frequently takes the form of denunciation of government—usually "big government"—in general, but it can also take the form of a preference for state or local action over federal action. On occasion it involves justifying the fragmentation of the executive branch of the government. In agriculture small geographic communities are glorified as "grass roots democracy." Their parallels in business are necessarily functional and the language takes the vocabulary of individualism, even where the unit of social reality involved is the large corporation. The voluntarism of labor exalts the national union, sometimes regarding even the federation with suspicion and often hailing the local union as the true home of union democracy—nearly the ultimate in the ideology of small units. Given the close association between ends and ideology, it should not be surprising that the materialistic aspects of American culture should be emphasized in the ideology by the proclivity of these narrowly based groups for concrete and specific ends.

The ideology of small units is the link between the strong American commitment to the autonomy of economic units and the still strong belief in the democratic value of autonomous small governmental units, whether they are states or localities. In the orthodox view there seems to be a definite progression in desirability from national government at the least desirable level, to state government, to large private units of organization, to local government (with a minor step to a fragment of local government such as a water district), to small private units. The abstractions of "big business" and "big labor" probably fall somewhere in the scale between big and small government.

Insofar as federalism is regarded as guaranteeing state

sovereignty, it receives the praise of the orthodox. Yet it is more evident in the explicitly political units of the states than in private organizations that autonomy is a means of discriminating among the members of the state's supposed constituency —as becomes transparent to most people when the cry of states' rights is raised; the implications for civil rights need no explanation today. But the internal pattern of state government poses the same large issue of internal distribution of benefits in a multitude of other ways.

One of the most serious problems of a system of decentralized political units in a liberal society is the consequent uneven sharing in power. Some segments of the population are excluded from effective participation in the benefits of the political process because, as Madison observed, small units have less diversity than large units; they thus allow greater opportunities for the oppression of those who are already weak. This is not merely a matter of extreme action by small majorities, as Madison seemed to suggest, for power often derives from factors other than sheer numbers. The force of whatever element in the unit is powerful is accentuated to the degree that the unit is small and homogeneous, whether its power is founded on numbers, wealth, or even violence. This is perhaps most evident on the social level of power. The pressures for conformity are most intense and extreme in units so small they lack formal institutions of government. Such pressures can be observed readily in small geographical communities but they exist in small communities of other kinds as well. The informal structures of relationships in these communities are similar to systems of rank. Frequently they coincide with differences in wealth; but in any case the relationships involved are relationships of power. In a very small society there may be so little open disagreement among the members that a massive consensus appears to exist. Nevertheless, as the contemporary illustration of rural communities in some Southern states may suggest, such consensus may not reflect the feelings and interests of Negroes, for example, with perfect accuracy.

One of the interesting features of government in small societies is the degree to which it reflects—or, perhaps, reproduces—this structuring of power relationships. In the United States the form by which this is accomplished is, ironically, the form which is often exalted as the purest democracy: direct participation in government by the members or citizens. The ideal is the town meeting, but in practice other means of approximating this ideal have had to be adopted. Sometimes these devices are regarded as means of majority rule, but the goal sought is usually much more than establishment of a majority; it is likely to be utter unanimity. Where this is true, the institutions of politics give no role to opposing parties and provide neither checks on leaders nor protection for dissenters.

The discriminatory effects of a decentralized politics are not limited to their impact within the boundaries of the respective constituent units. With public units a presumption exists that nobody is excluded from the constituency of some unit, and this at least moderates the discriminatory force of inequality of power within these units. But with private political units, or with the quasi-public functional units that have developed in so many fields, this presumption does not exist and many individuals are in fact excluded from any membership or effective participation in the system as a whole. Thus farm migrant workers, Negroes, and the urban poor have not been included in the system of "pluralist" representation so celebrated in recent years. However much these groups may be regarded as "potential interest groups," the important fact is that political organization for their protection within the pluralist framework can scarcely be said to exist. Such protection as they have had has come from the centralized features of the political order—parties, the national government, and the presidency. Where private functional groups exercise public powers of government, as in the grazing districts, the licensing of doctors, or where elections are held to determine the imposition of quotas on wheat or oil, the ambiguities of less-than-comprehensive constituencies are plain. The condition is not markedly different, however, where an area of policy is under the informal but effective control of an organized group that has successfully isolated that area from influence by a larger constituency.

Sometimes structures of power in one area confront other such structures with differing interests, sometimes, but not necessarily, producing moderation of the demands of both. Since the two contestants do not include all interests or all individuals within their combined constituencies, an alternative to compromise may be available: the two may join to seek the objectives of both—at the expense of those who are within neither constituency. This form of settlement has repeatedly marked the recent history of industrial relations in the steel industry. Moreover, the unstated assumption that the thesis of a given force will create its own antithesis is no more than the wishful metaphysics of countervailing power. Many interests are not represented at all.

Not the least of ironies is that political organization by small constituencies, while praised as a check on power and a restraint on extremism, at times actively encourages both. Since significant groups are excluded from influence over many important areas of policy, some being excluded from influence over any policy, logrolling is the typical means of accommodation. It occurs in Congress frequently, as where the claimants for a new levee project in one region align themselves with the claimants for a new dam in another area. Each group may be indifferent to the other's demand, but in alliance they regularly push through massive rivers-and-harbors bills of questionable merit. Logrolling also occurs within some of the private groups. It explains, for example, the support of solid family farmers in Illinois for the bleak labor policy put forward by the American Farm Bureau Federation serving the interests of corporation farms in California. Although the Illinois support clearly enhances the power of the California group, it does nothing to moderate the latter's labor policy, which becomes the policy of the national organization. Logrolling may promote peace among rivals, but it is not compromise and it offers little prospect of moderation of the demands of particular groups. Through the medium of alliance and federation, it can foster the creation of concentrated power on a functional plane while preserving the agreeable appearance of divided power on the geographical plane.

Although this pattern of largely autonomous structures of power with varying degrees of influence over important matters of general concern is widespread, it is not the only form of power in America. It is not true that every unit of government and every bit of public authority is captive to some tight cohesive interest group with unfailingly cunning leadership. Moreover, there are important differences of degree in the influence which apparently strong interest groups exercise. Some agencies apparently vulnerable to take-over by particular groups have managed to avoid the worst of these dangers and have established excellent reputations for impartiality. Certainly, it is interesting that much of the recent criticism of the independent commissions, for example, has been directed against two of them, the Federal Communications Commission and the Civil Aeronautics Board. And there is the impressive fact that public measures intended to alleviate poverty and protect Negro rights have become law despite active opposition armed with all the advantages a fragmented political system offers.

Plainly, the political order contains centralizing elements. The first of these is the presidency. The constituency of this majestic office is all the people. The prestige of its occupant is so great that when his power is husbanded and skillfully used he can make innovations of policy in the interest of those who are outside the pluralist scheme of rule. The second element of centralization is the party system. This much misunderstood and abused part of the political order has necessarily suffered from the federal context within which it has had to develop and act. It has been fashionable to regard the parties as more state than national phenomena, but the degree of truth in this view has perhaps been over-emphasized. Certainly it is interesting that many states are without genuine party organization of either label. At the supposedly vital "grass roots" level, moreover, party organization is found mainly in the large and diverse cities. Perhaps the alchemy of the large unity operates here as elsewhere to transmute base parochialisms and particularisms into something higher. The importance of the quadrennial presidential election compels the parties to transcend the narrow boundaries of their state organizations.

Much might have been said here of the fragmentary character of representation in Congress. Congressional constituencies are often narrow and suffer from all the defects outlined above. And Congress still betrays some of the evils described long ago by Woodrow Wilson; the problem of fragmentation deriving from the committee system is not solved.[8] Party discipline is often weak and interest groups are active and influential. Indeed, lobbyists, Congressmen, Senators and committees frequently act as components of the various sub-systems of politics commented on in these pages. Nevertheless, Congress itself is not the major source of the problems that have been discussed here. The important fact about Congress is that it embodies the localist aspect of federalism. This, rather than any deficiencies of procedure and custom, however real, is the major difficulty with Congress. And the specific problems of Congress may well have been over-emphasized; the party system and the presidency may be more influential in Congress than the day-to-day tumult and controversy in the Capitol suggest. Of the Supreme Court it is necessary only to mention its recent record. If it is proper in any sense to speak of the Court's constituency, that constituency is the whole nation.

II

Since the end of World War II the orthodoxy of private power has hardened. This is the result of many factors—the conservative mood that has seized the nation; the frustrations of the Cold War, despite a vast increase of national power; vivid memory of the horrors of the Nazi era; deep fear of Communism; the disorders of McCarthyism; the swift pace of technological change; and the arrival of great prosperity. All these factors have converged to produce a common inclination to justify American institutions. This has been particularly strong in discussions of the place of interest groups in the large political order. It has been marked among social scientists by disinterment of the work of Arthur Bentley, revived use of the word "pluralism," revulsion against ideology—even against any large goals in politics—and cynicism about the meaning of "the public interest." It has also involved discovery of a beneficent order in the workings of the pluralism of interest groups. The virtues of this order have been variously perceived as the guarantee of freedom, the preservation of diversity, the limitation of power, protection against mass movements and irrationality in politics, and the provision of meaning in common life. The list could be extended.

This attribution of almost all virtue to the institutionalization of what another era might have seen as narrow selfishness is a remarkable phenomenon, particularly since it comes from some of the more generous minds of our time. Perhaps it is to be regarded as the errant response to the ugly threats of contemporary Know-Nothingism and the movements that masquerade as today's conservatism. Certainly these black theologies call for explanation. The beginning of an explanation may lie in the theory of "status politics" and the discontents of a mobile society.[9] Nevertheless, concern with this problem has recoiled so far in horror of the irrational in current "rightist" mass movements that it has seemed to repudiate a major portion of the American democratic tradition. Although the discussions in which denunciations of "status politics" appear are scattered and diffuse, a question emerges from them that is itself more important than the possibly transitory mood that motivates it. Is a politics of narrow interest groups organized to serve specific material ends the alternative to a politics of ideology, mass movements, and irrationality?

An affirmative answer to this question might go somewhat as follows: The organization of political life on the basis of groups with specific, concrete, and material interests guarantees a limited and pragmatic politics. The contests that develop in it are for definite ends involving (usually minor) redistribution of income; they can be settled on a piecemeal basis and are always comprehensible. By contrast, there are no clear-cut solutions in status conflict. When politics is pitched on the plane of principles and generality there is an appeal to vague status anxieties, and the politics that develops is irrational in character, seeking scapegoats to symbolize the status threat. Antisemitism, xenophobia, and hatred of Wall Street emerge from their hiding places and a mob spirit develops.[10] When politics is allowed to escalate beyond the questions of a few more cents for this group or that, it becomes both meaningless and dangerous. Moreover, individual rights today derive from group rights, from membership in corporations, labor unions, farm organizations, and pressure groups, which are now the meaningful units of social action.[11]

This argument is an adaptation of the idea of anomie, the condition of rulelessness that follows from the breakdown of social classes and elites. Where anomie prevails, politics becomes a clash of empty ideologies and the danger of mass movements is great. Modern history has provided much evidence in support of this theory. Yet is the translation of the theory given above applicable to American conditions?

Much of the answer will depend on an assessment of the strength of contemporary "right" extremism. Such assessment calls for intuition, if not the gift of prophecy, and little of either can be offered here. From the evidence given in previous pages, however, it is possible to suggest that to the extent organized interest groups provide barriers to the rise of irrational mass movements, American politics is very safe indeed. A substantial portion of government is under the heavy influence of these groups, and the groups themselves are led by elites which work well together. To the degree that irrational mass movements threaten America, perhaps we may be grateful for the interest-group organization of politics which insures political preoccupation with mundane matters of wages, prices, and contracts.

Nevertheless, the specters of mass movements and totalitarianism may have blinded us to the implications of the defense offered for the narrow constituencies into which American politics is broken. First, the defense is an almost explicitly conservative justification of the power of interest-group elites. It has been seen that many interest groups vest much power in their leaders—power not only to influence public policy for the benefit of a particular group, but also to enforce discipline upon and guarantee the performance of members; and the rights of members in these groups are not always given equal guarantees. Second, to emphasize meaningful position within the small constituency of the interest group is little more than to grasp at a surrogate for the idealized status systems of traditional societies. Actually, there is great absurdity in perceiving the modern corporation and the trade union as the *Gemeinschaften* in whose bosoms modern man may find warmth and meaning for his life and work.[12] Third, such a defense of narrow interest groups involves a very particular conception of the locus of rationality in politics. Concrete demands are held to be rational, whereas general demands are irrational—for general demands may involve large constituencies, which presumably are incipient mobs or mass movements, while narrow, concrete, economic demands mean limited ends, and these are safe. Apparently, moreover, their interplay results in a beneficent balance. Whether an end, concrete or general, is rational, then, depends on the degree of danger of anomie and mass movements that exists, and not upon any intrinsic quality of the end itself. In practice, however, this line of thought leads to preference for selfish and material values.

It can be readily agreed that if explosive mass movements are a genuine threat to America, a politics of narrow constituencies might be desirable to counter the danger. Small associations probably do provide order and stability for any society. In the United States some associations may serve in this manner to a greater degree than others. The American Civil Liberties Union and the League of Women Voters have given notable service to American democracy. Trade unions and farm organizations have undoubtedly also been similarly useful at various times. Nevertheless, it should be clear that a substantial price is paid for any guarantee against mass movements provided by a pattern of small constituencies. That price is paid in freedom and equality. Although the price would be worth paying if the danger were grave, it can hardly be argued that such an extremity is present. Large constituencies, moreover, do not necessarily mean mass movements. The goals of Populism, the movement which has been offered as the native American prototype of mass irrationalism, were general and political, but the direct election of Senators, the regulation of monopoly, the initiative, and the referendum were neither dangerous nor absurd. The large constituencies of political parties and the presidency also have not destroyed the cohesion of American society. The real alternative to the politics of narrow interest groups lies here.

Preoccupation with the dangers of mass society and ideological politics has also obscured one of the genuine necessities of politics—the necessity to recognize power where it exists and to coopt it for the minimum needs of the large society. To a remarkable degree the American political system has shown ability to do this. On probably no other score have the American traits of flexibility and pragmatism better served the nation. Repeatedly, we have seen groups capable of seriously sabotaging large national efforts brought into the political order and given a share in the direction of the common adventure. Such cooptation is achieved at a cost; the potentially threatening groups are given additional power, even public authority, to exercise in their own spheres of interest. The phenomenon has been illustrated many times over during wartime. The use of industry advisory committees and the employment of WOCs has ensured the cooperation of industry when its less-than-energetic participation might have been disastrous. At less critical junctures, the endowment of farm elites with essentially public power on farming matters has prevented the eruption of serious farm discontent upon the political scene, and the appointment of labor leaders to occasional positions of direction in public affairs has limited their tendencies to cause disorder.

This is a process of accommodation of elites, however, and it involves not merely recognition of their power, but increase of it. To some extent it involves accommodation of their constituencies as well, but this need be so only to the degree that the elites and leaders are insecure in their leadership positions. There is something disingenuous in the widespread disinclination to avow the nature of the process and instead to celebrate the accommodation as designed to promote freedom, equality, and virtue. Much of the accommodation has been necessary —the condition under which the republic could continue to exist as such. But we have been less than clear or frank about what we have done.

Perhaps the greatest mark of American political genius has been federalism. It has been the means whereby local elites that could have turned their leadership to the ends of separatism have instead been induced to give limited commitment to national values. It has provided substantial autonomy to functional groups through geographical decentralization. There was something inspired in the original compromise, the implications of which were seen more clearly by James Madison than by many people today. Over time the real political contests of America have not been between state and national governments, but between functional, ethnic, religious, and other segments of the population. By preserving a substantial degree of the autonomy of these segments, federalism has kept them within the nation to however limited an extent while the process of developing a national culture went on. In recent times, federalism has been visibly a means by which national resources have been channeled piecemeal to different elites, which have generally been unfettered in their use of them. As the late Morton Grodzins pointed out, federalism is a system of sharing functions between state and national governments. More, it is a system of mobilizing private and public influence at local levels.[13] The process does gain the support of the various elites, but, again, at a substantial price—a large degree of acquiescence in local control of national programs for the benefit of small constituencies, control too often reflected in the imposition of narrow regional or local values upon measures supported by the nation. There have been no sadder examples than the racial discrimination exercised in federal programs in the South.

Like any compromise, federalism has always had two faces, the one looking to localism and the maintenance of existing power relationships, the other to nationalism and an alteration of those relationships. At any given moment it has been difficult to be certain that the compromise effected is a true reflection of the degree of existing local power on the one hand or of the desirability of change on the other. However, a survey of some of the specific measures by which the compromise has been effected inspires doubt that it was actually necessary to accommodate the groups to the extent that they have been accommodated. Refusal to yield to the importunities of tobacco or peanut growers, for example, would hardly have precipitated armed rebellion. Insistence that public works, whether new post offices or dams for irrigating vast new tracts of desert, should meet some rational test of national need, would probably not mean secession by any state. Nor has the direct placating of clamorous interests like the Western stockmen by endowing them with autonomous rule of the public domain been justifiable by any realistic fear of local riots.

Federalism and the interest group "pluralism" with which it is associated today are instruments of conservatism and particularism. The ideology of "grass roots democracy" and the gradual growth of power in small units by the institutional processes of accommodation have probably betrayed us into yielding too much of the republic's essential values of liberty and equality. The dangers to democracy in the United States have rarely been anomie and mass movements. The real threats, often adeptly met by cooptation of group leaders, have come from narrowly constituted interest groups. Yet it is all too apparent that often the leaders of such groups have coopted the United States instead.

The price paid for the boon of acquiescence by organized elites in the building of a nation has been greater than is immediately obvious. The ledger of accounts has been heavily glossed by the ideologies of *laissez faire*, grass roots, and the virtue of small units. Curiously, however, confusion has also come from a source from which it should perhaps have last derived—Progressivism. Most of the attacks upon the inequalities of political power have been in this tradition. Progressivism and its antecedents saw the rise of monopolies, the ruthless exercise of governmental power by railroads and financial institutions, the theft of public resources in too simple terms. Yet perhaps the simplest term of all was correct: here was evil. Nevertheless, Progressivism was unequipped either to analyze or to prescribe for the evil in the context in which it appeared. The Progressive diagnosis came down too readily either to the simple explanation that power existed and must be destroyed or to the denunciation of evil men who must be driven from the temples. Power did exist and must always exist if society is to go on; the practical problem is to organize it and to limit its exercise. Bad men have always existed and will continue to be with us. Yet not all of those denounced by the Progressives were evil, and even the evil did good. The castigation of the "special interests" and the unmasking of corruption may have served some public purpose, but the service has not been great. The "special interests" could always point to the guarantee of the First Amendment and lay proper claim to the blessings of liberty; the corruption uncovered has almost always been trivial and somehow boring.

In attempts to go beyond the punishment of outright bribery and theft of public land or other resources, the would-be reformers have found themselves adrift. By what criteria could they say that the malefactors of great wealth or power had done wrong? Judge Gary could persuade President Theodore Roosevelt that United States Steel had used its power for good.

Roger Blough could tell the American people that the public interest was simply the diverse lawful interests of each of the many million people who live in the republic, and that these interests included the right of United States Steel to raise its prices when it could. How could these men be gainsaid? How could the Federal Communications Commission or the Civil Aeronautics Board choose among the clamoring applicants before it when Congress gave only the public convenience, interest, or necessity as guides? How could the Forest Service decide upon the proper use of the vast tracts within its care when its doctrine held only that the test should be the greatest good of the greatest number in the long run? The translation of this dogma into the slogan of "multiple use" meant only an assertion of unlimited discretion in the disposal of public resources according to the personal tastes and power needs of the administrators. Here was a trackless wilderness in which men in office unlearned in reading the signs upon the land itself and ungifted with the sense of moral direction wandered before the pressures of all the winds that blew.

The problem of criteria has always been closely tied to the problem of government. A judicial model would serve well for government if standards existed on which men were agreed and which could be readily applied. There would be a problem of discovering wise and upright men to serve as rulers, but this would not be hopeless. But if the only standards recognized were those of science, as the Progressives seemed to suggest, the prospective judges would be without precedent, statute, or constitution when disputes came before them. Once the attention of a fickle public had turned away, the lonely judicial grandeur of agencies isolated from the influences of "politics" was vulnerable to the claims and charges of those very interests they had been established to regulate. Sometimes, indeed, strong-minded men in positions of such exposure found shelter in the orderly development of practice and made and followed precedent; here at any rate was, in time, a form of certainty and a set of guides leading away from the bottomless gulf of arbitrary choice. Often, however, handed the awful gift of governing without so much as this minimum and difficult guide, lesser men succeeding lesser men were unwittingly drawn into relationships of accommodation with the only segments of the public that could exercise influence. It was both less and more than corruption.

Probably the hypothesis that society tends toward order and stability is as good as, if not better than, its opposite. Certainly, behavior that steps over limits once thought impassable is less difficult the second time and even less so the third. With practice, accommodation becomes a pattern and other adjustments occur; so do systems of autonomous government grow. They cannot be termed irresponsible; they have their own constituencies, with which they gladly consult. The process is natural and so, perhaps, partakes of the sanction that nature gives.

It may be that small constituent units developed on functional lines in this manner and small units, drawn for whatever historical reason by geography, offer qualities of life that modern men crave—face-to-face human contact, a sense of place within a comprehensible world, warmth and abiding certainty. Yet the cost in loss of liberty and equality has been mentioned many times already. Another loss is in formality. To consider formality desirable is perhaps alien to the pragmatism of which Americans boast. Yet formality is a means of limitation and implies a set of bounds upon the possible. It curbs the whimsical and stays the hand of arbitrary action. In government and politics one of its fundamental gifts is the distinction between the public and the private. This, like many other formal principles, may well be arbitrary in its location, yet the distinction itself is far from arbitrary; it is close to the heart of constitutionalism. It has been compromised far more deeply than we like to acknowledge. In the grazing districts, for example, the meaning of public property has been almost lost. In states and localities, the public functions of licensure have often been given to private associations. The federal government has from time to time manned its offices with men paid by private industry. Boards and commissions composed of "representatives" of private groups, sometimes officially making policy and sometimes merely advising (another distinction often lost in practice), deal with public matters at all levels of government. These practices are so widespread that the very idea of constitutionalism sometimes seems to be placed in question.[14]

Often it is assumed that the role of government is that of arbiter or mediator among the many interests that exist within society. Neither role is possible where the distinction between public and private is lost. Where cleavage on one dimension of social difference is profound, as on the line of class or religion, politics is in danger of becoming a war to the finish unless it is separate and above the social conflict. Fortunately, this kind of division is not the condition in America, and the multitude of lesser divisions reflected in interest-group politics is a substantial safeguard against its development. If there is no real danger of such a disastrous condition, however, it does not follow that no loss is suffered when the line separating politics from other spheres of common life is allowed to disappear. By the same token that class conflict (where this is an overriding problem) is intensified, the struggle of interest groups is sharpened and the demands they enforce are made more extreme by destruction of the distinction between the political and the nonpolitical.

There is a comfortable assumption that interest groups will balance each other in their struggles and produce policies of moderation. But this is only partially true. Many of the structures of power described in previous chapters have no countervailing opposites, and many are nearly autonomous. Clashes, some serious, do occur. It is usually possible, however, either to reach accommodation by jurisdictional demarcation or to agree that each contestant should have everything it seeks. These solutions are available because not all interests have such structures of power and settlement can be made at the expense of those that do not. Where government is fragmented and the fragments are under the influence or control of such contestants, government can neither arbitrate nor mediate. The consequence is a series of policies more extreme than would otherwise emerge. The general public not only suffers the disruption caused by the conflict, but also pays the cost of settlement. At the same time, it is not clear that complete avoidance of conflict by jurisdictional agreement between interested parties produces results more generally satisfactory than those which emerge from open contest. Alongside the struggles and settlements achieved in the contests between the Army Corps of Engineers and the Bureau of Reclamation and between the steel industry and the steel union must be set the consequences of the peaceful arrangements between management and labor in the trucking industry.

A politics of interest groups and small-constituent units is unlikely to develop its own checks. Government offers the best means of limiting both the conflicts between such groups and the agreements by which conflicts are ended or avoided. To give this service, however, government must be formal and distinct. It cannot be either if it is broken into units corresponding to the interests which have developed power.

III

For many years it has been traditional to see the problem of private power as the antithesis between particular interests and the public interest. At times the whole career of Progressivism and its successor reform movements seems to have ridden on this distinction. To expose the predatory designs of "special interests" and to root out corruption in public life has always had the appeal of simple righteousness. Given the ruthlessness of corporate empire builders, the callousness of food packers and speculators, and the graft of machine politicians at the turn of the century, it was perhaps inescapable that the public interest to which all of these were opposed should seem to shine with an almost blinding intensity. In less dark a night, however, that beacon has grown dim. For all that Congress has repeatedly named the public interest as the guide for governmental action, uncertainty and doubt have cast a cloud about its meaning.

Paradoxically, the rise of democracy is itself responsible for this cloud. On the one hand, it carried the impulse by which special privilege and inequality were challenged; on the other, it lacked the criteria by which the products of power could be condoned or condemned. Ultimately, the only test seemed to be individual choice—not what was objectively good, but what each individual rightly or wrongly declared to be his own interest. So it has seemed that men in such great numbers and such diversity spread across so great a land have no common interest save that imposed by geography. With every man free and as good as the next, each was endowed with the right to seek his own destiny wherever it might lie. With so vast and so secular a priesthood of all men, how could a common good or a public interest be claimed in any sense save, perhaps, restraint of their contests to minimum levels of intensity? It is scarcely surprising that thoughtful men have at times concluded that the public interest is a myth,[15] that a totally inclusive interest does not exist,[16] or that the notion is so normative that nothing empirical can be said about it.[17]

These conclusions deserve much sympathy. As a term, "the public interest" has often served to disguise the selfish ends of narrow groups. In the sense in which "interest" was intended, it is difficult to name an interest all men would agree that they share. And as a universal principle of moral guidance, it appears to be above tests of mere fact. Nevertheless, these judgments carry too severe implications. It would indeed be gratifying if an overarching public interest could be demonstrated by empirical data to the satisfaction of all men. In a skeptical age, however, this is too much to ask. Although it may be true that no interest of any kind may be found that all members of the public will avow, neither does it follow that "the public" is meaningless or that nothing more may be said.

Perhaps the strongest solvent in which the idea of the public interest has recently been made to disappear is the alternative notion of group interest. Certainly American political science has unearthed abundant evidence that groups play an important role in political life. Nevertheless, the supposedly hard reality of any group tends to dissolve when it is recalled that all the members of any group do not have all interests in common—that, in fact, they have important differences, however much these may be disguised or suppressed. In this sense, the difference between "group" and "public" is a matter of degree. Both are abstractions and both are open to many of the same attacks.

The difference of degree is important, however. If the various politically active groups and the general public are placed on a continuum of inclusiveness of their constituencies, from the narrowest at one end to the broadest at the other, two interesting things appear. First, the groups with the narrowest constituencies are on the whole those with the least degree of formality in their governmental systems and the fewest guarantees for individual members. Second, different values are served by constituencies of different degrees of comprehensiveness.[18]

Most prominent of these values are liberty and equality. In general, the liberty of individuals is more secure in a large constituency than in a small. Moreover, the larger the constituency, the more probable is it that the group is committed to equality; the narrower and more exclusive the group, the more probably will it be a defender of inequality. Indeed, it often appears that the achievement and defense of particular status and privilege are the central goals of narrow and cohesive groups. These are not general or abstract goals, and they relate only to the specific spheres of overriding concern to the respective narrow groups. It is nevertheless obvious that if political life were exclusively in the hands of narrow groups the interests of many people in the general society would be discriminated against and some would be excluded from the political process entirely.

Other values of a more specific nature are also seen to be characteristic of constituencies of different sizes. Generally, the values served by groups with narrow constituencies are "hard," material and economic. Thus a trade union is more likely to seek a ten-cent wage increase than a reform of the electoral system, a farm commodity group is more likely to be concerned with increasing the price of beef that with improvement of foreign relations, a trade association is more likely to attempt to ease specific rigors of competition than to foster full employment. Where small constituencies have been established to govern particular activities values other than the "hard," the economic and the material have generally suffered. Thus soil conservation has not fared well at the hands of the grazing districts; expansion of medical services has been of less concern to the medical profession than the protection of its market; the constituent system of the Forest Service has discriminated in favor of sawlogs against the preservation of scenery.

Thus it is not meaningless to speak of public values. They are public in the sense that they are shared by broad constituencies; usually, they must be achieved through mobilization of large constituencies. If left to the array of narrow constituencies which make up so large a part of American politics, many of these values would have no spokesmen or even forums in which their claims could be advanced. A political order composed exclusively of small constituencies, whether drawn on lines of geography, function, or other dimensions, would exclude a variety of genuine values of real concern to the members of society. Fortunately, the American polity is not composed so exclusively of small constituencies. Yet it is questionable whether the political organization of the nation permits justice to be done to all the values Americans actually cherish. A cliché of foreign observers is that America is a nation of materialism and narrow self-interest, as is demonstrated by much of the behavior of government and by the ideology advanced in support of this behavior. Yet there is also abundant evidence that the cliché is seriously mistaken. The conclusion is too readily drawn that the values actually served are those the nation most esteems. The unspoken premise in this conclusion is that the institutions by which these values are legitimized are perfect.

The error here is both obvious and serious. Many of the values Americans hold in highest esteem can only be realized through large constituencies, some indeed only by a genuinely national constituency. It may be comforting to believe that since the people are the same whether they are ordered in small units or large ones, the consequences will be the same. In fact, however, the consequences are not the same, and for good reason.

Certainly not all virtues are public virtues. At many points narrow, even personal, interests should be preferred to general interests. Nevertheless, the political institutions of the United States have in many ways been designed more to gain the acquiescence of power-holding groups than to achieve a balance of public and private values. There has been great political virtue in this fact; indeed, it is probably the greatest of Americal political achievements that means have been found to gain the adherence and allegiance to a common society of so diverse an array of groups and interests, without foreclosure of change or hardening of class lines. Nevertheless, as a nation we have not been willing to acknowledge the nature of this achievement or to confess the cost it has involved.

The quest of the public interest is neither simple nor open to rapid achievement. One of the conclusions that must be drawn from the survey contained in these pages is that quick or large-scale reform in the United States is improbable. The tradition of the virtuous small constituency is deeply rooted in America, and the political order is built on an almost infinitely complex design of interlocking relationships which accommodate a multitude of small constituencies. Although these small constituencies often act as barriers to the realization of much that is best in American aspirations, they are not evil in themselves; indeed, they have repeatedly served to provide the organization and the means by which demands that might otherwise have erupted dangerously have been satisfied by shares in power, and it would be mistaken to seek their destruction. There are signs, however, that some of these small constituencies have even tightened their hold on segments of public authority. The consequence is that the prospect for achievement of public values is less than it otherwise might be.

The prescriptions which emerge from this examination are

neither simple nor easy to fill. In general, they ask the strengthening of those elements of the political order which tend toward the creation of a constituency of the entire nation. These include the party system, the presidency, and the national government. They also include reassertion of public values and a clearer understanding of the means by which these may be achieved. They involve an acceleration of that evolution of federalism which, however hesitantly, has led toward the building of a nation. They require rejection of the illusions that informality of government produces justice, that political power can be abolished, and that the surrender of public authority to private hands results in democracy. None of these requirements are radical.

There can be no guaranty that a truly national constituency would always produce policies that serve the public interest. Even in the limited sense in which the term is used here, the public interest will always carry large uncertainties of meaning. And there are other obstacles which may stand athwart its path. Nevertheless, its greatest difficulty is the common lack of a national constituency. American democracy has been one of the great adventures of history. Its career has been marked with danger, but repeatedly the danger has been overcome. That career deserves to proceed toward its fulfillment.

NOTES

Part I

CHAPTER 1: *The Open Secret*

1. This account is based on *Hearings before the Select Committee on Lobby Investigation*, U.S. House of Representatives, 63rd Cong., 1st Sess. (1913), 4 vols.
2. Committee on the Judiciary, *Subcommittee Hearings*, U.S. Senate, 63rd Cong., 1st Sess. (1913).
3. Committee on Banking and Currency, *Hearings on Farm Organizations*, U.S. House of Representatives, 66th Cong., 3rd Sess. (1922).
4. For full details of the investigation, see U.S. Federal Trade Commission, *Utility Corporations*, No. 72A.
5. *Hearings before the Special Subcommittee on Legislative Oversight*, U.S. House of Representatives, 85th Cong., 2nd Sess. (1958).
6. *Hearings before the Select Committee to Investigate Lobbying Activities*, U.S. House of Representatives, 81st Cong., 2nd Sess. (1950).
7. Special Committee to Investigate Political Activities, Lobbying and Campaign Contributions, *Report No. 395*, U.S. Senate, 85th Cong., 1st Sess. (1957). See also *Hearings before the Subcommittee on Privileges and Elections*, U.S. Senate, 84th Cong., 2nd Sess. (1956).
8. See for example, Robert Allen, *Our Sovereign State* (New York: Vanguard Press, 1949); and in still more popular vein, Lester Velie, "This is How Payola Works in Politics," *Readers Digest*, August 1960, vol. 77, no. 460, pp. 46–51.
9. Cf. Herbert Croly, *The Promise of American Life* (New York: Macmillan, 1909), p. 139.

10. Louis Hartz, *The Liberal Tradition in America* (New York: Harcourt, Brace & World, 1955), chap. I.

11. This, for example, was the principal conclusion of the report made by James M. Landis to President-Elect Kennedy on the problems of the independent regulatory commissions in late 1960. *Report on Regulatory Agencies to the President-Elect* (Washington, D.C., 1960).

12. See, for examples, Henry W. Ehrmann, *Interest Groups on Four Continents* (Pittsburgh: University of Pittsburgh Press, 1958). Also, Peter Self and Herbert Storing, *The State and the Farmer* (London: Allen and Unwin, 1962); Harry Eckstein, *Pressure Group Politics, The Case of the British Medical Association* (Stanford, Calif.: Stanford University Press, 1960).

CHAPTER 2: *The Progressive Legacy*

1. Richard Hofstadter, *The Age of Reform* (New York: Alfred A. Knopf, 1956), pp. 300ff.

2. We have recently been made acutely aware of the conservative (or "radical right") use of the theory of conspiracy. It is, however, endemic in American politics, and is the exclusive property of neither right nor left.

3. Henry Adams, quoted in Herbert Croly, *Progressive Democracy* (New York: Macmillan, 1914), pp. 33–34.

4. Charles Albro Barker, *Henry George* (New York: Oxford University Press, 1955), pp. 620–634.

5. The list is not complete. For a discussion of the ramifications of the muckraking movement see C. C. Regier, *The Era of the Muckrakers* (Chapel Hill, N.C.: University of North Carolina Press, 1932) and Louis Filler, *Crusaders for American Liberalism* (New York: Harcourt, Brace, 1939).

6. This is a central theme of Hofstadter, *op. cit.* It is also very conspicuous in the collection of essays in Daniel Bell, ed., *The New American Right* (New York: Criterion Books, Inc., 1955).

7. *The Autobiography of Lincoln Steffens* (New York: Harcourt, Brace, 1931), p. 349.

8. Thus, Franklin Hichborn, *The System* (San Francisco: Press of the James H. Barry Co., 1915). Hichborn was one of the California Progressives.

9. J. Allen Smith, *The Spirit of American Government* (New York: Macmillan, 1907), p. vii.

10. Parrington has said this book was "the most adequate expression" of the movement to democratize the Constitution. Vernon L. Parrington, *Main Currents in American Thought* (New York: Harcourt, Brace, 1930), vol. 3, p. 408.

11. This theme runs through Croly's *The Promise of American Life* (New

York: Macmillan, 1912), which provided Theodore Roosevelt with his slogan "the new nationalism." Senator Albert J. Beveridge also consistently emphasized it. Thus, a speech of his in 1911 began: "Mr. Chairman, Ladies and Gentlemen: The United States IS (applause) the American people are a Nation (applause)—not forty-six Nations." *Proceedings of the Second National Conservation Congress* (Washington, D.C., 1911), p. 152.

12. Herbert Croly, *Progressive Democracy* (New York: Macmillan, 1915), p. 245.

13. The best summary of Midwestern Progressivism, in ways so different from its other forms, is in Russel B. Nye, *Midwestern Progressive Politics* (East Lansing: Michigan State College Press, 1951), pp. 195–238. The entire work is perceptive and illuminating.

14. Cf. Theodore Roosevelt, "We do not propose to make mere size an offense. We do propose that there shall be hearty and generous recognition of exceptional ability if guided by a decent spirit of fair play, and if the reward is made to depend upon serving, and not upon swindling the public. We do propose to prevent growth by oppression. . . ." Introduction to S. J. Duncan-Clark, *The Progressive Movement*, (Boston: Small, Maynard and Co., 1913), p. xix.

15. Thus, Richard T. Ely remarked in that year, "If there is any serious student of our economic life who believes that anything substantial has been gained by all the laws passed against trusts, by all the newspaper editorials which have thus far been penned . . . this authority has yet to be heard from. Forms and names have been changed in some instances but the dreaded work of vast aggregation of capital has gone on practically as heretofore. The writer does not hesitate to affirm it as his opinion that efforts along lines which have been followed in the past will be equally fruitless in the future." *Monopolies and Trusts* (New York: Macmillan, 1900), p. 243.

16. Senator Albert Beveridge at the Progressive National Convention of 1912. Claude J. Bowers, *Beveridge and the Progressive Era* (New York: Macmillan, 1932), p. 427.

17. Robert M. La Follette, *La Follette's Autobiography* (Madison, Wis.: The Robert M. La Follette Co., 1919), 3d ed., p. 16.

18. *Progressive Democracy*, p. 311.

19. *Ibid.*, p. 343.

20. *The Promise of American Life*, p. 139.

21. Cross-filing was changed in 1952 by a provision that party affiliation of candidates could appear on the primary ballots. This device greatly reduced the possibility of any candidate's winning both party nominations. The survival of parties in California in any form has been largely due to the evolution of extra-legal party organizations. A similar development has occurred in Wisconsin; see F. J. Sorauf, "Extra-Legal Political Parties in Wisconsin," *APSR*, September 1954, pp. 692–704.

22. Hiram Johnson argued at the time: "There is nothing thus presented

to you that seeks to destroy or even to affect political parties *nation-ally*. The government of the state has become now a matter of efficient business management, and efficient business management may be best obtained without parties." (My italics)

23. For discussion of this see George E. Mowry, *The California Pro-gressives* (Berkeley and Los Angeles: University of California Press, 1951), p. 111; and Robert S. Maxwell, *La Follette and the Rise of the Progressives in Wisconsin* (Madison, Wis.: State Historical Society of Wisconsin, 1956), chap. v.

24. Charles McCarthy, *The Wisconsin Idea* (New York: Macmillan, 1912), p. 174.

25. *La Follette's Autobiography*, p. 359. Italics in the original.

26. *Progressive Democracy*, p. 365.

27. Pinchot's autobiography gives a vivid though biased account of this history. Gifford Pinchot, *Breaking New Ground* (New York: Harcourt, Brace, 1949).

28. This theme recurs constantly in the conservation speeches and articles. See, for example, Gifford Pinchot, *The Fight for Conservation* (New York: Doubleday, Page, 1910), pp. 80, 110.

29. *Ibid.*, p. 46.

30. This letter was reproduced in *The Use of the National Forest Re-serves*, the first manual of the United States Forest Service, 1905, pp. 10, 11.

31. *The National Forest Manual*, 1911, p. 11.

32. I have elsewhere discussed the development of the perplexities in Forest Service policy. See Grant McConnell, "The Multiple Use Concept in Forest Service Policy," *Sierra Club Bulletin*, October 1959.

33. Quoted in Eric Goldman, *Rendezvous with Destiny* (New York: Knopf, 1952), p. 240.

34. *The Age of Reform*, p. 212.

35. For a discussion of the California political pattern before the recent changes and of the influence of Progressivism in the forming of this pattern, see McConnell, "California Conundrum," *The Nation*, vol. 179, pp. 477, 478, Dec. 4, 1954.

36. See Lester Velie, "The Secret Boss of California," *Collier's*, Aug. 13, 1949 and Aug. 20, 1949. See also discussion *infra*, pp. 178, 179.

37. See *infra*, pp. 281, ff.

CHAPTER 3: *The Search for an Orthodoxy*

1. For example, Russell Kirk, *The Intelligent Woman's Guide to Con-servatism* (New York: Devin-Adair Company, 1957).

2. This mood is particularly apparent in J. K. Galbraith, *The Affluent Society* (Boston: Houghton Mifflin Company, 1958).

3. Thus, Gardiner Means explicitly raises the question of "legitimacy"

in his *Pricing Power and the Public Interest* (New York: Harper & Brothers, 1962), chap. II. See also Richard Eells, *The Government of Corporations* (New York: The Free Press of Glencoe, 1962).

4. Cf. Richard Hofstadter, *Social Darwinism in American Thought* (Boston: Beacon Press, 1944), chap. 2.

5. Francis X. Sutton, Seymour E. Harris, Carl Kaysen, James Tobin, *The American Business Creed* (New York: Schocken Books, 1956).

6. Daniel Bell, *The End of Ideology* (New York: Collier Books, 1961).

7. Ida M. Tarbell, *The History of the Standard Oil Company* (New York: McClure, Philips & Company, 1904).

8. U.S. Commissioner of Corporations, *Report on the Steel Industry*, Part I, 1911, pp. xx, xxi.

9. *Ibid.*, p. xxii.

10. See Ida M. Tarbell, *The Life of Elbert H. Gary* (New York: D. Appleton & Company, 1925), chap. 8, also p. 255.

11. I have discussed the events of 1952 and 1962 in *The Steel Seizure of 1952* (published by the University of Alabama Press, University, Ala., 1960, for the Inter-University Case Program); and *Steel and the Presidency* (New York: W. W. Norton and Company, 1963).

12. Cf. C. A. Pearce, *Trade Association Survey*, Monograph 18, U.S. Temporary National Economic Committee (Washington, D.C., 1941), p. 12.

13. Arthur Jerome Eddy, *The New Competition* (Chicago: A. C. McClurg and Company, 1915), title page. Italics in the original.

14. *Ibid.*, pp. 11, 13, 16. Italics in the original.

15. Federal Trade Commission, *Open Price Trade Associations*, Senate Document 226, 70th Cong., 2nd Sess. (1929).

16. His *Principles of Scientific Management* appeared in 1911 (New York: Harper & Brothers).

17. Quoted in Harwood L. Childs, *Labor and Capital in Politics* (Columbus, Ohio: State University Press, 1930), p. 13.

18. "If you can visualize a convention of able, if not the ablest, men of affairs in America—not so much the presidents and chairmen of boards, whose hard-working days are over, but the keen, dynamic, forceful, purposeful, transilient vice-presidents and managers and superintendents; not the men who are reputed to be doers, but the real doers of the colossal deeds of the titanic American industrial scene—removing their coats, rolling up their sleeves, and marching in a body to take agreeable, assigned positions in a super-corporation, you will view the War Industries Board." Grosvenor B. Clarkson, *Industrial America in the World War* (Boston and New York: Houghton Mifflin Company, 1923), p. 65.

19. Cf. Bernard M. Baruch, *American Industry in the War*, a report of the War Industries Board, 1921. (Reprinted by Prentice-Hall, Inc., New York, 1941, p. 22).

20. Clarkson, *op. cit.*, p. 73.

21. William C. Mullendore, *History of the United States Food Adminis-*

tration, 1917–1919 (Stanford, Calif.: Stanford University Press, 1941), p. 61.

22. Clarkson, *op. cit.*, p. 217.

23. *Ibid., loc. cit.*

24. *Ibid.*, p. 313.

25. *Ibid.*, p. 300.

26. Bernard M. Baruch, *Taking the Profit out of War* (Program presented to the War Policies Commission, 1931), reprinted as Book II of *American Industry in the War*, p. 401.

27. See Herbert Hoover, *Memoirs* (New York: Macmillan, 1951–52), vol. I, pp. 245ff.

28. See especially his early book, *American Individualism* (Garden City, N.Y.: Doubleday Page & Company, 1923).

29. *Ibid.*, p. 37.

30. Cf. *Memoirs,* vol. II, p. 169.

31. From speeches given in 1924, quoted in *Memoirs,* vol. II, pp. 171–173.

32. See, for example, the *Annual Report* of the Secretary of Commerce for 1923, pp. 18, 19. In each of Hoover's reports as Secretary this was a conspicuous theme.

33. During the war, decentralization was a major policy of the WFA because it gained local cooperation. See Hoover, *Memoirs*, vol. I, p. 250.

34. *Report* of the Secretary of Commerce, 1922, p. 29.

35. *Memoirs*, vol. II, p. 173n.

36. Cf. J. Danielian, *A.T. & T.* (New York: Vanguard Press, 1939).

37. *Historical Statistics of the United States* (Washington, D.C., 1949), p. 29; *Statistical Abstract of the United States, 1964* (Washington, D.C., 1964), p. 16.

38. This account is to be found in my *The Decline of Agrarian Democracy* (Berkeley and Los Angeles: University of California Press, 1953).

39. Thomas Jefferson, *Notes on Virginia*, Query XIX.

40. Taylor was a prolific writer. He may most easily be sampled in *Arator: Being a Series of Agricultural Essays, Practical and Political* (Petersburg, Virginia: printed by Whitworth and Yancy for John M. Carter, 1818).

41. Cf. *Report of the Commission on Country Life*, Senate Document 705, 60th Cong., 2nd Sess. (1909).

42. J. C. Bailey, *Seaman A. Knapp, Schoolmaster of American Agriculture* (New York: Columbia University Press, 1945), p. xi.

43. See Gladys Baker, *The County Agent* (Chicago: University of Chicago Press, 1939). See also A. C. True, *A History of Agricultural Education in the United States, 1785–1925*, U.S. Department of Agriculture Misc. Publ. No. 15, 1928.

44. *Report* of the Secretary of Agriculture for 1915, p. 40.

45. Dr. A. C. True in speech reprinted in *Hearings on Farm Organizations*, House Committee on Banking and Currency, 1922, p. 93.

46. Cf. Bailey, *op. cit.*, p. 178.

47. Speech by C. B. Smith, Chief of Extension Work, North and West, 1920 in *Hearings on Farm Organizations*, 1922, p. 94.

48. *Proceedings, Convention of Association of Land Grant Colleges and Universities*, 1947.

49. See, for example, the periodical *The Banker Farmer*, published by the Agricultural Commission of the American Bankers Association until 1928.

50. See testimony by the President of the American Farm Bureau Federation in *Hearings on Farm Organizations*, p. 227.

51. In a speech to the AFL convention of 1900, quoted in George G. Higgins, *Voluntarism in Organized Labor in the United States* (Washington, D.C.: Catholic University of America Press, 1944), p. 9.

52. Samuel Gompers, *Labor and the Common Welfare* (New York: E. P. Dutton and Company, 1919), p. 7.

53. Selig Perlman, *The Theory of the Labor Movement* (New York: Macmillan, 1928), p. 197.

54. *American Federationist*, XII, July 1905.

55. Felix Frankfurter and Nathan Greene, *The Labor Injunction* (New York: Macmillan, 1930).

56. Gompers in the 1914 AFL Convention, quoted in Higgins, *op. cit.*, p. 35.

57. Michael Rogin, *Voluntarism as an Organizational Ideology in the American Federation of Labor: 1886–1932*, unpublished master's thesis, University of Chicago, 1959, p. 12.

58. Sidney and Beatrice Webb, *Industrial Democracy* (London: Longmans, Green, 1897).

59. Rogin, *op. cit.*, p. 182.

60. Rogin, *op. cit.*, pp. 16off.

61. *Ibid.*, pp. 74ff.

62. For example, San Francisco. See Walton Bean, *Boss Rueff's San Francisco* (Berkeley: University of California Press, 1952).

63. Quoted in Louis S. Reed, *The Labor Philosophy of Samuel Gompers* (New York: Columbia University Press, 1930), p. 143. The capital letters are those of Gompers.

64. From the AFL Convention *Proceedings*, 1923. The manifesto is reprinted in Higgins, *op. cit.*, pp. 154–158.

65. Rogin, *op. cit.*, p. 151.

CHAPTER 4: *The Constituency*

1. Nevertheless, the International Social Science Council did launch an ambitious study of the effect of scale on policy, administration, and efficiency some years ago. There are also numerous studies of small social units that touch on political problems. See, for example, George

C. Homans, *The Human Group* (New York: Harcourt Brace, 1950); Robert A. Nisbet, *The Quest for Community* (New York: Oxford University Press, 1953); Sidney Verba, *Small Groups and Political Behavior* (Princeton, N.J.: Princeton University Press, 1961); Arthur J. Vidich and Joseph Bensman, *Small Town in Mass Society* (Princeton, N.J.: Princeton University Press, 1958).

2. There are many panegyrics to the virtues of rural life. See, for example, M. L. Wilson, *Democracy Has Roots* (New York: Carrick & Evans, Inc., 1939); also Baker Brownell, *The Human Community* (New York: Harper, 1950).

3. American literature is filled with fictional portrayals of this phenomenon. See, for example, Sinclair Lewis's *Main Street*, which stands for an almost endless parade of works with this theme.

4. Aristotle, *The Laws*, Book IV.

5. This is particularly characteristic of the "human relations" approach to industrial relations.

6. Cf. Frank Tannenbaum, *A Philosophy of Labor* (New York: Alfred A. Knopf, 1951).

7. Although the point is seldom made clearly, it is implicit in many statements of labor leaders. See statements quoted in Chapter 5.

8. See Harold J. Laski, *Authority in the Modern State* (New Haven: Yale University Press, 1927); *Foundations of Sovereignty* (London: G. Allen & Unwin, 1931); and *Studies in the Problem of Sovereignty* (New Haven: Yale University Press, 1912).

9. Perhaps an exception should be made for the work of Mary Parker Follett. See her *The New State: Group Organization the Solution of Popular Government* (New York: Longmans, Green, 1918).

10. On the problem facing churches in England, see J. N. Figgis, *Churches in the Modern State* (London and New York: Longmans, Green, 1914).

11. The argument even went beyond this to assert that political life should be reorganized about the representation of interests. See G. D. H. Cole, *Guild Socialism Restated* (London: L. Parsons, 1920).

12. This was a persistent theme in the works of Elton Mayo. See his *The Human Problems of an Industrial Civilization* (Cambridge, Mass.: Harvard University Press, 1946); *The Social Problems of an Industrial Civilization* (Cambridge, Mass.: Harvard University Press, 1945).

13. Distaste for government, of which the most essential characteristic is taken to be compulsion, is particularly evident in the works of Mayo.

14. Examples run from early Christianity through medieval guilds to contemporary Communist parties.

15. Ferdinand Tönnies, *Gemeinschaft und Gesellschaft* (Leipzig: Fues's Verlag, 1887).

16. See his essay "On Coleridge," first published in 1840. It appears in J. S. Mill, *Dissertations and Discussions: Political, Philosophical and Historical* (New York: Holt, 1874), vol. II, pp. 27–36.

17. A very useful summary and discussion of this outlook is contained in William Kornhauser, *The Politics of Mass Society* (Glencoe, Ill.: Free Press, 1959).

18. For example, in Ortega y Gasset, *The Revolt of the Masses* (New York: W. W. Norton, 1932).

19. This emerges perhaps most clearly in Emil Lederer, *The State of the Masses* (New York: W. W. Norton, 1940).

20. See Grant McConnell, "John Taylor and the Democratic Tradition," *Western Political Quarterly,* March 1951, pp. 17–31.

21. *The Federalist,* Number 10. Modern Library edition, pp. 53–62.

22. *Ibid.,* pp. 60–61. The most important recent development of this part of Madison's argument is in E. E. Schattschneider, *The Semi-Sovereign People* (New York: Holt, Rinehart & Winston, 1960), pp. 3–18.

23. The novelists have offered the strongest testimony here.

24. Cf. Cole, *op. cit.*

25. The word "class" has many connotations and definitions. With this ambiguity it is apt to be very misleading. In the present context the concept of power is central and the present reference is to inequalities in the holding of power. There is unfortunately no precise term referring to stratification on this dimension alone.

26. This appears to be one of the themes of the writers in Daniel Bell, ed., *The Radical Right* (Garden City, N.Y.: Anchor Books, 1964). Thus "status politics" expresses frustration and general anxiety and is thereby irrational; it is associated both with the Populism of the 1890s and the radical right of the second half of the twentieth century. See especially the essays by Bell, Viereck, and Lipset.

CHAPTER 5: *Private Government*

1. Cf. Robert A. Horn, *Groups and the Constitution* (Stanford, Calif.: Stanford University Press, 1956).

2. On the distinction between state and society as a liberal principle see Guido de Ruggiero, *The History of European Liberalism* (London and New York: Oxford University Press, 1927), pp. 383–386. See also Lord Acton, *Essays on Freedom and Power* (Glencoe, Ill.: The Free Press, 1949), pp. 247–248.

3. Classification of American writers as pluralists or nonpluralists is somewhat risky. However, to take one writer who is quite clearly in the pluralist tradition, Mary Parker Follett, it is evident that (whatever the confusions that may seem to exist in her writings) her purpose was liberal. Cf. *The New State* (New York: Longmans, Green, 1918).

4. Robert Michels, *Political Parties,* reprinted (Glencoe, Ill.: The Free

Press, 1949). The first English edition was printed in 1915, but the original German appeared in 1913.

5. For example, he is one of the real-life figures who appear in the early volumes of Jules Romains' *Men of Good Will.*

6. This is most particularly true in the English-speaking world. For example, see Sylvia Kopald, *Rebellion in Labor Unions* (New York: Boni and Liveright, 1924).

7. Alexis de Tocqueville, *Democracy in America* (New York: Alfred A. Knopf, 1945), vol. II, p. 106.

8. Cf. *National Organizations of the U.S.* (Detroit: Gale Research Co., 1961).

9. Thus "A business is a *government* because within the law it is authorized and organized to make rules for the conduct of its affairs. It is a *private* government because the rules it makes within the law are final and not reviewable by any public body." Beardsley Ruml, quoted in Richard Eells, *The Government of Corporations* (New York: The Free Press of Glencoe, 1962), p. vi.

10. Especially Robert Aaron Gordon, *Business Leadership in the Large Corporation* (Washington: The Brookings Institution, 1945). Most recently, Richard Eells, *op. cit.,* has become the most articulate advocate.

11. For example, Roger Blough, *Free Man and the Corporation* (New York: McGraw-Hill, 1959); also, "General Motors is People" (national advertising of General Motors).

12. Adolph A. Berle and Gardiner C. Means, *The Modern Corporation and Private Property* (New York: Macmillan, 1932).

13. See David Karr, *Fight for Control* (New York: Ballantine Books, 1956).

14. Cf. R. A. Gordon, *op. cit.,* p. 121.

15. Abram Chayes, "The Modern Corporation and the Rule of Law," in Edward S. Mason, *The Corporation in Modern Society* (Cambridge, Mass.: Harvard University Press, 1959). See also the article by Eugene V. Rostow, "To Whom and for What Ends Is Corporate Management Responsible?" in the same volume.

16. Arundel Cotter, *United States Steel: A Corporation with a Soul* (Garden City, N.Y.: Doubleday Page & Co., 1921).

17. Mr. Lewis D. Gilbert reportedly attended 150 annual meetings of different corporations during the annual meeting "season" of 1963. See his book, *Dividends and Democracy* (Larchmont, N.Y.: American Research Council, 1956).

18. Eells, *op. cit.,* chap. 2.

19. Bayless Manning, "Corporate Power and Individual Freedom: Some General Analysis and Particular Reservations," *Northwestern University Law Review,* vol. 55, no. 1 (March–April, 1960), pp. 38–53.

20. See the general indictment in William H. Whyte, Jr., *The Organization Man* (New York: Simon & Schuster, 1956).

21. See George E. Barnett, "The Government of the Typographical Union," in Jacob H. Hollander and George E. Barnett, eds., *Studies in American Trade Unions* (New York: H. Holt & Co., 1912), p. 19.

22. Much of what follows in the remainder of this chapter previously appeared in Grant McConnell: "The Spirit of Private Government," *The American Political Science Review*, vol. LII, no. 3 (September 1958), pp. 754–770.

23. The convention's similarities to the British Parliament are superficially greater. To press this analogy, however, is to ignore the strong constitutional restraints that have developed to circumscribe the actions of Parliament, a development that has not occurred in American trade union conventions. For a vivid description of the convention in the Teamsters Union see Sam Romer, *The International Brotherhood of Teamsters, Its Government and Structure* (New York: John Wiley & Sons, 1962), chap. 2. There is an extended account of the American Federation of State, County and Municipal Employees in Leo Kramer, *Labor's Paradox* (New York: John Wiley & Sons, 1962), chap. 3.

24. Quoted in J. Kovner, *Report on Conventions*, typescript, p. 337.

25. The incident is told in Grant McConnell, *The Steel Seizure of 1952* (Published by the University of Alabama Press, University, Alabama, 1960, for Inter-University Case Program), p. 17.

26. See Philip Taft, "Constitutional Power of the Chief Officer in American Labor Unions," *Quarterly Journal of Economics*, vol. 62 (May 1948), pp. 459–471. However, compare the tenor of that discussion with Taft's *The Structure and Government of Labor Unions* (Cambridge, Mass.: Harvard Univ. Press, 1954), chap. VIII.

27. See the tabulation and discussion in Philip Taft, "Judicial Procedure in Labor Unions," *Quarterly Journal of Economics*, vol. 59 (May 1945), pp. 370–385; however, see also his *The Structure and Government of Labor Unions*, pp. 123–125, for an apologia.

28. Constitution of the International Brotherhood of Electrical Workers, Art. xxvii, 15, 16.

29. Quoted in Kovner, *op. cit.*, p. 207.

30. S. M. Lipset, M. Trow, and J. Coleman, *Union Democracy* (Glencoe, Ill.: The Free Press, 1956).

31. John Mitchell, *Organized Labor* (Philadelphia: American Book and Bible House, 1903), pp. 75, 76.

32. Second object of the United Steelworkers of America, stated in Article II of its Constitution. The other two stated are to unite all eligible workers and to secure legislation safeguarding the economic security and social welfare of workers in the industry.

33. This argument has been previously advanced in Lloyd H. Fisher and Grant McConnell, "Labor Union Solidarity," in Kornhauser, Dubin, and Ross, eds., *Industrial Conflict* (New York: McGraw-Hill, 1954).

34. V. L. Allen, *Power in Trade Unions* (London: Longmans, Green, 1954), p. 10.

35. Cf. J. A. C. Grant: "The Gild Returns to America," *Journal of Politics*, vol. 4, pp. 303–336 and 458–477.

36. See Grant McConnell, *The Decline of Agrarian Democracy* (Berkeley and Los Angeles: University of California Press, 1953), pp. 52–54.

37. Cf. *Yale Law Journal*, May 1954; Oliver Garceau, *The Political Life of the American Medical Association* (Cambridge, Mass.: Harvard University Press, 1941).

38. However, it has been claimed that even in the ITU the party system is dying out. See Paul Jacobs, *Old Before Its Time: Collective Bargaining at 28* (Santa Barbara, Calif.: Center for the Study of Democratic Institutions, 1963), p. 28.

39. For example, the history of the Auto Workers. Cf. Jack Stieber, *Governing the U.A.W.* (New York: John Wiley & Sons, 1962), chap. 5.

40. This trait of the referenda was remarked on by Childs in his study of 1929. The point remained valid throughout the period in which the referendum was in use. See Harwood L. Childs, *Labor and Capital in National Politics* (Columbus, O.: Ohio State University Press, 1930), pp. 161–171.

41. This is the argument of Walter Galenson in the foreword to Morris A. Horowitz, *The Structure and Government of the Carpenters' Union* (New York: John Wiley & Sons, 1962), p. ix.

42. See Jack Stieber, Walter E. Oberer, and Michael Harrington: "Democracy and Public Review" (Santa Barbara, Calif.: Center for the Study of Democratic Institutions, 1960).

Part II

INTRODUCTION

1. Quoted by Philip M. Stern, "The Slow, Quiet Murder of Tax Reform," *Harpers*, December 1963, p. 68.

2. Arthur F. Bentley, *The Process of Government* (Chicago: The University of Chicago Press, 1908).

3. Leo Weinstein has analyzed the thought of Bentley and the legend that has grown up about him in *Arthur F. Bentley's Approach to the Study of Politics: A Critical Analysis*, unpublished doctoral dissertation, University of Chicago, 1958.

4. David B. Truman, *The Governmental Process* (New York: Alfred A. Knopf, 1951), pp. 50–51. There is perhaps a hedge in the sentence which followed, "In developing a group interpretation of politics, therefore, we do not need to account for a *totally inclusive interest*, because one does not exist." Italics mine.

5. Pendleton Herring, *The Politics of Democracy* (New York: W. W. Norton & Co., 1940).

6. Earl Latham has made this point about the English Pluralists in *The Group Basis of Politics* (Ithaca, N.Y.: Cornell University Press, 1952), p. 8.

7. For a justification, see Peter Woll, *American Bureaucracy* (New York: W. W. Norton & Co., 1963).

8. Morton Grodzins has emphasized the intermingled character of state and federal government in the U.S. in "Centralization and Decentralization in the American Federal System," an essay in Robert A. Goldwin, *A Nation of States* (Chicago: Rand, McNally Co., 1963).

CHAPTER 6: *The States*

1. The Commission on Intergovernmental Relations (Kestnbaum Commission) perhaps began with a presumption that the states had become dangerously weakened. As time went on, however, the presumption disappeared and the ultimate report took a very moderate view. The Commission's *Report* is dated June, 1955 (Washington, D.C.).

2. The American Assembly, *The Forty-Eight States* (New York: Columbia University Press, 1955), p. 65.

3. Information from *Book of the States* (Chicago: Council of State Governments, 1963), vol. 29, table, p. 12.

4. *Ibid., loc. cit.*

5. For example, ". . . one might wish they had constitutions more nearly limited to fundamental law so that they could make more appropriate demands on their voters and give their legislatures needed authority." Karl A. Bosworth in *The Forty-Eight States*, p. 90.

6. *Book of the States*, table, p. 13.

7. U.S. Advisory Commission on Intergovernmental Relations, *Apportionment of State Legislatures* (Washington, D.C., 1962), p. 15.

8. 369 U.S. 186 (1962).

9. *Colegrove v. Green*, 328 U.S. 549 (1946).

10. *Colegrove v. Barrett*, 330 U.S. 804 (1947).

11. "Control of the political institution of apportionment in American states . . . helps to arrest the political sentiments by protecting the vested rule in the status quo. It has placed a capitalized value on inaction. It has elevated the prospect of reapportionment almost into a threat to the social order." Thomas Page, quoted in *The Forty-Eight States*, p. 95.

12. Malcolm E. Jewell, *The State Legislature: Politics and Practice* (New York: Random House, 1963), p. 22.

13. For analysis of the arguments for the "federal plan" see Paul T. David

and Ralph Eisenberg, *State Legislative Redistricting: Major Issues in the Wake of Judicial Decision* (Chicago: Public Administration Service, 1962), pp. 8–9. See also Robert B. McKay, *Reapportionment and the Federal Analogy* (New York: National Municipal League, 1962).

14. *Book of the States*, table, Apportionment of Legislatures as of November 1, 1961.

15. See Chapter 4.

16. See article by D. R. Derge, "Urban-Rural Conflict: The Case of Illinois," in John C. Wahlke and Heinz Eulau, *Legislative Behavior* (Glencoe, Ill.: Free Press, 1959). See also discussion in Jewell, *op. cit.*, pp. 60–67.

17. Dayton McKean in *The Forty-Eight States*, p. 75. He apparently was following the estimate in Belle Zeller, ed., *American State Legislatures* (New York: Thomas Y. Crowell, 1954).

18. Jewell, *op. cit.*, pp. 10, 11.

19. V. O. Key, Jr., *Southern Politics in State and Nation* (New York: Alfred A. Knopf, 1949), p. 299. See chap. 14 *in toto*.

20. *Ibid.*, pp. 304–307. To this might be added the comment of Karl Bosworth: "Experience in one-party states makes clear that personal politics tends to displace issue-oriented politics." *The Forty-Eight States*, p. 87.

21. *Ibid.*, p. 307.

22. See Chapter 2, *supra*.

23. V. O. Key, Jr., *American State Politics* (New York: Alfred A. Knopf, Inc., 1956), p. 120.

24. John C. Wahlke, et al., *The Legislative System: Explorations in Legislative Behavior* (New York and London: John Wiley & Sons, 1962), p. 351. See also Key, *American State Politics*.

25. See Duane Lockard, *New England Politics* (Princeton, N.J.: Princeton University Press, 1959), pp. 14ff.

26. I outlined this explanation in "California Conundrum," *The Nation*, Dec. 4, 1954. A somewhat similar argument appears in Dean E. Cresap, *Party Politics in the Golden State* (Los Angeles: Haynes Foundation, 1954).

27. See pp. 42, 48.

28. Roland R. Renne, *The Government and Administration of Montana* (New York: Thomas Y. Crowell Co., 1958), p. 78: "It [Anaconda] works closely with key legislators in getting useful information into their hands, assists them with drafting bills, advances arguments for or against a particular measure, and develops strategy for getting the measure enacted into law."

29. Lockard, *op. cit.*, pp. 79–80.

30. Wahlke, *op. cit.*, p. 100.

31. A comparison of states for conflict along party lines ranked New Jersey, Ohio, California in that order. See Wahlke, *op. cit.*, p. 351.

32. William J. Keefe, cited in Neil F. Garvey, *The Government and*

Administration of Illinois (New York: Thomas Y. Crowell Co., 1958), p. 106. There were 2,324 roll call votes in the first session.

33. See, for example, Gilbert Y. Steiner and Samuel K. Gove, *Legislative Politics in Illinois* (Urbana, Ill.: University of Illinois Press, 1960), pp. 76–80. Few more remarkable devices for creating an illusion of unanimity exist than the "agreed bill" procedure in Illinois. See Gilbert Y. Steiner, *Legislation by Collective Bargaining: The Agreed Bill in Illinois Unemployment Compensation Legislation* (Urbana, Ill.: University of Illinois Institute of Labor and Industrial Relations, u.d.).

34. *Southern Politics,* p. 306n: "Comparative analysis of some southern and some northern states suggests the inference that theorists of the state reorganization movement have by and large failed to see the relation of political organization to the problem of state administrative organization. A state such as New York adapts itself to an integrated state administration under the direction of a governor who is the leader of a relatively cohesive and organized party. A governor in a loose factional system does not have organized about him social elements necessary to produce enough power to control the entire state administration. Nor does he occupy a position as party leader that makes him appear sufficiently accountable to warrant vesting him with broad authority for the direction of administration."

35. *Book of the States,* table, pp. 140, 141.

36. For a summary of the usual arguments for and against reform on this score see Ferrel Heady, *State Constitutions: The Structure of Administration* (New York: National Municipal League, 1961), pp. 2–5.

37. *Reorganizing State Governments* (Chicago: Council of State Governments, 1950).

38. The state "little Hoover Commissions" have tended to echo the preoccupation with the problem of orderliness found in their original model, the First Hoover Commission. I believe the concern is exaggerated and not accurately focused on the real evil that is involved.

39. See chart in *The Agency Plan for California,* summary prepared by California Department of Finance, April 1962 (mimeographed).

40. These examples and quotations are from *California State Government, A Guide to Organizations and Functions* (Sacramento: California State Department of Finance, 1951).

41. California *Government Code,* Section 65020.

42. Reorganization began in 1961 after a long preparatory campaign. It still continues. See Statement of Governor Edmund G. Brown, "Government Reorganization," March 20, 1963. See also *California State Government, Its Tasks and Organization,* The California State Assembly (Stanford, Calif.: Stanford University Press, 1956).

43. Lynton K. Caldwell, *The Government and Administration of New York* (New York: Thomas Y. Crowell Co., 1954), pp. 284, 285.

44. Coleman E. Ransome, Jr., *The Office of Governor in the United*

States (University, Ala.: University of Alabama Press, 1956), p. 270.

45. James W. Fesler, *The Independence of State Regulatory Agencies* (Chicago: Public Administration Service, 1942), p. 32.

46. J. A. C. Grant, "The Gild Returns to America," *Journal of Politics,* vol. 4 (1942), pp. 303–336, 459–477.

47. *Ibid.*, p. 316.

48. Council of State Governments, *Occupational Licensing Legislation in the States* (1952).

49. For a radical critique of licensure, see Milton Friedman, *Capitalism and Freedom* (Chicago: The University of Chicago Press, 1962).

50. Cf. Ransome, *op. cit.*, pp. 381–383.

51. Cf. the comments of Paul Dolan on the informal administrative process in Delaware, *The Government and Administration of Delaware* (New York: Thomas Y. Crowell Co., 1956), pp. 102–103.

52. Leslie Lipson may correctly have seen the long-term development of the office of governor, but the subtitle to his pioneering work was perhaps premature. Leslie Lipson, *The American Governor: From Figurehead to Leader* (Chicago: The University of Chicago Press, 1939).

53. Ransome, *op. cit.*, p. 152.

54. See Chapter 5.

55. For a development of the theme of corruption see Robert S. Allen, ed., *Our Sovereign State* (New York: The Vanguard Press, 1949). "In state government are to be found in their most extreme and vicious form all the worst evils of misrule in the country. Venality, open domination and manipulation by vested interests, unspeakable callousness in the case of the sick, aged and unfortunate, criminal negligence in law enforcement, crass deprivations of primary constitutional rights, obfuscation, obsolescence, obstructionism, incompetence, and even outright dictatorship are widespread characteristics" (p. vii).

CHAPTER 7: *Preemption*

1. On preemption, see Benjamin Horace Hibbard, *A History of the Public Land Policies* (New York: Peter Smitt, 1939), chap. IX.

2. On the Pinchot-Ballinger affair, still a topic of controversy, see Alpheus T. Mason, *Bureaucracy Convicts Itself* (New York: Viking, 1941), and literature cited therein.

3. On the Oregon and California lands, see Wesley C. Ballaine, "The Revested Oregon and California Railroad Grant Lands: A Problem in Land Management," in *Land Economics* (August 1953), pp. 219–232.

4. See Grant McConnell: "The Conservation Movement, Past and Present," *Western Political Quarterly,* (September 1954), pp. 463–478.

5. See Chapter 2.

6. Hibbard, *op. cit.*, p. 476.

7. *Ibid.*, p. 479.

8. Louis E. Peffer, *The Closing of the Public Domain* (Stanford, Calif.: Stanford University Press, 1951), p. 183.

9. Phillip O. Foss, *Politics and Grass* (Seattle: University of Washington Press, 1960), pp. 47–48.

10. *Ibid.*, pp. 51–52.

11. The Taylor Act is analyzed in Wesley Calef, *Private Grazing and Public Lands* (Chicago: The University of Chicago Press, 1960), pp. 52–57.

12. *Ibid.*, p. 57.

13. Foss, *op. cit.*, p. 82.

14. *Ibid.*, p. 119.

15. *Ibid.*, p. 121.

16. *The New York Times*, Sept. 10, 1961.

17. Calef, *op. cit.*, p. 81.

18. Foss, *op. cit.*, p. 62.

19. Calef, *op. cit.*, pp. 60, 61.

20. Half of the fees went to the state, one fourth to the District for range improvements and one fourth to the Federal Treasury. "I found it a startling exemplification of the political power of the range stockmen to discover that these funds were invariably turned over to the grazing district advisory boards to be expended for range improvements, in spite of the stringent needs of many western counties (particularly in the 1930's) for school, road, and other funds." Calef, *op. cit.*, p. 73. Fees have since been increased and their distribution changed.

21. Calef, *op. cit.*, p. 63.

22. See Foss, *op. cit.*, pp. 132–134. See also Calef, *op. cit.*, p. 77.

23. Foss, *op. cit.*, pp. 122–124. The average rate of voter participation in Oregon and Idaho districts was 9.9 per cent. In one district the voting was undertaken by mail. The number of votes cast sharply increased, but soon declined.

24. Calef, *op. cit.*, p. 117.

25. Foss, *op. cit.*, pp. 140–170.

26. Select Committee on National Water Resources, *Water Resources Activities in the United States,* U.S. Senate, 86th Cong., 1st Sess. (1959).

27. Joint Committee on Reorganization of the Executive Branch of the Government, *Reorganization of the Executive Department,* 68th Cong., 1st Sess. (1924).

28. House Report 1833, 72nd Cong., 2nd Sess. (1932).

29. The first was for the Senate select committee to investigate the executive agencies of the government, 75th Congress. The report was made by the Brookings Institution and was printed as Senate Report 1275, 75th Cong., 1st Sess. (1937). The second was the *Report of the*

President's Committee on Administrative Management, Senate Document 8, 75th Cong., 1st Sess. (1937).

30. The Commission on Organization of the Executive Branch of the Government (First Hoover Commission). *Report on the Department of the Interior*, House Document 122, 81st Cong., 1st Sess. (1949). The task force on natural resources also gave the familiar recommendation, while the task force on public works advocated a Department of Public Works.

31. *Report of the President's Water Resources Policy Commission, A Water Policy for the American People*, 1950.

32. *The Civil Function Program of the Corps of Engineers, U.S. Army*, House Committee Print No. 21, 82nd Cong., 2nd Sess. (1952). This was a subcommittee on public works.

33. Commission on Organization of the Executive Branch of the Government, *Report on Water Resources and Power*, 1955.

34. *Water Resources Policy, A Report by the Presidential Advisory Committee on Water Resources Policy* (Washington, D.C., 1955), p. 2.

35. See Arthur Maass, *Muddy Waters* (Cambridge, Mass.: Harvard University Press, 1951), pp. 21, 22.

36. See the general discussion in Chapter 4.

37. The memorandum is quoted in a case study for the Hoover Commission by Arthur Maass. *Task Force Report on Natural Resources*, Commission on Organization of the Executive Branch of the Government, 1949, p. 167. It is also recounted in Maass, *Muddy Waters*, chap. V.

38. Obviously, however, the pork barrel includes other projects as well—post offices and public buildings of various kinds. Today, moreover, highway building, as in the interstate program, overshadows even the building of dams and levees.

39. The quoted phrase is that of Maass, *op. cit.*, p. 63.

40. Maass, *op. cit.*, p. 74.

41. *Encyclopedia of Associations*, vol. 1, *National Organizations of the U.S.*, 3rd ed. (Detroit: Gale Research Co., 1961), p. 180.

42. See the account of such cooperation in Maass, *op. cit.*, pp. 46–51.

43. See the case study on the Kings River in the *Task Force Report on Natural Resources* of the First Hoover Commission, pp. 149–187.

44. *Ibid.*

45. The administrative organization of the bureau and the change in it are discussed in Charles McKinley, *Uncle Sam in the Pacific Northwest* (Berkeley, Calif.: University of California Press, 1952), pp. 118–123.

46. *Reclamation in Accomplishments and Constitutions, Report by the Library of Congress Legislative Reference Service*, printed for the Committee on Interior and Insular Affairs, 86th Cong., 1st Sess. (1959), p. 2.

47. *Encyclopedia of Associations*, p. 247.

48. This conflict is described in McKinley, *op. cit.*, pp. 619–626.
49. The problems of water in the Missouri Basin and the contests for their exploitation are described in Henry C. Hart, *The Dark Missouri* (Madison, Wis.: University of Wisconsin Press, 1957). A brief account of the story of the Pick–Sloan Plan appears in a case study by Edward Ackerman in *Task Force Report on Natural Resources*, First Hoover Commission, Appendix 6.
50. U.S. Department of Agriculture, *A Proposed Program of the U.S. Department of Agriculture within the Missouri Basin*, January, 1948.
51. "Project-type undertakings" is the oddly revealing bureaucratic term used by Gladwin E. Young, Deputy Administrator of SCS. See his "Where Does Watershed Development Fit into the Total Picture of Resources Development?" in E. S. Tolley and F. E. Riggs, eds., *Economics of Watershed Planning* (Ames, Ia.: Iowa State University Press, 1961), p. 19.
52. *Ibid.*, p. 22.
53. See *infra*, pp. 239, 240.
54. The Association, originally based in League City, Texas, now has a Washington headquarters and a membership of 2,900. It sponsors an annual Watershed Congress. *Encyclopedia of Associations*, p. 250.
55. This account is drawn from Irving K. Fox and Isabel Picken, *The Upstream–Downstream Controversy in the Arkansas White–Red Basins Survey* (published by the University of Alabama Press, University, Ala., 1960, for the Inter-University Case Program).
56. See Robert E. Lowry, "Organization for Watershed Planning in the Public Interest," in G. S. Tolley and F. E. Riggs, *op. cit.*, pp. 246–259.
57. Owen Stratton and Philip Sorotkin, *The Echo Park Controversy* (published by the University of Alabama Press, University, Ala., 1959, for the Inter-University Case Program), p. 93.
58. Keith S. Krause, "Statement for Comprehensive Water Pollution Control Programs," U.S. Public Health Service, 1964 (mimeographed).
59. See Chapter 3.
60. See William J. Block, *The Separation of the Farm Bureau and the Extension Service* (Urbana, Ill.: University of Illinois Press, 1960); also, Gladys Baker, *The County Agent* (Chicago: The University of Chicago Press, 1939).
61. See Arthur Capper: *The Agricultural Bloc* (New York: Harcourt, Brace & Co., 1922). Senator Capper was the Bloc's leader on the official side.
62. See McConnell, *The Decline of Agrarian Democracy* (Berkeley and Los Angeles: University of California Press, 1953) and literature cited therein.
63. Farm Bureau lobbying arrogance precipitated an investigation into its activities by the House Committee on Banking and Currency. *Hearings on Farm Organizations*, 66th Cong., 3rd Sess. (1922).
64. See, for example, C. W. Thompson: "How the Department of Agri-

culture Promotes Organization in Rural Life," U.S. Department of
Agriculture, *Yearbook of Agriculture*, 1915, pp. 272A–272P; also L. R.
Simons, *Organization of a County for Extension Work—The Farm
Bureau Plan*, U.S. Department of Agriculture, Circular No. 30 (1919).

65. The advice is cited by William Foote Whyte in his *Street Corner Society* (Chicago: The University of Chicago Press, 1943 and 1955), p. 276.

66. On this period, see *The Decline of Agrarian Democracy*, chap. 6.

67. *Ibid.*, chap. 7.

68. M. C. Wilson, *How and to What Extent Is the Extension Service Reaching Low Income Families?* Extension Service Circular 375 (1941).

69. Christina McFayden Campbell has suggested that the Farm Security Administration "embarked on an extensive program of reform" and thus aroused Farm Bureau hostility. By the time of the FSA, however, the "reform" program had become minor in the program. *The Farm Bureau and the New Deal* (Urbana, Ill.: University of Illinois Press, 1962), p. 165.

70. Another striking example during this period is the Forest Service-directed defeat of the President's reorganization plan. See Kenneth Crawford, *The Pressure Boys* (New York: J. Messner, Inc., 1939).

71. This nearly unbelievable attack may be sampled in *The Decline of Agrarian Democracy*, chap. 9, and literature (especially Congressional hearings) cited therein.

72. The text of the "Mount Weather Agreement" appears in John M. Gaus and Leon O. Wolcott, *Public Administration and the United States Department of Agriculture* (Chicago: Public Administration Service, 1940), pp. 463–465.

73. On the BAE, see Charles M. Hardin, "The Bureau of Agricultural Economics under Fire, A Study in Valuation Conflicts," *Journal of Farm Economics*, vol. 28 (August 1946).

74. From a study made for the Congressional Joint Economic Committee. See Dale E. Hathaway, *Government and Agriculture* (New York: Macmillan, 1963), p. 165. The situation was not notably changed by 1960; see the table on p. 51 of that book.

75. The little volume by Michael Harrington, *The Other America* (New York: Macmillan, 1962).

76. See Charles M. Hardin, *The Politics of Agriculture* (Glencoe, Ill.: The Free Press, 1952), chaps. 5 and 6 (especially *n.* 4, p. 72).

77. See the newsletters and bulletins of the Association for this period (League City, Texas). The tone is almost hysterical.

78. An aide to Secretary Benson is reported to have said, "We try to start out with our programs being independent of all the farm pressure groups, but we usually end up by buying just about what the Farm Bureau advocates." Stanley Andrews, *The Farmers' Dilemma* (Washington, D.C.: Public Affairs Press, 1961), p. 84.

79. Hathaway, *op. cit.*, pp. 205 and 293.

80. Don F. Hedwiger, "Discussion of Trends in the Political Position of the American Farmer," *Goals and Values in Agricultural Policy* (Ames, Ia.: Iowa State University Press, 1961), pp. 231–237.

81. See Julius Duscha, *Taxpayer's Hayride* (Boston: Little, Brown and Co., 1964).

82. For a vivid sense of the rich variety of business interests in agriculture, see Wesley McCune, *Who's Behind Our Farm Policy?* (New York: Praeger, 1956).

83. Hathaway, *op. cit.*, p. 233.

84. *Ibid.*, p. 197.

85. It should also be recalled that the Farmers Union is in part a commodity association for wheat growers and that some state Farm Bureaus are themselves nearly commodity organizations.

86. See Philip Selznick, *TVA and the Grass Roots* (Berkeley and Los Angeles: University of California Press, 1949).

87. The campaign that culminated in Congressional return of the oil "tidelands" to the states is a particularly striking example of the appreciation of the oil companies that their influence would be greater in the little pools of Sacramento, Austin, and Baton Rouge than in the big pool of Washington, D.C.

88. For a recent summary, see Fay Bennett, *The Condition of Farm Workers in 1963* (New York: National Sharecroppers Fund, 1964).

89. Theodore Lowi, "How the Farmers Get What They Want," *The Reporter*, vol. 30, no. 11 (May 21, 1964).

CHAPTER 8: *Self-regulation*

1. See Francis X. Sutton, Seymour E. Harris, Carl Kaysen, James Tobin, *The American Business Creed* (New York: Schocken Books, 1956).

2. Guido de Ruggiero, *The History of European Liberalism* (Boston: Beacon Press, 1959), p. 384. (The book was first published in English by Oxford University Press in 1927.)

3. The present debate begins with the publication of *The Modern Corporation and Private Property*, by Adolph A. Berle, Jr. and Gardiner C. Means (New York: Macmillan, 1932), although there was in 1932 already a large literature on monopoly. For a selection of evaluations of the general problem, see Edward S. Mason, ed., *The Corporation in Modern Society* (Cambridge, Mass.: Harvard University Press, 1960). See especially "The Financing of Corporations," by John Lintner, pp. 166–201.

4. See Carl Kaysen, "The Corporation: How Much Power? What Scope?" in Mason, *op. cit.*, pp. 99–105.

5. See C. Wright Mills, *The Power Elite* (New York: Oxford University Press, 1956).

6. Edward S. Mason in Mason, *op. cit.*, p. 4.

7. A. A. Berle, Jr., *The Twentieth Century Capitalist Revolution* (New York: Harcourt, Brace & Co., 1954), p. 51.

8. See Chapter 5.

9. J. K. Galbraith, *American Capitalism*, rev. ed. (Boston: Houghton Mifflin Co., 1956).

10. See the incisive critique of countervailing power by Walter Adams, "Competition, Monopoly and Countervailing Power," *Quarterly Journal of Economics*, vol. 67 (1953), 469–492.

11. See Grant McConnell, *Steel and the Presidency, 1962* (New York: W. W. Norton Co., 1963). For an account of the history of industrial relations in steel since World War II, see *Collective Bargaining in the Basic Steel Industry*, U.S. Department of Labor, January 1961.

12. See McConnell, *op. cit.*, p. 112.

13. Ida M. Tarbell, *The Life of Elbert H. Gary* (New York: D. Appleton & Co., 1925).

14. These charges were made by Louis Brandeis in his *The Curse of Bigness* (New York: Viking, 1934). They were also implied by the Commissioner of Corporations in 1905. They have more recently been renewed by the staff of the Senate Antitrust Committee. See also Gardiner C. Means, *Pricing Power and the Public Interest* (New York: Harper & Bros., 1962), chap. XVI.

15. Berle, *The Twentieth Century Capitalist Revolution*, chap. III.

16. Cf. Eugene V. Rostow, "To Whom and for What Ends Is Corporate Management Responsible?" in Mason, *op. cit.*, p. 67. However, see the suggestion of Gardiner Means, *op. cit.*, chap. XVII.

17. Berle's discussion of this in *The Twentieth Century Capitalist Revolution* (pp. 83–115) seems eminently reasonable.

18. Adolph A. Berle, *The American Economic Republic* (New York: Harcourt, Brace & World, Inc., 1963), p. 13.

19. See Chapter 3.

20. This summary is drawn from *Industrial Mobilization for War*, vol. I, U.S. Civilian Production Administration, 1947. See also Donald M. Nelson, *Arsenal of Democracy* (New York: Harcourt Brace & Co., 1946). For the period 1943–1945, see also Herman Miles Somers, *Presidential Agency* (Cambridge, Mass.: Harvard University Press, 1950).

21. See, for example, *Industrial Mobilization for War*, p. 19. Regarding criticism of "big business" orientation, General Hugh S. Johnson in a newspaper column attacked the War Resources Board as "politically and popularly impossible." *Dollar-A-Year and Without Compensation Personnel Policies*, Production Administration, Special Study No. 27, 1947, p. 3.

22. The list prices quoted were usually merely the starting point for bargaining. This example is drawn from the writer's experience in the Rubber Branch of the Price Division of the Office of Price Administration.

23. Nelson, *op. cit.*, p. 90.
24. *Ibid.*, p. 345.
25. John C. Whitridge, Director of the WPB Office of Industrial Advisory Committee, in Foreword to Carl Henry Monsees, *Industry–Government Cooperation* (Washington, D.C.: Public Affairs Press, 1944).
26. Monsees, *op. cit.*, p. 24.
27. Nelson, *op. cit.*, p. 347.
28. *Dollar-A-Year and Without Compensation Personnel Policies*, Appendix B, p. 106.
29. See footnote 22.
30. Special Senate Committee Investigating the National Defense Program, *Additional Report, Dollar-A-Year Men*, 77th Cong., 2nd Sess. (1942).
31. Nelson, *op. cit.*, p. 340.
32. U.S. Department of Commerce, *Consultation with Industry*, (Washington, D.C., 1953), pp. 5, 6.
33. There were two days of hearings before a House Committee and four days before a Senate Committee. *The Mobilization Program, Report of the Subcommittee on Study of Monopoly Power*, U.S. House of Representatives, 82nd Cong., 1st Sess. (1951), p. 5.
34. *Consultation with Industry*, p. 245.
35. *The Mobilization Program*, p. 24.
36. *Consultation with Industry*, p. 28.
37. *Ibid.*, pp. 126–130.
38. *The Mobilization Program*, pp. 31–33, 50.
39. *Ibid.*, pp. 79–82.
40. *Consultation with Industry*, pp. 138–139.
41. *Amendment to the Administrative Expense Act of 1946, Hearings before the Committee on Government Operations*, U.S. House of Representatives, 85th Cong., 1st Sess. (1957), p. 2.
42. *Interim Report of the Antitrust Subcommittee of the Committee on the Judiciary on WOCs and Government Advisory Groups*, U.S. House of Representatives, 84th Cong., 2nd Sess. (1956), pp. 7, 8.
43. *Ibid.*, p. 8.
44. *Ibid.*, pp. 10, 11.
45. *WOCs and Government Advisory Groups, Hearings before the Antitrust Subcommittee of the Committee on the Judiciary*, U.S. House of Representatives, 84th Cong., 1st Sess., part I (1955), p. 178.
46. *Interim Report*, p. 29.
47. *Hearings, WOCs and Government Advisory Groups*, pp. 339–344.
48. *Ibid.*, pp. 207–208.
49. *Ibid.*, p. 191.
50. *Interim Report*, p. 99.
51. Address by Walter S. Hallanan, Chairman, National Petroleum Council to American Petroleum Institute, 1955. Printed in *WOCs and Government Advisory Groups, Hearings before the Antitrust Sub-*

committee of the Committee on the Judiciary, U.S. House of Representatives, 84th Cong., 2nd Sess., part IV (1956), p. 2400.

52. *Ibid.*, pp. 2516, 2517.

53. The American Petroleum Institute, founded in 1919, has 11,000 members and a staff of 330. *Encyclopedia of Associations*, p. 156.

54. See, for example, letter of E. M. Callis in *Hearings*, p. 2271.

55. See remarks of Ralph K. Davies, Director of the Oil and Gas Division, 1946. *Hearings*, p. 2294.

56. *Hearings*, p. 2407.

57. See *Replies from Executive Departments and Federal Agencies to Inquiry Regarding Use of Advisory Committee, Committee on Government Operations*, U.S. House of Representatives, 84th Cong., 2nd Sess. (1956), pp. 2505–2535.

58. *Replies from Executive Departments*, vols. I, II, III, and IV (pp. 1219 ff.).

59. *Replies from Executive Departments*, pp. 2846–2849.

60. *Interim Report on the Business Advisory Council, Antitrust Subcommittee of the Committee on the Judiciary*, U.S. House of Representatives, 84th Cong., 1st Sess. (1955), pp. 3, 4.

61. *Ibid.*, p. 16.

62. *Ibid.*, p. 23.

63. *Ibid.*, pp. vii and 27.

64. *Ibid.*, p. 22.

65. *Ibid.*, p. 17.

66. Executive Order 11007, February 26, 1962.

67. The early history of these agencies is set forth in Robert E. Cushman, *The Independent Regulatory Commissions* (New York: Oxford University Press, 1941).

68. A summary of arguments for and against the Commission form appears in Marver H. Bernstein, *Regulating Business by Independent Commission* (Princeton, N.J.: Princeton University Press, 1955), pp. 24, 25.

69. *Report of the President's Committee on Administrative Management* (Washington, D.C., 1937), p. 32.

70. Committee on Administrative Procedure Appointed by the Attorney General, *Report on Administrative Procedure in Government Agencies* (Washington, D.C., 1941), p. 7. It is notable that the leading contemporary text on administrative law is much less restrictive: "The administrative process is the complex of methods by which Agencies carry out their tasks of adjudication, rule making, and related functions." Kenneth Culp Davis, *Administrative Law Text* (St. Paul, Minn.: West Publishing Co., 1959), p. 1.

71. *Report on Administrative Procedure*, p. 59.

72. Commission on Organization of the Executive Branch of the Government, *Regulatory Commissions* (Washington, D.C., 1949), pp. 3, 4.

73. Commission on Organization of the Executive Branch of the Govern-

ment, *Legal Services and Procedure* (Washington, D.C., 1955), pp. 84–88.

74. See Chapter 1.

75. Davis, *op. cit.*, p. 6.

76. This quotation appears in almost all critical discussions of the commissions, e.g., Davis, *op. cit.*, p. 7; Bernstein, *op. cit.*, p. 265. The letter itself was written by Richard Olney in 1892 to the president of the Burlington Railroad.

77. Samuel P. Huntington, *Clientalism: A Study in Administrative Politics*, Ph.D. dissertation, Harvard University, 1950, pp. 391, 392, 397.

78. Henry J. Friendly, *The Federal Administrative Agencies* (Cambridge, Mass.: Harvard University Press, 1962), pp. viii, 6, 7.

79. *Ibid.*, pp. 53–73.

80. *Ibid.*, p. 97.

81. Louis J. Hector, "Problems of the CAB and the Independent Regulatory Commissions," 69 *Yale Law Journal*, 939 (May 1960).

82. Quoted in Friendly, *op. cit.*, p. 97.

83. Huntington, *op. cit.*, pp. 32–35. Also Walton H. Hamilton, *The Politics of Industry* (New York: Alfred A. Knopf, Inc., 1957), pp. 61–62.

84. *Ibid.*, pp. 24–35, 94.

85. This example is termed by Friendly—with much justification—"a rather beautiful story." *Op. cit.*, pp. 27–35.

86. Bernstein, *op. cit.*, pp. 74–102.

87. Thus Davis, *loc. cit.*; Huntington, *op. cit.*, pp. 378–380; Emmette S. Redford, *Administration of National Economic Control* (New York: Macmillan, 1952), p. 386.

88. Thus, Emmette S. Redford, *The President and the Regulatory Commissions, Report Submitted to the President's Advisory Committee on Government Organization*, 1960; James M. Landis, *Report on Regulatory Agencies to the President-Elect* (Washington, D.C., 1960).

89. Landis, *op. cit.*

90. William O. Douglas, *Democracy and Finance* (New Haven, Conn.: Yale University Press, 1940), p. 82.

91. *Report of Special Study of Securities Market of the Securities and Exchange Commission*, part 4, U.S. House of Representatives, 88th Cong., 1st Sess. (1965), p. ix.

92. *Ibid.*, pp. 679–682.

93. *Securities and Exchange Commission Legislation, 1963, Report of the Committee on Banking and Currency*, U.S. Senate, 88th Cong., 1st Sess. (1963), pp. 41, 42.

94. Cf. John H. Bunzel, *The American Small Businessman* (New York: Alfred A. Knopf, 1962), p. 68 and *passim*; J. C. Palamountain, Jr., *The Politics of Distribution* (Cambridge, Mass.: Harvard University Press, 1955), pp. 235–262. See also Harmon Zeigler, *The Politics of Small Business* (Washington, D.C.: Public Affairs Press, 1961).

95. Mason, *op. cit.*, p. 51. See also the Berle statement. The large corpora-

tion has "*de facto*, at least, invaded the political sphere and has become in fact, if not in theory, a quasi-governing agency." *The Twentieth Century Capitalist Revolution*, p. 105.

96. Hamilton, *op. cit.*, pp. 50–51.

CHAPTER 9: *Autonomy*

1. See Chapter 3.
2. Philip Taft, *Organized Labor in American History* (New York: Harper & Row, 1964), pp. 418, 419.
3. Quoted in John Lombardi, *Labor's Voice in the Cabinet* (New York: Columbia University Press, 1942), p. 65.
4. *Ibid.*, p. 92.
5. See Taft, *op. cit.*, pp. 424–432.
6. It is worth observing that the NLRB has a considerably higher reputation than some of the other independent regulatory agencies. See, for example, Henry J. Friendly, *The Federal Administrative Agencies* (Cambridge, Mass.: Harvard University Press, 1962), pp. 36–52.
7. Florence Peterson, *American Labor Unions* (New York: Harper & Row, 1962), p. 43.
8. See Walter Galenson, *The CIO Challenge to the AFL* (Cambridge, Mass.: Harvard University Press, 1963).
9. See Philip Ross, "The Role of Government in Union Growth," *Annals of the American Academy of Political and Social Science*, November 1963, pp. 75–85.
10. Peterson, *loc. cit.*
11. Joel Seidman, *American Labor from Defense to Reconversion* (Chicago: the University of Chicago Press, 1953), pp. 91–108.
12. *Ibid.*, pp. 174–175.
13. See Grant McConnell, *The Steel Seizure of 1952* (published by the University of Alabama Press, University, Ala., 1960, for the Inter-University Case Program), pp. 7–10.
14. See Chapter 5.
15. Quoted in Taft, *op. cit.*, p. 690.
16. The committee assembled a large shelf of hearings under the title *Investigation of Improper Activities in the Labor or Management Field*, 85th Cong., 1st and 2nd Sess. (1957, 1958).
17. A clear example is the position of organized labor on legislation extending the program by which Mexican and Caribbean workers have been imported to work on American farms. The program met the official disapproval of the labor movement, but organized labor did relatively little to bring it to an end.
18. Alexander Heard, *The Costs of Democracy* (Chapel Hill, N.C.: University of North Carolina Press, 1960), p. 182.

19. Quoted in J. David Greenstone, *Labor Politics in Three Cities: Political Action in Detroit, Chicago and Los Angeles*. Unpublished doctoral dissertation, University of Chicago, 1963, p. 1.

20. Quoted in Taft, *op. cit.*, p. 617.

21. For example, Angus Campbell, *et al.*, *The American Voter* (Ann Arbor: University of Michigan Survey Research Center, 1960), p. 325.

22. Greenstone, *op. cit.*, chap. 3.

23. U.S. Bureau of Labor Statistics, *Monthly Labor Review*, September 1961, pp. 935–936.

24. This point was very clearly stated by William Goldner in 1952, well before pension plans had attained anything approaching the scale of today's plans. See "Trade Union Structure and Private Pension Plans," *Industrial and Labor Relations Review*, October 1951, pp. 62–72.

25. Robert F. Hoxie, *Trade Unionism in the United States* (New York: D. Appleton & Co., 1921), pp. 45, 46. Joseph Shister has rather aptly distinguished business unionism from today's "social unionism," which is more concerned with public policy and has a broader outlook. He notes that the latter requires a large membership base. "Unresolved Problems and New Paths for American Labor," *Industrial and Labor Relations Review*, April 1956.

26. The entire clause is quoted in Robert D. Leiter, *The Teamsters Union* (New York: Bookman Associates, 1957), pp. 61, 62.

27. Cf. footnote 16. For a list of other hearings on Teamsters affairs, see Leiter, *op. cit.*, pp. 287–289. Even this is not complete.

28. The spirit of the campaign to trap James Hoffa can be seen in Robert F. Kennedy, *The Enemy Within* (New York: Harper & Brothers, 1960).

29. Cf. Leiter, *op. cit.*, pp. 49, 50.

30. *Ibid.*, pp. 138–159.

31. J. B. Gillingham, *The Teamsters Union on the West Coast* (University of California, Berkeley: Institute of Industrial Relations, 1956), p. 40.

32. See Paul Jacobs, *The State of the Unions* (New York: Atheneum, 1963), pp. 5–70.

33. Cf. J. B. S. Hardman, "John L. Lewis, Labor Leader and Man: An Interpretation," *Labor History*, Winter 1961, p. 21.

34. Cf. A. H. Raskin: "The Obsolescent Unions," *Commentary*, July 1963, p. 23.

35. The UMW has consistently sought restriction of output. Cf. Morton S. Baratz, *The Union and the Coal Industry* (New Haven, Conn.: Yale University Press, 1955), pp. 69–74.

36. Burton H. Wolfe, "The Strange Twilight of Harry Bridges—A Labor Leader Turns Businessman," *Harper's*, March 1964, p. 79.

37. Cf. Grant McConnell, *The Steel Seizure of 1952*. (Published by the University of Alabama Press, University, Ala., 1960, for the Inter-University Case Program).

38. For an account of this general history see *Collective Bargaining in the*

Basic Steel Industry (Washington, D.C.: U.S. Department of Labor, 1961), Appendix A. This volume is usually known as "The Livernash Report" after E. Robert Livernash, who directed its preparation.

39. See these articles: Edward T. Townsend, "Is There a Crisis in the American Trade-Union Movement? Yes"; Philip Taft, "Is There a Crisis in the Labor Movement? No"; and Solomon Barkin and Albert A. Blum, "Is There a Crisis in the American Trade-Union Movement —The Trade Unionists' Views," in *Annals of the American Academy of Political and Social Science*, November 1963, pp. 1–9, 10–15, and 16–24, respectively.

40. See Chapter 3, footnote 52.

41. See Irving Bernstein, "The Growth of American Unions, 1945–1960," *Labor History*, Spring 1961, pp. 131–157. Also *Manpower Report to the President*, 1963.

42. See the bibliography at the end of the article by Maurice F. Neufeld, "The Historical Relationship of Liberals and Intellectuals to Organized Labor in the United States," *Annals*, November 1963, pp. 126–128.

43. Raskin, *op. cit.*; Jacobs, *op. cit.*, pp. 257ff. The quotation is from Raskin, p. 24.

44. Richard A. Lester, *As Unions Mature* (Princeton, N.J.: Princeton University Press, 1958), p. 25.

45. U.S. Department of Labor, "Union Security and Checkoff Provisions in Major Union Contracts, 1958–59," Bulletin No. 1272, March 1960.

46. Joseph A. Beirne: *New Horizons for American Labor* (Washington, D.C.: Public Affairs Press, 1962), pp. 70–71.

47. For example, Jacobs, *op. cit.*, p. 264; A. H. Raskin, "AFL-CIO: A Confederation or Federation? Which Road for the Future?" *Annals*, November 1963, p. 44.

48. Quoted in *Chicago Sun-Times*, Sept. 25, 1964.

CHAPTER 10: *The Quest of the Public Interest*

1. C. Wright Mills, *The Power Elite* (New York: Oxford University Press, 1956), p. 7.

2. David Riesman, with Nathan Glazer and Reuel Denney, *The Lonely Crowd* (Garden City, N.Y.: Anchor Books, 1956), pp. 246–251.

3. Cf. Douglass Cater, *Power in Washington* (New York: Random House, 1964), pp. 26–48; Jack Raymond, *Power at the Pentagon* (New York: Harper & Row, 1964).

4. Daniel Bell has developed this criticism. See "Is There a Ruling Class in America?" in *The End of Ideology* (New York: Collier Books, 1961), pp. 53–55.

5. See Marcus Duffield, *King Legion* (New York: Jonathan Cape &

Harrison Smith, 1931), p. 59: "So thoroughly has the Legion launched into its work that it has virtually taken over an arm of the government, the Veterans Bureau."

6. See U.S. Congress, Senate Committee on the Judiciary, *Hearings before the Subcommittee on Antitrust and Monopoly: Administered Prices*, 1957. Also, Richard Harris, *The Real Voice* (New York: Macmillan, 1964).

7. James B. Conant, *The Education of American Teachers* (New York: McGraw-Hill, 1963), pp. 19–20.

8. Woodrow Wilson, *Congressional Government* (New York: Meridian Books, 1956), pp. 82ff.

9. See the volume edited by Daniel Bell, *The Radical Right* (New York: Anchor Books, 1963), especially the articles by Daniel Bell (chap. 1), Richard Hofstadter (chaps. 3 and 4), Peter Viereck (chap. 7), and S. M. Lipset (chap. 13). See also Daniel Bell, *The End of Ideology*, chap. 6.

10. Cf. S. M. Lipset, "The Sources of the Radical Right," in Bell, *The Radical Right*, p. 309.

11. Cf. Bell, "The Dispossessed," in *The Radical Right*, p. 19.

12. The authors of *The Radical Right* do not make this claim. It is evident in the work of more avowed conservatives such as Elton Mayo.

13. Morton Grodzins, "Centralization and Decentralization in the American Federal System," in Robert A. Goldwin, ed., *A Nation of States* (Chicago: Rand, McNally Co., 1963); also Morton Grodzins, "Local Strength in the American Federal System," in Marian D. Irish, ed., *Continuing Crisis in American Politics* (Englewood Cliffs, N.J.: Prentice-Hall, Inc., 1963).

14. Henry S. Kariel has perceived a basic conflict between pluralism and constitutionalism in the United States. See his *The Decline of American Pluralism* (Stanford, Calif.: Stanford University Press, 1961).

15. Pendleton Herring, *The Politics of Democracy* (New York: W. W. Norton & Co., 1940), pp. 424–425.

16. David B. Truman, *The Governmental Process* (New York: Alfred A. Knopf, 1961), p. 51.

17. Glendon A. Schubert, *The Public Interest* (Glencoe, Ill.: The Free Press, 1961), pp. 219–224.

18. Robert A. Dahl, commenting on Madison's argument about the size of constituency, has remarked that he sees no way to demonstrate "that the restraints on the effectiveness of majorities imposed by the facts of a pluralistic society operate only to curtail 'bad' majorities and not 'good' majorities. . . ." *A Preface to Democratic Theory* (Chicago: The University of Chicago Press, 1956), p. 29. Inasmuch as demonstration of "good" or "bad" to determined skeptics may be difficult, his point is probably correct. To say only this, however, is to pass over the great differences among the values served by majorities drawn from constituencies of different sizes.

INDEX

GRANT McCONNELL was born in Portland, Oregon, in 1915. After graduating from Reed College, he went to Oxford as a Rhodes Scholar, returning to the United States at the outbreak of the war. He taught for a year at Mount Holyoke College and then went to Washington to work for the government; he later saw active service with the Navy in the western Pacific. After the war he returned to academic life, earning his doctorate from the University of California at Berkeley; he taught there before going in 1957 to the University of Chicago. He is now Professor of Political Science at the University of California at Santa Cruz. In recent years he has traveled extensively in Europe and Africa and has been visiting professor at Makerere College in Kampala, Uganda. He is the author also of *The Decline of Agrarian Democracy, The Steel Seizure of 1952,* and *Steel and the Presidency, 1962.*